CENTURY
OF CHAMPIONS

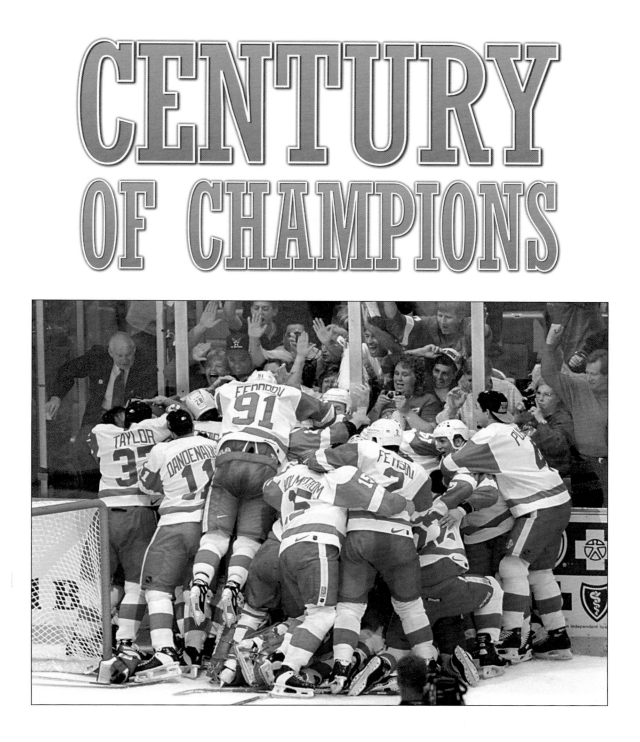

EDITED BY
GENE MYERS

WRITTEN BY
NICHOLAS J. COTSONIKA

DESIGNED BY
BRIAN JAMES

PHOTOS EDITED BY
ALAN R. KAMUDA

DIRECTED BY
STEVE SCHRADER

PRODUCED BY
BOB ELLIS

Detroit Free Press

CONTENTS

OUR CHAMPIONS

Chapter 1

Michigan sports in the 20th Century were filled with great teams, great players and even greater memories. We honor the best of the best. **Page 7.**

COBB'S CORNER, 1900-1929

Chapter 2

When troubled Ty Cobb came to Detroit, his fiery brand of baseball helped make the growing Motor City a major league town. *By Nicholas J. Cotsonika.* **Page 37.**

CITY OF CHAMPIONS, 1930-1947

Chapter 3

In one sweet span, the Tigers, Lions and Red Wings won titles and helped boost Detroit out of the Depression. *By Nicholas J. Cotsonika.* **Page 65.**

TWO DYNASTIES, 1948-1962

Chapter 4

No city boasted better hockey and football than Detroit: Gordie Howe's Red Wings and Bobby Layne's Lions were the classes of their leagues. *By Nicholas J. Cotsonika.* **Page 105.**

SOCK IT TO 'EM, 1963-1968

Chapter 5

After a race riot devastated Detroit in 1967, the Tigers brought the city together again by winning the World Series. *By Nicholas J. Cotsonika.* **Page 153.**

BO & WOODY, 1969-1978

Chapter 6

Michigan's Bo Schembechler spent 10 gripping seasons in Big Ten battles with his mentor, Ohio State's Woody Hayes. *By Nicholas J. Cotsonika.* **Page 181.**

HOOP DREAMS, 1979-1993

Chapter 7

Basketball boomed as Magic Johnson won a title at Michigan State, Isiah Thomas won two with the Pistons and Steve Fisher pulled off a miracle at Michigan. *By Nicholas J. Cotsonika.* **Page 211.**

NEW ICE AGE, 1994-1999

Chapter 8

After 42 years of failure and frustration, the Red Wings finally won another Stanley Cup — then added a second for a fallen comrade. *By Nicholas J. Cotsonika.* **Page 275.**

Detroit Lions

LEGENDARY LIONS LINEBACKER JOE SCHMIDT GAVE AN AMAZING
CENTURY OF SPORTS NOT JUST A HAND, BUT TWO!

Detroit Free Press

600 W. Fort Street
Detroit, Mich. 48226

To subscribe to the Free Press,
call 1-800-395-3300. Find the
Freep on the World Wide Web at
www.freep.com.

ISBN 0-937247-29-4

Manufactured by Quad/Graphics

Other recent books by the
Free Press sports staff:

The Corner
Believe!
MICHIGAN
Stanleytown
Live Albom IV
Live Albom III

To order, call 800-245-5082
or go to www.freep.com/bookstore

Editor's note: Statistics in
this book current through
Oct. 1, 1999.

Editor: Gene Myers
Author: Nicholas J. Cotsonika
Designer: Brian James
Scrapbook editor: Steve Schrader
Copy chief: Ken Kraemer
Production editor: Bob Ellis
Photo editor: Alan R. Kamuda
Photo technician: Jessica Trevino
Associate editors: George Sipple, Tom Panzenhagen,
Shelly Solon, Chris Clonts, Matt Fiorito, Owen Davis
Assistant editors: Doug Church, Bill Collison,
Tim Marcinkoski, Carlos Monarrez, Scott Talley
Project coordinator: Dave Robinson
Photo support: Robert Kozloff, Christine Russell,
Rose Ann McKean
Technical support: A.J. Hartley, Stephen Mounteer
Cover design: Brian James
Acknowledgements: Risa Balayem, Detroit Lions;
J.J. Carter, Detroit Pistons; Frederick Honhart, University
Archives and Historical Collections, Michigan State
University; Gregory Kinney, Bentley Historical Library,
University of Michigan; Rico Longoria, Sports Information
Department, Michigan State University
Special thanks: Harry Atkins, Richard Bak, Jeff Brown,
John C. Clor, Laurie Delves, Carole Leigh Hutton,
Robert G. McGruder, Heath J Meriwether, Michigan
Sports Hall of Fame, Germany Schrader, Andrew Topic,
Charlie Vincent.
Very special thanks: Beth Myers, Shelia Ellis,
Maggie Schrader, Alison Boyce
Free Press sports staff, October 1999: Mitch Albom,
Jo-Ann Barnas, Paul Barrett, Brad Betker, Doug Church,
Bill Collison, Nicholas J. Cotsonika, Steve Crowe,
Bernie Czarniecki, Owen Davis, Laurie Delves, Jim Dwight,
Bob Ellis, Perry A. Farrell, Matt Fiorito, Gene Guidi,
Jemele Hill, Christie Innes, Brian James, Ken Kraemer,
John Lowe, Tim Marcinkoski, David A. Markiewicz,
Mick McCabe, Carlos Monarrez, Brian Murphy,
Gene Myers, Sarah O'Rourke, Tom Panzenhagen,
Pete Reinwald, Bill L. Roose, Michael Rosenberg,
Helene St. James, Jack Saylor, Steve Schrader, Drew Sharp,
Eric Sharp, George Sipple, Shelly Solon, Curt Sylvester,
Scott Talley, Jeff Taylor

I f, as Karl Marx once said, religion is the opiate of the masses, then by the end of the 20th Century, sports cannot be far behind.

Think about it. On any given Sunday, people might oversleep church services, but they won't miss the football game. Midnight mass might be losing popularity, but midnight madness has never been bigger. We don't offer sacrifices at the altar anymore; we do, however, have the Super Bowl halftime show.

In the past 100 years, sports went from something a few people did as a diversion, to something many people did for a living. Who would have imagined, in 1901, that you could have a career as a sports agent, a triathlete, a punter, an ESPN announcer, or selling — *come on, be serious* — running shoes?

This will forever be the century that sports came to define us, particularly in America — and even more particularly in Detroit, the best sports town in the nation.

Some cities witness sports championships; Detroit *wears* them, on its chests, on its bumpers, on its car windows.

Some cities celebrate sports stars; we make them ambassadors.

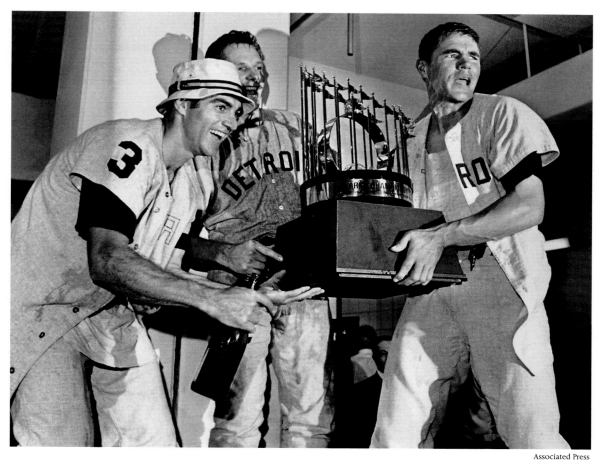

Associated Press

LIKE NO OTHER CITY, DETROIT EMBRACES SPORTS HEROES SUCH AS DICK McAULIFFE, JIM NORTHRUP AND MICKEY STANLEY, WHO WON THE 1968 WORLD SERIES WITH THE TIGERS.

Joe Louis *is* Detroit. Gordie Howe *is* Detroit. Magic Johnson *is* the state of Michigan.

Some cities record their sports stories: Detroit stitches them into the city's tapestry, passes them from father to son, from grandmother to granddaughter. *"I remember when my mother took me to my first Tiger game. . . . I remember when my grandpa took me to meet Hank Greenberg. . . ."*

So, when the Detroit Free Press takes a look back at a century of sports, it cannot help but take a look back at who we are, what we held dear. Ty Cobb putting the Tigers on the map at the turn of the century. Joe Louis embodying the grit of this city in the '30s. Bobby Layne practicing hard working and hard playing in the '50s. Steve Yzerman, hoisting the Stanley Cup in the '90s, symbolizing the perseverance of Detroiters, no matter how long it takes.

When Tiger Stadium closed in 1999, after nearly a century of use, the media came from around the country to witness the farewell. Reporters asked why this rusty, sagging,

paint-peeling structure could bring tears to the eyes of its final patrons.

"Because," Detroit fans replied, "this is where we go. This is where my father went. This is where his father went. This is what we do around here. We watch our sports teams. We root them on."

We root. We cheer. We make mental pictures. Every picture tells a story. Every story finds a family. Every family has a picture.

And every picture tells a story all over again.

Within these pages lie the stories and the pictures of Detroit and Michigan sports. Yours is in here, too. And, therefore, so are you.

Enjoy finding yourself.

Mitch Albom
Columnist
October 1999

I was born in cookie pollution.

As a sophomore in high school, nearly a quarter-century ago, I wrote that simple sentence. My life hasn't been the same since. It was the sentence that made all other sentences possible.

As the Free Press sports staff pulls a fortnight's worth of all-nighters to finish "Century of Champions," I can't help but think about how I reached this point, as the sports editor, about to enter my eighth year, and about how I love this newspaper business and the daily challenge of producing one of the country's best sports sections. And how much this book means to me, how I have thought about it for almost a decade, and how much I want everyone in Michigan to buy it, read it and enjoy it.

So I keep thinking about cookie pollution. I grew up less than a mile from a giant Nabisco factory in Philadelphia. Some days the wind carried the aroma of chocolate chip, other days it was Nilla Wafers. Cookie pollution. Every kid's dream.

When I wrote about it as a high school sophomore, my English teacher decided on the spot that I was her gifted student. She pushed me to write and write and write – for English classes, for the school paper and for the community papers. And so I wrote. By my junior year, I knew I wanted to be a sportswriter. So I wrote some more.

As a punk freshman at the University of Kansas I wanted to be on the school paper. Explaining why, I wrote about cookie pollution. When I pursued a summer internship at the Free Press, I wrote about cookie pollution. When I wanted a full-time job after college, in 1983, I wrote about cookie pollution for the Free Press once more.

I have never used it again until now. Once I discovered the wonders of Michigan, I never wanted to leave. For a sports journalist, no place can compare to Motown and the Great Lakes State. Michiganders live and die with their sports

teams and sports heroes. At least one team always seems in the midst of a potential championship run. And some big event, whether a prize fight or a golf tournament or an auto race, always is right around the corner.

Michigan sports have become central to the fabric of my life. There are those who would say that's shallow; I would counter that it's a blessing.

As the sports staff finishes this book, I think about how I purchased an engagement ring with the overtime pay generated by the Michigan Panthers' USFL title. I think about the excitement from the classic Free Press poster pages — *Gr-r-reat! Not Bad, Boys! Hail, Yes!* I think about the thrill of seeing Brendan Shanahan, in the champagne-soaked locker room with the national TV cameras rolling, holding aloft a Free Press extra edition bearing his photo.

That's why I don't view "Century of Champions" as a history book, even though it strives to tell the time line of Michigan sports better than any book out there. I view "Century of Champions" as a memories book.

So don't get caught up in why Bill Laimbeer is ranked ahead of Bob Lanier on our list of 100 sports heroes. Or why Michigan State's Game of the Century merits five pages and Michigan's Mad Magicians four. Our work isn't scientific or logical but personal. Choices were made from our hearts and from our memories.

So much happened in this century that a 10,000-page book wouldn't be large enough to cover every aspect of Michigan sports. But in these 336 pages, the Free Press proudly presents our version — our memories — of the 20th Century in Michigan sports.

Sit down with a couple of cookies and start reading.

Gene Myers
Sports Editor
October 1999

JULIAN H. GONZALEZ/Detroit Free Press

REVERSAL OF FORTUNE: AFTER WINNING THE STANLEY CUP, BRENDAN SHANAHAN COULDN'T WAIT TO CHECK OUT THE FREE PRESS. . . .

WHILE WORKING ON THE PAPER, SPORTS EDITOR GENE MYERS COULDN'T WAIT TO HOIST THE CUP WHEN IT MADE A TOUR OF DOWNTOWN OFFICES.

STEVE SCHRADER/Detroit Free Press

CHAPTER 1

OUR CHAMPIONS
MICHIGAN'S ATHLETIC GIANTS

Our Favorites
By the numbers

00 Otto Moore, William Bedford

0 George Plimpton, Olden Polynice

1 Terry Sawchuk, Anthony Carter, Lou Whitaker, Andre Rison, Billy Martin, Ray Oyler

2 Charlie Gehringer, Black Jack Stewart, Charles Woodson, Slava Fetisov, Gary Bergman

3 Alan Trammell, Eddie Murray, Lisa Brown-Miller, Dick McAuliffe, Marcel Pronovost

4 Jim Harbaugh, Joe Dumars, Red Kelly, Bill Gadsby, Angela Ruggiero, Chris Webber, Aurelio Rodriguez, Jason Hanson

5 Hank Greenberg, Jim Northrup, Marcel Dionne, Courtney Hawkins, Gordon Bell, Jalen Rose, Nick Lidstrom

6 Larry Aurie, Al Kaline, Tyrone Wheatley, Terry Mills, Ali Haji-Sheikh

7 Ted Lindsay, Norm Ullman, Garry Unger, Red Berenson, Rick Leach, Kelly Tripucka, Korie Hlede, Rocky Colavito, Chris Sabo

8 Morten Andersen, Igor Larionov, Don Wert, Ron LeFlore, Dennis Polonich, Eddie Brinkman

9 Gordie Howe, Dennis Franklin, Damion Easley, Kip Miller, Brendan Morrison

10 Rusty Staub, Alex Delvecchio, Dale McCourt, Brad Van Pelt, Dennis Rodman, Mayo Smith, Tony Taylor, Charlie Batch

11 Greg Landry, Mark Ingram, Sparky Anderson, Isiah Thomas, Bill Freehan, Bob McAdoo, the Wistert brothers, Bobby Hebert

12 Sid Abel, Bruce MacGregor, George Yardley, Errol Mann

13 Lance Parrish, Slava Kozlov

14 Dave Bergman, Joe Reed, Nick Libett, Dave Yarema, Brendan Shanahan, Eddie Miles, Earl Morrall, Eric Money, Brian Griese, Jim Bunning, Mike Donnelly

15 Joe Coleman, Paul Woods, Vinnie Johnson, Shelley Looney, John Mengelt

MARY SCHROEDER/Detroit Free Press

TIGERS G-MEN CHARLIE GEHRINGER (LEFT) AND HANK GREENBERG HAD THEIR NUMBERS RETIRED IN 1983.

16 Hal Newhouser, Bob Lanier, Vladimir Konstantinov, Gary Danielson, Charlie Baggett, Henry Boucha, Barry Larkin

17 Denny McLain, Tony Clark, Tim Ecclestone, Gerard Gallant

18 Herman Weaver, John Hiller, Tobin Rote, Bailey Howell, Curtis Rowe, Danny Gare, Bryan Watson

19 Steve Yzerman, Joe Niekro, Scott Mitchell, Paul Henderson, Bill Munson, Doyle Alexander, Dave Rozema

20 Mark Fidrych, Mickey Redmond, Lem Barney, Billy Sims, Barry Sanders, Campy Russell, Vaclav Nedomansky, Mickey Tettleton

21 Dave Bing, Desmond Howard, George Kell, Rumeal Robinson, Tshimanga Biakabutuka, Andy Bathgate, Danny Grant, Guillermo Hernandez, Enos Cabell, Steve Smith

22 Bobby Layne, Dave DeBusschere, Dino Ciccarelli, Alexi Lalas, John Salley, Bill Buntin, Brad Park, Ben Oglivie

23 Kirk Gibson, Willie Horton, Mark Aguirre, Levi Johnson, Jamie Morris, Bill Lochead

24 Sonny Grandelius, Mel Farr, Butch Woolfolk, Bob Probert, Travis Fryman, Jimmy Walker, Mickey Stanley, Rickey Green, Dexter Bussey, Spencer Haywood

25 Pat Studstill, Norm Cash, John Long, Juwan Howard, Earl McCullough, Harlan Huckleby, John Ogrodnick, Buddy Bell, Danny Meyer, Terry Furlow

26 Herb Adderley, Gates Brown, Dick Jauron, Clinton Jones

27 Frank Mahovlich, Harold Snepsts, Frank Tanana, Barbaro Garbey

28 Reed Larson, Bob Timberlake, Yale Lary, Mike Weger, James Hunter, Tom Timmerman

29 Jim Rutherford, Mickey Lolich, Mike Vernon, Aurelio Lopez

30 Jason Thompson, James Jones, M.L. Carr, Chris Osgood, Rogatien Vachon

31 Ed Giacomin, Larry Herndon, Ed Shuttlesworth, Vern Ruhle, Robert Fick

32 Greg Kelser, Ralph Simpson, Nick Pietrosante

33 Steve Kemp, Sedrick Irvin, Kris Draper, Magic Johnson, Grant Hill, Cazzie Russell

34 Lorenzo White, Andre St. Laurent, Chet Lemon

35 Ralph Houk, Tico Duckett, Don Dufek, Thom Darden, Walt Terrell

36 Steve Owens, Bennie Blades, Dan Schatzeder, Bill Gullickson

37 John Pingel, Doak Walker

38 J.D. Carlson, Brian Moehler

39 Leonard Thompson, Wayne Fontes, Mike Henneman, Milt Wilcox

40 Ron Simpkins, Charlie West, Nick Eddy, Ron Johnson, Bill Laimbeer

41 Ed Mio, Rob Lytle, Terry Barr, Tom Yewcic, Darrell Evans, Terry Tyler, Glen Rice, Jack Billingham

42 Chuck Nevitt, Roy Tarpley, Altie Taylor, Billy Taylor, Terry Duerod

43 James Pace

44 Rick Mahorn, Juan Berenguer, Dan Majerle

45 Cecil Fielder, Rudy Tomjanovich, Adrian Dantley, Dave Tobik

46 Harry Newman, Dan Petry, Bruce Kimm

47 Bennie Oosterbaan, Jack Morris

48 Gerald Ford, Percy Snow

49 Larry Walton, Bob Chappuis, John Offerdahl

50 Charley Ane, Paul Naumoff

51 Steve Everitt, Alex Grammas

52 Jim Laslavic, Rod Payne

53 Mike Lucci, James Edwards, Dick Tracewski

54 Chris Spielman, Ed Flanagan, Robert Traylor

55 Tiger Williams, Wayne Walker, Keith Primeau, Ed O'Neil, Larry Murphy

56 Joe Schmidt, Pat Swilling, Billy Muffett

57 John Corker, Ray Bentley, Stephen Boyd

58 Mike Hennigan

59 Charlie Weaver, Joe DeLamielleure

60 Bubba Baker, Mike Utley

61 Willis Ward, Ron Goovert

62 Lynn Boden

63 Jon Morris, Julius Franks

64 Jeff Hartings

65 Reggie McKenzie, Eric Andolsek

66 Bob Kowalkowski

67 Hank Bullough

68 Joe Cocozzo

69 Matt Elliott

70 Marty Huff

71 Alex Karras

72 Dan Dierdorf, Ed Muransky, Jumbo Elliott, Walt Downing

73 Russ Bollinger, Bill Dufek

74 Larry Hand

75 Greg Skrepanek, Lomas Brown, Jim Yarborough, Bubba Paris

76 Rockne Freitas, Lou Creekmur, Jim Brandstatter, Roger Brown, Flozell Adams

77 Paul Coffey, John Woodcock, Paul Seymour, Jon Jansen

78 Don Coleman, Darris McCord, Doug English

79 Tony Mandarich

80 Cloyce Box, Herb Orvis, Jerame Tuman

81 Night Train Lane, David Hill

JOHN C. HILLERY/Reuters

ISIAH THOMAS LENT A HAND WHEN FELLOW BAD BOY BILL LAIMBEER HAD HIS NUMBER RETIRED AT THE PALACE IN 1995.

82 Leon Hart

83 Jim Mitchell, Jim Doran, Paul Seal

84 Gene Washington, Herman Moore

85 Chuck Hughes, Petr Klima

86 David Sloan

87 Ron Kramer

88 Larry Bethea, Jim Mandich, Charlie Sanders, Sam Williams

89 Gail Cogdill, Ron Jessie

90 George Webster

91 Sergei Fedorov, Robert Porcher

92 Marc Spindler

93 Jerry Ball, Sam Sword

94 Luther Elliss

95 Bubba Smith

96 Tom Mack, Calvin O'Neal

97 Chris Hutchinson

98 Tom Harmon

99 Jeff Burton, Joel Smeenge

— Ty Cobb

Our Favorite Teams

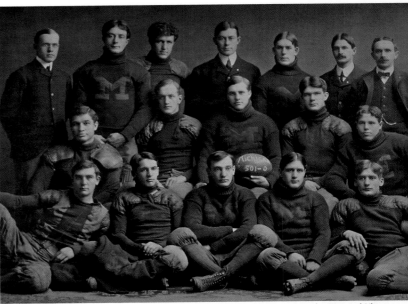

Bentley Historical Library

① 1901 MICHIGAN WOLVERINES   RECORD: 11-0.   COACH: FIELDING H. YOST.

A new era started at Michigan: Fielding H. Yost became coach; he unleashed his "Point-a-Minute" attack; the Wolverines outscored their opponents, 550-0; and U-M captured its first national championship. Michigan won the title the next three years, too. The season ended with a 49-0 victory over Stanford in the first Rose Bowl, which was so disappointing to the Tournament of Roses committee that a second Rose Bowl wasn't held until 1916. The committee unsuccessfully switched to polo, chariot races and ostrich races.

② 1979 MICHIGAN STATE SPARTANS

RECORD: 26-6.
COACH: JUD HEATHCOTE.

TERRY
DONNELLY

It was the Magic season and it was Magic's game. Sophomore Earvin (Magic) Johnson scored 24 points and grabbed seven rebounds as the Spartans beat Larry Bird and unbeaten Indiana State, 75-64, for their first NCAA basketball championship. More key Spartans: Greg Kelser, Jay Vincent, Terry Donnelly, Mike Brkovich and Ron Charles.

③ 1997 DETROIT RED WINGS

RECORD: 38-26-18.
COACH: SCOTTY BOWMAN.

MIKE
VERNON

The Red Wings ended Detroit's 42-year wait for its eighth Stanley Cup. After a so-so regular season, the Wings stormed through the playoffs, beating St. Louis in six, Anaheim in four, Colorado in six and Philadelphia in four. Goalie Mike Vernon won the Conn Smythe. More key Wings: Captain Steve Yzerman, Nick Lidstrom, Brendan Shanahan and Igor Larionov.

④ 1968 DETROIT TIGERS

RECORD: 103-59.
MANAGER: MAYO SMITH.

MAYO
SMITH

In the Year of the Pitcher, Denny McLain won the AL Cy Young and MVP awards by winning 31 games. But Mickey Lolich's heroics brought Detroit its first World Series title since 1945. He beat St. Louis three times, including the decisive Game 7 against Bob Gibson, 4-1. Other key Tigers: Al Kaline, Willie Horton, Mickey Stanley and Jim Northrup.

⑤ 1989 DETROIT PISTONS

RECORD: 63-19.
COACH: CHUCK DALY.

VINNIE
JOHNSON

The Pistons won their first NBA championship when the best of their Bad Boys-era teams swept Magic Johnson's Los Angeles Lakers. The Pistons lost only two of 16 playoff games, both to Chicago. Joe Dumars, who averaged 27.3 points against LA, was the playoffs' MVP. Other key Pistons: Captain Isiah Thomas, Bill Laimbeer and Vinnie Johnson.

6 1935 DETROIT TIGERS

RECORD: 93-58.
MANAGER: MICKEY COCHRANE.

GOOSE
GOSLIN

After failing in four World Series, the Tigers finally won the title, despite Hank Greenberg's broken wrist in Game 2. The decisive run came in the bottom of the ninth in Game 6 against the Chicago Cubs, when Goose Goslin singled in Mickey Cochrane with two out. Other key Tigers: Charlie Gehringer, Schoolboy Rowe, Tommy Bridges and Billy Rogell.

7 1966 MICHIGAN STATE SPARTANS

RECORD: 9-0-1, 7-0 BIG TEN.
COACH: DUFFY DAUGHERTY.

GENE
WASHINGTON

The '65 Spartans won a national championship but the '66 team played the "Game of the Century," a controversial 10-10 tie with Notre Dame. Irish coach Ara Parseghian ran out the clock instead of trying to win. MSU finished No. 2 in the polls behind the Irish. Key Spartans: George Webster, Bubba Smith, Gene Washington and Jimmy Raye.

8 1959 HAMTRAMCK LITTLE LEAGUE

RECORD: 13-0.
MANAGER: GENE PIOTKOWSKI.

The Hamtramck Nationals won the state's only Little League World Series championship, at Williamsport, Pa. Art (Pinky) Deras won seven of the 13 tournament games and was selected player of the year. In the 7-1 semifinal victory over Kailua, Hawaii, Deras struck out 17 and came within an out of a no-hitter. In the 12-0 final victory over Auburn, Calif., Deras struck out 14 and hit a three-run homer. That gave him a streak of 75 scoreless innings. For the summer, he had 10 no-hitters and 296 strikeouts in 108 innings. The team was flown to California to appear on the "Lawrence Welk Show." Two years later, as a 14-year-old, Deras led virtually the same team to the national Pony League championship.

Special to the Free Press

9 1952 DETROIT RED WINGS

RECORD: 44-14-12.
COACH: TOMMY IVAN.

TOMMY
IVAN

Perhaps the strongest of the Gordie Howe-led teams, the Wings won their fourth straight regular-season title with 100 points and then won all eight playoff games. Goalie Terry Sawchuk had two shutouts against Toronto in the semifinals and two against Montreal in the finals. He gave up only five goals for an unbelievable 0.63 goals-against average.

10 1957 DETROIT LIONS

RECORD: 8-4.
COACH: GEORGE WILSON.

TOBIN
ROTE

To win their third NFL championship of the '50s, the Lions overcame: the resignation of coach Buddy Parker right before the season; Bobby Layne's broken ankle in the final home game; and a 27-7 deficit at San Francisco in a divisional playoff. George Wilson coached, Tobin Rote quarterbacked, and the Lions beat Cleveland, 59-14, in the championship game.

➤

11 1984 DETROIT TIGERS

JACK
MORRIS

RECORD: 104-58.
MANAGER: SPARKY ANDERSON.

The Tigers sprinted to a 35-5 start, led wire-to-wire, and beat the San Diego Padres in five games for their first World Series title since 1968. Bless You Boys! Jack Morris threw a no-hitter in April. Kirk Gibson belted a classic home run against Goose Gossage in Game 5. Larry Herndon caught the final out. Alan Trammell was MVP of the Series.

12 1968-75 HUDSON HIGH TIGERS

TOM
SAYLOR

RECORD: 72 CONSECUTIVE VICTORIES.
COACH: TOM SAYLOR.

Hudson High won 72 straight football games in 1968-75, breaking the national record set by Jefferson City, Mo., in 1958-66, with a 24-14 victory over Kalamazoo Hackett on Nov. 15, 1975. The streak ended in the first Class C state title game, 38-22 to Ishpeming. The Michigan Sports Hall of Fame has inducted one team: the Hudson Tigers, in 1976.

MARY SCHROEDER/Detroit Free Press

13 1983 MICHIGAN PANTHERS

RECORD: 12-6.   COACH: JIM STANLEY.

Although the team existed only two years — and the USFL three — the Panthers captured the hearts of fans. Why? Detroit's teams had been basically awful since the '68 Tigers. In the playoffs, 60,237 saw the Panthers beat the Oakland Invaders, 37-21, and thousands ripped down the Silverdome goalposts and ripped up the turf. In the title game, at Denver's Mile High Stadium, the Panthers beat the Philadelphia Stars, 24-22. Bobby Hebert, MVP of the title game, connected with Anthony Carter on a 48-yard, game-clinching touchdown late in the fourth quarter. (Above, Carter and kicker Novo Bojovic celebrated it.)

14 1992 MICHIGAN WOLVERINES

JUWAN
HOWARD

RECORD: 25-9.
COACH: STEVE FISHER.

The Fab Five. Chris Webber, Juwan Howard, Jalen Rose, Jimmy King and Ray Jackson, who started a fashion trend by wearing baggy shorts, had the nation buzzing when they led Michigan to the NCAA championship game as freshmen. Jackson was the last to join the starting lineup, against Notre Dame in February. Duke, though, won the title, 71-51.

15 1934 STROH'S BOHEMIAN BEER

JOE
NORRIS

Stroh's was the first of the great beer teams that dominated bowling for two decades. In 1934, one year after it was formed by captain Joe Norris, Stroh's became the first team from Detroit to win the ABC national tournament and won the first of five World Match Game titles. The original team was Norris, Phil Bauman, John Crimmins, Cass Grygier and Walter Reppenhagen. Fred Gardella sometimes replaced Crimmins.

Our Favorite column

Mitch Albom came to the Detroit Free Press in July 1985 as a 27-year-old with a background as an amateur boxer, nightclub singer and pianist, and degrees in sociology, business administration and journalism.

Michiganders embraced him from the start. And so did the critics. He won every sportswriting award around — most several times over. The Associated Press Sports Editors selected him the country's top columnist 12 times; no one else had won the award more than once. Albom also worked in TV and radio and even wrote a song, "Cookin' For Two," that was nominated for a Cable Ace Award. He wrote several books, including best-sellers "Bo," "Fab Five" and "Tuesdays With Morrie."

For "Century of Champions," he was asked to select his favorite column. He said he couldn't. But he said readers continue to mention the following column, published Dec. 18, 1994.

BY MITCH ALBOM

As the year fades to dust, we mourn an old friend in sports. His name was Grace. He passed away in 1994. Cause of death was neglect. They found him wrapped in a blanket, frozen and forgotten, in an alley behind a TV studio. He left no survivors.

You may recall Grace from your youth — if you're old enough. He played for many teams. Many sports. Once upon a time, when his legs were strong, he was welcome on any playing field in America.

He was best known for tipping his cap in the baseball stadium, or speaking humbly with reporters in small towns. You saw him respecting a referee's decision in tennis, or handing the ball to the ref after a touchdown.

He could dunk a basketball — but gently, without yelling obscenities. He could grind for a hockey puck — but never pushed the stick into an opponent's throat.

He even boxed a little, and after victories, he was humble. "I'm lucky tonight," he would say. "That man is a fine fighter."

This was long ago, before commercial endorsements, before ESPN highlights, before players practiced dance steps in front of the locker room mirror.

Grace was a hero then. He never made a lot of money. In fact, he never took a paycheck for anything he did.

He died penniless.

People laughed at his "lack of marketing."

SPORTS AS A VEHICLE

These are the same people who see sports as a star-making machine: shoe companies, agents, TV networks, media "pals."

The same people who bring you a new CD this Christmas, featuring rap songs by NBA players. One is called "Livin' Legal and Large" by Seattle's Gary Payton:

*I'm just a superstar, rolling down
the boulevard in my $50,000 car.*

It doesn't matter that most of America doesn't know who Payton is — or that he's never won an NBA title, or that, as a point guard, he ranked 17th in assists last season. The NBA is about 'tude. Payton has 'tude.

Grace did not have 'tude.

He didn't even know what it meant.

Grace knew how to lose. He never would hire a hit man to whack an opponent, and he didn't blame reporters when he made a mistake. He wouldn't throw firecrackers at fans, like Vince Coleman, or desert his team to be with Madonna, like Dennis Rodman.

Remember Joe Louis, when he said, "Every man's got to get beat sometime"?

Grace taught him that.

He knew how to lose.

More important, he knew how to win. He knew that for every great play he made, many others were trying to do the same. He refused to rub their noses in his success. When he made an interception, he did not wiggle down the sideline, laughing at the opposing team, the way Deion Sanders does today.

And when he hit home runs, he did not flip the finger to opposing dugouts, as Ken Griffey Jr. did last season.

In June, during the NBA playoffs, Scottie Pippen dunked over Patrick Ewing. Ewing fell and Pippen stood over him, so Ewing had to stare up into his crotch. Pippen glared. Later he said, "You wait your whole career for a moment like that."

Grace would never have understood that.

THE SCREAMERS TAKE OVER

Throughout his sports career, Grace never wore his name on his uniform. He never held out of camp, or demanded that a contract be renegotiated. "A deal's a deal," he once said.

Later, when Grace retired from active sports, he coached. For a while, he worked with men like UCLA's John Wooden. Men who taught. Men who kept things in perspective.

But soon, Grace was driven out of coaching. He was squashed by obnoxious types like Buddy Ryan and greedy types like Rollie Massimino, who made a dirty deal with a university, then demanded they pay him off.

In the twilight of his career, Grace tried broadcasting. An understated voice, never intruding. Men like Ernie Harwell and Vin Scully shared the booth with Grace.

But soon, he went out of fashion, tossed aside for screamers like Dick Vitale, Chris Berman and John Madden. Grace never understood them. Never understood becoming bigger than the game itself. "They sure are loud," he would say, trying to be kind.

After that, Grace disappeared. No one seems to know exactly when, but those who loved him felt his absence like a cold wind.

Now he is gone.

Reaction to his death was mild. Only a few of today's athletes — Joe Dumars, Stefan Edberg, Barry Sanders — seemed to care about his tradition. Others were busy pulling off their helmets and pointing at TV cameras.

And so this is it, the obituary, the death of Grace. His last request concerned his funeral. For all he had done, he wanted only this: "Something small, something quiet, something dignified."

Hmm. Does anyone know how to do that anymore?

◆

All-time Red Wings

SCOTTY BOWMAN
RED WING: 1993-
LEGACY: Won back-to-back Stanley Cups. Posted NHL-record 62 victories in 1995-96.

JACK ADAMS
RED WING: 1927-62. LEGACY: Built the foundation. Won seven Cups, 12 regular-season titles (seven straight).

MIKE ILITCH
RED WING: 1982-
LEGACY: Paid Norris family around $10 million in 1982; now worth $185 million.

JULIAN H. GONZALEZ/Detroit Free Press

GORDIE HOWE AND TED LINDSAY SHARE STANLEY'S SPOTLIGHT WITH STEVE YZERMAN.

FIRST TEAM

LW **TED LINDSAY**

RED WING: 1944-57, '64-65.
GOALS: 335. ASSISTS: 393.
LEGACY: "Terrible Ted." Retired as NHL's highest-scoring left wing and leader in penalty minutes. First-team all-star eight times. Won four Stanley Cups.

C **STEVE YZERMAN**

RED WING: 1983-
GOALS: 592. ASSISTS: 891.
LEGACY: At 21, youngest captain in team history. Longest-serving captain in NHL history. Scored 50 goals five times. Won two Cups. Conn Smythe in 1998.

RW **GORDIE HOWE**

RED WING: 1946-71.
GOALS: 786. ASSISTS: 1,023.
LEGACY: Mr. Hockey. League MVP six times. Leading scorer six times. Retired as NHL's all-time scoring leader. Won four Stanley Cups.

D **RED KELLY**

RED WING: 1947-60.
GOALS: 154. ASSISTS: 297.
LEGACY: Won very first Norris Trophy as the NHL's top defenseman in 1954. First-team all-star six times. Won four Cups with Detroit, plus four more with Toronto.

D **MARCEL PRONOVOST**

RED WING: 1949-65.
GOALS: 80. ASSISTS: 217.
LEGACY: Twice a first-team all-star, twice on second team. Made debut during '50 playoffs, helping injury-depleted team win Stanley Cup. Won three more in Detroit.

G **TERRY SAWCHUK**

RED WING: 1949-55, '57-64, '68-69.
RECORD: 352-244-130.
AVG.: 2.46. SHUTOUTS: 85.
LEGACY: More games, more victories, more shutouts than any other NHL goalie. Won three Cups in Detroit.

SECOND TEAM

RW	Larry Aurie	1927-39
C	Alex Delvecchio	1950-74
LW	Sid Abel	1938-43, '45-52
D	Jack Stewart	1938-43, '45-50
D	Ebbie Goodfellow	1929-43
G	Harry Lumley	1943-50

All-time Lions

FIRST-TEAM OFFENSE

QB BOBBY LAYNE
LION: 1950-58.

RB BARRY SANDERS
LION: 1989-98.

RB DOAK WALKER
LION: 1950-55.

OG HARLEY SEWELL
LION: 1953-62.

OT LOU CREEKMUR
LION: 1950-59.

C ALEX WOJCIECHOWICZ
LION: 1938-46.

OG DICK STANFEL
LION: 1952-55.

OT LOMAS BROWN
LION: 1985-95.

TE CHARLIE SANDERS
LION: 1968-77.

WR CLOYCE BOX
LION: 1949-50, '52-54.

WR HERMAN MOORE
LION: 1991-

PK JASON HANSON
LION: 1992-

KR MEL GRAY
LION: 1989-94.

FIRST-TEAM DEFENSE

DE BUBBA BAKER
LION: 1978-82.

DT ALEX KARRAS
LION: 1958-62, '64-70.

NG LES BINGAMAN
LION: 1948-54.

DT ROGER BROWN
LION: 1960-66.

LB WAYNE WALKER
LION: 1958-72.

LB JOE SCHMIDT
LION: 1953-65.

LB CHRIS SPIELMAN
LION: 1988-95.

CB LEM BARNEY
LION: 1967-77.

CB DICK (NIGHT TRAIN) LANE
LION: 1960-65.

S YALE LARY
LION: 1952-53, '56-64.

S JACK CHRISTIANSEN
LION: 1951-58.

P YALE LARY
LION: 1952-53, '56-64.

PR JACK CHRISTIANSEN
LION: 1951-58.

COACH

BUDDY PARKER
LION: 1951-56.
LEGACY: Coach for NFL titles in '52 and '53, runner-up in '54. His .671 winning percentage (50-24-2) is team's best.

EXECUTIVE

EDWIN ANDERSON
LION: 1948-73.
LEGACY: President, 1949-61; GM, 1962-73. Praised in '50s; ripped in '60s, when players hung him in effigy from goalposts.

SECOND-TEAM OFFENSE

QB Dutch Clark
1934-38

RB Billy Sims
1980-84

RB Nick Pietrosante
1959-65

OT Rockne Freitas
1968-77

OG John Gordy
1957, '59-67

C Ed Flanagan
1965-74

OG Kevin Glover
1985-97

OT Keith Dorney
1979-87

WR Gail Cogdill
1960-68

WR Leon Hart
1950-57

TE David Hill
1976-82

PK Eddie Murray
1980-91

KR Pat Studstill
1961-67

SECOND-TEAM DEFENSE

DE Larry Hand
1964-77

DT Doug English
1975-79, '81-85

DT Jerry Ball
1987-92

DE Darris McCord
1955-67

LB Ox Emerson
1934-37

LB Mike Lucci
1965-73

LB Charlie Weaver
1971-81

CB Dick LeBeau
1959-72

CB Jim David
1952-59

S Don Doll
1949-52

S Bennie Blades
1988-96

P Jim Arnold
1986-93

PR Mel Gray
1989-94

All-time Tigers

SPARKY ANDERSON
TIGER: 1979-95.
LEGACY: Won World Series in 1984. Twice AL manager of year. Club record for games (2,579), victories (1,331), losses (1,248).

 1B HANK GREENBERG

TIGER: 1930, '33-41, '45-46.
AVERAGE: .319. GAMES: 1,269.
HOMERS: 306. RBIs: 1,202.

 2B CHARLIE GEHRINGER

TIGER: 1924-42.
AVERAGE: .320. GAMES: 2,323.
HOMERS: 184. RBIs: 1,427.

 SS ALAN TRAMMELL

TIGER: 1977-96.
AVERAGE: .285. GAMES: 2,293.
HOMERS: 185. RBIs: 1,003.

 3B GEORGE KELL

TIGER: 1946-52.
AVERAGE: .326. GAMES: 826.
HOMERS: 25. RBIs: 414.

 C MICKEY COCHRANE

TIGER: 1934-37.
AVERAGE: .313. GAMES: 315.
HOMERS: 11. RBIs: 152.

LF HARRY HEILMANN

TIGER: 1914, '16-29.
AVERAGE: .343. GAMES: 1,989.
HOMERS: 164. RBIs: 1,442.

DOUGLAS C. PIZAC/Associated Press

GEORGE KELL SPENT PARTS OF SEVEN SEASONS IN A TIGERS UNIFORM – AND MOST OF FOUR DECADES IN A TIGERS BROADCAST BOOTH.

 **CF TY COBB**

TIGER: 1905-26.
AVERAGE: .368. GAMES: 2,805.
HOMERS: 112. RBIs: 1,804.

 **RF AL KALINE**

TIGER: 1953-74.
AVERAGE: .297. GAMES: 2,834.
HOMERS: 399. RBIs: 1,583.

 **PH GATES BROWN**

TIGER: 1963-75.
AVERAGE: .257. GAMES: 1,051.
HOMERS: 84. RBIs: 322.

RHP DENNY McLAIN

TIGER: 1963-70.
RECORD: 117-62. ERA: 3.13.
K's: 1,150. SHUTOUTS: 26.

LHP HAL NEWHOUSER

TIGER: 1939-53.
RECORD: 200-148. ERA: 3.07.
K's: 1,770. SHUTOUTS: 33.

RP JOHN HILLER

TIGER: 1965-70, '72-80.
RECORD: 87-76. ERA: 2.83.
GAMES: 545. SAVES: 125.

BILL LAJOIE
TIGER: 1968-91.
LEGACY: Best known as GM in 1983-91. Built '84 and '87 teams through draft and trades. Quit over low pay, tight budgets, Sparky's veto power.

FRANK NAVIN
TIGER: 1902-35.
LEGACY: Turned ragtag franchise into AL power. Started as bookkeeper in 1902. Built Navin Field in 1912. Died five weeks after first World Series title in '35.

SECOND TEAM

1B	Norm Cash 1960-74	**3B**	Aurelio Rodriguez 1971-79	**CF**	Sam Crawford 1903-17	**RHP**	Jack Morris 1977-90
2B	Lou Whitaker 1977-95	**C**	Bill Freehan 1961, '63-76	**RF**	Kirk Gibson 1979-87, '93-95	**LHP**	Mickey Lolich 1963-75
SS	Billy Rogell 1930-39	**LF**	Willie Horton 1963-77	**PH**	Bob Fothergill 1922-30	**RP**	Guillermo Hernandez 1984-89

All-time Pistons

COACH

CHUCK DALY
PISTON: 1983-92.
LEGACY: Back-to-back NBA titles.

GM

JACK McCLOSKEY
PISTON: 1979-92.
LEGACY: Hired Daly. Drafted NAIA's Dennis Rodman.

OWNER

BILL DAVIDSON
PISTON: 1974-
LEGACY: Built Palace, bought plane.

SECOND TEAM

F Bailey Howell 1959-64

F Kelly Tripucka 1981-86

C Bill Laimbeer 1981-94

G Joe Dumars 1985-99

G John Long '78-86, '88-89, '90-91

6th Vinnie Johnson 1981-91

FIRST TEAM

F GRANT HILL

PISTON: 1994-
G: 361. **PTS:** 20.7. **REB:** 8.1.
LEGACY: Co-rookie of year in 1995. One of only three NBA players to lead his team in scoring, rebounding and assists at least two seasons. First-team All-NBA once.

F DAVE DeBUSSCHERE

PISTON: 1962-68.
G: 440. **PTS:** 16.1. **REB:** 11.2.
LEGACY: Hall of Fame in 1982. Named to NBA 50th anniverary team. At 24, became youngest-ever coach in NBA after second season. Pistons' player-coach for three seasons (79-143).

C BOB LANIER

PISTON: 1970-80.
G: 681. **PTS:** 22.7. **REB:** 11.8.
LEGACY: Hall of Fame in 1991. No. 16 retired in '93. All-Star Game MVP in '74. Led team in scoring eight times, rebounding seven. First overall pick in '70 draft out of St. Bonaventure.

G ISIAH THOMAS

PISTON: 1981-94.
G: 979. **PTS:** 19.2. **AST:** 9.3.
LEGACY: Guaranteed a championship as a rookie and made good on promise in 1989 and '90. Finals MVP in '90. All-Star Game MVP twice. Named to NBA 50th anniversary team.

Detroit Pistons

IN 1976, A SEASON AFTER BEING TRADED BY THE PISTONS TO THE WASHINGTON BULLETS, DAVE BING WAS THE ALL-STAR GAME'S MVP.

G DAVE BING

PISTON: 1966-75.
G: 675. **PTS:** 22.6. **AST:** 6.4.
LEGACY: First Piston to have No. (21) retired. Rookie of year in 1967. Named to NBA 50th anniversary team. First-team All-NBA twice, second-team once. Hall of Fame in 1989.

6TH DENNIS RODMAN

PISTON: 1986-93.
G: 549. **PTS:** 8.8. **REB:** 11.5.
LEGACY: Defensive player of year in 1990, '91. All-Defensive team 1989-93. Rebounding champ in '92, '93. On two Bad Boys title teams. Single-game team rebounding record (34).

All-time MSU basketball

FIRST TEAM

 **GREG KELSER**

SPARTAN: 1975-79.
G: 115. PTS: 17.5. REB: 9.5.
LEGACY: "Special K." Co-captain (with Magic) of 1979 NCAA championship team. Career leader in rebounds. All-America in 1979.

(F) **TERRY FURLOW**

SPARTAN: 1972-76.
G: 100. PTS: 17.8. REB: 6.3.
LEGACY: In 1976, had school's best single-season scoring average (29.4) and scored most points in a game − 50 − against Iowa. All-America in '76.

(C) **JOHNNY GREEN**

SPARTAN: 1956-59.
G: 63. PTS: 16.9. REB: 16.4.
LEGACY: "Jumpin' Johnny." Big Ten MVP and All-America in 1959. Had school-record 392 rebounds in 1957-58. Career leader in rebound average. MSU's first first-round NBA pick.

JULIAN H. GONZALEZ/Detroit Free Press
THE SPARTANS, LED BY STEVE SMITH, WON THE BIG TEN TITLE IN 1990.

 **EARVIN JOHNSON**

SPARTAN: 1977-79.
G: 62. PTS: 17.1. AST: 7.9.
LEGACY: "Magic." Beat Larry Bird for 1979 NCAA title. Holds school record for single-game assists (14) in Big Ten game, season steals overall (75). All-America, Big Ten MVP in 1979.

 **STEVE SMITH**

SPARTAN: 1987-91.
G: 122. PTS: 18.5. REB: 6.1.
LEGACY: Big Ten MVP in 1990. Two-time All-America ('90, '91). MSU's second all-time leading scorer. Big Ten scoring champ (23.2) in 1991. Led team to Big Ten title in '90.

 **SCOTT SKILES**

SPARTAN: 1982-86.
G: 118. PTS: 18.2. AST: 5.5.
LEGACY: All-time assists leader (645) and third all-time scorer. Co-captain and Big Ten MVP in 1986. Big Ten scoring champ (29.1) in '86, when he led Spartans to regional semifinals.

SECOND TEAM

F	Julius McCoy	1954-56
F	Ralph Simpson	1970
C	Jay Vincent	1978-81
G	Mateen Cleaves	1997-
G	Shawn Respert	1991-95
6th	Sam Vincent	1982-85

All-time MSU football

FIRST-TEAM OFFENSE

 QB **EARL MORRALL**
SPARTAN: 1953-55.

 RB **LORENZO WHITE**
SPARTAN: 1984-87.

 RB **CLINTON JONES**
SPARTAN: 1964-66.

 OG **DAVE BEHRMAN**
SPARTAN: 1960-62.

OT **DON COLEMAN**
SPARTAN: 1949-51.

C **DICK TAMBURO**
SPARTAN: 1950-52.

OG **JOE DeLAMIELLEURE**
SPARTAN: 1970-72.

OT **TONY MANDARICH**
SPARTAN: 1985-88.

TE **BILLY JOE DuPREE**
SPARTAN: 1970-72.

WR **GENE WASHINGTON**
SPARTAN: 1964-66.

WR **KIRK GIBSON**
SPARTAN: 1975-78.

 **PK** **MORTEN ANDERSEN**
SPARTAN: 1978-81.

 KR **DERRICK MASON**
SPARTAN: 1993-96.

FIRST-TEAM DEFENSE

 **DE** **SAM WILLIAMS**
SPARTAN: 1956-58.

 **DE** **BUBBA SMITH**
SPARTAN: 1964-66.

 **DT** **FRANK KUSH**
SPARTAN: 1950-52.

 **DT** **BUCK NYSTROM**
SPARTAN: 1953-55.

 **LB** **CARL BANKS**
SPARTAN: 1980-83.

R **GEORGE WEBSTER**
SPARTAN: 1964-66.

 **LB** **PERCY SNOW**
SPARTAN: 1986-89.

DB **GEORGE SAIMES**
SPARTAN: 1960-62.

CB **HERB ADDERLEY**
SPARTAN: 1958-60.

S **BRAD VAN PELT**
SPARTAN: 1970-72.

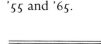 **S** **LYNN CHANDNOIS**
SPARTAN: 1946-49.

 P **RAY STACHOWICZ**
SPARTAN: 1977-80.

 **PR** **DERRICK MASON**
SPARTAN: 1993-96.

COACH

DUFFY DAUGHERTY
SPARTAN: 1947-72.
LEGACY: UPI national champion in '65. Coach of year in '55 and '65.

ASSISTANT

BIGGIE MUNN
SPARTAN: 1947-71.
LEGACY: National championship in '52. Coach of year in '52. Head coach, 1947-53.

SECOND-TEAM OFFENSE

QB	Steve Juday	1963-65
RB	John Pingel	1936-38
RB	LeRoy Bolden	1951-54
OT	Flozell Adams	1994-97
OG	Don Mason	1948-49
C	Dan Currie	1955-57
OG	Ed Bagdon	1946-49
OT	Jerry West	1964-66
TE	Mark Brammer	1976-79
WR	Andre Rison	1985-88
WR	Bob Carey	1949-51
PK	John Langeloh	1987-90
KR	Eric Allen	1969-71

SECOND-TEAM DEFENSE

DL	Dorne Dibble	1949-50
DL	Don Dohoney	1951-53
DL	Larry Bethea	1974-77
DL	Sid Wagner	1933-35
LB	Rich Saul	1967-69
LB	Ron Goovert	1963-65
LB	Dan Bass	1976-79
DB	James Burroughs	1977-79, '81
DB	Allen Brenner	1966-68
DB	James Ellis	1951-53
DB	Bill Simpson	1971-73
P	Greg Montgomery	1985-87
PR	Jesse Thomas	1948-50

All-time U-M basketball

FIRST TEAM

F GLEN RICE

WOLVERINE: 1986-89.
G: 134. **PTS:** 18.2. **REB:** 6.4.
LEGACY: Top scorer in Michigan history. Scored NCAA-record 184 points in six games to help Michigan win 1989 title. All-America in '89.

F CHRIS WEBBER

WOLVERINE: 1992-93.
G: 70. **PTS:** 17.4. **REB:** 10.0.
LEGACY: Only player to make NCAA all-tourney team as freshman and sophomore. Led Fab Five to two NCAA finals appearances.

C BILL BUNTIN

WOLVERINE: 1963-65.
G: 79. **PTS:** 21.8. **REB:** 13.1.
LEGACY: Two-time All-America. Three-time All-Big Ten. School MVP award named in his honor. First Wolverine drafted by NBA.

G CAZZIE RUSSELL

WOLVERINE: 1964-66.
G: 80. **PTS:** 27.1. **REB:** 8.5.
LEGACY: Only U-M basketball player to have number (33) retired. Three-time All-America. Career scoring-average leader. Three Big Ten titles.

Detroit Free Press

HAMTRAMCK NATIVE RUDY TOMJANOVICH AVERAGED 25.1 POINTS AT MICHIGAN. HE WOULD GO ON TO COACH THE HOUSTON ROCKETS TO TWO NBA TITLES.

G RICKEY GREEN

WOLVERINE: 1976-77.
G: 60. **PTS:** 19.7. **AST:** 4.1.
LEGACY: Speedy fast-break specialist from juco ranks. All-Big Ten twice. All-America and runner-up to Marques Johnson as player of year in '77.

6TH RUDY TOMJANOVICH

WOLVERINE: 1968-70.
G: 72. **PTS:** 25.1. **REB:** 14.4.
LEGACY: Averaged 30.1 points, 15.7 rebounds as All-America in '70. U-M's all-time leading rebounder with 1,039. Twice led Big Ten in rebounding.

All-time U-M football

FIRST-TEAM OFFENSE

 QB RICK LEACH
WOLVERINE: 1975-78.

 RB TOM HARMON
WOLVERINE: 1938-40.

 **RB ROB LYTLE**
WOLVERINE: 1974-76.

OT DAN DIERDORF
WOLVERINE: 1968-70.

 OG REGGIE McKENZIE
WOLVERINE: 1969-71.

C ERNIE VICK
WOLVERINE: 1918-21.

 OG JULIUS FRANKS
WOLVERINE: 1941-42.

OT GREG SKREPENAK
WOLVERINE: 1988-91.

E RON KRAMER
WOLVERINE: 1954-56.

 **E BENNIE OOSTERBAAN**
WOLVERINE: 1925-27.

WR ANTHONY CARTER
WOLVERINE: 1979-82.

PK REMY HAMILTON
WOLVERINE: 1994-96.

 KR DESMOND HOWARD
WOLVERINE: 1989-91.

FIRST-TEAM DEFENSE

 **DL BILL YEARBY**
WOLVERINE: 1963-65.

 **DL FRANCIS WISTERT**
WOLVERINE: 1931-33.

 **DL ALBERT WISTERT**
WOLVERINE: 1940-42.

 **DL MARK MESSNER**
WOLVERINE: 1985-88.

 **LB GERMANY SCHULZ**
WOLVERINE: 1904-05, '07-08.

LB ERICK ANDERSON
WOLVERINE: 1988-91.

 **LB RON SIMPKINS**
WOLVERINE: 1976-79.

 **CB CHARLES WOODSON**
WOLVERINE: 1995-97.

CB THOM DARDEN
WOLVERINE: 1969-71.

 **S TRIPP WELBORNE**
WOLVERINE: 1987-90.

S TOM CURTIS
WOLVERINE: 1967-69.

 **P HARRY KIPKE**
WOLVERINE: 1921-23.

 **PR GENE DERRICOTTE**
WOLVERINE: 1944, '46-48.

COACH

FIELDING H. YOST
U-M: 1901-41.
LEGACY: National titles in '01-04, '18, '23. Went 56 straight without loss in '01-05.

ASSISTANT

BO SCHEMBECHLER
U-M: 1969-90.
LEGACY: Won or tied for 13 Big Ten championships. Ten Rose Bowls.

SECOND-TEAM OFFENSE

QB Benny Friedman 1924-26
RB Ron Johnson 1966-68
RB Willie Heston 1901-04
OT Jumbo Elliott 1984-87
OG Albert Benbrook 1908-10
C Charles Bernard 1931-33
OT Tom Mack 1964-65
OG Stefan Humphries 1980-83
TE Jim Mandich 1967-69
WR Desmond Howard 1989-91
WR Jim Smith 1973-76
PK J. D. Carlson 1989-91
KR Anthony Carter 1979-82

SECOND-TEAM DEFENSE

DL Curtis Greer 1976-79
DL Otto Pommerening 1927-28
DL Alvin Wistert 1947-49
DL Chris Hutchinson 1989-92
LB John Anderson 1974-77
LB Calvin O'Neal 1974-76
LB Maynard Morrison 1929-31
DB Pete Elliott 1945-48
DB Rick Volk 1964-66
DB Bump Elliott 1946-47
DB Dave Brown 1972-74
P Monte Robbins 1984-87
PR Derrick Alexander 1989-90, '92-93

All-time College hockey

Michigan State University

Michigan State's Kip Miller won the
Hobey Baker Award in 1990.

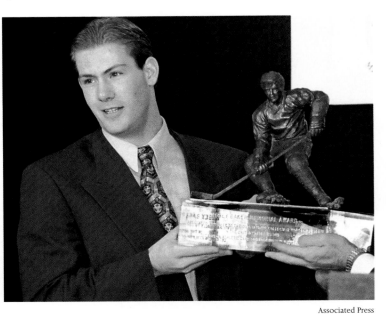

Associated Press

Brendan Morrison, who won the Hobey in 1997, became
Michigan's all-time leading scorer (102 goals, 182 assists).

COACH

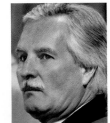

RON MASON
MSU: 1979-
LEGACY: Owns NCAA record for victories (837-354-70). Won national title in 1986 and has record 19 NCAA tourney appearances. Coached 29 All-America players and 40 who went to NHL.

ASSISTANT

JOHN MacINNES
MICH. TECH: 1956-82.
LEGACY: Built national power and won NCAA championships in 1962, 1965 and 1975. Started Great Lakes Invitational in Detroit. Sixth on the all-time victory list with 555.

FIRST TEAM

F RED BERENSON

MICHIGAN: 1959-62.
GOALS: 78. **ASSISTS:** 59.
LEGACY: Two-time All-America. Scored school-record 43 goals — including nine hat tricks — in 28 games in 1961-62 season, ending with third-place NCAA finish.

F MIKE ZUKE

MICHIGAN TECH: 1972-76.
GOALS: 133. **ASSISTS:** 177.
LEGACY: Ranks second all-time in NCAA scoring. Two-time first-team All-America, played in three straight national championship games, winning one, in 1975.

F BRENDAN MORRISON

MICHIGAN: 1993-97.
GOALS: 102. **ASSISTS:** 182.
LEGACY: 1997 Hobey Baker Award winner. Scored NCAA championship-winning goal in overtime in 1996 against Colorado College. Wolverines' all-time leading scorer.

D WAYNE GAGNE

WESTERN MICHIGAN: 1983-87.
GOALS: 42. **ASSISTS:** 199.
LEGACY: Hobey Baker runner-up in 1987. Two-time All-America. WMU career leader for points as a defenseman, third overall. Twice top-scoring defenseman in the country.

D BRAD WERENKA

NORTHERN MICH.: 1987-91.
GOALS: 40. **ASSISTS:** 88.
LEGACY: Was first-team All-America in 1991 during dream season capped by Wildcats' only national championship. Eventually played in NHL with Pittsburgh.

G TONY ESPOSITO

MICHIGAN TECH: 1964-67.
RECORD: 38-10-3. **AVG.:** 2.55.
LEGACY: Three-time first-team All-America. Led Huskies to NCAA championship in 1965 before going on to a Hall of Fame career with Chicago Blackhawks.

SECOND TEAM

F Kip Miller
Michigan State
1986-90

F Tom Ross
Michigan State
1972-76

F Gary Emmons
Northern Michigan
1984-87

D Keith Aldridge
Lake Superior State
1992-96

D Don McSween
Michigan State
1983-87

G Marty Turco
Michigan
1994-98

One hundred heroes

100 YEARS

①

JOE LOUIS
May 13, 1914—
April 12, 1981

Heavyweight boxing champion. Born in Alabama, moved to Detroit as child. Started at Brewster Gym. "The Brown Bomber" reigned as heavyweight champ '37-49. Great left jab, left hook. Record was 68-3 with 54 knockouts. Quiet and modest, Louis was popular with black and white fans. Popularity peaked in '38 by knocking out German Max Schmeling, who gave him first loss in '36. Retired in '49 but returned in '50, struggling to settle problems with IRS. Final bout an eight-round KO by Rocky Marciano in '51. Inducted into International Boxing Hall of Fame in '54.

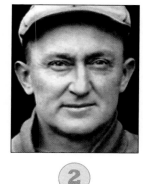

②

TY COBB
Dec. 18, 1886—
July 17, 1961

Tigers centerfielder 1905-26. "The Georgia Peach" was baseball's fiercest and greatest competitor. Some regard him as best player ever. His temper, on and off the field, was infamous — the stories ranged from sharpening his spikes to injure players to killing a man on the street. Owns highest lifetime average (.367). Holds record for runs (2,245). Second in hits (4,191), triples (297). Fourth in doubles (724), steals (892). From 1907 to '20, won batting title 12 of 13 seasons. Went to three World Series with Tigers ('07-09), never won. Was Tigers' player-manager '21-26.

③

GORDIE HOWE
March 31, 1928—

Red Wings right wing 1946-71. "Mr. Hockey." Won four Stanley Cups ('50, '52, '54, '55). Won Hart Trophy as league MVP six times and Art Ross Trophy as top scorer six times. First-team All-Star 12 times, second-team nine times. Played a record 26 NHL seasons, the last of which, at 51, was with sons Mark and Marty with Hartford. Also played with them for six WHA seasons. Record 1,767 games. Second with 801 goals, 1,850 points. Third with 1,049 assists. Retired from Wings in '71; inducted into Hockey Hall of Fame in '72. Joined WHA Houston Aeros at age 45; MVP of WHA in '74.

④

ISIAH THOMAS
April 30, 1961—

Pistons guard 1981-94. When drafted second overall in '81, Indiana star guaranteed Detroit an NBA championship. Delivered with back-to-back titles in '89 and '90 as captain of Bad Boys. MVP of '90 NBA Finals. Selected as one of NBA's all-time 50 greatest players. First-team All-NBA three times, second-team twice. Played in 12 All-Star Games, 11 as starter; twice All-Star MVP ('84, '86). Pistons retired his No. 11. Team leader in points (18,822), steals (1,861), assists (9,061). Had falling-out with Pistons and bounced around in retirement: VP with Toronto, TV analyst for NBC, owner of CBA.

⑤

MAGIC JOHNSON
Aug. 14, 1959—

Michigan State guard 1977-78, '78-79. As sophomore, All-America led MSU to first NCAA title, defeating Larry Bird and Indiana State in the most-watched final ever. In '77 led Lansing Everett to Class A state title, beating Birmingham Brother Rice, 62-55, in overtime. Earvin Johnson Jr., one of the NBA's greatest players, proved a 6-9, 250-pounder could be a point guard. Helped make Showtime Lakers the team of the '80s, winning five NBA titles. Retired in '91, revealing he was HIV positive. Made brief comebacks, won gold in '92 Olympics, tried coaching, became successful businessman.

➤

(6)

AL KALINE
Dec. 19, 1934—

Tigers rightfielder 1953-74. Inducted into Baseball Hall of Fame in '80. Selected to 18 All-Star Games. Ten-time Gold Glove winner. In '55, his second full season, had 200 hits and won batting crown with .340 average at age 20, the youngest batting champion ever. Tigers leader in games played (2,834) and home runs (399). Batted .379 against the Cardinals in '68 World Series. Retired in '74 with 3,007 hits. First Tiger to have his number (6) retired. A Tigers television broadcaster since '76.

(7)

BOBBY LAYNE
Dec. 19, 1926—Dec. 1, 1986

Lions quarterback 1950-58, including NFL championships in '52, '53 and '57. Inducted into Pro Football Hall of Fame in '67. Lions' all-time passing leader in attempts (2,193), completions (1,074), yards (15,710), touchdowns (118). All-Pro in '52, '56. Passed for 196 TDs in his 15-year career with four teams. Traded after two games in 1958 to Pittsburgh for QB Earl Morrall and two draft choices. Ended career with Steelers in 1962. Basically invented the now-common two-minute drill.

(8)

STEVE YZERMAN
May 9, 1965—

"The Captain." Red Wings center 1983-present. Led Red Wings to back-to-back Stanley Cups ('96-97, '97-98), ending 42-year title drought. Playoffs MVP in '97-98. Fourth pick in '83 draft. At 21, youngest captain in team history in '86-87 and eventually longest-serving captain in NHL history. Second to Gordie Howe in team scoring with 592 goals, 891 assists, 1,483 points after '98-99. Had at least 50 goals five times (60-plus twice). All-Star Game choice nine times. Arena named for him in Nepean, Ontario.

(9)

BO SCHEMBECHLER
April 1, 1929—

Michigan football coach 1969-89. Ninth all-time in Division I-A coaching victories with 234. Coach at Miami (Ohio) in '63-68. Record at U-M: 194-48-5 (.796). Led Wolverines to 13 Big Ten championships (outright or tied) and 17 bowls, including 10 Rose Bowls. His 96-10-3 regular-season record in the '70s was best in nation. U-M athletic director 1988-90. "Bo" is a nickname, full name is Glenn Edward Schembechler. Tigers president 1990-92. Inducted into College Football Hall of Fame in '93.

(10)

DUFFY DAUGHERTY
Sept. 8, 1915—Sept. 25, 1987

Michigan State football coach 1954-72. 109-69-5 record (.609), including national championship (UPI coaches poll in '65). Won two Big Ten titles. 1965, '66 teams combined had one loss, one tie. Coach of year in '55 (coaches association) and '65 (football writers). Inducted into College Football Hall of Fame in '84. Worked as TV analyst. Duffy, whose first name was Hugh, well-known for his "Duffyisms." When a reporter asked at the start of a season whom he was happiest to see returning, his reply: "Me."

(11)

CHARLIE GEHRINGER
May 11, 1903—Jan. 21, 1993

"The Mechanical Man." Tigers second baseman 1924-42. Fowlerville native. Inducted into Baseball Hall of Fame in '49. Considered among top five second sackers ever. Batted .375 in 1935 World Series. American League MVP in 1937 after career-high .371 average. Had 60 doubles in '36, still a Tigers record for a left-handed hitter. Hit over .300 in 13 seasons with a .320 lifetime average. Tigers general manager '51-53, vice president till '59. His No. 2 retired June 12, 1983, same day as Hank Greenberg's No. 5.

(12)

HANK GREENBERG
Jan. 1, 1911—Sept. 4, 1986

"Hammerin' Hank." Tigers first baseman 1933-46. Inducted into Baseball Hall of Fame in '56. Two-time AL MVP ('35, '40). Led AL with 36 homers and 170 RBIs as Tigers won first World Series in '35. Four-time RBI leader and four-time HR champion. Hit 58 in '38. Had 183 RBIs in '37. Hit ninth-inning grand slam on final day of '45 season to win pennant in first game of a doubleheader; Tigers then won second World Series. Among first to go to war; lost three-plus seasons to WWII, returned in '45.

(13)

BARRY SANDERS
July 16, 1968—

Lions running back 1989-98. Second in NFL career rushing with 15,269 yards, 1,457 behind Walter Payton. Possibly most exciting back ever. NFL records included: 150 yards rushing (25 games), consecutive 1,000-yard seasons (10), career TD runs of 50 yards (15). Retired with 16 Lions rushing records, including yards, total TDs (109), rushing TDs (99). Rushed for 2,053 yards in '97. Won Heisman Trophy in '88 as a junior at Oklahoma State. Announced retirement July 27, 1999, on eve of training camp.

One hundred heroes 100 YEARS

14

JOE SCHMIDT

Jan. 18, 1932—

Lions linebacker 1953-65. Won about every honor a middle linebacker could. Seventh-round pick out of Pitt. Lions captain '56-65. League MVP in '60. All-Pro nine times, Pro Bowl 10 straight years ('55-64). Was four-time Lions MVP. Played on two NFL championship teams ('53, '57). Had 24 career interceptions. Lions leadership award named after him. Went 43-34-7 as Lions coach ('67-72). '70 team went 10-4, lost in playoffs to Dallas, 5-0. Inducted into Pro Football Hall of Fame in '73.

15

TOM HARMON

Sept. 28, 1919—March 17, 1990

"Ol' 98." Michigan running back 1938-40. U-M's first Heisman Trophy winner, in '40. AP male athlete of year in '40. One of last triple-threat single-wing tailbacks. Ran and passed for 3,438 yards, scored then-Big Ten-record 33 TDs, kicked two field goals. Also threw 16 TD passes. Inducted in College Football Hall of Fame in '54. Drafted first overall by Bears in '41, but never signed. Played briefly for New York Americans in AFL before serving as pilot in WWII. Successful career as radio and TV sportscaster.

16

GAR WOOD

Dec. 4, 1880—June 19, 1971

"Gray Fox From Algonac." Speedboat racer and inventor. As internationally famous as Bobby Jones and Jack Dempsey. Won five straight Gold Cups on Detroit River ('17-21). Held famed Harmsworth Trophy longer than any other person, winning it from England in '20 for the U.S., where it remained until '59. Miss America X, last of his string of Miss Americas to defend the trophy, set his final world speedboat mark at 124.91 m.p.h. in '32. Made fortune off "Wood hydraulic hoist."

17

FIELDING H. YOST

April 30, 1871—Oct. 20, 1946

Michigan football coach 1901-23, '25-26 and athletic director '21-41. Compiled 165-29-10 record (.833), including 56-game unbeaten streak in 1901-05. The '01-05 "Point-a-Minute" teams outscored foes, 2,821-42. Won national titles in '01-04 and 10 Big Ten titles. Staked claims to national titles in '18, '23. As AD, built Michigan Stadium, golf course, nation's first intramural building, and nation's first multi-purpose field house, known today as Yost Ice Arena. Inducted College Football Hall of Fame in '51.

18

TERRY SAWCHUK

Dec. 28, 1929—May 31, 1970

Red Wings goalie 1949-55, '57-64, '68-69. Won three Cups in Detroit, one in Toronto. Holds NHL record for games (971), wins (447), shutouts (103). Won '52 Cup in minimum eight games with four shutouts. Rookie of year in '50-51. Four-time Vezina Trophy winner ('51-52, '52-53, '54-55; '64-65 with Toronto). First-team All-NHL three times, second-team four. Elected to Hockey Hall of Fame in '71. Wings retired No. 1 in '94. Died at 40 of injuries from backyard brawl with Rangers teammate Ron Stewart.

19

GEORGE WEBSTER

Nov. 25, 1945—

Michigan State roverback 1964-66. In '69, named "the greatest Spartan in MSU football history." All-America in '65 and '66. His No. 90 was retired. Named to MSU's Centennial Super Squad in '96. Redefined roverback position, lining up on strong side as DL, LB or DB. Led MSU to national championship in '65. Drafted in first round by Houston Oilers. AFL rookie of year in '67. LB on all-time AFL team picked in '70. Picked for three Pro Bowls. Inducted into College Football Hall of Fame in '87.

20

TARA LIPINSKI

June 10, 1982—

Figure skater. Moved from Texas to join Detroit Skating Club in December '95. At 14, became the sweetheart of nationals and was crowned youngest U.S. champion, in '97. A month later in Switzerland, became youngest world champion. Became youngest Olympic gold medalist in February '98 in Nagano, Japan, beating Michelle Kwan. Turned pro two months before 16th birthday. Returned to Texas and pursued other interests, including acting on soap opera "The Young and the Restless."

21

ERNIE HARWELL

Jan. 25, 1918—

Tigers broadcaster. Voice of Tigers almost 40 years. Received Ford Frick Award, presented by Baseball Hall of Fame for broadcasting excellence, in '81. Inducted National Sportscasters Hall of Fame in '89. Handled numerous network assignments. Called first major league game in '48. Joined Tigers in '60. Fired in early '90s in widely unpopular move. Missed only '92 before returning in some form on radio or TV. Full-time radio voice again starting in '98, at age 80. Songwriter and author. ➤

22
CHARLES WOODSON
Oct. 7, 1976—

Michigan cornerback, kick returner, part-time receiver 1995-97. As a junior in '97 won Heisman Trophy, first primarily defensive player to win it. Started all but one game in three years. Team and Big Ten MVP on '97 team that won Rose Bowl and national title. Two-time All-America ('96, '97), Big Ten defensive player of the year twice. Named national defensive player of year and won Jim Thorpe Award as nation's top defensive back in '97. Skipped senior season. Drafted fourth overall by Oakland Raiders.

23
JOE DUMARS
May 24, 1963—

Pistons guard 1985-99. Played more seasons (14) and more games (1,018) than any other Piston. MVP of '89 NBA Finals as Pistons won first world title. Starter on '90 championship team. Second to Isiah Thomas in all-time scoring (16,401), assists (4,612). First in three-pointers. Played in six All-Star Games. NBA all-defensive first team four times, second team once. All-NBA second team in '93. Captained Team USA that won gold in '94 World Championships. Became VP of player personnel after retiring.

24
TED LINDSAY
July 29, 1925—

"Terrible Ted." Red Wings left wing 1944-57 and '64-65. Although small (5-8, 160), was one of toughest players in NHL history. First-team All-Star eight times, second team once. Retired as NHL's highest-scoring left wing and all-time leader in penalty minutes. Led league in scoring in '49-50 (78 points) as he won first of four Stanley Cups. Captain 1952-56. Traded in '57 to Chicago as punishment for role in players union. Elected to Hockey Hall of Fame in '66. His No. 7 retired in '91. Also Wings GM and coach.

25
HAL NEWHOUSER
May 20, 1921—Nov. 10, 1998

"Prince Hal." Tigers left-handed pitcher 1939-'53. Detroit-born and raised. Only pitcher to win back-to-back MVP awards ('44, '45). Won AL's pitching Triple Crown in '45 (25 wins, 212 strikeouts, 1.81 ERA). Won 29 games in '44. All-Star six times. Led AL in victories four times, strikeouts and ERA twice. Won Game 7 vs. Cubs in '45 World Series. His No. 16 became fourth Tigers number retired, in '97. Elected to Baseball Hall of Fame in 1992. Voted left-hander (with Mickey Lolich) by fans on all-time Tigers team in '99.

26
JIM ABBOTT
Sept. 19, 1967—

Flint native, born without right hand. Major league pitcher 1989-99. National hero to people with disabilities. Played baseball and football at Flint Central High, quarterbacking his team to the state football playoffs in '84. Played baseball at Michigan, winning the Sullivan Award as the nation's top amateur athlete. Pitched U.S. to Olympic gold medal in 1988. Skipped minors, went into majors after being drafted by California. Pitched no-hitter against Cleveland as NY Yankee in '93. Posted 87-108 record.

27
THOMAS HEARNS
Oct. 18, 1958—

"Hit Man." Boxer fighting out of Detroit's Kronk Gym won seven world titles. Was AAU and Golden Gloves champ in '77. Titles won: WBA welterweight in '80 (vs. Pipino Cuevas), WBC junior middleweight in '82 (vs. Wilfred Benitez), WBC light-heavyweight in '87 (vs. Dennis Andries), WBC middleweight in '87 (vs. Juan Roldan), WBO super middleweight in '88 (vs. James Kinchen), WBA light-heavyweight in '91 (vs. Virgil Hill), WBU cruiserweight in '95 (vs. Lenny Lapaglia). 59-4-1 (46 KOs).

28
NIGHT TRAIN LANE
April 16, 1928—

Lions defensive back 1960-65. Started with LA Rams '52-53 and Chicago Cardinals '54-59. Inducted into Pro Football Hall of Fame in '74. All-Pro four times with Lions, five overall. Played in seven Pro Bowls. Intercepted record 14 passes in a 12-game season as a rookie. Intercepted 68 passes. As a Ram, Dick Lane spent a lot of time with Tom Fears, who constantly played the record "Night Train." One day a teammate came into Fears' room, saw Lane and exclaimed, "Hey, there's Night Train."

29
JACK ADAMS
June 14, 1895—May 1, 1968

Red Wings coach 1927-47, general manager 1927-63. His teams won seven Stanley Cups and 12 regular-season titles (including seven straight, 1948-49 to '54-55). Had .512 winning percentage, .500 in playoffs. In 36 years, Wings missed playoffs only seven times. At one time, NHL had a division named for him. Jack Adams Award honors the NHL coach of the year. First winner of Lester Patrick Trophy for service to U.S. hockey, in '66. Inducted into the Hockey Hall of Fame in '59.

One hundred heroes _{100 YEARS}

30

DOAK WALKER
Jan. 1, 1927—Sept. 27, 1998

Lions halfback 1950-55. He did it all: running back, wide receiver, quarterback, defensive back, kicker, punter, returner. Scored 534 points, 34 touchdowns, 183 extra points, 49 field goals. Played on '52, '53 NFL championship teams. All-Pro four times, Pro Bowl five times. Won Heisman Trophy at Southern Methodist in '48. Doak Walker Award given annually to top college running back. Member of College and Pro Football halls of fame. Paralyzed in a skiing accident in January '98.

31

BUBBA SMITH
Feb. 28, 1945—

Michigan State defensive end 1964-66. Two-time All-America. Possibly best collegiate lineman ever. Helped MSU win national title in '65, when Spartans had nation's top-ranked defense. Named to MSU's Centennial Super Squad in '96. Inducted into College Football Hall of Fame in '88. First pick in '67 draft, by Baltimore. Dominator for Colts, Oakland and Houston before retiring in '76. Became successful businessman and actor. Remember "Police Academy" films and Miller Lite commercials?

32

SPARKY ANDERSON
Feb. 22, 1934—

Tigers manager 1979-95. Led wire-to-wire Tigers to '84 world championship. His 1,331 wins are team record. Twice AL manager of year ('84, '87). Ended 26-year career with 2,194 victories, third all-time behind Connie Mack (3,731) and John McGraw (2,763). First to win 100 games in one season in each league and a World Series in each league. Won two Series as Reds manager, '75-76. Noted for his malapropisms and bad grammar. Upon leaving Tigers in October '95, he proclaimed: "I ain't here no more."

33

CHUCK DALY
July 20, 1930—

"Daddy Rich." Pistons coach 1983-92. Won back-to-back NBA titles ('89, '90), the first in franchise history. Made nine straight playoff appearances. Teams had five straight trips to the Eastern Conference finals and five straight seasons of 50 or more victories. Record: 467-271 (.633), playoffs 71-42 (.628). No. 2 retired Feb. 12, 1997, in honor of NBA titles won. Coached first Dream Team that won 1992 Olympic gold medal. Also coached Cavaliers, Nets and Magic. Elected to Basketball Hall of Fame in '94.

34

SCOTTY BOWMAN
Sept. 18, 1933—

Red Wings coach since 1993. Most successful coach in NHL history. Produced back-to-back Stanley Cups ('97, '98). Has won eight Cups as a coach, tying mentor Toe Blake for the record. Recorded his 1,000th career regular-season victory Feb. 8, 1997. Only coach to win Cups with three franchises. Only coach to guide a team to 60-win season, did it twice — '96 with Detroit (62) and '77 with Montreal (60). Record for most NHL games coached with more than 1,900. Inducted into Hockey Hall of Fame in '91.

35

EMANUEL STEWARD
July 7, 1944—

Boxing trainer and manager. Made Kronk Gym in Detroit a world-famous destination for fighters. His list of pupils reads like a who's who of boxing. Trained and/or managed Thomas Hearns, Evander Holyfield, Michael Moorer, Julio Cesar Chavez, Oliver McCall, Lennox Lewis. Won Golden Gloves bantamweight title in '63. Three times trainer of year, twice manager of year, as picked by Boxing Writers Association of America. Inducted into the International Boxing Hall of Fame in '96.

36

MICKEY COCHRANE
April 6, 1903—June 28, 1962

Tigers catcher-manager 1934-37. One of the finest catchers ever. Played nine seasons in Philadelphia, took over as Detroit player-manager in '34, and led Tigers to back-to-back American League pennants and first World Series title in '35. Scored winning run in the bottom of the ninth on Goose Goslin's single. Career ruined when Yankees' Bump Hadley hit him with fastball in temple. He was unconscious 10 days. Lifetime average of .320. Inducted into Baseball Hall of Fame in '47.

37

BIGGIE MUNN
Sept. 11, 1908—March 18, 1975

Michigan State football coach 1947-53. Most successful Spartans coach by percentage, compiling a 54-9-2 record (.846) in seven seasons. Included in his tenure were a national championship ('52), a Rose Bowl victory ('54), a 28-game unbeaten streak, and a Big Ten co-championship ('53). Named coach of the year in '52. Beginning in '54, MSU's athletic director for 18 years. MSU's hockey arena is named after him. Inducted into the College Football Hall of Fame in '59.

➤

38

DON CANHAM
April 29, 1918—

Michigan athletic director 1968-88. Introduced pro-style marketing to college sports. Turned football Saturdays into full-blown events with 100,000-plus crowds. Track coach and star at U-M. Helped found former U.S. Track & Field Federation. Founded and directed NCAA Indoor Track championships at Cobo Hall. Coached U-M to 12 Big Ten titles in track and cross-country. NCAA high jump champion and set record 6-7¼ in '40. Member of National Track and Field Hall of Fame.

39

SID ABEL
Feb. 22, 1918—

Red Wings forward 1938-43 and '45-52. Center of the famed "Production Line." Won Hart Trophy as MVP in '49. Wings captain '42-43, '46-52. Won three Stanley Cups. First-team All-Star twice, second team twice. Still 11th on all-time Wings scoring (463 points). Inducted into Hockey Hall of Fame in '69. Wings coach '57-68, '69-70; Wings GM '62-71. Second all-time in team victories (340), behind Jack Adams. Longtime Wings broadcaster, too. His No. 12 retired April 29, 1995.

40

DUTCH CLARK
Oct. 11, 1906—Aug. 5, 1978

Lions quarterback 1934-38, coach '37-38. Led team in rushing, passing and scoring in '34. Also kicked field goals and extra points. Quarterbacked '35 NFL championship team. Tied for two Lions records: most points in game (24) and touchdowns in game (four). Inducted into Pro Football Hall of Fame in '63. Began career with Portsmouth in '31. Coached Cleveland Rams '39-42. University of Detroit football coach and athletic director '51-53. Full name was Earl Harry Clark.

41

HARRY HEILMANN
Aug. 3, 1894—July 9, 1951

Tigers outfielder and first baseman 1914-29. One of the best hitters in his era, "Slug" hit .390 or higher four times, including .403 in '23. Won AL batting title four times ('21, '23, '25, '27). Lifetime average of .342. Batted over .300 in 1919-29. Finished career with Reds, hitting .333 in '30. Second to Babe Ruth three times in AL slugging percentage. Second to Lou Gehrig for AL MVP in 1927. Drove in 100 runs eight times. Tigers radio broadcaster '34-51. Baseball Hall of Fame in '52.

42

ALEX DELVECCHIO
Dec. 4, 1932—

Red Wings center 1950-74. "Fats." Only Gordie Howe played more NHL seasons (26-24) or games (1,767-1,549). Captain '62-73. Second-team All-Star twice ('53, '59). Played in 13 All-Star Games. Won three Stanley Cups ('52, '54, '55). Won Lady Byng Trophy three times ('59, '66, '69). Received Lester Patrick Trophy in '74 for outstanding service to U.S. hockey. Third in Wings history with 1,281 points. Elected to Hockey Hall of Fame in '77. His No. 10 retired Nov. 10, 1991. Also coach ('73-76) and GM ('74-77).

43

CAZZIE RUSSELL
June 7, 1944—

Michigan basketball guard 1964-66. His dominant play had many calling Crisler Arena, built after he left, "The House That Cazzie Built." As senior, voted national player of the year, was a three-time All-America and Big Ten MVP twice. Averaged 27.1 career points and 30.8 as senior, both U-M records. Led team to Final Four as freshman and sophomore. Drafted first overall by Knicks in '67. Averaged 15.1 points in 12 NBA seasons. U-M retired No. 33 on Dec. 11, 1993. Successful CBA and small-college coach.

44

FRED BEAR
March 5, 1902—April 27, 1988

Father of modern bowhunting. Moved to Detroit in 1923 from Pennsylvania. Created Bear Archery Tackle, moving it to Grayling in '47. Started publicizing his and other early bowhunters' exploits in '50s. Appeared on TV with fellow hunter Arthur Godfrey. Made famous by a Life magazine spread of him killing a world-record Kodiak bear at 20 yards. Hunted into his 80s and used his bows to kill record-book bears, moose, tiger, lion, cape buffalo, elephant. Immortalized in song by Ted Nugent.

45

ALEX KARRAS
July 15, 1935—

Lions defensive tackle 1958-62, '64-70. Small for his position at 6-2, 250, watched game films to learn blocking techniques and tendencies of opponents. All-Pro '60-62; suspended in '63 for gambling on NFL games. Tried pro wrestling. Returned to Lions in '64, All-Pro again in '65. Won '57 Outland Trophy as nation's top lineman at Iowa. Lions' top draft choice (10th overall) in '58. "Mad Duck." Best known as actor. Starred in "Paper Lion," "Blazing Saddles," "Porky's" and TV's "Webster" with wife Susan Clark.

One hundred heroes

46

BENNIE OOSTERBAAN
Feb. 24, 1906—Oct. 25, 1990

Three-time All-America end at Michigan, 1925-27. Considered one of U-M's greatest all-around athletes. Won nine letters, in football, basketball, baseball. All-America in basketball, leading Big Ten in scoring ('28). Also led Big Ten in batting. Football coach '48-58, with 63-33-4 record. National coach of the year in '48, when U-M went 9-0 and won national title. Won three Big Ten titles and 1951 Rose Bowl. Head basketball coach '38-46, with 81-72 record. Inducted into College Football Hall of Fame in '54.

47

RED KELLY
July 9, 1927—

Red Wings defenseman 1947-60. Won four Stanley Cups with Wings ('50, '52, '54, '55). First recipient of Norris Trophy as NHL's top defenseman, in '54. Traded to Rangers, but deal fell through two days later when Kelly wouldn't report; traded three days later to Toronto, where he played until '67 and won four more Cups. First-team All-NHL six times, second-team twice. Won Lady Byng three times with Wings, once with Leafs. Inducted into Hockey Hall of Fame in '69. Coach '67-77 with three teams.

48

SUGAR RAY ROBINSON
May 3, 1921—April 12, 1989

Born Walker Smith Jr. in Detroit. Pound-for-pound, greatest fighter ever. Won 174 bouts, 109 by knockout, losing only 19. Welterweight and five-time middleweight champion. Fought 12 times in Detroit; most notable were two at Olympia with Jake LaMotta, whom Robinson fought six times. Nickname reportedly from a sports writer who pronounced his fighting style "sweet as sugar." Inducted into Boxing Hall of Fame in '67. Didn't spend much time in Detroit but always called it home.

49

EARL MORRALL
May 17, 1934—

Michigan State quarterback 1953-55, Lions QB '58-64. Muskegon native considered finest prep passer ever. Led '55 team that was 9-1 and won Rose Bowl. All-America in '55, fourth in Heisman voting. Passed for 274 yards against Marquette in '55, record that stood until '69. Played 21 years in NFL, won three of four Super Bowls (one with Baltimore, two with Miami). Replaced injured Bob Griese as Dolphins went 14-0 in '72 regular season. Was league MVP replacing injured Johnny Unitas in '68.

50

NORB SCHEMANSKY
May 30, 1924—

World champion weight lifter. Born in Detroit. Four-time medalist in four Olympics — '48, silver in heavyweight division; '52, gold in middle-heavyweight; '60, bronze in heavyweight; '64, bronze in heavyweight. One of two athletes to win individual medals in four Olympics. Was 40 when he won bronze in '64 in Tokyo, making him the oldest weight lifter to capture Olympic medal. Won three world championships. Set 26 world records. Member of National Weightlifting Hall of Fame.

51

SAM CRAWFORD
April 18, 1880—June 15, 1968

Tigers rightfielder 1903-17. Helped win consecutive AL pennants '07-09. Most prolific triples hitter in history, led AL five times, NL once with Cincinnati. Hit more than 20 triples in a season five times, finishing his career with a major league-record 312 (15 more than Ty Cobb). Ended career 36 hits short of 3,000. Batted .309 lifetime. Led AL in RBIs three times. Outstanding defensive player. Elected to Baseball Hall of Fame in '57. Why "Wahoo Sam"? He was born in Wahoo, Neb.

52

FRITZ CRISLER
Jan. 12, 1899—Aug. 19, 1982

Michigan football coach 1938-47, athletic director '41-68. One of most powerful, innovative men in college sports. Designed the winged helmet first used in '38. Coach of year in '47 when "Mad Magicians" were voted national champion in disputed AP poll taken after 49-0 win over Southern Cal in Rose Bowl. Posted 71-16-3 record (.806). U-M basketball arena named for Crisler, who was nicknamed Fritz by Amos Alonzo Stagg while at the University of Chicago, after the German violinist Fritz Kreisler.

53

WALTER HAGEN
Dec. 21, 1892—Oct. 6, 1969

"Sir Walter." Professional golfer. Regarded as greatest pro for half-century. Colorful personality who helped popularize golf. Dominated in 1914-36, winning 75 titles (including 11 majors). Won '14 U.S. Open and was head pro at Oakland Hills when he won '19 U.S. Open in playoff. Kept residence in Detroit. Won five PGA Championships, including a record four straight, when it was match play. His 40 PGA Tour victories tied for seventh on all-time list. Also won four British Opens.

54

DAVE BING
Nov. 24, 1943—

Pistons guard 1966-75. Drafted second overall (behind Cazzie Russell) out of Syracuse. His 22.6 scoring average second all-time among Pistons, behind Bob Lanier's 22.7. Rookie of year in '67. All-NBA first-team twice, second-team once. Played in All-Star Game six times with Pistons, once with Washington — when he was MVP in '76. Elected to Basketball Hall of Fame in '89. First Piston to have jersey (No. 21) retired (in '83). Named one of 50 greatest players by NBA. Became a successful businessman.

55

RON KRAMER
June 24, 1935—

Michigan end 1954-56. Two-time All-America. Won nine letters, in football, basketball, track. His No. 87 retired after senior season. Basketball MVP all three years. Standout high jumper, despite 230 pounds. Drafted by Packers in first round. Prototype of modern tight end. All-Pro in '62, devastating blocker. Caught 37 passes for 555 yards, seven TDs in '62. Played for Lions in '65-67. Inducted into College Football Hall of Fame in '78. At East Detroit High, all-state in football, hurdles, shot put, high jump.

56

JUD HEATHCOTE
May 27, 1927—

Michigan State basketball coach 1976-'95. Known for matchup zone defense, intensity, sense of humor and "Jud Thuds" (pounding his head with his fists). All-time MSU leader with 340 victories (against 220 losses). Led Magic Johnson and Spartans to first national title in '79. Made nine NCAA tournament and three NIT appearances. Retired as fifth in all-time Big Ten victories. Won three Big Ten titles. National coach of the year in '90. NBA drafted 22 of his players.

57

RON MASON
Jan. 14, 1940—

Michigan State hockey coach since 1979. Most successful college coach in North America with more than 800 victories. Turned MSU into national powerhouse. Under Mason, MSU has had only three losing seasons, one in the past 17 years. Won five CCHA championships and NCAA championship in '86. Coached more than 20 All-Americas. More than 37 NHL players were coached by Mason. National coach of the year in '92. Won NAIA national championship at Lake Superior State in '72.

58

BILL MUNCEY
Nov. 12, 1928—Oct. 18, 1981

One of powerboat racing's most successful drivers. The Mario Andretti of unlimiteds was born in Ferndale, attended Royal Oak High (now Dondero). Won his first race, the Hearst Trophy on the Potomac River, at age 20. Won record 62 unlimited races, including eight Gold Cups — breaking Gar Wood's mark of five — seven national championships and four world championships. Only Chip Hanauer, a protege and friend, has won as often. Muncey was killed in a hydroplane accident during a race off Acapulco.

59

GREG BARTON
Dec. 2, 1959—

World champion kayaker. Born in Jackson, grew up on a Homer pig farm. Four-time Olympic medalist. First American to win Olympic gold in kayaking; in Seoul in '88, captured gold in 1,000-meter singles and doubles 90 minutes apart. Known as greatest American paddler. Won bronze medals in '84 Los Angeles and '92 Barcelona Olympics. Qualified for '80 Moscow Olympics, but U.S. boycotted. In '94 won the Clean Water Challenge, a 744-mile race from Chicago to New York City.

60

DAVE DeBUSSCHERE
Oct. 16, 1940—

University of Detroit basketball and baseball player 1958-62, Pistons forward '62-68. Second in Titans career scoring with 1,985 points; he averaged 24.8. Pitched for White Sox for two seasons, then quit to become Pistons' player-coach. Posted 79-143 record. Traded to the Knicks in '68 and was named to six straight all-defensive teams. On Knicks' NBA champions in '70, '73. Later Knicks GM and executive vice president. Elected to Basketball Hall of Fame in '82. Led Detroit Austin to '58 Class A basketball title.

61

HUGHIE JENNINGS
April 2, 1869—Feb. 1, 1928

Tigers manager 1907-20. "Hustling Hughie." One of most colorful managers in baseball history. Famous for "Eeyah" cry from third-base coaching box. Led teams that featured Ty Cobb, Harry Heilmann and Sam Crawford. Won consecutive league titles in 1907-09, losing in World Series each time. Posted 1,131-972 record (.538) with Tigers. An outstanding shortstop, batted .313 in 17 seasons. After leaving baseball, practiced law in Pennsylvania. Elected to Baseball Hall of Fame in '45.

One hundred heroes 100 YEARS

62
LEM BARNEY
Sept. 8, 1945—

Lions cornerback/kick returner 1967-77. Wore No. 20. Second-rounder out of Jackson State. Defensive rookie of the year in '67, when he intercepted 10 passes and scored three TDs. Shares Lions record for return touchdowns (11), leads in interception-return yards (1,077), interceptions returned for touchdowns (7). Averaged 9.2 yards per punt return and 25.5 yards per kickoff return. Had 56 career interceptions. All-Pro twice, Pro Bowl seven times. Elected to Pro Football Hall of Fame in '92.

63
BILLY SIMS
Sept. 18, 1955—

Lions running back 1980-84. Wore No. 20. NFL rookie of the year in '80. Dazzling runner. Ranks second to Barry Sanders in Lions rushing and career rushing touchdowns. Gained 5,106 yards, scored 42 touchdowns. Three-time Lions offensive MVP and three-time Pro Bowl selection. Knee injury Oct. 21, 1984, against Minnesota ended his career. Won the Heisman Trophy in '78 at Oklahoma. Inducted into College Football Hall of Fame in '95. After retiring, faced severe financial and legal troubles.

64
BILL LAIMBEER
May 19, 1957—

Acquired from Cleveland in 1982, was Pistons center until '94. Punched by some, loathed by many, he was the baddest of Detroit's "Bad Boys." His image often overshadowed superior shooting, rebounding and defensive skills. Helped Pistons to back-to-back championships in '88-89 and '89-90. Was 19th to reach 10,000 points, 10,000 rebounds. Holds Pistons record for career rebounds (9,430) and is fifth in scoring (12,664). His No. 40 was retired in '95. Now a successful businessman, owner of Laimbeer Packaging.

65
KIRK GIBSON
May 28, 1957—

Tigers outfielder 1979-87 and '93-95; All-America in football and baseball at Michigan State. Dynamic wide receiver, '75-78. Caught 42 passes for 806 yards as senior, when he was all-time leader in receptions (112) and receiving yards (2,347). Drafted in the first round by Tigers in '78. Hit dramatic, last-game homer for Tigers in '84 World Series. Pinch-hit a two-run homer in the bottom of the ninth for Dodgers to win Game 1 of the '88 series. Was NL MVP that season. Landed in Tigers broadcast booth.

66
BUDDY PARKER
Dec. 16, 1913—March 22, 1982

Lions coach 1951-56. Guided them to NFL championships in '52 and '53 and Western Division title in '54. Highest winning percentage (.671) among Lions coaches. Was 50-24-2. With quarterback Bobby Layne, developed the two-minute drill. Was a back for Lions' 1935 championship team. Also coached Chicago Cardinals and Pittsburgh Steelers. Quit as Detroit coach on the eve of '57 season, saying Lions couldn't win (they won fourth NFL title) and went to Pittsburgh, where he finished his career in '64.

67
EDDIE TOLAN
Sept. 29, 1909—Jan. 30, 1967

Detroit sprinter. Michigan Wolverine 1929-31, U.S. Olympian 1932. Won gold medals in 100 and 200 meters at '32 Los Angeles Olympics, becoming first African-American to win two gold medals. His time of 10.3 seconds in 100 set world record and his 21.2 seconds in the 200 set an Olympic record. At U-M, Tolan won the NCAA 220-yard dash in '31 and won various AAU national sprint titles, including the 100 and 220 dashes. Member of National Track and Field Hall of Fame.

68
ALETA SILL
Sept. 9, 1962—

One of best, if not the best, female professional bowlers in history. Born in Detroit, moved to Dearborn. In '99 became first woman to reach $1 million in career earnings. Tied for Professional Women's Bowling Association lead with 30 career titles. After winning '98 U.S. Open, became first bowler, man or woman, to win Triple Crown — U.S. Open, Sam's Town Invitational and WIBC Queens — twice. Great ambassador for her sport. Inducted into Women's Professional Bowling Hall of Fame in '88.

69
WILLIE HORTON
Oct. 18, 1942—

Homegrown hero and Tigers outfielder 1963-77. Helped win '68 World Series after hitting .285 with 36 homers, 85 RBIs in season. Four All-Star teams as a Tiger. Traded to Texas in '77. In '79 was DH of the year, batting .279 with a career-high 106 RBIs with Seattle. Signed with Tigers after his junior year at Detroit Northwestern. In PSL title game at Tiger Stadium in '59, hit a homer that landed on the roof, striking the bottom of the right-centerfield light standard. Retired after '80 with .273 average, 325 homers, 1,163 RBIs. ➤

70

ANTHONY CARTER
Sept. 17, 1960—

Michigan wide receiver/return specialist 1979-82. So talented, Bo Schembechler was forced to pass more. All-America three times. Big Ten MVP and fourth in Heisman voting in '82. On two Big Ten title teams and helped Bo win his first Rose Bowl in '81. Only 5-11, 160. Holds U-M records for receptions (161), receiving yards (3,076), TD catches (37). Won '83 USFL title with Michigan Panthers. Joined Vikings in '85 and became one of NFL's most dangerous wide receivers. Played final two seasons with Lions ('94, '95).

71

DESMOND HOWARD
May 15, 1970—

Michigan wide receiver/return specialist 1989-91. Second Wolverine to win Heisman, in '91. Did so by second-largest margin ever. Set or tied five NCAA records and 12 single-season U-M records in '91. Holds U-M records for TD catches (19), total TDs (23), points (138) in season. Drafted No. 4 by Washington in '92. Never matched success in NFL, but found niche as returner. MVP of Super Bowl XXXI with Packers, with 90 yards on six punt returns, 154 on four kick returns, including a 99-yarder.

72

SHIRLEY MULDOWNEY
June 19, 1940—

"Cha Cha." Drag racer from Mt. Clemens. First woman licensed by National Hot Rod Association. Drove a hot-pink car as her trademark. Was first driver, male or female, to win two world championships and won a third in '82. Won U.S. Nationals in '82. Won Winston world championship in '80. Only woman to have won NHRA top-fuel title ('77, '80, '82). Wrecked in Montreal in '84 and spent 18 months in rehabilitation before returning in '86. Subject of the critically acclaimed film "Heart Like a Wheel."

73

MICKEY LOLICH
Sept. 12, 1940—

Tigers pitcher 1963-75. Won Games 2, 5 and 7 in '68 World Series. Named Series MVP with 3-0 record, three complete games, 1.67 ERA and the only home run of his career. Tigers season leader in strikeouts (308). Career leader in games started (459), strikeouts (2,679), shutouts (39). Also team record in strikeouts in a game (16). Named to three All-Star Games. Finished second in Cy Young voting in '71 (25-14, 29 complete games). Finished career in San Diego. Opened doughnut shop after retiring.

74

GLEN RICE
May 28, 1967—

Michigan basketball, 1985-89. Led U-M to '89 national championship by setting an NCAA tournament scoring record (184 points in six games). Selected most outstanding player. All-Big Ten first team in '88, '89 and MVP in '89. Holds U-M records in career scoring (2,442 points), season scoring (949), scoring in NCAA tournament game (39). Played on one of great prep teams ever, Flint Northwestern, winning Class A titles in '84, '85 with Andre Rison. Miami Heat's top pick, fourth overall, in '89.

75

HARRY KIPKE
March 26, 1899—Sept. 14, 1972

Michigan halfback 1921-23 and football coach 1929-37. All-America in '22, largely because of amazing punting skills. Earned nine letters, in football, basketball, baseball. Went 3-4-1 as Michigan State coach in '28, then became U-M coach in '29 (5-3-1). Went 31-1-3 in 1930-33, winning four Big Ten and two national titles. Struggled to 10-22 final four seasons. Called his system "a punt, a pass and a prayer." Also coined: "A great defense is a great offense." Inducted into College Football Hall of Fame as a player in '58.

76

LARRY AURIE
Feb. 8, 1905—Dec. 11, 1952

"Little Dempsey." Right wing 1927-39 with Detroit Cougars/Falcons/Red Wings. Only 5-feet-6, 148 pounds. The Wings' first star player. All-NHL first team in '37. Played on '36-37 Stanley Cup winners, but didn't play in '37 playoffs because of injury. First Wing to have his number (6) retired. (Modern Wings, though, haven't hung a banner for him, just say No. 6 is "out of circulation.") Tied for league scoring lead with 23 goals in '37. Led Wings in scoring 1933-34.

77

DENNY McLAIN
March 29, 1944—

Tigers pitcher 1963-70. In '68, became last pitcher of century to win 30 games and first since '34. Finished 31-6 with 1.96 ERA; league leader in starts (41), complete games (28) and innings (336). He won MVP and Cy Young awards in '68 and shared Cy Young in '69 (24-9, 2.80). Named male athlete of year by AP in '68. Flame-out starting in '69. Suspensions, injuries, trades. Went 10-22 for Senators in '71. Out of baseball before 30. After retirement suffered financial, legal troubles, including two prison terms.

One hundred heroes 100 YEARS

BOB LANIER
Sept. 10, 1948—

Pistons center 1970-80. All-Star seven times with Detroit, once with Milwaukee. Third on Pistons all-time scoring list (15,488), top scoring average (22.7). Drafted with first overall pick in '70 out of St. Bonaventure, where he was all-time scoring and rebounding leader. MVP of '74 All-Star Game. In his quest for NBA title, he was traded to Milwaukee in February '80. Won five division titles in five years there but never reached Finals. Basketball Hall of Fame in '91. Pistons retired No. 16.

CHRIS WEBBER
March 1, 1973—

Michigan basketball, 1991-93. Birmingham Detroit Country Day star won Mr. Basketball Award in '91. Third all-time leading scorer in state prep history. Leader of U-M's "Fab Five." Big Ten freshman of year. Led U-M to NCAA championship game in '92 and '93. All-America in '93. Drafted first overall by Orlando Magic in '93, rights traded to Golden State Warriors. Career controversies: Called time-out U-M didn't have in '93 final against North Carolina, brushes with law as a pro.

MIKE ILITCH
July 20, 1929—

Little Caesars Pizza founder and owner purchased Red Wings in '82 and Tigers in '92. Established, then sold Drive (arena football), Rockers (indoor soccer). Wings franchise at rock bottom, lousy on the ice, no fans in stands. With wife Marian rebuilt it, won back-to-back Stanley Cups in '97 and '98. Not much success turning around Tigers. Scheduled to move into new downtown Comerica Park in 2000. Sponsors Little Caesars amateur hockey, baseball and soccer.

BILL DAVIDSON
Dec. 5, 1922—

Pistons majority owner and managing partner. Also owns Vipers (IHL), Shock (WNBA), Tampa Bay Lightning (NHL), Palace (Auburn Hills) and several entertainment venues. Earned fortune with Guardian Glass. Bought Pistons from Fred Zollner in '74. Moved team from Cobo Arena to Silverdome to Palace, which he privately financed. Among first to buy plane for a team (Roundball One). Pistons won back-to-back NBA titles in '89 and '90. Was city-champion half-miler at Detroit Central.

FRANK NAVIN
April 22, 1871—Nov. 13, 1935

Tigers majority owner and president 1907-35. Started as bookkeeper in '02 and always known as penny-pincher. Under Navin, unsteady Tigers organization became one of baseball's most stable, with many thanks to Ty Cobb, of course. Died from heart attack a month after Tigers won first World Series in '35. For about $300,000, built new park on the same location as Bennett Park, moving home plate from what was rightfield to its famous location. Navin Field opened April 20, 1912.

TURKEY STEARNES
May 8, 1901—Sept. 4, 1979

Outfielder for Detroit Stars of Negro National League 1923-31. Some statistics suggest Detroit native hit most home runs in Negro leagues history. Held many of Stars' records. Star of Mack Park hit .352 lifetime in black leagues, .313 against barnstorming white major leaguers, .474 in playoff games. A shy man, he never attracted attention or was part of the lore that helped other Negro leaguers get into Hall of Fame. Nickname referred to the way Norman, who was very fast, ran the bases, flapping his arms.

TERRY McDERMOTT
Sept. 20, 1940—

Olympic gold medal speedskater. Essexville native. Won only U.S. gold medal at '64 Innsbruck Winter Games, in 500-meter speedskating. His victory, a huge upset, and his story got nation interested in speedskating. People who never paid any attention to the sport read about the 23-year-old barber who raced on skates he borrowed from team coach. Won silver medal in '68 Olympics in Grenoble, France. Later became a speedskating official. Took Olympic oath on behalf of athletes at '80 Games.

LOFTON GREENE
Feb. 11, 1919—

River Rouge basketball coach and athletic director. Served Rouge for 41 years. Won more state boys basketball titles than any other Michigan coach. Won Class B championships in '54-55, '59. Won five straight in '61-65 and four straight in '69-72. Was runner-up four times in state finals. Won 151 state tourament games. Two-time Michigan coach of the year. National High School Coaches Association basketball coach of the year in '72. Member of National High School Hall of Fame.

➤

86
BOB CHAPPUIS
Feb. 24, 1923—

Michigan halfback 1942, '46-47. Triple threat for "Mad Magicians" disputed national championship team of '47. Led 10-0 team with 1,674 yards of total offense. Set Rose Bowl record for total offense (230 yards) in '48. Finished U-M career with 3,487 yards total offense. Finished second in '47 Heisman voting to Johnny Lujack of Notre Dame. Career interrupted by WWII; shot down over Italy. Two seasons in AAFC before career in labor relations. Inducted into College Football Hall of Fame in '88.

87
GUS DORAIS
July 2, 1891—Jan. 3, 1954

University of Detroit football coach 1925-42 and Lions coach '43-47. Had a 112-48-7 record (.692) as U-D coach, including unbeaten streak of 22 games ('27-29). Went 20-31-2 with Lions. Played quarterback at Notre Dame in 1910-13. Four-year roommate with Knute Rockne. Became first player to throw football in an overhand manner, making the pass an effective weapon in 1913. Inducted into College Football Hall of Fame as a coach in '54. Served on Detroit's City Council '40-47.

88
RED BERENSON
Dec. 8, 1939—

"The Red Baron." Michigan hockey player 1959-62, U-M coach since 1984. Two-time All-America, his 43 goals in '61-62 still a U-M record. First college player to go directly to NHL. One of only seven to score six goals in NHL game, with St. Louis in '68. Played five seasons with Red Wings ('70-75). Finished with 261 goals in 987 games for Montreal, Rangers, Blues and Wings. At U-M, won NCAA titles in '96, '98. In the top 25 all-time in college coaching victories. NHL coach of the year in '81 with Blues.

89
JULIE KRONE
July 24, 1963—

Jockey born in Benton Harbor, grew up in Eau Claire. First female jockey to win a Triple Crown race, winning '93 Belmont Stakes riding Colonial Affair. By that time, she already was considered one of the best jockeys in country. In '87-89 was among the top five in the nation in races won. On Aug. 30, 1993, she recorded five victories at Saratoga, tying track record. In her career the 4-foot-10, 98-pounder suffered a broken arm, cardiac contusion and shattered ankle. Her last outing as a jockey was in April '99.

90
HAYES JONES
Aug. 4, 1938—

Olympic hurdler from Eastern Michigan and Pontiac Central High. Bronze medal in 110-meter hurdles in '60 Rome Olympics. Won gold in '64 Tokyo Games. Donated gold medal to the children of Pontiac. Was the AAU outdoor champion three years ('58, '60, '61) and the indoor champion four times ('58, '60-62). Won NCAA title in '59, when he also was the Pan-Am Games champion. In '61, ran on 400-meter relay team that set world record. Member of the National Track and Field Hall of Fame.

91
ROGER PENSKE
Feb. 20, 1937—

Owner of Team Penske Racing and Penske Motorsports Inc. Runs the most successful Indy-car racing team in history with 99 victories. Owned first car to top 180 m.p.h. at Indianapolis. Team has won 10 Indianapolis 500s, nine Indy-car national championships and 119 poles. Owns NASCAR team, too. Helped lift auto racing to a major form of American entertainment. Owns five tracks across the country, including Michigan Speedway in Brooklyn. Penske Auto Parts stores based at Kmart.

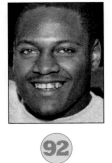

92
LORENZO WHITE
April 12, 1966—

Michigan State running back 1984-87. All-America in sophomore and senior seasons. In '88, led MSU to first Rose Bowl since '66, rushing for 1,572 yards (added 113 in bowl). Fourth in Heisman voting in '85 after rushing for 1,908 yards (added 158 more in All-American Bowl). Career leader in rushing yards (4,887), rushing TDs (43), 100-yard games (23). Named to MSU's Centennial Super Squad in '96. Drafted in first round by Houston in '88, played last of eight seasons with Cleveland.

93
DENNIS RODMAN
May 13, 1961—

Pistons forward 1986-92. Known for defensive skills, hair colors and outrageous behavior on and off the court, "Worm" led NBA in rebounding average seven straight years. Drafted in second round in 1986 as obscure 25-year-old from Southeastern Oklahoma State. Key member of Pistons championship teams in '89 and '90, he also won titles with Chicago in '96, '97, '98. NBA defensive player of year in '90 and '91. Seven-time NBA all-defensive team. Pistons leader in rebounds with 34 in game.

One hundred heroes

94

BOB CALIHAN
Aug. 2, 1918—Sept. 23, 1989

University of Detroit basketball coach 1948-69. U-D basketball player 1938-40. Was school's first basketball All-America, twice earning the honor ('39, '40). U-D athletic director '65-77. Posted 306-237 hoops record, leading U-D to one NCAA tournament ('62) and three NIT appearances. In '77, school's basketball arena (Memorial Building) was named Calihan Hall. Played in National Basketball League, leading the Detroit Eagles to league title in '41 and also playing for Chicago and Rochester.

95

LISA BROWN-MILLER
Nov. 16, 1966—

Women's ice hockey player. Pioneer in her sport. Helped United States win gold medal in first women's Olympic competition, '98 Nagano. Unknown to her, she was pregnant at time with son Alexander. Left wing from Union Lake had one goal, two assists and a plus-six rating at Olympics. Member of inaugural national team in '90. College player of year in '88 as a senior at Providence. Finished with 154 points in her college career. Compiled a 60-45-5 record as head coach at Princeton '91-96.

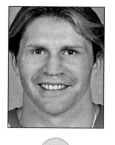

96

VLADIMIR KONSTANTINOV
March 19, 1967—

Red Wings defenseman 1991-97. Recognized as one of NHL's top defensemen. Also one of its roughest. Helped the Wings win Stanley Cup in '97. Six days later, suffered massive head injuries when limousine in which he was a passenger hit a tree. His efforts to recover inspired teammates and the city. Celebrated '98 Cup from wheelchair on the ice. Made NHL all-rookie team in '92 and All-NHL second team in '96. Captain of Central Red Army team and Soviet national team.

97

JEAN HOXIE
March 17, 1903—May 6, 1970

Tennis coach from Hamtramck. Coached Hamtramck High boys to 18 Class A state championships, '49-59, '61-64, '67-69, and runner-up finishes in '60, '65, '66. With husband Jerry, turned Hamtramck into mecca for junior tennis in '50s and '60s. Top teen players from all over the country came to Hamtramck to train with Hoxie, a hard-nosed disciplinarian who developed more than 200 national and international champions. She conducted clinics all over the world.

98

KARCH KIRALY
Nov. 3, 1960—

Volleyball player. Possibly the best player the world has seen. Born in Jackson but grew up mainly in Ann Arbor while his father, Laszlo, earned three degrees. Led UCLA to three NCAA championships ('79, '81, '82). Member of the U.S. national team in '81-89. Team won gold medals at '84 and '88 Olympics. Named world's top player after '86 world championship. Also starred in beach volleyball, winning dozens of tournaments and first Olympic gold (with Kent Steffes) in '96.

99

DOUG KURTIS
March 12, 1952—

Marathon runner from Northville. Ran in 190 marathons in 25 countries and holds the world records for most victories with 39 and the most sub-2:20 marathons with 76. Won a record six straight Free Press marathons in 1987-92. Retired from marathon competition in '97. A systems analyst at Ford Motor Co., he became director of Detroit Free Press/Flagstar Bank International Marathon. Also coaches elite Detroit area runners and is the director of Northville's Roadrunner Classic.

100

ALAN TRAMMELL AND LOU WHITAKER
Feb. 21, 1958—   *May 12, 1957—*

Tigers shortstop 1977-96. Won four Gold Gloves ('80, '81, '83, '84), selected to six All-Star Games ('80, '84, '85, '87, '88, '90). Got his 2,000th career hit Aug. 15, 1991 against Chicago White Sox. Career batting average .285; career fielding average .977. Was MVP of World Series as Tigers won in '84. In '87 hit .343 (third in AL) with 28 homers, 105 RBIs, 205 hits, finishing second to George Bell in AL MVP voting, 332-311. Voted shortstop by fans on Tigers' all-time team. Became Tigers' hitting instructor.

Tigers second baseman 1977-95. Sweet Lou and Trammell were longest-running double play combination in baseball history, establishing a league record in '95 with 1,918 appearances as teammates. AL rookie of year in '78. First Tiger since Norm Cash to reach 1,000 RBIs (in '94), finishing his career with 1,084. Got 2,000th hit in New York on June 6, 1992. Had 2,369 hits, 244 home runs. Selected to five All-Star Games ('83-87). Won three Gold Gloves ('83-85). Had .276 batting average, .984 fielding percentage.

Michigan
Numerology

The **1** extra seat at 107,501-seat Michigan Stadium, saved for Fritz Crisler. T.C. Chen's first-round **2** on the par-five second hole at Oakland Hills in 1985; it was the first double-eagle in U.S. Open history. Mickey Lolich's **3** victories in the '68 World Series. Tobin Rote's **4** touchdown passes in the '57 NFL title game. The Fab **Five**. Syd Howe's **6**-goal game. Vinnie Johnson's jumper with **.7** second left. The quadruple-bogey **8** T.C. Chen took on No. 5 during the final round at Oakland Hills. No. **9**, Gordie Howe. The Big **Ten** (even though it has **11** members). Lofton Greene's **12** Class B basketball titles with River Rouge. Terry Mills' NBA-record **13** straight three-pointers in '96. **14** grams of cocaine in Bob Probert's underwear. Tara Lipinski, Olympic champion at **15**. San Francisco vs. Cincinnati in Super Bowl **XVI** at the Silverdome. Sparky Anderson's **17** seasons with the Tigers. Rudy York's **18** homers in August 1937. Mark Fidrych's **19** victories as a rookie. Al Kaline, baseball's youngest batting champion at age **20**, when he hit .340 in '55. Steve Yzerman, the Wings' youngest captain at age **21**. Dave Bing's **22.6** scoring average for the Pistons. Larry Aurie's league-leading **23** goals in 1936-37. Kirk Gibson's **24** TD catches. Gordie Howe's **25** seasons with the Wings. The **26.2** miles of the Free Press Marathon. Michigan sophomore Rudy Tomjanovich's **27** rebounds in the first game played in Crisler Arena, a 96-79 loss to Kentucky. Ernie Irvan's mangled No. **28** car. Hal Newhouser's **29** victories in '44. Aleta Sill's **30** titles and million-dollar career. Denny McLain's **31** victories in 1968. **32** touchdown passes by Scott Mitchell in '95. Larry Bethea's **33** sacks for Michigan State. The Spartans' **34-31** victory over Michigan in the last meeting of the century. The '84 Tigers' **35-5** start. Blake Ezor's **36** points against Northwestern. Anthony Carter's **37** touchdowns for Michigan. Sergei Fedorov, the $**38**-million man. Lou Gehrig's ironman streak ending at Briggs Stadium in '**39**. Ernie Harwell's **40** years in Detroit. Michigan's **41**-game home unbeaten streak in 1969-75. **42** years without a Stanley Cup. Lorenzo White's **43** touchdowns for Michigan State. Hal Newhouser's back-to-back MVP awards in '**44** and '**45**. Brendan Shanahan's **46** goals in 1996-97. Tyrone Wheatley's **47** rushing touchdowns. Bobby Hebert's game-clinching, **48**-yard TD pass to Anthony Carter in the '83 USFL title game. Michigan's **49-0** victory over Stanford in the first Rose Bowl. The Lions' team-record **50** touchdowns in '95. Cecil Fielder's **51** homers in 1990. Mickey Redmond's **52** goals in 1972-73. Charlie Batch's **53** touchdown passes for Eastern Michigan. Joe Louis' **54** knockouts. The Wings' Cup in '**55**. Kelly Tripucka's Pistons-record **56** points against Chicago. The Lions' last NFL championship, in '**57**. Hank Greenberg's **58** homers in 1938. Lions **59**, Browns 14, in 1957 NFL championship game. The Lions' **60** games on Thanksgiving Day. Kalamazoo College's **61** consecutive MIAA men's tennis titles. The NHL-record **62** victories by the 1995-96 Wings. Tom Dempsey's **63**-yard field goal against the Lions. Gordie breaking the Rocket's goal-scoring record with his 545th in '**64**. Steve Yzerman's **65** goals in '88-89. Duke Christie's **66** points – 10 touchdowns, six PATs – as Escanaba beat Ishpeming, 102-0, in a 1920 football game. Ben Hogan's final-round **67** to win the '51 U.S. Open at Oakland Hills. The '68 Tigers. Ralph Guldahl's final-round **69** that won the 1937 U.S. Open at Oakland Hills. Drew Henson's national-record **70** career homers for Brighton High. Reggie Jackson's homer in the '**71** All-Star Game at Tiger Stadium. Hudson High's **72**-game football winning streak. David Thompson's **73** points against the Pistons. The Wings' **74** seasons. Bubba Baker's **75½** sacks for the Lions. Speedskater Sheila Young-Ochowicz's three medals at the '**76** Olympics. The Wings' drafting Dale McCourt No. 1 in '**77**. Carney-Nadeau's **78**-game winning streak in girls basketball in 1989-91. Magic Johnson vs. Larry Bird in the '**79** NCAA final. Michigan's **80-79** victory over Seton Hall in the 1989 NCAA final. The Pistons' drafting Isiah in '**81**. The Pistons' acquiring Laimbeer in '**82**. The Panthers' USFL title in '**83**. The Roar of '**84**. Terry Sawchuk's **85** shutouts for the Wings. Pistons **186**, Nuggets 184 (3 OT), the NBA's highest-scoring game, Dec. 13, 1983. The Tigers' pennant drive in '**87**. **88** years of Tiger Stadium. The '**89** Pistons. The '**90** Pistons. Thumbs Up for the Lions in '**91**. Butch Woolfolk's **92**-yard run against Wisconsin. Desmond Howard's **93**-yard punt return for a TD against Ohio State in 1991. The '**94** World Cup games at the Silverdome. The Wings' return to the finals in '**95**. Ty Cobb's record **96** stolen bases in 1915. Ed Burling's **97** points for Crystal Falls in a 1911 basketball game against Iron River. Ol' **98**. Barry Sanders' **99** rushing touchdowns. **100** great years of sports.

By Nicholas J. Cotsonika

At the dawn of the 20th Century, Detroit was a pretty, peaceful place. Known as City Beautiful for its shaded streets and gracious homes, it already held dear a quiet distinction, celebrating its bicentennial in 1901. Only 285,704 people called it home, making it just the 13th-largest town in the United States, and all lived within four miles of city hall.

But suddenly, in two decades, it became a bustling center of big-time big business. Newcomers from around the globe poured into what became known as Dynamic Detroit and later, of course, the Motor City. Local companies experimenting with horseless carriages made advances in design and production, and newfangled automobile assembly lines provided unskilled workers with well-paying jobs. By 1910, the city's population was

After Ty Cobb left Georgia for the big city, baseball and Detroit would never be the same.

466,000. By 1920, it was 1 million. With the world on wheels, Detroit shed its sleepy skin and boomed, its fast-paced streets crowded by loud-mouthed machines that belched black smoke.

As Detroit began growing into a big-league industrial giant, it began growing into a big-league sports center as well, almost out of necessity: All those new residents needed something to jeer and cheer after their mind-numbing workdays. At first, they looked west to Ann Arbor, where Fielding H. Yost was building the nation's preeminent college football program at Michigan, his teams posting what seemed like a point a minute, winning championships consistently. Then, when a terrible tyrant of a man arrived from Georgia, the fans looked back to baseball, completely captivated by the period's only professional team sport of consequence.

The city's baseball history dates to 1881, when a National League franchise alternately called the Detroits and Wolverines began an eight-season run that included a world title in 1887. The club moved to Cleveland in 1888, making Detroit a minorleague town, but the sorrow was fairly short-lived. In 1894, Western League organizer Byron Bancroft (Ban) Johnson awarded the city a franchise, which was dubbed the Tigers in a Free Press headline. In 1901, Johnson changed the Western League's name to the American League, winning full major

---

Ty Cobb was called a genius in spikes. When he left Georgia to play baseball, his father told him: "Don't come home a failure."

league status for his brainchild in 1903.

For a while, the Tigers played poorly and drew poorly. There was even talk of moving them to Pittsburgh. But that all began to change dramatically in '05. The Tigers trained in Augusta, Ga., where colorful infielder Germany Schaefer pointed out a local prospect to management. "He's the craziest ballplayer I ever saw," Schaefer said. "He tries to stretch every hit. He tries to steal when the pitcher is holding the ball. Wait till you see him." The prospect was a slight, speedy 18-year-old who had bounced around the low bushes. His name was Tyrus Raymond Cobb.

Late that season, a rash of injuries plagued the Tigers, and secretary-general manager Frank Navin needed a warm body

for his outfield. He had the right to take any player from the Augusta Tourists' roster for $750, as part of a deal in which he had loaned young pitcher Eddie Cicotte to them in lieu of paying rent for training facilities. Navin wanted a player named Clyde Engle, but he settled for Cobb. Engle's hitting had been tailing off, and Cobb, highly recommended by certain scouts, was leading the league with a .326 average.

Cobb debuted at the corner of Michigan and Trumbull on Aug. 30, 1905, before 1,200 fans at Bennett Park, the forerunner of Navin Field. He ripped a run-scoring double, the first of 4,191 career base hits. Navin didn't know it, but he had introduced perhaps the most compelling character — and most venomous villain — that the sporting world ever would

---

April 6, 1900: James Jeffries knocked out challenger Jake Finnegan in the first round in Detroit.
It was the first-ever first-round KO in a heavyweight title fight.

PETE ROSE, THE ONLY PLAYER TO SURPASS COBB IN CAREER HITS — 4,256 TO 4,189 — HAD A WHOPPING 2,624 MORE AT-BATS THAN HIS PREDECESSOR.

see. He didn't know it, but he also had introduced the first famous figure of a glorious 100-year athletic era for the proud Motor City, an era rightly titled the Century of Champions.

THE FURY GROWS

Days before his arrival in Detroit, Ty Cobb experienced a personal tragedy so horrific, he spent the rest of his life living in a rage and rancor, which many experts theorized was brought on by some sort of mental illness. Someone — his mother or a possible lover of hers — blew off his father's head with a double-barreled shotgun at the Cobb family home in Royston, Ga.

The shooting occurred Aug. 8, 1905. William Herschel Cobb, a prominent man and state senator known as the Professor, dined with his family that evening, announced unexpectedly that he was leaving on a business trip, and departed around 6 p.m. His wife, Amanda, testified that she retired to her bedroom around 10:30, then was jolted from sleep after midnight by a scratching sound at a window. She looked up and saw by moonlight the outline of a large, ominous figure she assumed was a robber. The scratching con-

APRIL 25, 1901: THE TIGERS MADE THEIR AMERICAN LEAGUE DEBUT WITH A 14-13 VICTORY
OVER MILWAUKEE BEFORE 10,000 AT BENNETT PARK.

tinued. She grabbed the gun, alone, panic-stricken, and fired. Twice.

When she crept toward the body, according to her testimony, she barely could identify her husband. His stomach was torn open. Not much above his neck was left. Doctors arrived and pronounced him dead around 1:30 a.m.; they found a six-shot revolver in his pocket. Almost immediately, rumors buzzed around town. Amanda was a young, shapely woman. The Professor was out of town often. Although no one ever proved Amanda was unfaithful or that anyone but her pulled the trigger, many assumed that Amanda had a lover and that the Professor, suspecting so, laid a trap and was killed because of it. There was no other way to explain why the Professor had been outside the window. Amanda escaped punishment.

Cobb went pale at the news, leaving the Tourists in Augusta and rushing home. "I'll never get over this," he said. As his beloved father was buried, he said: "There goes the best man I ever knew." Cobb had clashed with his father repeatedly on the subject of baseball; the Professor, whom he deeply admired, had wanted him to use his brains instead of his muscles and go to college, preferably West Point. But recently they had made peace. Since Cobb had kept pursuing a career in the game with dogged determination, the Professor relented and encouraged his tenacity, telling him pointedly: "Don't come home a failure." Those words went straight to his broken heart.

Shortly after the incident, Cobb, in deep depression, never having seen an official major league game, departed for Detroit. "I wasn't so much scared as nervous and anxious," he told his biographer, Al Stump. "Nothing was familiar. I didn't know anyone between the train depot and the boondocks. Hell, I didn't even know where the Tigers' ballpark was located." And then, unbelievably, things got worse. Much worse.

Everything about him rubbed his crusty teammates the wrong way: his youth, his confidence, his Southern accent, his ability to take someone's job. They openly ignored him — but only when they didn't haze him severely. They threw things at him. They spit tobacco juice on his clothes and uniform. They nailed his shoes to the floor. They even destroyed his homemade bats, which Cobb considered his pride and joy.

Consumed by fury, Cobb fought back. He confronted the team's biggest star, Wahoo Sam Crawford, an outfielder and future Hall of Famer who got his nickname because of his hometown of Wahoo, Neb. Cobb beat the living daylights out of Ed Siever, a veteran pitcher who was orchestrating some of the abuse. But his actions just contributed to a most vicious cycle. Cobb's teammates disliked him even more, and he kept fighting. Everyone. And everything. Everywhere.

Sometimes to the death.

FIGHTING TO KILL

Cobb's soul was tortured so badly, he spent part of the '06 season in a suburban Detroit sanatorium, suffering from a nervous breakdown. He had little sense of humor, especially if the joke was on him. He was cold and cruel, on the field and off. He was a bigot, his racist mind rooted in Confederate country. Although he had soft spots for children and dogs, giving scholarships to the former and homes to the latter, he was full of hate.

Few befriended Cobb, and those who did quickly reversed course.

Associated Press

TY COBB'S BATTING STANCE, EVEN WHEN HE WAS AN 18-YEAR-OLD ROOKIE, WAS DESIGNED FOR SPRAY HITTING RATHER THAN PURE POWER. HE FINISHED HIS CAREER WITH 3,052 SINGLES, 724 DOUBLES, 297 TRIPLES AND 118 HOME RUNS.

Richard Bak Collection

COBB — FLANKED BY FELLOW OUTFIELDERS BOBBY VEACH AND WAHOO SAM CRAWFORD — WAS FEARED, IF NOT RESPECTED, BY TEAMMATES.

Writer Ernest Hemingway once went big-game hunting with Cobb in Wyoming. But when Cobb decked a guide with a rifle for taking them down the wrong trail, Hemingway had had enough. "I packed out next day and after that avoided him," said Hemingway, who later gave Cobb this title: "Ty Cobb, the greatest of all ballplayers — and an absolute s---."

From the beginning, Cobb was far more feared for his volcanic temper than his considerable skill. After being hazed one day, Cobb began carrying a snub-nosed Frontier Colt pistol. He would carry a weapon for the rest of his life, laying a revolver on the nightstand next to his deathbed. "I was catching hell by the handful," he told Stump. "That gun was forced on me."

Special to the Detroit Free Press

TY COBB TRADEMARKS — A HIGH SLIDE, A STEAL OF HOME AND A BUNT. HE PILFERED HOME PLATE A RECORD 50 TIMES IN HIS CAREER.

Cobb never shot anyone, to the public's knowledge. He came close several times, however, and everyone knew he didn't need to fire his gun to draw blood. Once, he pounced upon an abrasive fan — although the fan had no hands. To Detroiters, his most famous fight occurred in 1908, when he accidentally stepped into some freshly poured asphalt outside the original Pontchartrain Hotel at Michigan and Woodward. He spat several choice racial epithets at Fred Collins, a black laborer, then assaulted him. But there were far more disturbing tales of his ready violence.

During training in '07, Cobb found one of his four-fingered gloves mangled maliciously. He assumed the black groundskeeper, Bungy Davis, was behind the dirty deed. So one morning, when Davis tried to shake Cobb's hand and clap him on the shoulder, Cobb attacked him, punching him to the ground and kicking his head. When Davis' wife intervened, Cobb, all 6-feet-1 and 190 pounds of him, slammed her to her knees and began choking her. He didn't stop until catcher Charlie (Boss) Schmidt tore him away.

Richard Bak Collection

At a Cleveland hotel in 1909, Cobb grew angry when a black watchman, George Stansfield, told him he would have to walk up to his room because the elevators didn't run past midnight. After an argument, Stansfield pulled his nightstick and the two began brawling. Cobb pulled a pocketknife and slashed Stansfield all over — in the ear, shoulder and hands — before kicking him in the head. A desk clerk and janitors saved Stansfield's life by jumping on Cobb, whose only punishment was this: He had to avoid Ohio justice by taking trains through Canada to Pittsburgh for the World Series.

One night in 1912, Cobb encountered three muggers on Trumbull while in his car with his wife. In the midst of the fight, one of them knifed Cobb in the back. As the gang ran away, Cobb pulled out his

Richard Bak Collection

Detroit Free Press

TY COBB COLLECTED 12 BATTING
TITLES, HIT BETTER THAN .400
THREE TIMES AND FINISHED
WITH A .367 CAREER AVERAGE,
HIGHEST IN BASEBALL HISTORY.

OCT. 3, 1903: CHESTER BREWER COACHED HIS FIRST FOOTBALL GAME FOR MICHIGAN AGRICULTURAL, A 12-0 LOSS
AT NOTRE DAME. BREWER'S AGGIES POSTED 49 SHUTOUTS IN HIS 88 GAMES OVER THREE STINTS AT THE SCHOOL.

TYRUS RAYMOND COBB
1886 — 1961

GREATEST TIGER OF ALL
A GENIUS IN SPIKES

"My idea was to go on the attack and never relax it. An offensive attitude is the key to making any play, and if it meant gambling and getting tough, I was willing. If they roughed me up, I knocked them kicking with my spikes. I used my legs like an octopus when I was thrown out."

TY COBB

Special to the Detroit Free Press

pistol, which would not fire, then decided to *chase* his assailants. He caught one of them in an alley, beat him with the butt of his gun, and presumed him dead. "Left him there, not breathing, in his own rotten blood," Cobb told Stump proudly about 50 years later. Days after the incident, an unidentified body was found in an alley off Trumbull.

"I fight to kill," Cobb said. "If I'd been meek and submissive, instead of fighting back, the world never would have heard of me."

THE TYGERS

Playing against Cobb required courage, a strong stomach for steel, and blood. In 1906, Joe Jackson of the Free Press referred to Cobb as "a peach of a player," then as the "Georgia Peach." But Cobb's demeanor was anything but peachy. He studied books on Napoleon, and he aspired to do battle like him. He left lasting impressions on infielders who dared block his way to the bag, sliding with sharpened spikes high, slicing and dicing his way to safety. He was called a "genius in spikes." But he was a devil in them, too.

To Cobb, baseball was a game of cunning, to be won not with power but with precise placement hitting, tight defense, hit-and-run plays, disguised bunts, sacrifice flies, squeeze plays and steals. All kinds of steals. Delayed steals. Double steals. In-your-face-I'm-coming-home steals. He stole home a record 50 times. Cobb believed the batter's box and base paths belonged to him, and as the meanest monster in the game, he aggressively defended his turf. If a pitcher tried to bean him, for instance, Cobb would bunt down the first-base line and slam the pitcher as he tried to cover. That would teach him.

"My idea was to go on the attack and never relax it," Cobb said. "An offensive attitude is the key to making any play, and if it meant gambling and getting tough, I was willing. If they roughed me up, I knocked them kicking with my spikes. I used my legs like an octopus when I was thrown out."

Associated Press

Ty Cobb was in his 20th season — fourth as Tigers manager — in this photo from 1924, a year in which the 37-year-old smacked 211 hits and batted .338.

One incident cemented his reputation. Against the Athletics in Philadelphia during the '08 season, Cobb seemed like a dead duck as he approached third base. He faked a hook slide to his left and whipped his right leg across to the bag, severely stabbing star infielder John

Franklin (Home Run) Baker, who dropped the ball in pain. Safe. Baker called the spiking a "Cobb's Kiss" and claimed "it was on purpose." Although Cobb denied intent, A's manager Connie Mack called him a "no-good ruffian." Afterward, Philly fans joined the rest of the nation in detesting him.

Intimidation was a key factor in Cobb's sheer domination of the game. And, oh, he *did* dominate the game. After hitting .240 in 41 games his first season, he hit better than .300 for the rest of his career. That's 23 straight years. Mostly in the dead-ball era. He hit better than .400 three times, the best of which was .420 in 1911. He stole 892 bases. He won a record 12 batting titles, nine straight at one point, and finished with a .367 career average, by far the best of the century.

"Good as I was, I never was close to Cobb, and neither was Babe Ruth or anybody else," said Cobb's foil, Hall of Famer Tris Speaker, the only man to beat Cobb for the batting title from 1907 to 1919 (.386 to .371 in 1916). "The Babe was a great ballplayer, sure. But Cobb was even greater. Babe could knock your brains out, but Cobb would drive you crazy."

Cobb played 22 seasons in Detroit before ending his career by playing two more in Philadelphia. For most of that time, the Tigers were mediocre. Only the intrigue Cobb created spun the turnstiles enough to make the building of Navin Field in 1912 such a necessity. Losing badly bothered Cobb, because he desperately wanted to make up for his only on-field failure: subpar performances in three straight World Series.

Above: Burton Historical Collection   Below: Richard Bak Collection

The Tigers often were called the Tygers, because Cobb rose above them all — even Crawford and animated manager Hughie Jennings, another future Hall of Famer. But after winning pennants, setting the burgeoning city alight in delight with parades of torchbearers, they were called many other names. In the 1907 and '08 World Series, the Tigers lost to the Chicago Cubs, in four straight the first time (after a tied Game 1 was called on account of darkness in the 12th), in five games the second. In 1909, the Tigers lost to the Pittsburgh Pirates in seven. Cobb had his moments. He hit .368 in the '08 Series, and he stole home to spark a victory in Game 2 of the '09 Series, his last. But Cobb, who always felt as if his late father were watching him, wasn't satisfied. His lifetime Series batting average was a dismal .262.

TY COBB — BEHIND THE WHEEL OF A 1910 OWEN — MADE A FORTUNE BY INVESTING IN AUTOMOBILES AND COCA-COLA. HE ALSO WAS A PITCHMAN FOR THE ATLANTA-BASED SOFT DRINK.

BUSTIN' THE BABE

When Babe Ruth began hammering homers for the New York Yankees in the '20s, Cobb couldn't stand it. For Cobb's taste, Ruth's homers were changing the game for the worse, and he was getting far too much fame. A rivalry brewed, and run-ins were inevitable. Cobb snarled and hurled racial slurs at Ruth, although Ruth was white, and the two once came to blows. But Cobb got back at Ruth in more than just fights. Two moments in particular made him flash his crooked smile.

A COMMON MISCONCEPTION HOLDS THAT THE LONG-BALL HITTING SULTAN OF SWAT HULKED OVER THE WIRY GEORGIA PEACH, BUT BABE RUTH IN HIS HEYDAY CAME TO THE PLATE AT 6-FEET-2, 215 POUNDS, WHILE COBB SWUNG AWAY AT 6-1, 190.

THREE FUTURE HALL OF
FAMERS CAPPED OFF THEIR
CAREERS IN PHILADELPHIA
(FROM LEFT): EDDIE
COLLINS, TY COBB AND
TRIS SPEAKER.

Burton Historical Collection

Burton Historical Collection

WHILE TY COBB HAD FEW FRIENDS, EVEN IN RETIREMENT, HE SOMETIMES RETURNED TO THE CORNER OF MICHIGAN AND TRUMBULL,
WHERE FANS GREETED HIM FONDLY. HE DIED JULY 17, 1961, IN ATLANTA.

Cobb was player-manager of the Tigers for his final six seasons in Detroit, despising every moment of it, because his
players never could attain his lofty standards. Outfielder
Harry Heilmann, a future Hall of Famer he had scouted, was
not of his class, although Heilmann beat him for batting titles
in 1921, '23, '25 and '27. Neither was outfielder Heinie Manush,
who won the batting title in '26. But despite his foul moods,

Cobb had some fun as manager. One day in 1923, he openly
instructed his pitcher, Hooks Dauss, to intentionally walk
Ruth. But he was faking. With the Babe relaxed on each pitch,
Dauss fired strikes, and Cobb came out in mock anger to
scold him each time. Babe struck out, stunned, with his bat
on his shoulder. Tricked by Ty. "A once-in-a-lifetime setup
play," Cobb said. "I flattered Ruth with that walk-the-man

stuff, and he fell for it."

On May 5, 1925, Cobb became fed up with the attention Ruth's homers were receiving. So he told reporters something truly newsworthy: "For the first time in my life, I will be deliberately going for home runs. For years, I've been reading comparisons about how others hit, as against my style. So I'm going to give you a demonstration." That day, he went 6-for-6, with three homers, two doubles and a single. The next day, he homered twice more and added another single. "There's no doubt in my mind that Ty is the best all-around hitter who ever lived," Speaker said. "He can bunt, chop-hit, deliver long drives or put balls out of sight."

Ruth gave Cobb an awestruck, grudging respect. "Cobb's the meanest, toughest (expletive) who ever walked onto a field," Ruth once told Jimmie Reese, a former Yankees infielder. "He gave everybody hell — me included — because he couldn't stand to lose. All he wanted was to beat you on Saturday and twice on Sunday. Otherwise, he was miserable."

Cobb retired after batting .323 in 1928, his record unstained by a games-fixing scandal that also involved Speaker, just before Detroit became known as the City of Champions. But Cobb never mellowed. Never. He drank hard, having picked up the habit for the first time during a brief stint in World War I. He played hard, once gruffly storming through a group on a golf course that included President Dwight Eisenhower. He stayed surly, a paranoid penny-pincher, always worried someone would steal the multi-million-dollar fortune he made by shrewdly investing in automobiles and Coca-Cola. He remained alone, devoid of friends, divorced from two wives, estranged from five children.

Demons of the past continued to haunt him. When he died in 1961 at age 74, there weren't a quartermillion people to file past his casket or two-day services at New York's St. Patrick's Cathedral, as there were for the beloved Ruth in 1948. Only three men from all of baseball — Tigers Hall of Fame catcher Mickey Cochrane, fellow Hall of Famer Ray Schalk, an old-time catcher, and Nap Rucker from his minor league days — showed up to bury him on a hot day in Georgia. The first man elected to the Hall of Fame went to his grave with only one comfort: the knowledge that he was the most ferocious of all Tigers, that his furious, fiery success had kept him from coming home a failure.

"My father," he had said, "how proud he would have been if he hadn't left for the other side." ◆

Detroit Free Press

TY COBB HAD A SOFT SPOT FOR CHILDREN, INCLUDING HIS GRANDDAUGHTER, MARY MCLAREN. MORE THAN HALF A CENTURY AFTER THE VEXING DEATH OF HIS FATHER, COBB WAS LAID TO REST IN THE FAMILY VAULT IN HIS HOMETOWN OF ROYSTON, GA. THE TOWN STILL PROCLAIMS ITSELF AS "HOME OF BASEBALL'S TY COBB."

BILLY BOWLES/Detroit Free Press

BILLY BOWLES/Detroit Free Press

Fielding (Hurry-Up) Yost

A point a minute

By Michael Rosenberg

Fielding H. Yost arrived in Ann Arbor for the 1901 football season determined to make Michigan a national power. A year later, in his 13th game as coach, Yost saw an opponent score on Michigan for the first time. A year after that, in his 30th game as coach, Yost saw his team finish a game without a victory for the first time when it tied Minnesota, 6-6. And two years after that, in his 57th game as coach, Yost finally ended up a loser, 2-0 to the University of Chicago. Soon after that, in the final poll of Yost's fifth season, one of Yost's teams finished without a national championship for the first time.

So if Michigan fans have unrealistic expectations for their team, blame Yost. He set standards that will never again be reached, for excellence and for charisma. Without Yost, Michigan probably would still have an athletic department, but it wouldn't have an aura.

Yost was everything U-M athletics have ever wanted to be and everything U-M athletics have ever been accused of being. He was the ultimate winner, a brilliant innovator, a pioneer, a showman and a marketing wizard. He also was an egomaniac, a racist and a rule-breaker, even in an era when there were not many rules.

From his arrival in 1901 until he retired as athletic director in 1941, Yost always got what he wanted. When people questioned the wisdom of building a new football stadium, Yost designed it and had it built. He even put in double footings to allow for expansion. Yost envisioned a capacity of 300,000, but Michigan Stadium opened in 1927 with a mere 84,401 seats. For its time, it was indeed the Big House, and it kept getting bigger, eventually reaching a capacity of 107,501 for the 1998 season. That never would have been possible without Yost's double footings.

For 40 years, the U-M athletic department's every move was orchestrated by Fielding H. Yost. He was an immovable object to his detractors but an irresistible force to his many fans. Ann Arbor was Yost's town, and for one reason: He made it that way as soon as he arrived.

Bentley Historical Library

Under Fielding H. Yost's tutelage, the Wolverines became Champions of the West, going unbeaten in the first 56 games he coached.

Oct. 18, 1913: Michigan Agricultural beat Michigan for the first time, 12-7 at Ann Arbor, en route to its first perfect season (7-0).

THE 1901 SQUAD WAS UNBEATEN AND UNSCORED UPON. AMONG ITS VICTIMS: ALBION, CASE, BUFFALO, CARLISLE, CHICAGO AND BELOIT.

Yost's first five seasons were the most successful in college football history. They also were the most influential five seasons in U-M history, perhaps in the state's history. Yost's phenomenal success begot his overwhelming popularity, which ensured that his vision for U-M would become reality.

Yost came to Ann Arbor from Stanford in 1901. Three years earlier, U-M music student Louis Elbel had penned "The Victors," dubbing his school "the champions of the West." Yost turned the fight song from fantasy to fact.

That 1901 team not only went 11-0 with a national title, it outscored its opponents, 550-0, an offensive feat made all the more remarkable by the fact that the forward pass was still illegal and touchdowns were worth only five points. The press tabbed the new coach "Point-a-Minute" Yost, and the nickname endured long after Yost died. The quick-scoring offense also earned Yost the nickname "Hurry-Up."

A LITTLE BROWN JUG TURNED INTO ONE OF COLLEGE FOOTBALL'S OLDEST TROPHIES AFTER SOME GOPHERS PINCHED THE VESSEL IN 1903.

After finishing its 10-game regular season, U-M made an unprecedented trip to California, where organizers in Pasadena were looking for something to spice up their annual Tournament of Roses Parade on New Year's Day. Yost's new team went out to face his old team, Stanford, and despite U-M's lopsided regular season, some on the West Coast wondered whether the Wolverines could compete with Stanford for a full game. As it turned out, they never played a full game. U-M built a 49-0 lead, gaining 527 yards to Stanford's 67, and Stanford captain Ralph Fisher conceded the game with eight minutes remaining.

Fullback Neil Snow scored four touchdowns, but Willie Heston was the star of the game, rushing for 170 yards on 18 carries. Heston was the dominant player of his era, a two-time All-America who scored many of the points for the "Point-a-Minute" teams.

Heston was so fast and had such great feet that Yost felt the need to create a new position for him, the better to get him the ball quickly. Heston lined up a few yards behind the line of scrimmage and

THE 1901 WOLVERINES TOOK A JOY RIDE OUT WEST BEFORE RAMBLING IN THE
ROSE BOWL. STANFORD GAVE UP AFTER MICHIGAN BUILT A 49-0 LEAD.

Bentley Historical Library

THE 1902 SQUAD ALSO WAS UNDEFEATED AND WALLOPED
OPPONENTS BY AN AVERAGE SCORE OF 59-1.

became the game's first tailback.

But there was no shortage of stars on those teams, and some of them even were actual students. Yost's players often were accused of skipping classes, even semesters. At the time, however, there was no such thing as an NCAA violation, and Yost and his players went mostly unpunished.

Besides, few fans were complaining, especially after the 1902 Wolverines also went 11-0 and won the national title. They might even have improved from the year before, outscoring their opponents, 644-12.

Yet for all his team's success — perhaps because of it — Yost's most memorable game at U-M was the first he didn't win. On Halloween in 1903, the Wolverines played at Minnesota, one of the game's powers. The Golden Gophers were 10-0 at the time, and their crowd of 20,000 — huge at the time — was raucous. Yost doubted Minnesota would provide safe drinking water, so he ordered equipment manager Tommy Roberts to purchase a jug for water.

Bentley Historical Library

FULLBACK NEIL SNOW,
WHO SCORED FOUR
TDS IN THE FIRST ROSE
BOWL, WAS A 10-LETTER
WINNER IN FOOTBALL,
BASEBALL AND TRACK.

With uncontaminated water at hand, U-M took a 6-0 lead, but Minnesota tied the game, 6-6, with two minutes left. Nobody had ever come close to tying a Yost U-M team, and the Gophers fans went crazy, climbing trees and telephone poles and rushing the field. The game was called and the Wolverines darted back to Ann Arbor — without their jug.

When Yost requested that the jug be returned, Minnesota athletic director L. J. Cooke wrote back: "If you want it, you'll have to come up and win it." In 1909, the Wolverines would recapture the Little Brown Jug, 15-6, the oldest trophy in Division I-A football.

The tie with Minnesota didn't prevent U-M from claiming the national title that year, and the Wolverines won another in 1904. U-M was 10-0, outscoring its opponents, 567-22 — the lowest point differential yet for a Yost team. In the season's final game, the Wolverines defeated Chicago, 22-12. Nobody had ever scored in double digits against Yost's Wolverines.

A year later, Chicago, under Amos Alonzo Stagg, finally ended U-M's unbeaten streak with a 2-0 victory in Chicago. In Yost's first 56 games, U-M had gone 55-0-1 and outscored its opponents, 2,821-40.

This was no small accomplishment, and Yost made no attempt to downplay it. With the press he was "Quote-a-Minute" Yost, a man who never ran out of things to say,

OCT. 30, 1920: MICHIGAN AGRICULTURAL BEAT OLIVET, 109-0, FOR ITS

BIGGEST ROUT. THE AGGIES WERE 4-6 IN GEORGE (POTSY) CLARK'S ONLY SEASON.

FOOTBALL GIANTS: WALTER CAMP (LEFT), WHO TURNED YALE INTO A GRIDIRON POWERHOUSE IN THE LATE 1800S, WAS KNOWN AS THE FATHER OF AMERICAN FOOTBALL. FIELDING H. YOST (RIGHT) FOLLOWED IN HIS FOOTSTEPS.

usually about himself. Legendary sports writer Ring Lardner was asked once whether he ever spoke to Fielding H. Yost, and he supposedly replied, "No. My father taught me never to interrupt."

Because he was so charismatic, Yost was a favorite of the press, and because he won so often, he was a favorite of the fans. Thus armed with the support of two important camps, Yost tried to ensure that U-M would be everything he wanted it to be. For better or worse, it was.

Yost engineered the school's disastrous 1908 exit from the Western Conference. Within a decade, it became apparent that U-M needed the conference more than the conference needed U-M, and the school meekly returned to the conference for the 1917 season, which included 10 schools for the first time.

Yost also never coached a black athlete. The son of a Confederate soldier, Yost didn't change his philosophy on race when he went to Ann Arbor, and it wasn't until after he left that black athletes made serious inroads at U-M.

But Yost's mistakes eventually were overcome, and his accomplishments secured his legacy. He didn't just build the stadium; he built an entire athletic complex, unmatched in its era and a huge reason for U-M's success. He saw that games would be more popular if there was some entertainment besides football, and so it was under his watch that the Michigan marching band grew in popularity.

At the end of the 20th Century, the Wolverines were still playing in the stadium Yost built. Most of the other facilities that were built at his behest were still in use. The Wolverines had won more football games than any other school and were one of the most popular teams in the country. The U-M athletic tradition is still secure, still on double footings.

Yost asked to be buried at the highest point in Ann Arbor, and his grave lies in Forest Hill Cemetery next to campus. On his tombstone there is a quote from Yost, who was born in West Virginia but was never happier than when he was in Ann Arbor: I WISH TO REST WHERE THE SPIRIT OF MICHIGAN IS WARMEST.

A few feet away lies the tombstone of broadcaster Bob Ufer, who for years filled the Midwest airwaves with the gospel of Michigan. He never called it "Michigan," though. Ufer always said *"Meeech-igan,"* his take on Yost's West Virginia accent, his way of making sure the dreams of Fielding H. Yost would echo from Michigan Stadium long after the man who built the U-M legend had died.

Detroit Free Press

FIELDING YOST GREETED A PAIR OF RETURNING LETTERMEN IN 1939 — WILLIE HESTON (ALSO SHOWN BELOW LEFT), WHOSE PLAYING DAYS WERE 1901-04, AND GERMANY SCHULZ (BELOW RIGHT), WHO PLAYED 1904-05, '07-08.

Bentley Historical Library

Bentley Historical Library

SEPT. 24, 1926: DETROIT BUSINESSMEN WERE GRANTED AN NHL FRANCHISE, WHICH THEY STOCKED WITH PLAYERS FROM THE VICTORIA COUGARS IN THE WESTERN HOCKEY LEAGUE.

TACKLE-BACK-RIGHT PLAY.

Bentley Historical Library

THE WOLVERINES RODE ROUGHSHOD OVER STANFORD IN THE FIRST ROSE BOWL.
THE FINAL WAS 49-0 ON JAN. 1, 1902. THEY ALSO RODE IN THE ROSE BOWL PARADE,
WHICH PREDATES THE GAME ITSELF.

Bentley Historical Library

NOV. 18, 1926: THE NHL'S DETROIT COUGARS — PLAYING THEIR INAUGURAL SEASON
ACROSS THE DETROIT RIVER AT WINDSOR ARENA — LOST THEIR FIRST GAME TO BOSTON, 2-0.

A major league stadium

Opening Day

Osborn Engineering Co.

WHEN NAVIN FIELD OPENED IN 1912, AN "IMMENSE THRONG" OF 26,000 SAW THE TIGERS DEFEAT CLEVELAND, 6-5, IN 11 INNINGS.

BY TOM PANZENHAGEN

Detroit had a major league team as early as 1881, but it didn't become a major league city until 1912. That's the year Navin Field opened, the year Detroit's baseball future was set in concrete.

Baseball has been played in Detroit since the middle of the 19th Century. By the time Ty Cobb arrived in 1905, a generation of Detroiters knew the charms of the grand old game. In 1887, the Wolverines — Detroit's entry in the National League — won the pennant and what was then called the "world's series" by defeating the St. Louis Browns.

The Wolverines disbanded after the 1888 season, but in 1896 a minor league team called the Tigers began playing at the corner of Michigan and Trumbull. Those Tigers joined the fledgling American League in 1901, and once again Detroit could boast a major league team. But at rickety Bennett Park, the game's future was on shaky ground.

Shaky ownership also placed the Tigers in a precarious

position, and in 1903 the team almost moved to Pittsburgh. Then in 1904, Bill Yawkey, whose family had made a fortune in lumber, bought the club. Yawkey's millions put the Tigers on solid ground but, more important, Yawkey opened the door for Frank Navin to buy stock in the team and run its operations.

Under Navin's leadership, the franchise that almost bolted for Pittsburgh became one of the most successful in baseball, on and off the field.

Despite improvements, Bennett Park remained one of a dying breed of wobbly wooden parks and, in the fall of 1911, down it came. In its place — at a cost of about $300,000 — rose Navin Field, a modern 23,000-seat facility, the embodiment of baseball's future in Detroit.

The Tigers' new home covered an area almost twice the size of Bennett Park. The outfield dimensions were 340 feet to left, 365 to right and 400 to center, with a 125-foot flagpole

NOV. 20, 1926: THE FIELDING H. YOST ERA ENDED AT MICHIGAN WITH A 7-6 VICTORY AT MINNESOTA.
U-M FINISHED 7-1 AND SHARED THE BIG TEN TITLE WITH NORTHWESTERN.

NAVIN FIELD —
PICTURED SOON
BEFORE ITS GRAND
OPENING — STOOD
ON THE NORTHWEST
CORNER OF
MICHIGAN AND
TRUMBULL, WHERE
BASEBALL HAD BEEN
PLAYED SINCE 1896.

in fair territory in centerfield.

Here's how the Free Press described the first Opening Day — Saturday, April 20, 1912 — under the headline "Immense Throng Sees Tigers Win Opening Battle."

"There will be no further talk to the effect that Detroit isn't a good baseball town, and it probably will be several weeks before anyone informs us again that the franchise is shortly to be transferred to some other city. Nearly 26,000 fans, of whom 24,384 paid cash for the privilege of attending, proved yesterday afternoon not only that the City of the Straits is a good supporter of the national pastime but that it is one of the very best in the entire country.

"Incidentally, the Tigers demonstrated that they are the sort of a ball club which deserves patronage. In spite of the baneful effects of much preliminary celebrating, in which the Jungaleers nearly were killed with kindness, they wrenched a 6 to 5 victory from Cleveland at 11 innings of battling that had the fans chewing their finger nails and whooping themselves hoarse throughout the afternoon.

"Only five cities in the country, New York, Chicago, Boston, Pittsburgh and Philadelphia, have turned out larger crowds than that which honored the dedication of the splendid concrete stadium known as Navin Field. There were more people inside the gates than the entire population of Battle Creek, as shown by the census of 1911, and only eight cities in the state have as many inhabitants as there were fans within the concrete walls of the Tigers' new home."

The hero of the game was The Georgia Peach. According

to the Free Press:

"Baseball's brightest luminary, Tyrus R. Cobb, of course, could not let an opportunity of displaying his charms to 26,000 persons pass, so he put on the whole show, with a few interpolated numbers for good measure. A whole column could be written on the Peach's performance alone and even a bare list of his feats takes up considerable space. He got two hits, stole two bases, including home, failed by a very small margin in an attempt to perform his favorite stunt of scoring from second on an infield out, and made two catches in center field that were easily the defensive features of the game."

Navin Field had been constructed of concrete and steel and featured grandstands stretching from first to third in a horseshoe configuration, which allowed for several stages of expansion in the 1920s and 1930s.

In 1919, the Tigers led the league in attendance for the first time, drawing 643,805. In 1924, with capacity increased to 30,000, the Tigers became the second team to top the one-million mark in a season.

By 1938, the stadium that replaced antiquated Bennett Park had become the first in the majors to be completely enclosed by double-decked grandstands.

Capacity: 53,000.

Navin Field's construction and expansion had indeed turned Detroit into a major league city.

◆

NOV. 22, 1927: THE COUGARS PLAYED THEIR FIRST GAME IN OLYMPIA STADIUM, A 2-1 LOSS TO OTTAWA.
DETROIT'S JOHNNY SHEPPARD SCORED THE BUILDING'S FIRST GOAL.

Speed racer

Associated Press

GAR WOOD AT THE HELM AND ORLIN JOHNSON RIDING SHOTGUN FORMED AN ALMOST UNBEATABLE COMBINATION ON ANY BODY OF WATER.

BY DAVID A. MARKIEWICZ

It isn't easy for a sports figure to stand out in the memory of a state that has seen the colorful and controversial likes of Ty Cobb, Bobby Layne and Dennis Rodman. Especially when the figure left the spotlight nearly 70 years ago and engaged in what is now the little-publicized sport of powerboat racing.

But Garfield Arthur Wood, known around the world as "Gar," once was every bit as big on the Michigan sports scene, and even bigger

internationally, than our hometown baseball and college football heroes.

Wood was known as the "Gray Fox," a nod to his thatch of silvery hair as well as his wily ways on the water. And though Wood, who died at 90 in Florida in 1971, isn't remembered for a rollicking nightlife or especially eccentric behavior, he did demonstrate a flair for the dramatic, the kind of style that modern-day TV cameras would have loved.

MARCH 31, 1928: GORDIE HOWE WAS BORN
IN FLORAL, SASKATCHEWAN.

For example, described as "ungentlemanly" for his use of an airplane engine in a racing boat, Wood and Orlin Johnson, his ridealong mechanic, responded by showing up at one competition in white tie, tails and top hat, secured by strings under their chins. As an added touch, Wood even outfitted his two lucky teddy bears, Teddy and Bruin, in formal attire. After Wood and Johnson won the race going away, Wood drove to the judges' stand as immaculate as he had started, accepted the trophy and declared: "You see, this really is a gentleman's boat."

Over the course of his life, Wood, an Iowa native, made millions in business and gained fame and prosperity from numerous mechanical inventions. He became a close friend of Henry Ford, and he owned a mansion on Grayhaven Island in the Detroit River until 1968.

But most of Wood's fame as well as his place in Detroit history flowed from his prowess on the water. A pioneer in his sport, he also was the dominant powerboat racer of his time, an era when that meant much to the public. He was to his sport what Bobby Jones was to golf, what Babe Ruth was to baseball.

The son of a Great Lakes ship captain, Wood first grabbed the attention of sports fans and society in 1917, seven years after moving to Detroit, when he won speedboat racing's Gold Cup in his Miss Detroit, his first racing boat. He repeated the feat in 1918, 1919, 1920 and 1921.

His capture three years later of the Harmsworth Trophy in England catapulted Wood to trans-Atlantic prominence. The Harmsworth was the America's Cup of its time. Wood, the cocky American interloper, went across the pond, took the trophy in the match races, and brought it home to the United States.

He successfully defended his championship several times in the 1920s and the 1930s, spreading his celebrity and securing his place in history.

Wood was speed-crazy, the fastest man on the water. He reached a record 124.86 miles an hour in his Miss America X — in 1932. He was the first to average 70 miles an hour in a

Detroit Free Press

GAR WOOD, AN AMERICAN INVENTOR, AND KAYE DON, A BRITISH FLYING ACE, WERE BITTER RIVALS ON THE WAVES.

Detroit Free Press

GAR WOOD DIDN'T MIND PUTTING HIS LIFE ON THE LINE IN A SPEEDING BOAT — AS LONG AS TEDDY AND BRUIN WERE ALONG FOR THE RIDE.

Gold Cup race and the first to go 100 miles an hour in a straightaway mile. He even staged a timed race with a train, from Miami to New York; in 1921, he beat the train, the Havana Special, by 12 minutes up the Eastern Seaboard.

Wood never shirked competition and that occasionally caught him up in controversy. In the 1931 Harmsworth Trophy race, Wood and World War I British flying ace Kaye Don engaged in some spirited (some would say meanspirited) competition, during which Don's boat sank. In England, Wood was pilloried for what was viewed as gamesmanship.

Wood handled the matter in a customary way. "The truth is," he told a writer 40 years later, "his boat was no damn good."

After Wood won the Harmsworth the following year, 500 friends and admirers greeted him for a celebration at Grayhaven.

"It's probably cost me a million dollars to defend that trophy — but it's worth it," Wood said. Then he waved his two teddy bears to the crowd. "Well, the sons-a-guns!" he said. "I couldn't race without them." His wife found the bears in a novelty shop in 1910 and sewed life jackets for them. He had them aboard for every race, and at various times they were doused, singed and almost lost overboard.

Wood jabbed at his British rival, Don, by saying that if he ever wanted to win the Harmsworth, he should find some lucky bears.

Wood's racing career ended in 1933, when he was 52, but he was just beginning a life of even greater significance beyond sport. He invented a hydraulic lift for dump trucks, a device that made him a $50-million fortune and became standard equipment in trucks the world over, saving industry time and money.

And his introduction of airplane engines in marine craft led directly to the production of PT boats, crucial to the Allied cause in World War II.

Whether on water or on land, it could be said, Gar Wood was a giant.

◆

NOV. 17, 1928: FORMER MICHIGAN STAR HARRY KIPKE WAS ONLY 3-4-1 IN HIS LONE SEASON
AS MICHIGAN STATE COACH, BUT THE SPARTANS WERE IMPRESSIVE THIS DAY IN A 3-0 LOSS AT ANN ARBOR.

Our scrapbook

NEXT GENERATION	
Good-bye	Hello
Bennett Park	Navin Field

CALLED STRIKE

Manager Hughie Jennings liked to say a Tigers season wasn't complete unless Ty Cobb went into the stands to attack a fan. So it was no surprise when Cobb did just that in New York on May 15, 1912.

This particular fan was a well-dressed man named Claude Lucker, who liked to sit in the bleachers and razz opposing players. He and Cobb exchanged insults, often obscene, for several innings. But when Lucker brought up Cobb's mother, the outfielder had heard enough.

An enraged Cobb climbed into the stands and attacked Lucker viciously, beating him about the head, kicking him, and even spiking him behind the ear. Cobb apparently failed to notice that Lucker was missing one hand and three fingers from the other.

As fate would have it, American League president Ban Johnson was in the stands that day and immediately suspended Cobb. Unfairly, Tigers players thought, and they fired off a telegram to Johnson threatening to strike if the suspension wasn't rescinded.

The strike was to occur May 18 in Philadelphia, three days after the incident (in between, the Tigers had a rainout and beat the Athletics without Cobb, 6-4).

Jennings and Tigers president Frank Navin were fearful of the repercussions of not fielding a team, so Jennings prepared for the strike by rounding up players from Philadelphia's sandlots. When Cobb wasn't allowed to play, the Tigers handed their uniforms over to the replacement players, who were paid $10 each.

The replacements took a 24-2 shellacking (they scored their runs on a throwing error). Cobb's replacement in centerfield, Bill Leinhauser, managed to get hit on the head with a fly ball, prompting Jennings to advise him, "Forget about catching them, son, just play them off the wall."

When Johnson heard what happened, he canceled the next day's game and threatened to banish the strikers from baseball. After a meeting with Johnson, the players agreed to return.

Johnson fined each player $100. Cobb was fined $50 and received a 10-day suspension. The suspension later was made retroactive to May 16, and Cobb was back in the lineup May 26.

OLD YELLER

"Eeyah!"

Hughie Jennings liked to yell. He yelled often from the coach's box. He'd hold his arms in the air, kick one leg up, and let fly: *"Eeyah!"* He said he learned the word from a Hawaiian native, pitcher Johnnie Williams, and that in Hawaiian it meant "watch out."

Yes, Jennings — the Tigers' manager in 1907-20 — was a character. In addition to yelling, he also liked to get hit by pitches; he got plunked 49 times in 1896 while playing for Baltimore, a record that stood for 75 seasons.

Hughie's head took a beating over the years. Once he dove into a dark swimming pool, not knowing it had no water, and spent a month in the hospital with a fractured skull. He fractured it again in a car accident.

Another time, Jennings, a shortstop, dove into an unruly mob of Chicago fans for a foul ball. He was found unconscious — and holding the ball.

"As I shot over their heads," Jennings said, "someone of the gang slugged me on the jaw. The blow made the catch possible because it threw me over far enough to make it. That's all I remember."

Jennings was an extremely popular man who lasted 14 years with the Tigers. He was a player-manager for four of those seasons, but had just three hits in nine at-bats. His 1,131 victories were the most by a Tigers manager until Sparky Anderson came along and won 1,331.

OUR FAVORITE GERMANYS

GERMANY SCHAEFER, a Tigers utility player in 1905-09 and one of the great flakes of his day. For example, one time he stole second base. On the next pitch, apparently just to annoy the pitcher, he stole first. Real first name: Herman.

GERMANY SCHULZ, an All-America Michigan center in 1907. First of the roving centers — sort of a precursor to a linebacker — he's in the College Football Hall of Fame. Real first name: Adolph.

COBB BY THE NUMBERS

TIGERS	G	AB	R	H	2B	3B	HR	RBI	BB	SO	SB	AVG
1905	41	150	19	36	6	0	1	15	10	NA	2	.240
1906	98	350	45	112	13	7	1	41	19	NA	23	.320
1907	150	605	97	212	29	15	5	116	24	NA	49	.350
1908	150	581	88	188	36	20	4	108	34	NA	39	.324
1909	156	573	116	216	33	10	9	107	48	NA	76	.377
1910	140	509	106	196	36	13	8	91	64	NA	65	.385
1911	146	591	147	248	47	24	8	144	44	NA	83	.420
1912	140	553	119	227	30	23	7	90	43	NA	61	.410
1913	122	428	70	167	18	16	4	67	58	31	52	.390
1914	97	345	69	127	22	11	2	57	57	22	35	.368
1915	156	563	144	208	31	13	3	99	118	43	96	.369
1916	145	542	113	201	31	10	5	68	78	39	68	.371
1917	152	588	107	225	44	23	7	102	61	34	55	.383
1918	111	421	83	161	19	14	3	64	41	21	34	.382
1919	124	497	92	191	36	13	1	70	38	22	28	.384
1920	112	428	86	143	28	8	2	63	58	28	14	.334
1921	128	507	124	197	37	16	12	101	56	19	22	.389
1922	137	526	99	211	42	16	4	99	55	24	9	.401
1923	145	556	103	189	40	7	6	88	66	14	9	.340
1924	155	625	115	211	38	10	4	74	85	18	23	.338
1925	121	415	97	157	31	12	12	102	65	12	13	.378
1926	79	233	48	79	18	5	4	62	26	2	9	.339
A's	G	AB	R	H	2B	3B	HR	RBI	BB	SO	SB	AVG
1927	134	490	104	175	32	7	5	93	67	12	22	.357
1928	95	353	54	114	27	4	1	40	34	16	5	.323
Totals	3034	11429	2245	4191	724	297	118	1961	1249	357	892	.367

Associated Press

FASHION STATEMENTS

Ty Cobb's spikes, worn sharp and high.

AND THE WINNNER IS ...

Ty Cobb: American League MVP in 1911.

LET'S PLAY TWO

Baseball: On Sept. 26, 1906, Tigers pitcher George Mullin went the distance in both ends of a doubleheader, beating the Washington Senators, 5-3 and 4-3. Detroit's Ed Summers matched it Sept. 25, 1908, when he beat the Philadelphia Athletics, 7-2 and 1-0. The feat has been accomplished 10 times in the American League, but not since 1926.

Football: New coach Harry Kipke won two games faster than any other in Michigan history. For three seasons starting in 1929, the Wolverines opened with a doubleheader to spur ticket sales. Some 16,412 watched as they beat Albion, 39-0, and Mt. Union, 16-6. In 1930, U-M beat Denison, 33-0, and Michigan Normal (now Eastern Michigan), 7-0, and in '31 beat Central State Teachers College (now Central Michigan), 27-0, and Normal, 34-0.

Burton Historical Collection

ED SUMMERS

Burton Historical Collection

GEORGE MULLIN

Our scrapbook

BEST NICKNAMES

The Georgia Peach   The Little Rag Man   Hurry-Up Yost

The Mechanical Man   Wahoo Sam Crawford

POINT/COUNTERPOINT

The Tigers won their first pennant in 1907 and played the Chicago Cubs in the World Series. But Detroit's standing as a baseball town failed to impress at least one visiting sportswriter, after only 11,306 and 7,370 showed up at Bennett Park for the final two games of the Cubs' sweep.

"The attendance at the two games in Detroit was a serious reflection on the patriotism of the citizens. . . . I look for the disappearance of Detroit from the major league map within a few years," wrote Cy Sanborn of the Chicago Tribune.

But another journalist, Basil O'Meara, sports editor of the Ottawa Journal, had high expectations for Detroit as a hockey town. In a 1926 letter to John C. Townsend,

part of the Detroit Athletic Club consortium that was awarded an NHL franchise, O'Meara wrote: "When Boston came in, they selected the very unappealing name of Bruins, which did not register very well with their following. . . . The advent of Detroit into hockey is going to be a big thing for the game, and also for Detroit in an amusement way. Once they (get) going with a team that is well sustained by a 'bally-hoo' there is no telling just what a splendid proposition it will turn out to be."

That first team turned out to be the Victoria Cougars, and for the time being, it kept the Cougars nickname when it moved to Detroit.

HIT PARADE

What was the most-played song of the 20th Century in Michigan? Could it be "The Victors"?

The Wolverines' fight song actually was penned in 1898 by fan Louis Elbel, who was inspired after watching U-M win its season finale, 12-11, at Chicago, clinching its first conference title.

In April 1899, John Philip Sousa, left, and his band, appearing in Ann Arbor at University Hall, gave "The Victors" its debut public performance. Two nights later, the words were sung in public for the first time at the U-M Minstrels concert.

ON THE LINKS

A "boney-legged" Englishman (or so the papers described him) defeated one of the world's greatest golfers in the 1924 U.S. Open at Oakland Hills.

Diminutive Cyril Walker posted a 297 total, beating Robert T. (Bobby) Jones by three shots. The two were

tied after nine holes in the final round, but Walker gained two strokes on No. 10. Walker put the tournament away with a beautiful second shot into the teeth of a gale on No. 16. The ball landed 10 feet from the cup, and Walker made the putt for birdie.

MUSICAL COACHES	
Out	**In**
Langdon (Biff) Lea	Fielding H. Yost
Charles Bemies	George Denman
George Stallings	Frank Dwyer
Frank Dwyer	Ed Barrow
George Denman	Chester Brewer
Ed Barrow	Bobby Lowe
Bobby Lowe	Bill Armour
Bill Armour	Hughie Jennings
Chester Brewer	John Macklin
John Macklin	Frank Sommers*
John Macklin	George Gauthier*
Frank Sommers	George Gauthier
George Gauthier	Chester Brewer
Elmer Mitchell	E.J. Mather
Chester Brewer	George (Potsy) Clark
George Gauthier	Lyman Frimodig
Hughie Jennings	Ty Cobb
George (Potsy) Clark	Albert Barron
Lyman Frimodig	Fred Walker
Albert Barron	Ralph Young
Fielding H. Yost	George Little
Fred Walker	John Kobs
George Little	Fielding H. Yost
John Kobs	Benjamin VanAlstyne
Art Duncan	Duke Keats
Duke Keats	Jack Adams
Fielding H. Yost	Tad Wieman
Ralph Young	Harry Kipke
E.J. Mather	George Veenker
Ty Cobb	George Moriarty
Harry Kipke	Jim Crowley**
Tad Wieman	Harry Kipke**

*Early in the century, some Michigan State coaches coached both football and basketball. That's why Macklin was replaced by two men.

**After one season coaching football at Michigan State, Kipke switched to Michigan, his alma mater.

GHOST STORY

If he wasn't the greatest of all time, Illinois' Red Grange was the most storied running back of sports' Golden Age in the '20s, the age of Ruth, Gehrig, Dempsey, Tunney, Rockne and the Four Horsemen, Hagen, Tilden and Weissmuller.

And a game against Michigan contributed mightily to the legend of the Galloping Ghost. It was Oct. 18, 1924, and the Wolverines brought a 15-game winning streak to Champaign to help the Illini christen their new Memorial Stadium.

Grange, No. 77, took the opening kickoff, stepped to his right, cut back up center, broke through a wave of charging Wolverines, and ran 95 yards for a touchdown.

It was only the beginning of a magical day for Grange, a junior. He scored the next three times he handled the ball — on runs of 67, 56 and 44 yards — all in the first quarter. The game was barely 12 minutes old, and Grange had four touchdowns and gained 265 all-purpose yards, although he had his hands on the ball only six times.

"After the fourth touchdown, we called a time-out," Grange said. "When our trainer came with water, I said to him, 'I'm dog-tired. You'd better tell Coach (Bob) Zuppke to get me out of here.' When I got to the bench, Zup said to me, 'You should have had five touchdowns. You didn't cut right on one play.' Nobody could get a swelled head around Zup."

In the second half, Grange got his fifth touchdown (still a record for a Michigan opponent) on a 15-yard end run and passed for a sixth as Illinois won, 39-14. He rushed for 212 yards and finished with 402 yards of all-purpose offense.

Legendary sports writer Grantland Rice of the New York Tribune called Grange that day "a streak of fire, a breath of flame, eluding all who reach and clutch, a gray Ghost thrown into the game that rival hands may never touch; a rubber bounding, blasting soul, whose destination is the goal."

Legendary University of Chicago coach Amos Alonzo Stagg called it "the most spectacular single-handed performance ever made in a major game."

Grange, whose name was synonymous with college football in his day, went on to help the fledgling NFL gain acceptance when he barnstormed with the Chicago Bears in 1925.

He died in 1991 at age 87.

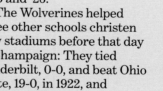

Bentley Historical Library

ILLINOIS' RED GRANGE GALLOPED FOR FIVE TOUCHDOWNS AGAINST MICHIGAN IN 1924.

THE REST OF THE STORY

Footnotes to Grange's great day against Michigan:

Fielding H. Yost, right, had retired the year before, and George Little coached the Wolverines in '24. The loss to Illinois apparently prompted Yost, still the athletic director, to come back to coach U-M in 1925 and '26.

The Wolverines helped three other schools christen new stadiums before that day in Champaign: They tied Vanderbilt, 0-0, and beat Ohio State, 19-0, in 1922, and defeated Michigan Agricultural, 7-0, in '24.

DON'T FEED THE WOLVERINE

Yost was envious when he saw Wisconsin parading live badgers around at football games, so in 1923 he set out to find wolverines for Michigan. Letters to 68 trappers produced no wolverines, but he did find a stuffed wolverine in '24.

Finally, in 1927, Yost procured 10 wolverines from Alaska and placed them in the Detroit Zoo. On game days, two were brought to Michigan Stadium and paraded around in cages. The practice lasted only one year, however, as the wolverines grew larger, more ferocious and more interested in taking a bite out of the Michigan men carrying them.

Our scrapbook

ICONS

The Little Brown Jug   Gar Wood's teddy bears

OLYMPIC MOMENTS

The 1904 games in St. Louis were the Michigan Olympics: Four current, one future and one former Wolverine won nine medals (six gold, two silver and two bronze). Archie Haun led the way with golds in three sprints: 60, 100 and 200 meters. He also won the 100 at Athens in '06.

In 1912 at Stockholm, another U-M sprinter outclassed the field, as Ralph Craig won the 100 and 200.

But no U-M athlete was more productive in those early games than Ralph Rose, who won six medals in three Olympics — three gold, two silver and a bronze in field events at St. Louis, London and Stockholm.

At the Paris Olympics in 1924, the University of Michigan's William DeHart Hubbard won the long jump with a leap of 24 feet, 5 inches, the first black athlete to earn an individual Olympic gold medal.

These games produced some pretty historic names. Paavo Nurmi, the Flying Finn, won five gold medals in track, including two in an hour. And Great Britain's gold medalists included Eric Liddell in the 400 meters and Harold Abrahams, who inspired the movie "Chariots of Fire," in the 100.

OLYMPIC MEDALISTS

Paris, Summer, '00
CHARLES DVORAK, Michigan, track and field: silver in pole vault.
HOWARD HAYES, Michigan, track and field: silver in 800 meters.
JOHN MCLEAN, Menominee, track and field: silver in high hurdles.

St. Louis, Summer, '04
WILLIAM COE, Michigan, track and field: silver in shot put.
CHARLES DVORAK, Michigan, track and field: gold in pole vault.
ARCHIE HAHN, Michigan, track and field: gold in 60, 100, 200.
HENRY JAMISON (JAM) HANDY, Michigan, swimming: bronze in 440 breaststroke.
RALPH ROSE, Michigan, track and field: gold in shot put, silver in discus, bronze in hammer.
FRED SCHULE, Michigan, track and field: gold in 110 hurdles.

Athens, Summer, '06
ARCHIE HAHN, Michigan, track and field: gold in 100.

London, Summer, '08
JOHN GARRELLS, Michigan, track and field: silver in 110 hurdles, bronze in shot put.
RALPH ROSE, Michigan, track and field: gold in shot put.

Stockholm, Summer, '12
RALPH CRAIG, Michigan, track and field: gold in 100 and 200.
RALPH ROSE, Michigan, track and field: gold in shot put combined, silver in shot put.

Antwerp, Summer, '20
CARL JOHNSON, Michigan, track and field: silver in long jump.
MARGARET WOODBRIDGE PRESLEY, Detroit, swimming: silver in 300 freestyle, gold in 400 freestyle relay.

Paris, Summer, '24
JAMES BROOKER, Michigan, track and field: bronze in pole vault.
HENRY JAMISON (JAM) HANDY, Michigan, water polo: bronze.
WILLIAM DEHART HUBBARD, Michigan, track and field: gold in long jump.

Amsterdam, Summer, '28
FREDERICK P. ALDERMAN, Orleans, track and field: gold in 1,600 relay.
GARNET AULT, Michigan, swimming: bronze in 800 relay (for Canada).
LEE BARTLET, Albion, track and field: bronze in javelin.
KEN DOHERTY, Michigan, track and field: bronze in decathlon.
PAUL SAMSON, Michigan, swimming: gold in 800 relay.

HOW DID THEY BECOME ...

The Tigers: Some baseball historians credited Phillip J. Reid, editor of the Detroit Evening News, with first using the name in print in 1896. The team's manager that season, George Stallings, also took credit for the name because, he said, the black-and-brown stockings he selected for the team reminded fans of tiger stripes.

But the Tigers' press guide gives credit to an unidentified Free Press headline writer. According to the Tigers, the name appeared a year earlier in the Free Press in a headline that read "Strouther's Tigers Showed Up Very Nicely," and another item labeled "Notes of the Detroit Tigers of 1895."

The Wolverines: This one's a real mystery. No one can remember when Michigan's teams weren't called the Wolverines, even though the species apparently never was indigenous to the state. Fielding H. Yost theorized in Michigan Quarterly Review in 1944 that wolverine pelts were traded at Sault Ste. Marie, and they might have been referred to as "Michigan wolverines."

Eight years later in the same publication, Albert H. Marckwardt put forth the theory that Michigan's early French settlers were known for their voracious — or "wolverine-like" — appetites, and perhaps the nickname evolved from that.

The last theory comes from the Ohio border dispute of 1803, when Michiganders began being called wolverines. It's unclear, however, whether Michiganders adopted the nickname to show their tenacity, or Ohio's side intended it as an insult. But Michigan did become the Wolverine State at that time.

The Spartans: In 1925, Michigan Agricultural College became Michigan State College, so the school ran a contest to replace its Aggies nickname. But Lansing State Journal sports editor George S. Alderton decided the winner, the Michigan Staters, was too long for newspaper use. He asked to see the other entries, and selected the Spartans nickname.

Alderton began using the name in print sparingly (although he spelled it "Spartons" for the first two days) and it caught on in other publications. Unfortunately, he neglected to write down the name of the person who submitted the Spartans entry and couldn't remember it.

CHAPTER 3

CITY OF CHAMPIONS
1930-1947

CITY OF CHAMPIONS,
1930-1947

By Nicholas J. Cotsonika

Detroit's success in sports and economics always seemed to parallel one another during the first half of the century, for better or worse, leaving the streets at once full of pure, tingling excitement or complete, utter exasperation.

As Ty Cobb rose to national prominence, slapping hits and spiking enemies, Detroit rose to national prominence along with him, designing better cars and churning out more of them for the masses. So naturally, when Cobb sent the Tigers into a tailspin by leaving for Philadelphia after the 1926 season, the city lost more than a great ballplayer. It soon lost its swagger, too.

In 1929, the auto industry provided more than 500,000 jobs in Detroit. The Big Three cornered 85 percent of the market. Ford employed 101,000 workers at its sprawling, state-of-the-art

Detroit was the biggest winner of all — the Tigers, Red Wings and Lions won titles at the same time.

Rouge plant alone. But then Detroit descended into the Great Depression, an era that seared the soul of the city's blue-collar core. Nearly 225,000 auto workers were unemployed by '31, and when they turned to sports for relief, the Great Depression gained new meaning.

Several football teams failed and folded. The new hockey team failed to find an identity, calling itself by three different names, and nearly went broke. The only established draw, the Tigers, failed to crawl out of mediocrity and, worse, watched sadly as their Hall of Famers faded away. Premier second baseman Charlie Gehringer remained. But Cobb did not. Neither did Harry Heilmann, a four-time batting champion who recorded a .342 lifetime average. Neither did Heinie Manush, another former batting champion, who hit .330 lifetime. Poor pitching and an unstable infield had kept the Tigers from winning a pennant since 1909, but at least the fans had been able to watch some of baseball's best hitters. Now they were gone.

But the city and its teams battled back from despair together, beginning another pattern, one that would carry through the rest of the century. Mickey Cochrane and Hank Greenberg rescued the Tigers. Jack Adams and James Norris Sr. rescued the hockey team, eventually settling on a permanent nickname: the

---

PRECEDING PAGE: IN 1934, HUDSON'S HUNG A SEVEN-STORY BANNER
DOWNTOWN IN HONOR OF DETROIT'S TOP CATS.

Photograph by Burton Historical Collection

Richard Bak Collection

THE KING OF THE RING, JOE LOUIS, AND THE DEAN OF THE DIAMOND, TIGERS MANAGER AND CATCHER MICKEY COCHRANE, MET BEFORE THE 1936 OPENER.

Red Wings. A new football team arrived from Ohio, became known as the Lions, and actually found a foothold. An old football team, the University of Michigan, reinforced its marquee status. A young boxer named Joe Louis started attracting attention.

By the mid-'30s, life improved dramatically, in all facets. Auto production increased by 30 percent from 1934 to '35. Many auto workers regained their jobs, and they started to buy tickets. Labor unions came of age, waging war against stingy companies for the common man. The Wolverines claimed national championships in '32 and '33; the Tigers and Lions won their first World Series and NFL championships in '35; the Wings won their first Stanley Cup in '36 and their second in '37; and Louis won the world heavyweight title in '37.

Glory days.

The Motor City revved up and experienced perhaps the most volatile, vigorous and victorious period it would know. Best of all, it earned a proud new nickname: City of Champions. Even World War II couldn't slow down Detroit. As the city became the Arsenal of Democracy, using a swelling population to produce tanks and planes instead of cars, the Wings won their third Cup, in '43, and the Tigers won their second Series, in '45.

"It seemed that all you had to do was throw on a Detroit jersey," Wings forward Pete Kelly said, "and you'd win."

BLACK MIKE

The Depression destroyed the dreams of thousands of Detroiters, but it also provided them with a jug-eared, dark-faced man who would lead the New Deal Tigers to their first

JULY 16, 1932: JAMES NORRIS BOUGHT THE FINANCIALLY STRAPPED DETROIT FALCONS, FORMERLY THE COUGARS, AND RENAMED THEM THE RED WINGS.

Burton Historical Collection

IN THE EARLY PART OF THE
CENTURY, CIGAR-CHOMPING
BILL YAWKEY OWNED THE
TIGERS, BUT FRANK NAVIN
CALLED THE SHOTS. NAVIN
(FACING YAWKEY, AND
RIGHT) EVENTUALLY TOOK
OVER BUT DIED A FEW WEEKS
AFTER THEIR FIRST
CHAMPIONSHIP, IN 1935.

Burton Historical Collection

Detroit Free Press

THE FIRST YEAR MICKEY COCHRANE SERVED AS PLAYER/MANAGER, 1934,
THE TIGERS WON THE PENNANT AND BLACK MIKE WAS THE MVP. A
YEAR LATER, DETROIT HAD ITS FIRST WORLD CHAMPION.

pennant in a generation and their first World Series championship.

Connie Mack's Athletics were in financial trouble, owing $250,000 to Philadelphia banks. With creditors hounding him, Mack made his players available for sale, and that caught the attention of Frank Navin, who had become the Tigers' principal owner. He was worried sick about his empty stands and empty bank accounts. In 1933, the Tigers drew just 320,972 fans, the second-lowest total since the building of Navin Field in 1912. Something had to be done. Soon.

First, Navin thought about attempting to acquire none other than Babe Ruth, a surefire gate attraction, but Ruth's salary demands were too high. Next, he contacted Mack about Cochrane, the inspirational leader of pennant-winners in 1929, '30 and '31 and two Series winners in Philadelphia, the game's best defensive catcher, a consistent .300 hitter. "Cochrane has been baseball poison for Detroit ever since he's been in the league," Navin said. "I would rather have him with us than against us."

Mack's asking price was $100,000. Navin didn't have the money, but his silent partner, the stern and extravagant industrialist Walter Briggs, did. Briggs had known Navin since 1907, when he convinced Navin to admit him into the first game of the sold-out World Series, and loved the team dearly. He quietly coughed up the cash, and the deal was made. "If Cochrane's a success here," Briggs said, "he may be a bargain at that price."

Cochrane became the Tigers' player-manager — and turned out to be a bargain indeed. Known as Black Mike as much for his dark disposition as his deeply tanned face, Cochrane seemed as fiery a competitor as Cobb ever was. "For the Tigers as a ballclub," Cochrane said, "we have only one idea: fight and hustle. The ballplayer who doesn't whip himself mentally after losing a game isn't in the proper mental condition." Cobb himself, having played with Cochrane in Philadelphia, respected Cochrane's drive. "One night after we had lost a game to the Braves we should have won," Cobb said, "Mike came in the room, flung off his cap, and then walked over and jumped up and down on it."

Cochrane and Cobb shared many similarities: Both were great players, intelligent, aggressive, enthusiastic and hard-nosed. Both experienced nervous breakdowns during their careers because of their overwrought intensity. Both were ornery combatants. And both preferred speed over power, the

NOV. 18, 1933: A 0-0 TIE WITH MINNESOTA IN THE NEXT-TO-LAST GAME MARRED MICHIGAN'S
PERFECT RECORD, BUT 7-0-1 WAS STILL GOOD ENOUGH FOR THE NATIONAL TITLE.

Detroit Free Press

OUR HEROES: FLEA CLIFTON, RAY HAYWORTH, CHARLIE GEHRINGER, HANK GREENBERG, MICKEY COCHRANE AND PETE FOX.

JUNE 30, 1934: GEORGE RICHARDS HEADED A GROUP THAT PURCHASED THE PORTSMOUTH (OHIO) SPARTANS
FOOTBALL TEAM AND MOVED IT TO DETROIT.

Associated Press

MICKEY COCHRANE (RIGHT) STUCK CLOSE TO HIS SUPERSTITIOUS SUPERSTAR,
SCHOOLBOY ROWE, WHO WON 16 STRAIGHT GAMES IN 1934.

Detroit Free Press

UNDER COCHRANE'S WATCHFUL
EYE, TOMMY BRIDGES WON 22, 21
AND A LEAGUE-LEADING 23 GAMES
IN 1934-36.

Detroit Free Press

DURING THE SAME SPAN, ROWE —
THE OTHER HALF OF COCHRANE'S
1-2 PUNCH — WON 24, 19 AND
19 GAMES.

hit-and-run over the home run, steals and sacrifices and squeezes over sit-back-and-slug-it-out strategies.

But Cochrane differed from Cobb in many important ways: He wasn't prone to punching people on a whim. He didn't carry a gun everywhere he went. In fact, intense as he was, he handled people and pitchers with aplomb, got along with umpires, and even had the respect of his players and the opposition.

"We were like a family," pitcher Eldon Auker said. "We followed him around like kids, and we would do anything Mike wanted us to do. He was very inspirational. There wasn't anything we felt we couldn't do. He really handled our pitching staff."

In the end, Cochrane left Detroit, baseball and life sadly. In 1937, a beanball by Bump Hadley nailed him on the temple, nearly killing him and ending his playing career. Cochrane returned as manager afterward but was fidgety and foul-tempered. "He'd outguess himself," Gehringer said. In '38, the Tigers struggled, and Cochrane disintegrated, second-guessed by everyone — including his owner. In August, the Tigers were in fifth place, and Briggs called Cochrane into his office.

"Well, what is the alibi for today?" he asked.

"You haven't got the players to win," Cochrane said.

"That's not what you said in the spring," Briggs said. "Maybe it isn't the players. Maybe you are the cause, and it would help matters if you quit."

With that, Briggs fired Cochrane. So many Detroiters were distraught, a large crowd hurried to the airport to see him off. Cochrane never held a major baseball job again and died, bloated and broke, at age 59, heartbroken over the death of his only son in World War II. "He never got over being let out as manager by Mr. Briggs," Greenberg said. "He never got over the hurt. This wasn't getting hit on the head. Mike's hurt was in the heart."

But Cochrane's Detroit legacy always will be one of success. In 1934, the Yankees' Lou Gehrig won the Triple Crown. Yet Cochrane, not Gehrig, was selected the American League's most valuable player, because Cochrane's Tigers, not Gehrig's Yankees, won the pennant. "He was simply one of the greatest," Auker said. "He was the reason we won in '34 and '35."

HAMMERIN' HANK

Cochrane's Detroit teams were full of personalities. His best pitchers were curveballer Tommy

SEPT. 23, 1934: RENAMED THE LIONS, THE TEAM WON ITS FIRST GAME, 9-0, OVER NEW YORK AT THE UNIVERSITY OF DETROIT.
THE LIONS LOST THEIR LAST THREE, FINISHED 10-3 FOR COACH POTSY CLARK AND MISSED THE PLAYOFFS.

Detroit Free Press

A PLAY YOU DON'T SEE EVERY DAY: AFTER STARTING FOR HOME, CHARLIE GEHRINGER REVERSED COURSE AND
SLID BACK INTO THIRD BASE UNDER THE TAG OF ST. LOUIS' HARLOND CLIFT.

Bridges and towering righthander Lynwood (Schoolboy)
Rowe, who won 16 straight games in '34 and was famous for
his superstitions. Among his good-luck charms were a
Canadian penny, a copper coin from the Netherlands, two
Chinese trinkets, a rabbit's foot, a jade elephant figurine, and
four feathers plucked from a three-legged rooster.

There was heavy-hitting Rudy York, and then there were
the G-Men: Gehringer, Greenberg and Leon (Goose) Goslin.
Nicknamed for his large nose, Goslin was a veteran presence
and a powerful hitter. Quiet and efficient, Gehringer was the
best-fielding second baseman of his time and known as the
Mechanical Man. He was in the midst of a 19-year career in
which he won the batting title with a .371 average and the
American League's most valuable player award in '37. Warm
and generous, Greenberg was known as Hankus Pankus or
Hammerin' Hank — and was the most beloved of them all. He
was voted MVP twice during a brilliant career that was interrupted by nearly four years of military service, and he challenged Ruth's single-season record of 60 homers in '38 by hitting 58.

Greenberg first gained national attention during the heat
of the 1934 pennant race. Greenberg, who was Jewish, decided to sit out on Yom Kippur that season. But a local rabbi

Associated Press

HALL OF FAMERS HANK GREENBERG, CHARLIE GEHRINGER AND
MICKEY COCHRANE CAUGHT UP WITH A FUTURE FAMER, 25-YEAR-OLD
AL KALINE, IN LAKELAND, FLA., IN 1959.

NOV. 29, 1934: THE LIONS HOSTED THEIR FIRST THANKSGIVING DAY GAME, A 19-16 LOSS TO CHICAGO.
TWO OF THEIR THREE CLOSING LOSSES WERE TO THE DIVISION-CHAMPION BEARS, WHO FINISHED 13-0.

Richard Bak Collection

gave him permission to play on Rosh Hashanah, the first day of the Jewish new year, and he hit two home runs — the second in the bottom of the ninth inning — in a 2-1 victory over Boston at Navin Field. *"Leshono tovo tikosayva"* read a Free Press headline, Yiddish for "Happy New Year!"

While Greenberg hammered hits, he was getting hammered. "Of all the ballplayers I played with and against, nobody took the abuse that Greenberg took," said Billy Werber, an American League infielder in the '30s. "The ballplayers would call him every name you can think of. All manner of things. He wasn't married at the time, so they used to accuse him of everything along those lines. The language can be pretty rough coming out of that dugout."

But Greenberg, a serious man and a hard worker, became a symbol of athletic success for a generation of Jewish youngsters. "I don't think anybody can imagine the terrific importance of Hank Greenberg to the Jewish community," said Bert Gordon, a Navin Field regular, in a book by author Richard Bak. "He was a god, a true folk hero. That made baseball acceptable to our parents. For once they didn't mind if we took a little time off from the big process of getting into college."

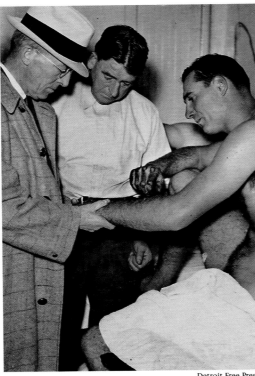

IN 1935, WHEN THIS WORLD SERIES PHOTO WAS TAKEN, FANS STILL HAD A VIEW OF DOWNTOWN DETROIT BEYOND THE SINGLE-DECKED RIGHTFIELD LINE. SOMETHING FANS DIDN'T WANT TO SEE WAS AN INJURED FIRST BASEMAN, BUT HANK GREENBERG WAS FORCED OUT OF THE LINEUP WITH A BROKEN WRIST IN GAME 2 OF THE SERIES.

Detroit Free Press

Later, after Cochrane departed Detroit, a new star emerged, one especially dear to the city. Hal Newhouser, a Detroit native, became baseball's dominant pitcher of the World War II years. Kept out of combat boots by a heart murmur, Prince Hal became the only pitcher to win back-to-back MVP awards. In 1944, he finished with 29 victories and 187 strikeouts, outshining teammate Paul (Dizzy) Trout, who finished with 27 victories and 144 strikeouts. In 1945, Newhouser became the third pitcher to lead the league in victories (25), strikeouts (212) and earned-run average (1.81).

HIGHS AND LOWS

The era was one of trial and triumph for the Tigers.

In the 1934 World Series, they faced St. Louis. Soon to be known as the Gashouse Gang, the Cardinals boasted a star pair of pitching brothers: Jay (Dizzy) Dean, who won 30 games, and Paul (Daffy) Dean, who won 19. The Deans went 4-1 with a 1.43 ERA to beat the Tigers in a hotly contested seven games — games that frustrated fans to the point of

DEC. 9, 1935: THE LIONS (7-3-2) FOLLOWED THEIR FIRST DIVISION TITLE WITH A 26-7 VICTORY OVER NEW YORK FOR THEIR FIRST NFL CHAMPIONSHIP.

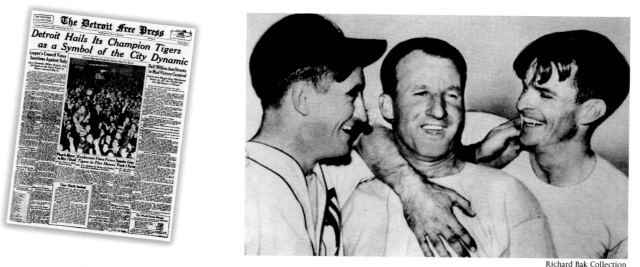

"The City Dynamic," as the Free Press dubbed Detroit, sported confetti-covered streets after (from left) Mickey Cochrane, Goose Goslin and Tommy Bridges helped the Tigers cage the Cubs in the 1935 Series. Goslin drove in Cochrane with the winning run in the bottom of the ninth in Game 6.

mayhem.

In the sixth inning of Game 7, the Cardinals led handily before 40,902 in Detroit, when Ducky Medwick spiked Tigers third baseman Marv Owen. Medwick tried to take the field afterward, but spectators in the leftfield bleachers pelted him with fruit, vegetables and garbage, and commissioner Kenesaw Mountain Landis removed him from the game to prevent a riot and a Tigers forfeit.

Fans left Navin Field that day after the 11-0 loss moaning about a hex, a curse, a bout of bad luck. Four World Series. Four disappointments. As the Tigers began the '35 Series,

they moaned even more, because Greenberg suffered a broken wrist. "Are we destined to never win one of these things?" Navin grumbled. But in a few days, a happy, dramatic ending made them all delirious.

In Game 6, the Cubs' Stan Hack led off the top of the ninth with a triple, threatening to break a 3-3 tie. But Bridges set down the next three hitters, and in the bottom of the inning, Goslin singled home Cochrane with two out. The moment Cochrane touched the plate, the city rejoiced, throwing an all-night celebration unlike any other it had seen. People blew horns, pounded drums, hoisted drinks and threw confetti

April 11, 1936: A 3-2 win at Toronto gave the Wings a 3-1 series victory and their first Stanley Cup in the best-of-five finals. Pete Kelly scored the winner at 9:45 of the third period.

Detroit Free Press

HAMMERIN' HANK GREEENBERG, ALWAYS A FAVORITE, WAS VOTED BY FANS TO THE ALL-TIME TIGERS TEAM IN 1999.

Associated Press

BABE RUTH MADE SURE THE COMBATANTS — DIZZY DEAN AND
FRANKIE FRISCH OF THE CARDINALS, MICKEY COCHRANE AND
SCHOOLBOY ROWE OF THE TIGERS — SHOOK HANDS BEFORE THE 1934
WORLD SERIES. THE SIDES WEREN'T SO CIVIL AFTER THAT.

well into dawn. Some even fired machine guns out of office windows.

Champions. Finally.

"The entire town was gaga," Gehringer said. "I tried to take a friend downtown, but golly, everything was blocked up. You couldn't cross the streets, the city was such a mess. Seemed like everybody was downtown, whoopin' and hollerin'." The Tigers had done the city a service. "I believe we helped bring Detroit out of the Depression," Auker said. "We helped change the attitude of the state. We gave people hope, and they became proud of Detroit and their Tigers. They were crazy for us."

Navin walked around with a smile creasing what usually was a placid poker face. The Tigers had led the league in attendance, topping the 1-million mark for just the second time. Profits were pouring in. "I have waited 30 years for this day," Navin said. Five weeks later, he died. While horseback riding on Belle Isle, the 64-year-old suffered a heart attack.

As the city mourned, Briggs bought the club from Navin's widow for $1 million. Rapidly, he settled in as the Tigers' new owner, spending another $1 million to renovate Navin Field for the '38 season. He increased its capacity to 53,000, made it the first park in the nation to be enclosed and completely double-decked — and renamed it Briggs Stadium, of course. "Navin Field was nice," Auker said. "But when the stadium was remodeled, it was more like the major leagues."

In 1940, the Tigers beat Cleveland for the pennant by one game. But as Nazi Germany ransacked Europe, inducing a half-million Detroiters to sign up for the draft, the Tigers lost the World Series

APRIL 12, 1936: HORTON SMITH, WINNER OF THE INAUGURAL TOURNAMENT IN 1934, CHIPPED IN FROM 50 FEET
FOR A BIRDIE ON NO. 14 ON HIS WAY TO A ONE-STROKE VICTORY IN THE MASTERS.

Richard Bak Collection

State Archives of Michigan

HANK GREENBERG, FLANKED BY PITCHERS TOMMY BRIDGES
AND BOBO NEWSOM, BROUGHT HOME A PENNANT FOR OWNER
WALTER BRIGGS IN 1940, BUT THE TIGERS WERE FOILED BY
CINCINNATI IN THE WORLD SERIES. BRIGGS (LEFT) WAS ONE
OF THE MOST DESPISED INDUSTRIALISTS IN DETROIT DURING
THE DEPRESSION.

SEPT. 22, 1936: THE TIGERS SWEPT THE ST. LOUIS BROWNS, 12-0 AND 14-0,
THE BIGGEST DOUBLE SHUTOUT IN MODERN MAJOR LEAGUE HISTORY.

YOU'RE THE MOST: HAL NEWHOUSER (LEFT) WON TWO MVP AWARDS, IN 1944 AND 1945. HANK GREENBERG ALSO WON TWO, IN 1935 AND 1940.

to the Cincinnati Reds in seven games. Their only real hero was Bobo Newsom, who went 21-5 during the season and 2-1 in the Series, during which his father died of a heart attack before Game 2. Fifteen Tigers soon went off to war.

Not until 1944 did good times return, when the Tigers soothed the sting still left from a race riot that scarred the city in '43. They lost the pennant by one game to the St. Louis Browns, then kept their momentum into '45, when they gave Detroit more to celebrate not long after V-J Day. Needing one victory to clinch the pennant, they played a rain-soaked doubleheader on the last day of the season. In the ninth inning of the first game, Greenberg, not long out of the military, approached the plate with two out and the bases loaded. He hit a rocket into the leftfield stands for a flag-clinching grand slam.

In the Series, once again against the Cubs, Greenberg continued to shine. In Game 2, he hit a three-run homer to help win a 4-1 game for Virgil Trucks, pitching less than a week after being discharged from the Navy. Greenberg finished with two homers, seven RBIs and a .304 average. The Tigers won in seven games and sent the city into another frenzy. When they returned from Chicago as champions, tens of thousands of people were waiting.

"People were packed solid all the way from (Michigan Central Station) to the Book-Cadillac Hotel downtown," Newhouser said. "It was a joy to walk off that train. I was also a little scared. They were grabbing at you, trying to congratulate us. I was afraid they were going to collapse on us. It was a great reception, something I'll never forget."

It was the last Series celebration Detroit would see for 23 years.

A NEW BREED OF CAT

Baseball was a big deal to Detroit in the early part of the century, but football was not. The American Professional Football Association was founded in 1920 at an auto dealership in Canton, Ohio. Two years later, it became known as the National Football League. No matter what the fledgling league was called, it couldn't support a franchise in Detroit for more than a decade. Teams named the Heralds, Tigers, Panthers and Wolverines all tried to capture the imagination of the market. Most even played at Navin Field. None was successful.

But in 1930, the seed of a future Detroit champion began growing on the fertile fields of Portsmouth, Ohio, a steel-mill town of 42,560 hearty souls located 90 miles south of Columbus along the Kentucky border. The Portsmouth Spartans, an independent team, joined the NFL. George (Potsy) Clark was coach. Tailback Chuck Bennett, fullback Mayes McClain and tackle Forrest Douds were stars. They won their first game, 13-6, over the Newark Tornadoes, and they beat the Chicago Bears, 7-6, while completing a 5-6-3 season.

Over the next two seasons, the Spartans improved dra-

Detroit Free Press

HARRY HEILMANN WAS A TIGER FOR 15 SEASONS AND A TIGERS BROADCASTER FOR ANOTHER 17. THAT WAS DIZZY TROUT TALKING INTO THE WXYZ MICROPHONE WHILE BIRDIE TEBBETTS LOOKED ON.

Richard Bak Collection

THE TIGERS CONGRATULATE WINNING PITCHER HAL NEWHOUSER AFTER BEATING THE CHICAGO CUBS IN GAME 7 OF THE 1945 WORLD SERIES. DETROIT WON, 9-3. IN THE SERIES, NEWHOUSER WENT 2-1 WITH 22 STRIKEOUTS.

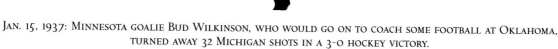

JAN. 15, 1937: MINNESOTA GOALIE BUD WILKINSON, WHO WOULD GO ON TO COACH SOME FOOTBALL AT OKLAHOMA, TURNED AWAY 32 MICHIGAN SHOTS IN A 3-0 HOCKEY VICTORY.

Richard Bak Collection

DUTCH CLARK, A STRONG RUNNER, PASSER AND
BLOCKER, PLAYED FIVE SEASONS FOR THE LIONS AND
CAPTAINED THE 1935 NFL CHAMPIONS. HE ALSO
COACHED THE TEAM IN 1937-38, BUT GOT FED UP
WITH OWNER GEORGE RICHARDS.

matically. Halfbacks Earl (Dutch) Clark of Colorado College and Glenn Presnell of Nebraska, as well as linemen George Christensen of Oregon and Grover (Ox) Emerson of Texas, joined the Spartans in '31, when they won their first eight games and finished second to Green Bay with an 11-3 record. Fullback Leroy (Ace) Gutowsky of Oklahoma City joined the Spartans in '32, when they played in the first — and by far most bizarre — NFL title game in history.

The Spartans lost their third game of the fall to Green Bay, but they came back to beat the Packers, 19-0, in the Spartans' season finale to finish 6-1-4. Thinking the season was over, Dutch Clark left for his off-season job as the basketball coach at Colorado College. But the Bears finished their season the next week at 6-1-6, and since ties didn't count in the standings, Chicago and Portsmouth boasted the NFL's best records with winning percentages of .857. Knowing Clark couldn't return in time to play another game, the league office still decided to set up its first playoff game so a single champion could be crowned.

It was to be played Dec. 18 at Chicago's Wrigley Field. But heavy snow and bitter cold gripped the Windy City that week, convincing Bears coach George Halas to move the game.

Indoors.

In what was perhaps a precursor to the Arena Bowl, the Spartans and Bears squared off before 11,198 inside a smelly, dank Chicago Stadium, which days before hosted a circus. There was room only for a dusty, dirty 80-yard field, surrounded by a fence three feet from each sideline. The cramped quarters resulted in several rules alterations for the game: Each time a team crossed midfield, it was penalized 20 yards, in effect making the field 100 yards long. The goalposts were moved from the end line to the goal line, and the end zones were not regulation size.

The teams, which had tied one another twice during the regular season, held one another scoreless for three quarters. Then came a controversial ending. Chicago's Bronko Nagurski carried the ball to the Portsmouth 7 for a first down. On the next play, he took it to the 2. Soon afterward, with the ball still on the 2, quarterback Carl Brumbaugh handed off to Nagurski, who faked a plunge into the line, backed up two steps and fired a pass to Red Grange in the end zone.

At the time, NFL rules stated that forward passes had to be thrown from at least five yards behind the line of scrimmage. Potsy Clark thought Nagurski had broken the rule, and he screamed for justice. He wasn't heard. The touchdown counted. Just before the end of the game, the Bears added a safety and won, 9-0. The game was such a success, the NFL split into two divisions afterward and decided to hold an annual title game.

In 1933, Dutch Clark retired from pro football to stay in Colorado to coach his alma mater. The Spartans finished in second place in the Western Division with a 6-5 record. But in '34, Clark came out of retirement because of an exciting development. George Richards, owner of Detroit radio station WJR, purchased the Spartans for $15,000 — plus $7,952.08 to pay off the team's debts — and moved them to Detroit. He sponsored a radio contest to pick a new nickname for the team, and the fans

Detroit Free Press

DUTCH CLARK'S LEGEND MAY HAVE FADED, BUT IN THE 1950S, CHICAGO'S GEORGE HALAS CALLED HIM THE GREATEST OF PRO PLAYERS.

NOV. 20, 1937: A 21-0 LOSS TO OHIO STATE WAS HARRY KIPKE'S LAST GAME AS MICHIGAN COACH.
IT WAS THE FOURTH STRAIGHT NON-WINNING SEASON FOR THE 4-4 WOLVERINES.

IN ONLY THEIR SECOND SEASON IN DETROIT, THE LIONS REIGNED AS NFL CHAMPIONS OF 1935. THEY BEAT NEW YORK, 26-7, IN THE TITLE GAME.

chose one that provided their beloved Tigers with some feline friends.

The Lions signed an agreement to play their home games at 25,000-seat Dinan Field on the campus of the University of Detroit. Wearing striking silver-and-blue uniforms in their first game, they defeated the New York Giants, 9-0, before an estimated 12,000 fans. They won their next nine, including six straight shutouts, before suffering a 3-0 loss to Green Bay. Although they lost their final two games, both to the Bears, the Lions finished their first Detroit season in second place at 10-3, established themselves in the city, and began a dear tradition: the Thanksgiving Day game. Richards arranged for a coast-to-coast radio broadcast, with Graham McNamee calling the play-by-play for 94 stations. The game aroused so much interest, 26,000 tickets were sold.

During their inaugural season, the Lions "collected not only the customers' money, but their wholehearted loyalty as well," Detroit Times sports editor Bud Shaver wrote. "Until the Lions put up their game stand against the Bears, professional football was still just an enterprise which had most of Detroit's best wishes, but little else. In their last home game, the Lions . . . became Detroit's own team, just as the Tigers and Red Wings are Detroit's own."

Detroit's own teams roared even louder in 1935. As the Tigers won their first World Series, the Lions used a rumbling rushing offense to win the Western Division with a 7-3-2 record. Dutch Clark, whom Halas often called the best player in the sport's history, led the league in scoring with 55 points and finished fourth in rushing. Wingback Ernie Caddel and fullback Bill Shepherd joined Clark in the top five in rushing. Caddel finished second, Shepherd fifth.

Before an estimated 15,000 fans at Dinan Field on Dec. 15, the Lions cruised in the NFL championship game, beating the Giants, 26-7, on a day when wind, rain, sleet and snow turned the field into an icy, slippery swamp. The Giants relied on a passing game, so the weather and two broken ribs sustained

JAN. 1, 1938: MICHIGAN STATE PLAYED IN ITS FIRST BOWL BUT GAINED ONLY TWO FIRST DOWNS AND 57 YARDS IN A 6-0 LOSS TO AUBURN IN THE ORANGE BOWL.

by league-leading receiver Tod Goodwin never gave them a chance against the smashmouth Lions, who scored on the first series of the game. Gutowsky, Clark, Caddel and Raymond (Buddy) Parker all ran for touchdowns.

Finally, football was in Detroit to stay.

Hockey soon would be, too.

COUGARS, THEN FALCONS

Detroit's hockey history began with Charles Hughes, a sports writer and schmoozer who once was Teddy Roosevelt's public relations man. Hughes helped convince the city's power brokers to build the Detroit Athletic Club in 1915 and hire him as its manager. Then, in '26, he convinced his contacts at the club that the city needed a professional hockey franchise — if it wanted serious consideration as a big-league town.

Hughes rounded up 73 local investors, including industrialist Edsel Ford, department store magnate S.S. Kresge and newspaper publisher William Scripps. The group paid the NHL a $100,000 franchise fee, then paid another $100,000 to purchase the rights to 15 members of the Victoria Cougars, a Western Hockey League club that had won the '25 Stanley Cup. Hughes signed nine of the players to contracts, including player-manager Art Duncan and superstar forward Frank Fredrickson, and kept the Cougars nickname, thinking that it was an appropriate continuation of the theme set by the Tigers.

The Cougars' first season was anything but spectacular. They were a permanent road team in 1926-27, playing home games at 6,000-seat Border Cities Arena across the Detroit River in Windsor, Ontario, while waiting for the million-dollar Olympia Stadium to be built at Grand River and McGraw. They lost their Nov. 18, 1926, debut to the Boston Bruins, 2-0, shuffled their aging lineup extensively, and finished 12-28-4 in the American Division. Dead last. Smarting from an $84,000 loss, Hughes, in desperation, asked NHL president Frank Calder for help in finding a coach and general manager. Word traveled throughout the league, and it reached the ears of Jack Adams, a sometimes gruff, sometimes gregarious 32-year-old who had been a forward and assistant coach with the Stanley Cup-winning Ottawa Senators in 1927.

Adams brashly called Calder and said: "I'm the man for the Detroit job!" Calder, taken aback, took him at his word and arranged for an interview, in which Adams told Hughes what he had told Calder so bluntly before. "I'd been involved in winning the Stanley Cup for Ottawa," Adams said, "so I told Hughes that he needed me more than I needed him."

Hughes couldn't argue with Adams, a hockey vagabond who once played with a professional team in Calumet, Mich., with Notre Dame football legend George Gipp. So Hughes hired him on May 16, and Adams went to work immediately. Among his first moves was injecting young legs into his lineup. He acquired a small, combative winger named Larry Aurie, whom he soon was fond of calling "the best two-way player in hockey."

The Cougars opened the '27-28 season on the road with a 6-0 victory in Pittsburgh and a 5-2 loss in Boston, then competed on

WHEN LARRY AURIE JOINED DETROIT'S LINEUP IN 1927-28, THE TEAM WAS CALLED THE COUGARS. BEFORE HE SKATED AWAY, AFTER PLAYING ONE GAME IN THE 1938-39 SEASON, THE TEAM HAD BECOME THE RED WINGS AND WON BACK-TO-BACK STANLEY CUPS IN 1936 AND 1937.

SEPT. 9, 1938: THE LIONS BEAT PITTSBURGH, 16-7, IN THEIR FIRST GAME AT BRIGGS STADIUM (THE NEW NAME FOR NAVIN FIELD, WHICH HAD BEEN EXPANDED TO 53,000 SEATS).

Detroit Free Press

A WING AND A PRAYER: JACK ADAMS — PICTURED
WORKING OUT THE DETAILS FOR A CHARITY GAME
WITH MONSIGNOR JOHN M. DOYLE — TOOK OVER
A FLEDGLING CLUB IN 1927 AND, OVER THE NEXT
35 YEARS, TURNED IT INTO ONE OF THE NHL'S
PREMIER TEAMS.

Detroit Free Press

DURING 14 YEARS WITH THE
RED WINGS — FIVE AS CAPTAIN
— EBBIE GOODFELLOW LED THE
TEAM IN SCORING TWICE AND
WON THREE STANLEY CUPS.

Detroit ice for the first time. The opening of Olympia
on Nov. 22 was a festive affair. A standing-room-only
crowd of more than 10,000 was there. So was Mayor
John Smith, who presented Adams bunches of
chrysanthemums. So was the University of Michigan
band, which played throughout the game. So was a
group of figure skaters, who performed between
periods. So was Foster Hewitt — the first man to
make the call "He shoots! He scores!" — who broadcast the game on radio station WGHP.

The Cougars lost to Ottawa, 2-1, but weren't dis-
couraged. Improving under Adams, they finished the
season 19-19-6 and barely missed the playoffs. In
1928-29, they finished 19-16-9, made the playoffs for
the first time, lost in the first round, but pulled in a
tidy $175,000 profit. Aurie and center Ebbie
Goodfellow held great promise for the future. Things
were going quite well.

But then the Depression hit. Attendance plum-
meted so badly, Adams went door-to-door on Grand
River trying to sell tickets and even allowed a fan into
a charity exhibition one night for five bags of pota-
toes. "We took his spuds," Adams said, "and gave him standing
room." The Cougars' performance in the '29-30 season matched
the economic malaise: They went 14-24-6 and missed the playoffs again.

After the season, the team tried to drum up interest by holding a contest in the newspapers to determine a new nickname.
The fans chose Falcons over other suggestions, such as Trojans,
Wanderers and Magnetos. New uniforms with gold letters were
introduced, marking the only time the team would wear a color
other than red and white.

But the hoopla failed to make an impact. The Falcons finished
next to last in '30-31, then lost to the Montreal Maroons in the
first round in '31-32 — then almost ceased to exist because of
financial problems.

RED WINGS

By the spring of 1932, the team had defaulted on its mortgage,
and its property had been put into receivership — although
Adams had been so tight with money, players weren't allowed to
travel in sleeping cars on road trips and ate cheese sandwiches
wrapped in waxed paper for meals. Investors kept their hands
in their pockets. The Olympia was padlocked. "We were this
depressed: If Howie Morenz, the great Montreal star, had been
available for $1.98, we couldn't have afforded him," Adams said.

The team needed help. It needed James Norris. A Montreal
native and ardent puckhead, Norris had moved to Chicago and
become a millionaire in the grain business. But the 53-year-old
tycoon missed hockey badly and yearned for an NHL franchise
— in the Windy City, where he already owned an interest in
Chicago Stadium, or anywhere else. When the opportunity
arose to buy the Detroit team for $100,000, Norris pounced on
it — and put pressure on Adams. "I'll give you a year on proba-

OCT. 1, 1938: FRITZ CRISLER COACHED HIS FIRST GAME FOR MICHIGAN,
A 14-0 VICTORY OVER MICHIGAN STATE THAT PROPELLED THE WOLVERINES TO A 6-1-1 SEASON.

Special to the Detroit Free Press

WITH THE LINE OF LARRY AURIE, MARTY BARRY AND HERBIE LEWIS, THE RED WINGS IN 1936 AND 1937 BECAME THE FIRST U.S.-BASED TEAM TO WIN CONSECUTIVE STANLEY CUPS. IN 1944, THE RED WINGS STARTED A HALL OF FAME. THE THREE LINEMATES WERE IN THE FIRST CLASS.

MAY 4, 1939: BOSTON ROOKIE TED WILLIAMS, FACING DETROIT PITCHER BOB HARRIS, BECAME THE FIRST BATTER TO HIT A HOME RUN OUT OF BRIGGS STADIUM. HARRIS WAS TRADED TO THE ST. LOUIS BROWNS NINE DAYS LATER.

Detroit Free Press

JACK ADAMS SURROUNDED
HIMSELF WITH CAPTAINS IN THE
PHOTO ABOVE (CLOCKWISE FROM
TOP LEFT) — HERBIE LEWIS
(1933-34), EBBIE GOODFELLOW
(1934-35, '38-42) AND CARSON
COOPER (1931-32). ADAMS CUT
A FINE FIGURE WHEN HE LACED
UP THE SKATES, TOO. HE WON
STANLEY CUPS PLAYING FOR THE
TORONTO ARENAS IN 1918 AND
THE OTTAWA SENATORS IN 1927.

Detroit Free Press

tion," he told him, "with no contract."

Norris was known as Pops to distinguish him from his oldest son, James Jr., who became a co-owner of the Black Hawks in 1946. And like any Pops, he was no-nonsense. He got his way. An innovative man, Norris solidified the team's identity with one bold move. Borrowing the name and emblem of a team for which he used to play — the Montreal Winged Wheelers, who won the first Stanley Cup in 1893 — he renamed the Falcons the Red Wings on Oct. 5, 1932, figuring the blood-red sweaters and automobile-tire emblem with a flying wing would fit in well with the Motor City's image. He also instituted the league's first season-ticket plan and matinee games. "Pops was the bankroll and the boss," Adams said. "After he took over, Detroit hockey never looked back."

Spurred by Norris' mandate and aided by his wallet, Adams retooled the team. He kept forwards such as Aurie, Goodfellow, Herbie Lewis and John Sorrell, adding young center Carl Voss. Adams kept bone-crushing defenseman Doug Young, adding veteran defenseman John Gallagher. Most important, he added veteran goaltender John Ross Roach, a 5-foot-5, 130-pounder who played extremely big, registering 10 shutouts and a 1.88 goals-against average. He became the first Detroit player named a first-team All-Star.

The Wings finished the '32-33 season 25-15-8 and advanced to the second round of the playoffs. They lost to the New York Rangers but made noticeable strides. "There isn't a man on that team who should make any All-Star team," Rangers coach Lester Patrick said. "But, as a group, they are almost unbeatable. It only goes to show what harmony, loyalty, pep and cohesion can accomplish when linked together and wisely directed."

Winning made the Wings a hot ticket. For years, Detroit hockey crowds consisted largely of Canadians, who openly booed the home team. But in '33-34, Canadians were replaced with celebrities: Mayor Frank Murphy, city council president James Couzens and Michigan football coach Harry Kipke. Olympia became the place to see and be seen in the winter as the Wings rolled to a 24-14-10 record and their first appearance in the Stanley Cup finals.

Adams kept making moves that season. He traded Voss to Ottawa for center Cooney Weiland and, when Roach was injured, acquired goaltender Wilf Cude on loan from Montreal. But the Wings weren't quite ready to be champions; Adams still had work to do. They lost the best-of-five finals to Chicago in four games, and in '34-35, they missed the playoffs altogether, largely because Montreal recalled Cude.

Still tinkering with the roster, Adams acquired forward Syd Howe, defenseman Ralph Bowman and goaltender Normie Smith. He converted Goodfellow to defense. And then he made perhaps his most important move. During the '35 Cup finals in Montreal, Boston coach Frank Patrick told Adams: "If I had Cooney Weiland, my club would be here." Adams responded: "If I had (Bruins center) Marty Barry, we'd win the Cup." That summer, Adams sent Weiland and defenseman Walt Buswell to Boston for Barry and right wing Art Giroux.

He proved to be a prophet.

OCT. 21, 1939: TOM HARMON RAN FOR TWO TOUCHDOWNS, PASSED FOR TWO MORE, AND KICKED A FIELD GOAL
AND THREE EXTRA POINTS AS MICHIGAN BEAT CHICAGO, 85-0, IN THE LAST GAME OF THIS ONCE-VICIOUS RIVALRY.

Photos by the Detroit Free Press

JAMES NORRIS WAS
THINKING OF THE
MONTREAL WINGED
WHEELERS — A TEAM
HE ONCE PLAYED FOR
— WHEN HE BOUGHT
THE DETROIT FALCONS
AND RENAMED THEM
THE RED WINGS IN
1932.

THREE CUPS

Barry became invaluable. Playing between Lewis and Aurie in '35-36, he scored 21 goals, led the Wings to a 24-16-8 record, and guided them through a thrilling playoff run, which included the longest game of the century and culminated with Detroit's first Stanley Cup.

In the first round against the Maroons, the defending champions, the Wings survived a five-hour, 51-minute, six-overtime endurance race and won, 1-0. Maroons goaltender Lorne Chabot made 61 saves, but Smith made 89. The showdown ended at 2:25 a.m., when forward Mud Bruneteau, a seldom-used rookie recalled from the minors just two weeks earlier, drove to the net, took a pass from Hec Kilrea and scored the game-winner at 4:47 after 176:30 of play — the longest game in NHL history. In the end, even the puck was too exhausted to move. "It was the funniest thing," Bruneteau said. "The puck just stuck there in the twine and didn't fall on the ice."

EBBIE GOODFELLOW
EVENTUALLY MOVED TO
DEFENSE, AND IN 1937
SMILED FOR A PHOTO
WITH JOHN
GALLAGHER (LEFT)
AND BUCKO
MCDONALD (RIGHT).

OCT. 28, 1939: TOM HARMON GAINED A CAREER-HIGH 206 YARDS
IN MICHIGAN'S 27-7 VICTORY OVER YALE.

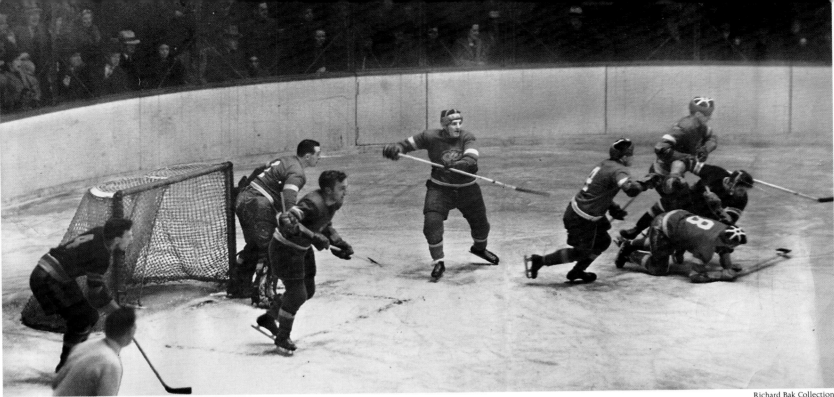

EARL ROBERTSON WAS IN GOAL FOR THE RED WINGS IN THE FIFTH AND FINAL GAME OF THE 1937 STANLEY CUP FINALS AGAINST THE NEW YORK RANGERS.

Bruneteau grinned at the Montreal Forum crowd while jamming money into his gloves and sweater, given to him by appreciative fans happy just to have the game over. He told reporters that he hoped his father, who never appreciated anything he did, had been listening on the radio at home in Manitoba. The team went out to celebrate. "I really found out how tired I was afterwards when we went to the Lumberbacks Club in Montreal, and I had one bottle of ale," Smith said. "That set me right back on my heels." But Bruneteau was wide awake in his room at the Windsor Hotel at 5 a.m.

Someone knocked on the door. Bruneteau got up and opened it. In the hallway stood Chabot. "Sorry to bother you, kid," the goaltender said. "But you forgot something when you left the rink." Chabot flipped Bruneteau the puck with which he had scored the game-winning goal, and with that, the Wings launched their first Ice Age. They finished a three-game sweep of the Maroons and beat the Maple Leafs in the finals, 3-1, winning their first Cup just months after the Lions and Tigers won their first championships.

"There were no TV cameras then," Pete Kelly said. "We didn't parade around the ice with the Cup. It was presented to us later, at the Royal York Hotel (in Toronto). There were quite a few fans from Detroit crowded in there, I remember." For the first time, Detroit had gone Cup crazy. "When we got back to Detroit after the game, the town had gone wild," Goodfellow said. "There seemed to be thousands of people at the railway station, and we were driven in a procession to Olympia, where another celebration took place."

The momentum of the victory carried the Wings to another celebration in '37. They finished 25-14-9, led the NHL in scoring and defense and dominated the All-Star first team. Aurie, Barry, Goodfellow and Smith made it. Aurie led the league with 23 goals, Barry won the Lady Byng Trophy, and Smith won the Vezina Trophy. Young and Aurie didn't appear in the playoffs because of injuries, and Smith was injured in the first round, but the Wings still beat the Canadiens and Rangers in five games apiece to become the first American team to win two straight Cups.

Adams was so overwhelmed when the Wings won that he fainted in the dressing room. Perhaps he was delirious at the beginning of the next season, too, because he made a foolhardy proclamation. "We should run away with it again," he said. If the Wings should have, they didn't. Adams kept his roster intact, but his players looked worn-out. The Lewis-Barry-Aurie line combined for only 32 goals in 1937-38, compared to 54 the previous season. "I'll never again make the mistake of hanging onto players for too long," Adams said after the Wings missed the playoffs with a 12-25-11 record. "When it comes to dealing with my teams, I'm going to have ice water in my veins."

The Wings returned to the finals six times from 1939 to 1949. But they were swept three times and were deeply disappointed to win only one more Cup, with a four-game sweep of Boston in 1943. They became known as chokers by becoming the first team in history to blow a 3-0 lead in the finals, which they did to Toronto in '42. The series turned at the end of Game 4, when Adams, incensed by the calls of referee Mel Harwood, chased Harwood into the officials' dressing room. Adams was suspended for the rest of the series. The Maple Leafs won the Cup, and Adams, ashamed, called the collapse "the bitterest blow" of his career.

Little did he know how well the Wings, starring a big new kid from the Canadian prairie, would make up for the losses in the coming years, joining forces with the Lions to keep Detroit atop the sporting world. ◆

JAN. 6, 1940: MICHIGAN STATE DEDICATED JENISON FIELD HOUSE
WITH A 29-20 BASKETBALL VICTORY OVER TENNESSEE.

THE 1935-36 RED WINGS WON THE STANLEY CUP IN TORONTO. "WHEN WE GOT BACK TO DETROIT AFTER THE GAME, THE TOWN HAD GONE WILD," EBBIE GOODFELLOW SAID. "THERE SEEMED TO BE THOUSANDS OF PEOPLE AT THE RAILWAY STATION, AND WE WERE DRIVEN IN A PROCESSION TO OLYMPIA, WHERE ANOTHER CELEBRATION TOOK PLACE."

Photograph from Detroit Free Press archives

Greatest sprinter ever

Fast Eddie

By Scott Talley

Chewing gum and wearing a pair of horn-rimmed glasses held on his face with adhesive tape, Eddie Tolan of Detroit blazed to a gold medal in the 100 meters at the 1932 Olympics.

His victory in Los Angeles was historic for several reasons: Tolan became the first black athlete to win the Olympic 100. Judges needed several hours to view a film of the race to determine he had won by two inches. His time of 10.3 seconds tied the world record and stood as an Olympic record until 1960. He became the third sprinter from the University of Michigan to win the Olympic 100, following Archie Hahn in 1904 and 1906 and Ralph Craig (Detroit Central) in 1912.

Two days later, Tolan returned to win the 200 meters, this time by six feet, making him the only male double-gold medalist in track and field that year.

So this is how a 5-foot-4½, 149-pound schoolteacher from Detroit came to be regarded at the time as the greatest sprinter ever. In more than 300 amateur races, he was defeated seven times.

Growing up, June Tolan thought the world of her older brother, Eddie, but she never considered him a fast runner until a fall day in Salt Lake City in the early 1920s.

Bentley Historical Library

EDDIE TOLAN OF DETROIT WAS PROCLAIMED AS THE GREATEST SPRINTER EVER AFTER WINNING THE 100- AND 200-METER DASHES AT THE 1932 LOS ANGELES OLYMPICS.

"We were at Liberty Park and a coach wanted my brother Hart to race a kid from Provo," recalled June, youngest of four Tolan children. "Hart was in his football gear, but he said, 'My younger brother Eddie' could race the kid.

"I knew Eddie played football at the junior high, but I didn't think he was a speedster or anything. And Eddie beat the kid. It was pretty shocking, he beat this ace runner who came all the way from Provo, and I think Eddie was wearing street clothes."

The Tolan family moved to Detroit in 1924 in search of a better education for the children. At Cass Tech High School, Eddie Tolan won the 100- and 220-yard dashes three years in a row at the Class A state finals. He starred as a 131-pound quarterback, scoring six touchdowns in a victory over Western in 1926, which he always called his greatest athletic thrill, not his gold medals.

"Tolan was good, but he was never stuck up," said Robert Sampson, one of Tolan's track teammates. "He was just a good-hearted guy and he always had that calm disposition. I don't think I ever saw him false-start. He was always very smooth, very calm."

NOV. 23, 1940: IN TOM HARMON'S FINAL, HEISMAN TROPHY-CLINCHING GAME, OL' 98 RUSHED FOR 149 YARDS AND TWO TDS, PASSED FOR TWO TDS, MADE FOUR EXTRA POINTS AND AVERAGED 50 YARDS A PUNT AS MICHIGAN BEAT OHIO STATE, 40-0.

Associated Press

Tolan headed to Michigan, hoping to be a quarterback for the school Fielding H. Yost made famous, but the track coach talked him into switching dreams. "The track team did a lot more traveling then," Tolan said. "So I saw the opportunity to travel on a Pullman and see the country. People would say on the streets of Chicago when they saw me, 'That's Eddie Tolan of Michigan.' "

Competing for the Wolverines in 1929-31, Tolan was the Big Ten 100-yard dash champion in 1929 and '31, and his '29 time of 9.5 seconds set the world record. In '31, he was the Big Ten and NCAA champion in the 220. He also won four national AAU sprint titles.

And in July 1930 at a meet in Vancouver, British Columbia, Tolan ran 100 meters in a blistering 10.2 seconds. That beat the world record, but could not be recognized for technical reasons.

However, his success on the track did not spare him from the indignities that confronted many blacks. "There were times when Eddie was discriminated against, but he took it and sacrificed for the generation behind him," June Tolan said.

That was the case in September 1930, soon after his unofficial world record. Tolan and two blacks on a national AAU team — Gus Moore and John Lewis — were denied lodging at the Illinois Athletic Club and the Chicago Athletic Club, where their teammates were staying for a meet against Great Britain.

Detroit Free Press

When Tolan threatened to leave the team, he was told by an AAU official that he would "be through in athletics forever." Following the urging of his family, Tolan competed in the meet and stayed at a black-owned hotel on Chicago's south side.

"He couldn't stay in the hotels, and he had a lot of bad experiences," June Tolan said. (In 1999, she lived with her sister Martha in Southfield, and had many of her late brother's awards.) "I guess the lesson that anyone can learn from Eddie's life is never give up. He never gave up, and he was always kind. That was just Eddie."

The easy-going exterior camouflaged his competitive fire. After earning a bachelor's degree in education from Michigan, he began preparing for the 1932 Olympics. "He would train at West Virginia State, where he was teaching, and after the school year ended he would run at Belle Isle or Northwestern — wherever he could find a place to run," June Tolan said. "He was self-trained."

Tolan won his 100-meter gold in a photo finish over American Ralph Metcalfe. In the 200, Tolan said he didn't want another close finish; he won by two-tenths of a second, in 21.2.

"You just have to wonder what Eddie Tolan could have done if he had starting blocks, lightning-fast tracks and weight training like they do today," said track historian Jim Moyes of Muskegon. "It would have been mind-boggling."

After the Olympics, to help support his family, Tolan agreed to do a vaudeville act with Bill (Bojangles) Robinson. At first it was a rousing success, but their bookings soon were canceled because of the Depression. Athletic officials decided Tolan had lost his amateur status.

He ran professionally for a while, winning a world pro sprint championship in Australia, where he was a celebrity on and off the track. He would later share his wisdom and experiences as a teacher in the Detroit Public Schools system, where he worked until his death in 1967.

"There have been people who have posted faster times in Michigan, but they didn't run on the tracks that Eddie did," Moyes said. "To me, Eddie Tolan is the best to ever come out of this state. And on top of it, he was just a heck of a nice guy. Everyone liked Eddie Tolan." ◆

A punt and a prayer

Great depression

By Michael Rosenberg

From 1930 to 1933, Michigan put together an incredible run, going 31-1-3 and winning outright or sharing four conference and two national titles. Four years later, the coach was fired.

It was a tumultuous period, featuring one of the highest peaks and lowest valleys in U-M football history.

When Harry Kipke took over for the 1929 season, greatness was expected in Ann Arbor for two reasons. First, Kipke himself had been great, one of the best punters and halfbacks of his era. Second, Kipke had been great for Fielding H. Yost, the legendary U-M coach who could do no wrong in the eyes of many, including himself.

At that time, it was widely assumed that the best players made the best coaches. So as one of Yost's favorites, Kipke's rise as a coach was assured. Nonetheless, it was startlingly quick. An All-America halfback in 1922, Kipke earned nine letters (in football, basketball and baseball) before his graduation in 1925. By 1929, he was Michigan's head coach, hired after one year in charge at a school then known as Michigan State College.

Faced with unfairly high expectations, Kipke actually exceeded them. Thanks mostly to superior line play, the Wolverines quickly developed into the nation's best team. Three linemen made All-America at least once in 1931-33. Center Maynard Morrison was the first, in 1931, starring as a blocker and a linebacker. Charles Bernard did it twice, in 1932 and 1933, giving U-M an All-America center for three straight seasons.

The other All-America lineman might have been the third-best among them, but eventually it was his number that was retired. His name was Francis (Whitey) Wistert, No. 11. After Wistert's brothers Albert and Alvin also made All-America wearing No. 11, the school decided nobody else would wear

Associated Press

Harry Kipke had been an All-America warrior on the field for Fielding H. Yost in the early '20s.

the number.

A loaded line in this era was often enough to win a championship, but in 1932 U-M had something else: an All-America quarterback, possibly the best player in the country. When Harry Newman played the position, a quarterback was expected to do it all, and Newman did. His passing, running and kicking were unequaled. U-M scored 83 points in Big Ten play; 57 of them were scored by Newman.

To put that in perspective, consider that in winning all eight of its games, U-M gave up just 13 points. The Wolverines avenged their only loss of 1931 with a 14-0 victory over Ohio State in Columbus. They also shut out five other teams. Toward the end of the season, U-M won tight games at Indiana (7-0) and Minnesota (3-0) to seal its perfect record.

Those games epitomized Kipke's philosophy: Play great defense, punt your way out of trouble, and you'll find a way to win. Yost had felt the same way; he used to say that every football victory could be traced to a successful kick.

Newman was gone in 1933, but it hardly mattered. The Wolverines went 7-0-1, with the only blemish a 0-0 tie with Minnesota at Ann Arbor. That was no shame; Kipke himself referred to the Gophers' 1934 team as the best he had ever seen.

That 1934 Minnesota team whipped the Wolverines, 34-0, but almost everybody beat U-M that year. Instead of seriously pursuing a third national title, the Wolverines went 1-7 and never scored in double digits. A year later, they went 4-4, followed by 1-7 and 4-4 seasons.

That put Kipke on shaky ground, and it didn't help that there were questions about his integrity. There were reports of a slush fund for athletes. Players allegedly were paid for summer jobs they never performed. The governing process for collegiate athletics

Special to the Detroit Free Press

DID IT PLAY MORE THAN "THE VICTORS"? HARRY KIPKE RECEIVED A NEW VARSITY RADIO AS A PROMOTION BY A CHICAGO COMPANY.

IN 1932,
QUARTERBACK
HARRY NEWMAN
WON THE DOUGLAS
FAIRBANKS AWARD,
THE PREDECESSOR
TO THE HEISMAN
TROPHY.

Associated Press

was still in its embryonic stage, so Kipke might not have violated any rules. But the faculty wasn't happy, and because the team was losing, the fans weren't happy. Yost had to fire Kipke.

The firing came after Yost had said that U-M didn't fire people for losing games, so there were questions about the motives behind it. The alleged ethical breaches were never presented as the reason.

Yost's fingerprints are all over the Kipke era. Kipke played for Yost and was hired because of Yost, and even after he won his two national championships, he still stood in his old coach's shadow. Eventually, Kipke succumbed in part because of the same thing that often hurt Yost — namely, Fielding H. Yost.

As his pupil's teams suffered, Yost was not shy about speculating what was wrong. Although Yost supported Kipke, eventually much of the public did not. Yost had made his own mistakes after winning national titles in his first four years, but he survived because of his charisma and unprecedented success. Kipke could not live off his national titles; Yost had set the bar high and national success was expected.

Kipke remained loyal to U-M, even serving on the Board of Regents. And in time, he would be remembered mostly for his success. After Kipke was fired, U-M hired Fritz Crisler, and the school returned to its winning ways. The Harry Kipke era was short, but for four years it was as successful as almost any era anywhere.

FEB. 5, 1943: JAKE LAMOTTA HANDED SUGAR RAY ROBINSON HIS FIRST LOSS
IN A 10-ROUND DECISION AT DETROIT.

CITY OF CHAMPIONS, 1930-1947

Harmon of Michigan

Ol' 98

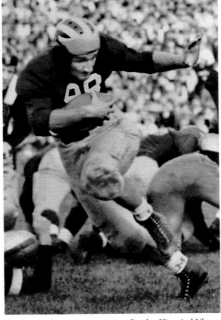

By George Puscas

Tom Harmon — "Ol' 98," as he often called himself — was perhaps the greatest of the legendary football players who made Michigan an enduring power in the collegiate game. Name the great players in 120 years of U-M football — Willie Heston, Germany Schulz, Benny Friedman, Bennie Oosterbaan, Ron Kramer, Desmond Howard, Charles Woodson — and leave room at the top for Harmon.

Never on old Ferry Field or in the huge stadium that became the home of Wolverines football has there ever been his all-around equal.

Death came to Harmon in 1990 at age 70 in Los Angeles, where he had lived since the late 1940s. He had been a nationally syndicated radio sportscaster until his retirement in 1988. He was stricken with a heart attack shortly after picking up airplane tickets at a travel office; the tickets were for a visit to former U-M star Forest Evashevski in Ft. Lauderdale, Fla. Evashevski, from Detroit's Northwestern High, was Harmon's blocking back.

"I always felt Tom was the best football player of all time," Evashevski said. "He was a complete player. Maybe a lot of guys could run like him, but he could pass, kick, play defense — do anything that was needed to win a game."

Harmon won the last sports competition he entered. Shortly before he died, he and a partner won a match in a golf tournament at Bel-Air Country Club.

In his time at U-M, Harmon was as widely applauded as young collegians ever get, not only in Michigan and among his own. Rival fans from California to Pennsylvania and in cities throughout the Big Ten marveled over his play.

His U-M teams of 1938-40 were 19-4-1. But although they never won a championship, national magazines regularly featured stories on him. Harmon won the 1940 Heisman Trophy and was named the nation's outstanding male athlete. Hollywood even made a movie — "Harmon of

Michigan" — extolling the kid from Gary, Ind., and his football career.

All of this came to Harmon before television could create instant heroes of athletes. It happened because his exploits were followed by millions via network radio and the newspapers.

Fielding H. Yost, the fabled U-M coach and athletic director, once called Harmon football's best player since Heston, the Wolverines' immortal from Yost's "Point-a-Minute" powerhouses opening the 20th Century.

Fritz Crisler, who with Harmon as his foil made the single-wing offense the most appealing and devastating attack of its day, said his star certainly was "better than Red Grange," the fabled Galloping Ghost from Illinois. "Tom could do more things," Crisler said. "He ran, passed, punted, blocked, kicked off and kicked extra points and field goals, and was a superb defense player."

Harmon was a 60-minute player when that type was fading from the gridiron. His unusual uniform number — 98 — became as widely known as Grange's 77 had been in the 1920s. Harmon's number was retired when he graduated.

Harmon was an awesome runner, big, powerful, quick, with that peculiar instinct of all great runners to find the open field and reach it. The Harmon cutback — drifting wide to his right, then turning sharply to his left and slicing back through tackle — was classic in his day.

He made the single wing so much a part of U-M football that for years after he departed, Michigan teams lined up in the formation and then shifted to whatever set they really intended to run.

Harmon's best game might have been his last — Nov. 23, 1940, when Michigan beat Ohio State at Columbus, 40-0. Harmon rushed for 139 yards, completed 11 of 12 passes for 151 yards, ran for two touchdowns, passed for two, kicked four extra points, averaged 50 yards with his punts despite a

Bentley Historical Library

TOM HARMON REALLY MOVED — IN THE AIR AS A WORLD WAR II BOMBER, ON THE GROUND AS A WOLVERINE.

wet ball, and intercepted three passes, returning one for a touchdown.

"He finished in one of those flaming flares of gridiron fame such as few college ball players ever know," Grantland Rice wrote.

With 15 seconds left, Crisler pulled Harmon from the game. Ohio State fans gave him an unprecedented ovation and swarmed over him, tearing pieces from his jersey for souvenirs.

"I didn't think anybody would remember that game," he said almost a half-century later, "because it wasn't a close one. We didn't even win a championship because we had lost earlier to Minnesota."

The Gophers claimed the national championship; Michigan, which lost all three games to Minnesota during Harmon's career, was third behind Stanford.

Harmon scored 33 touchdowns, then a Big Ten career record (Grange had 31). In three years and 24 games, Harmon gained 2,134 yards rushing, averaging 5.4 yards, and passed for 1,304 yards and 16 touchdowns. Harmon (1939-40) and Billy Sims (1978-79) were the only players in modern college football to win successive scoring titles.

The Chicago Bears made Harmon the NFL's No. 1 draft pick in December 1940, but he never played for them. After graduation, Harmon and several of his teammates, including Evashevski, later head coach at Iowa, starred in his movie.

During the making of the movie in Hollywood, Harmon met actress Elyse Knox. They were married in Ann Arbor before 500 guests. Her wedding dress was made from the silk of Harmon's parachute (he was a fighter and bomber pilot in World War II). Pictures of it were carried on the national news wires. They used a sword to cut the cake.

Their family included actor Mark Harmon, a one-time starting quarterback at UCLA; and daughters Kelly, former wife of auto magnate John DeLorean, and Kristin, who was married to the late singer Rick Nelson.

Harmon twice parachuted from his aircraft during World War II. In 1943, his bomber crashed and he was presumed dead. The nation mourned. Six days later, Harmon walked out of the jungle.

Later that year, in a battle with Japanese Zeroes over China, he parachuted into a lake and spent a month returning to his base with the aid of Chinese guerrillas.

"If you didn't have religion before the war, you did then," Harmon said. He was awarded the Silver Star and Purple Heart.

He had a brief pro football career following the war, with the Los Angeles Rams in 1946-47, but his legs were shot. He then turned to broadcasting. At one time, his nightly radio sports show was carried on more than 400 stations across the country.

"He kept in touch with his friends," said Don Canham, the longtime U-M athletic director. "He had a word processor and, geez, he'd write three-page letters. He'd do things for people no one ever knew about."

Bentley Historical Library

TOM HARMON SCORED 33 TDS, SURPASSING RED GRANGE'S BIG TEN RECORD BY TWO. "TOM COULD DO MORE THINGS," FRITZ CRISLER SAID OF THE TWO.

Special to the Detroit Free Press

TOM HARMON'S SON MARK PLAYED QB AT UCLA AND NUMEROUS ROLES IN HOLLYWOOD.

NOV. 20, 1943: A 45-7 VICTORY OVER OHIO STATE CLINCHED A 6-0 BIG TEN MARK AND A SHARE (WITH PURDUE) OF THEIR FIRST LEAGUE TITLE SINCE 1933 FOR FRITZ CRISLER'S 8-1 WOLVERINES.

The Brown Bomber

And still champion

By Nicholas J. Cotsonika

The legend of Joe Louis begins not in the boxing ring itself, but in the neighborhoods of Detroit. Whenever he fought, the streets of his hometown sat in silent standstill, from Black Bottom on the fringe of downtown, to the Jewish sector out on Dexter Avenue, into the enclaves of ethnics on the city's north and west sides. Everywhere, everything was deserted, everyone glued to the blow-by-blow accounts of his exploits crackling over the radio.

History does not accord Louis the distinction of being boxing's all-time greatest; that belongs to Muhammad Ali, although Louis reigned as world heavyweight champion longer than any other man, from 1937 to '49. But Louis played a special, central role in shaping the century's sports landscape — and its social landscape, too. With the exception of Babe Ruth, no other athlete captivated Detroit's — and the rest of the nation's — sports fans more before 1950, no matter what his race.

For perhaps the first time ever, blacks and whites rooted with all their hearts for *their* guy. The same guy. Together. Combining power with politeness, the Brown Bomber threatened white folks in the ring only. He wasn't considered uppity, as Jack Johnson was years before, and he wasn't considered brash, as Ali would be years later. "I never thought about any race thing," he said. He was a disinterested pioneer, a simple, quiet young man with no aggressions or agendas outside the ring, making him universally popular and admired.

"I've always said that Joe Louis is not black; he's not white; he's just Joe Louis," said John Condon, president of Madison Square Garden Boxing when Louis died in 1981 at age 66. "He was one of the finest people I ever met in my life. He was a good piece of the foundation of the sport."

Richard Bak Collection

JOE LOUIS AND JESSE OWENS (RIGHT) ERASED THE MYTH OF ADOLF HITLER'S ARYAN IDEAL.

Detroit Free Press

WITH MEAN FISTS THAT LOVED TO HAMMER HEADS, JOE LOUIS KNOCKED OUT 54 OPPONENTS IN SANCTIONED BOUTS.

FEB. 3, 1944: SYD HOWE SCORED SIX GOALS IN THE RED WINGS' 12-2 VICTORY OVER THE NEW YORK RANGERS.

Louis was the perfect man for a less-than-tolerant time, the perfect man to pave the way for the greater changes to come. "He opened up boxing to every black fighter," said Teddy Brenner, a predecessor of Condon's. "He even led the way for guys like Jackie Robinson in other sports. Every black athlete that followed owes a debt of gratitude to Joe Louis."

The racial majority learned to pay attention to Louis' skills, rather than his skin color. He was not a crafty boxer. He was a puncher. A spectacular, mind-numbing puncher. A puncher with so much might, with so much efficiency, he could condense a whole night's work in a single, gorgeous moment of speed and thunder. His unabashed head-hunting and deadpan, no-gloating principle made him dark and dramatic. Of his 68 professional victories in 71 bouts, 54 were by knockout. Arenas and stadiums filled to their rafters with those eager to see him.

Louis loved to fight. He won so many exhibition bouts — even while in the military during World War II — that his opponents were called collectively the Bum-of-the-Month Club. Among those bums was bigotry. Much like Jesse Owens did in the '36 Berlin Olympics, Louis confounded Nazi dictator Adolf Hitler's Aryan ideal. His two most memorable fights were in the mid-to-late '30s against German Max Schmeling, an eventual good friend who, in the heat of the moment, represented to those outside the ring an evil oppression of unwise, unholy and unjust ideas. Ali once called Louis an "Uncle Tom" because of Louis' passive political nature. But in time, even Ali became humbled by Louis' influence.

"When Joe's in the room," Ali said, "I am not the Greatest."

VIOLINS TO VIOLENCE

His name actually was Joseph Louis Barrow, and he came into the world by the light of a kerosene lamp on the morning of May 13, 1914, in the east-central Alabama town of Lafayette. He was the grandson of slaves and the seventh child of Monroe and Lillie Barrow.

The Barrow home was a windowless, ramshackle affair, like many of the sharecropper houses that peppered the red clay of Lafayette. Monroe leased 120 acres of mean farmland

Detroit Free Press

JOE LOUIS LEARNED TO BOX AT DETROIT'S BREWSTER RECREATIONAL CENTER, POLISHED OFF OPPONENTS, THEN POLISHED HIS TROPHIES. THIS ONE WAS FOR WINNING THE 1933 GOLDEN GLOVES TOURNAMENT, SPONSORED LOCALLY BY THE FREE PRESS.

that grudgingly yielded some cotton and, when he got lucky, a little wheat. But it was the kind of land that could break a man, and by the time Joe was 2 years old, it had broken Monroe. He was taken to the Searcy State Hospital for the Insane, where he lived until 1959 with no awareness of his son's achievements.

Lillie, a strict Baptist disciplinarian, later married Patrick Brooks, a widower with five children. Faced with the dreary prospect of a lifetime of tenant farming, Brooks went north, liked the opportunities that seemed to be available in Detroit, and returned south to bring the Barrow-Brooks family to the Motor City. They moved in with friends on Macomb Street on the city's east side, then shifted to a Catherine Street tenement when Patrick landed a job at the Ford Rouge plant.

At age 13, Joe became a fifth-grade student at Duffield School. His academic record was poor, leaving one teacher to prophetically observe that "he's going to have to make a living with his hands." For the moment, that meant enrollment in the Bronson Trade School, where Joe was to learn the craft of cabinet making. When an injury and a sagging economy threw Patrick out of work, Joe took a job delivering coal and ice, contributing his earnings to the family's upkeep.

However bad things became, Lillie got her children to church and saw that some of them received music lessons. For Joe, that meant the violin. Before he had taken enough lessons to play even a scale, however, he secretly was using his violin money to pay for boxing lessons at the Brewster Recreational Center. When Lillie learned what her son had been doing, she encouraged him to pursue boxing. So did his violin teacher. But with Patrick out of work, there was little time for the ring. Joe left Bronson to push truck bodies on the assembly line at Briggs Manufacturing.

In 1932, Joe managed to land a bout with U.S. Olympic boxer John Miler, who knocked him down seven times and convinced him that his future lay not in boxing, but in an auto plant. But before long, Joe was back at Brewster, training under a professional middleweight named Holman Williams. In his second amateur fight, Joe won by knockout after throwing just two punches.

Joe began a heavy schedule of amateur bouts and entered

JOE LOUIS MADE ABOUT $4.7 MILLION FROM HIS PRO BOUTS, PART OF WHICH HE USED FOR HIS SPRINGHILL FARMS IN UTICA, MICH.

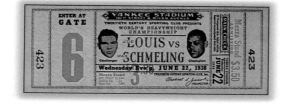

Associated Press

JOE LOUIS' TICKET TO IMMORTALITY CAME IN 1938.
AFTER SUFFERING THE FIRST LOSS OF HIS CAREER
TO MAX SCHMELING IN '36, LOUIS WON THE
HEAVYWEIGHT TITLE IN '37. THEN HE AVENGED HIS
DEFEAT, POUNDING SCHMELING AT YANKEE STADIUM.

Associated Press

the Golden Gloves tournament, then sponsored locally by the Detroit Free Press. He won the Gloves' national championship in the light-heavyweight division, but lost in the Amateur Athletic Union's light-heavyweight title fight. In all, Joe fought 58 amateur matches, losing only four. Lack of money forced him to substitute sneakers for boxing shoes and to use the same wrappings over and over to bandage his knuckles in the ring.

And then, Joe met a Detroit entrepreneur named John Roxborough. The man who was to change Joe's life was a study in contrasts: He began his money-making career as a bail bondsman, then went into the numbers business and, to some degree, politics. A philanthropist, he also underwrote college educations for many young blacks in the city and supported black teams and athletes.

After watching Joe spar in the Brewster ring, Roxborough took the youngster aside and asked his name.

"Name's Joe Louis Barrow," Joe said.

"That's too long," Roxborough replied. "We'll just call you Joe Louis."

LOUIS VS. SCHMELING

Joe Louis was a hit from the beginning under Roxborough's direction. His first professional opponent was Jack Kracken, Chicago's best heavyweight. When they met July 4, 1934, in the Bacon Casino on the Windy City's south side, a local fight manager predicted a mismatch. "Kracken will kill that boy," he said. "Louis is in over his head." Louis took a little less than two minutes of the first round to knock out Kracken, an achievement that earned the 20-year-old a whopping purse of $59.

The victory began a quick rise for Louis, who in 1935 beat Primo Carnera and Max Baer, both former heavyweight champions, and became a wealthy celebrity in Detroit and soon the rest of the nation. By February of '36, he had compiled a phenomenal record: 27 victories, 23 knockouts, no losses. None.

But then he met Schmeling for the first time.

Max Schmeling was 31, hoping to regain the form he had as heavyweight champion from '30 to '32. He was a 10-to-1 underdog, and few were impressed with him. Only 45,000 fans showed up for the fight June 19, 1936, at Yankee Stadium, about half of what was expected. Louis spent much of his training time on the golf course.

In the first round, Schmeling landed almost no punches, while Louis nearly closed one of his eyes. The fight continued somewhat in the same vein until the fourth round, when Schmeling suddenly landed a right that sent Louis to the canvas for the first time in his professional career. Louis took a count of only two but, as he later recalled, "never fully recovered from that blow."

As the bell rang to end the fifth round, Louis took another hard right from Schmeling. As Schmeling began scoring more rights in the sixth round, friends escorted Louis' mother from the stadium. In the 12th round, Schmeling landed another right, his last of the fight. Louis slumped to the canvas. He later recalled that "when the referee counted, it came to me faint, like somebody whispering."

It was Louis' first loss in 28 professional fights. When he left Yankee Stadium afterward, he hid his face behind a straw hat. Hitler and Nazi Germany rejoiced. All of Detroit was downcast. The Brown Bomber had been beaten — and beaten by the worst kind of opponent, a man whose home nation was championing the cause of racial rage.

When Louis stepped into the Yankee Stadium ring with Schmeling the second time, the world was watching. The date was June 22, 1938 — exactly one year after Louis had won the heavyweight championship by knocking out James J. Braddock. Schmeling, by losing a couple of bouts after the first Louis fight, had forfeited the right to a title shot.

The rematch for the heavyweight title proved more political than pugilistic. With horrifying descriptions of German concentration camps starting to reach the United States, Americans had begun fearing for the lives of relatives abroad. Weeks before the fight, Louis had been invited to dinner at the White House, where President Franklin Roosevelt, feeling the champ's biceps, had told Louis: "Joe, we need muscles like yours to beat Germany."

When Jewish organizations protested the fight, officials told them that the contest was really one of America vs. Germany and that the fight should take place so that the world could see Louis knock out Schmeling. The same officials told Louis that his boxing career might be over if he didn't win. Meanwhile, a newspaper reporter claimed to have found a full-dress Nazi uniform hanging in the training camp closet of Max Machon, Schmeling's trainer and confidant.

In Berlin, the Nazi government, which had virtually ignored the first fight, was lavish in its praise of Schmeling. German newspapers claimed the U.S. boxing world was alive with conspiracies aimed at guaranteeing a Schmeling loss. Before the fight, Schmeling received a cable that read: "To the coming World's Champion, Max Schmeling. Wishing you every success." It was signed by Hitler.

Against this chaotic, combustible backdrop, more than 70,000 fans poured into Yankee Stadium. Louis let go with everything he had from the moment the first bell rang. He opened with a series of left jabs. Schmeling responded with the right cross that had worked so well in the previous fight. This time, however, it never touched Louis. Schmeling threw another right. It landed, but it had no effect.

Within seconds, Louis had Schmeling hanging on the ropes. Referee Arthur Donovan scored that as a knockdown. Schmeling made for the middle of the ring, but Louis caught him again. When the champ continued to pound his opponent, Schmeling's handlers threw in the towel. Donovan ignored it at first, then realized that Schmeling, indeed, was finished.

In all, Louis threw about 40 punches, knocking Schmeling down four times. The fight had taken only two minutes and four

TONY SPINA/Detroit Free Press

JOE LOUIS NEVER SAW COMBAT DUTY DURING WORLD WAR II, BUT HE FOUGHT ALL THE TIME AND WENT ON GOODWILL TOURS. FACING ALL COMERS, HE APPEARED IN EXHIBITIONS FOR THE ARMY AND ADDED TO HIS REPUTATION.

OCT. 16, 1946: GORDIE HOWE SCORED A GOAL IN HIS FIRST GAME WITH THE RED WINGS, A 3-3 TIE AT HOME WITH TORONTO.

> ## "His people say he was a credit to his race.
> ## They sell him short. He was a credit to the human race."
>
> **JIMMY CANNON, SPORTS COLUMNIST**

seconds. In the Schmeling camp, someone cut the wire that was carrying a broadcast of the fight back to Germany.

"I had nothing personally against Max," Louis said. "But in my mind, I wasn't champion until I beat him. The rest of it — black against white — was somebody's talk. I had nothing against the man, except I had to beat him for myself."

AND STILL CHAMPION

After beating Schmeling, Louis made 17 title defenses, donating some of his purses to Army and Navy war-relief funds, before enlisting in the Army. During and after World War II he fought numerous exhibitions and defended his title four more times before retiring as heavyweight champion — never beaten as the champ — on March 1, 1949.

Louis, who had continued a heavy schedule of exhibitions, made a comeback in 1950. Thirteen years after he first won the title, weighing 197 pounds at age 23, he faced Ezzard Charles while weighing 218 at age 36. The added pounds and years had a telling effect, as Louis lost to Charles in 15 rounds on Sept. 27. "I just didn't have it," said Louis, who then began a long, slow, sad spiral toward personal problems.

After eight more bouts, Louis on Oct. 26, 1951 faced Rocky Marciano, who with 37 straight victories (32 knockouts) was on his way to becoming the next heavyweight champion. The fight probably was prompted more by Louis' need for money to pay tax debts than by any notion of recapturing his crown via a comeback. By the seventh round, Louis' legs gave out. By the eighth, Louis was snared by the ropes, halfway out of the ring.

Las Vegas News Bureau

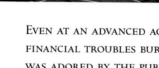

EVEN AT AN ADVANCED AGE, WHEN PERSONAL AND FINANCIAL TROUBLES BURDENED HIM, JOE LOUIS WAS ADORED BY THE PUBLIC AND THE BOXING COMMUNITY. THOMAS HEARNS (LEFT) AND ONE OF HEARNS' OPPONENTS, HAROLD WESTON, WANTED TO TOUCH HIM. THE U.S. POSTAL SERVICE WANTED TO HONOR HIM.

"My boy," said Marciano's manager, Al Weill, "knocked out the great Joe Louis." Roxborough laughed at that. "Your boy," Roxborough told Weill, "didn't knock out the great Joe Louis. He beat Joe Louis' shadow."

For the rest of Joseph Louis Barrow's life, he would play the roles of two men: the great Joe Louis, and Joe Louis' shadow.

Joe Louis' shadow had trouble with the IRS; blew his fortune and was broke because of his carelessly generous nature; ran through four marriages to three wives; suffered a temporary mental breakdown reminiscent of his father's; and turned to working as a greeter at Caesars Palace in Las Vegas to make ends meet.

But the great Joe Louis remained, winner and still champion. He remained lifelike in memory, a symbol of strength and unity so powerful, the city of Detroit named an athletic arena after him and built statues of him. His sparing but brilliant quotes became part of the American vernacular. *There's nothing wrong with America that Hitler can cure. . . . Nobody got hurt but the customers. . . . We are on God's side. . . . He can run, but he can't hide.*

Despite his faults, his ability to bring the neighborhoods of a nation together next to the radio for more than a decade, to show that a black kid from a hard-working industrial town like Detroit could take down any man of any color anytime anywhere under any kind of pressure, that amazing ability, well, it made him immortal.

In the words of legendary New York sports columnist Jimmy Cannon: "His people say he was a credit to his race. They sell him short. He was a credit to the human race." ◆

SEPT. 27, 1947: BIGGIE MUNN LOST HIS FIRST GAME AS MICHIGAN STATE COACH, 55-0, TO MICHIGAN AT ANN ARBOR. BUT THE SPARTANS REBOUNDED FOR A 7-2 RECORD AND THEIR FIRST OF SEVEN STRAIGHT WINNING SEASONS UNDER MUNN.

Our scrapbook

THE OTHER HOWE

Detroit Free Press

FROM THE LEFT: SYD HOWE, BUCKO MCDONALD AND WALLY KILREA PLAYED ON THE RED WINGS' FIRST STANLEY CUP WINNER IN 1936.

Syd Howe, who played in Detroit in 1934-46, was no relation to and nothing like the Howe named Gordie.

Syd was smallish at 5-feet-9 and 165 pounds, shot left-handed, and was not nearly as cantankerous as the other guy. But, oh, he could score.

Especially on Feb. 3, 1944, when Howe scored six goals in a 12-2 victory over the New York Rangers, one short of the NHL-record seven Joe Malone scored for the Quebec Bulldogs in 1920. (At the time, it was thought Howe had set the record, but the NHL has since recognized Malone's feat.)

When Howe retired in 1946, he left as the NHL's all-time leading scorer with 237 goals and 528 points.

One more footnote. When the Wings acquired Howe from the St. Louis Eagles in 1935, he came with another namesake: Scotty Bowman (also no relation).

JUST A BIG KID

The Red Wings signed 17-year-old Gordie Howe in 1945 for $2,300 and a team jacket. He joined the team the next year, the youngest player in the NHL.

"Away from the ice he is a typical teenage youngster," the Wings' press guide said. "He enjoys swing music and malted milks. He is shy and afraid of the opposite sex."

IF THE SHOE FITS

Ralph Guldahl, the golfer with movie-star looks, set an Open record with a score of 281, beating Sam Snead by two strokes in the 1937 U.S. Open at Oakland Hills. Guldahl shot a final-round three-under 69, despite an approach shot on No. 15 that bounced off a spectator's shoe and into a sand trap. Guldahl blasted out, saving par.

THE WINNER IS ...

CARL VOSS: NHL's Calder Trophy in 1933.

MICKEY COCHRANE: American League's most valuable player in 1934.

HANK GREENBERG: American League's most valuable player in 1935 and '40.

MARTY BARRY: NHL's Lady Byng Trophy in 1937.

NORMIE SMITH: NHL's Vezina Trophy in 1937.

CHARLIE GEHRINGER: American League's most valuable player in 1937.

EBBIE GOODFELLOW: NHL's Hart Trophy in 1940.

TOM HARMON: Heisman Trophy in 1940.

JOHNNY MOWERS: NHL's Vezina Trophy in 1943.

HAL NEWHOUSER: American League's most valuable player in 1944 and '45.

WAR GAMES

Professional sports went on during World War II, even though many top athletes were serving in the military. But some people — even sports types, such as boxer Gene Tunney — called for sports to be suspended during the war.

Not Lt. Tom Harmon. Addressing the Detroit Downtown Quarterback Club in '44, he said: "Not as an Army man but merely as Tom Harmon, a former football player, I take issue with Gene Tunney, whose interests are against competitive sports.

"The boys on the front line want sports to continue."

Harmon, who served in the Army Air Corps, was awarded the Silver Star and Purple Heart. His plane crashed in South America, and he survived six days in a jungle. His plane was shot down in China, and he survived more than a month along the Yangtze River.

1. LEATHERNECK ERNIE HARWELL. 2. FIGHTING TIGER MICKEY COCHRANE. 3. JOE LOUIS IS IN THE ARMY NOW. 4. LT. TOM HARMON. 5. SCHOOLBOY ROWE, LEFT, IN THE NAVY. 6. TIGERS PITCHER TOMMY BRIDGES, LEFT, DID HIS TIME IN THE ARMY. 7. HARRY HEILMANN SHOWED OFF HIS STANCE TO THE TROOPS. 8. LT. COMM. HARRY KIPKE. 9. SGT. HANK GREENBERG WAS A HIT IN THE ARMY AIR CORPS. 10. EX-LION AND FUTURE SUPREME COURT JUSTICE WHIZZER WHITE SERVED IN THE SOUTH PACIFIC.

Photographs: 1. H.T. ALLEN/Detroit Free Press; 2. Detroit Free Press; 3. Detroit Free Press; 4. Associated Press; 5. Associated Press; 6. Associated Press; 7. U.S. Army; 8. Detroit Free Press; 9. Associated Press; 10. Associated Press

1930-1947
Our scrapbook

Associated Press

IT WAS A SAD DAY AT BRIGGS STADIUM WHEN THE YANKEES' LOU GEHRIG
TOOK A SEAT AND ENDED HIS STREAK ON MAY 2, 1939.

MUSICAL COACHES

Out	In
George Veenker	Franklin Cappon
Bucky Harris	Del Baker
Jim Crowley	Charlie Bachman
Del Baker	Mickey Cochrane
Potsy Clark	Dutch Clark
Mickey Cochrane	Del Baker
Harry Kipke	Fritz Crisler
Franklin Cappon	Bennie Oosterbaan
Dutch Clark	Gus Henderson
Gus Henderson	Potsy Clark
Potsy Clark	Bill Edwards
Del Baker	Steve O'Neill
Bill Edwards	Gus Dorais
Bennie Oosterbaan	Ozzie Cowles
Jack Adams	Tommy Ivan
Charlie Bachman	Biggie Munn

OLYMPIC CHAMPIONS

Los Angeles, Summer, '32
JAMES CRISTY, Michigan, swimming:
bronze in 1,500 freestyle.

RICH DEGENER, Michigan, diving:
bronze in springboard.

EDDIE TOLAN, Michigan, track and field:
gold in 100 and 200 meters.

Berlin, Summer, '36
SAM BALTER JR., Detroit, basketball:
gold.

RICH DEGENER, Michigan, diving: gold
in platform.

THE IRON HORSE

Lou Gehrig pulled himself from the New York Yankees' lineup May 2, 1939, in Detroit. It was the first time the man nicknamed the Iron Horse had not started for the Yankees in 2,130 consecutive games covering 14 seasons.

Gehrig, then 35, never played again and died two years and one month later of amyotrophic lateral sclerosis, a degenerative nerve disease that later would bear his name. He had been struggling with a loss of strength and coordination for weeks when he decided to end his historic

streak — a record that stood for 56 years until Baltimore's Cal Ripken Jr. broke it in 1995 — at Briggs Stadium.

Teammate Tommy Henrich said the rest of the Yankees didn't know Gehrig wasn't going to start until he delivered the lineup card to the umpires at home plate before the game, to a standing ovation from the 11,379 Tigers fans in attendance.

"When he came back to the dugout, that was really something," Henrich said. "You never saw a more somber ballclub."

Henrich and pitcher Lefty Gomez were

standing on the top step of the dugout. Behind them sat Gehrig, crying.

"This was a tough moment," Henrich said. "Finally Gomez walked slowly past Lou and said, 'Aw, what the heck, Lou. Now you know how a pitcher feels when he gets knocked out of the box.' Lou laughed."

Legend has it that Gehrig then dressed, walked down the street to Shea's pub on Michigan Avenue, and had lunch while he listened to the game on the radio. But Henrich and many fans there that day say he watched the game from the dugout.

THE EXPLOITS OF OL' 98 — MICHIGAN'S 1940 HEISMAN TROPHY WINNER, TRIPLE-THREAT TOM HARMON — WERE EVEN CELEBRATED ON THE SILVER SCREEN.

MIGHTY GOPHERS

It's difficult for Michigan fans to attach much importance to the Little Brown Jug — the symbol of football supremacy between the Wolverines and Minnesota — since the Golden Gophers lost the last 12 meetings of the century. In fact, U-M was 29-2 in the series since 1968.

But it wasn't always that way. There was a time when the Gophers had their way with Michigan, winning nine straight games in 1934-42. The Wolverines were shut out four times in that stretch, not counting a 0-0 tie in '33.

FASHION STATEMENTS

New coach Fritz Crisler introduced Michigan's distinctive winged helmets in 1938. Was it to make Wolverines receivers more visible to quarterbacks, or did Crisler just like the look? Take your pick, because Crisler told both stories.

WEIRDEST PLAY

It was one of those Tom Harmon days on Sept. 28, 1940. Fun if you're a Michigan fan, but not if you're rooting for the other guys.

Harmon ran the opening kickoff back 94 yards for a touchdown against California at Memorial Stadium. Then he ran a punt back 72 yards for another score.

When Ol' 98 broke loose on another long run for the end zone, Bud Brennan had seen enough. He jumped out of the stands, ran for the field, and tried to tackle Harmon at the 3.

Harmon eluded him, of course — even though Brennan had played a little high school ball himself at Oakland Fremont — and scored on an 86-yard run en route to a 41-0 Wolverines rout.

No harm done, the two men even kept in touch with each other over the years. And they died of heart attacks within months of each other in 1990.

PUBLIC SERVICE

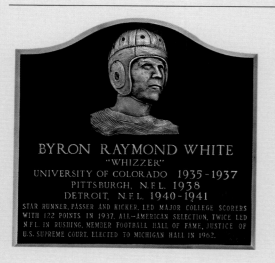

Who says football players are dumb?

Byron (Whizzer) White led the NFL in rushing in 1940, the last Lion to do so before Barry Sanders came along. And White went on to serve on the Supreme Court.

Gerald Ford, right, played center for Michigan in 1932-34. And he went on to serve in Congress and become president of the United States.

Our scrapbook

ICONS

Sugar Ray Robinson's pink Cadillac

Sparty, a 10½-foot statue, dedicated in June 1945

SWEET SCIENCE

Pound for pound, boxing pundits will tell you, Detroit native Sugar Ray Robinson was the greatest fighter who ever lived.

And pounding for pounding, Jake LaMotta — the Raging Bull — was his greatest rival.

"He was the greatest boxer that ever lived," promoter Bob Arum said of Sugar Ray. "He was an absolute master in the ring. He was the complete fighter — defense, offense, movement. His fights with Jake LaMotta were the best that boxing ever produced."

Robinson, a five-time middleweight champion, fought LaMotta six times and won five. Two of the fights were 10-rounders in Detroit in 1943.

They were brutal fights, mostly because LaMotta absorbed all the punishment Robinson could deliver, and continued fighting. All but their last bout — a 13th-round TKO by Robinson — went the distance.

"You don't fight somebody six times unless the fights are close," LaMotta said.

Robinson had started his pro career with 40 straight victories before losing to LaMotta in a Feb. 5, 1943, slugfest at Olympia Stadium. But three weeks later, on Feb. 26, Robinson avenged that defeat, again at Olympia.

The first fight was decisively LaMotta's; he had a 16-pound weight advantage. He won a unanimous decision and scored the only knockdown, when Robinson was saved by the bell in the eighth.

When a rematch was announced, few gave the smaller Robinson a chance. But this time he used his speed to avoid LaMotta, tied him up when he could, and scored enough points to win a unanimous decision. Again, LaMotta scored the only knockdown, in the seventh.

"I knew I would have to stay away and never let him get me on the ropes," Robinson said. "He really hurt me with a

SUGAR RAY ROBINSON WAS KNOWN FOR HIS FLASHING FISTS AND FLASHY TASTES.

Associated Press

left in the seventh round. I was a little dazed and decided to stay on the deck for the count of eight. That was the only time I was in trouble, and my plan of staying away worked the rest of the time."

Four days later, Robinson reported for service in the Army.

Robinson, who was born in Detroit but moved to New York as a child, retired at the age of 44 on Dec. 10, 1965, with a record of 174-19-6 and 109 knockouts.

When the flamboyant Robinson died April 12, 1989, at age 67, he had a star-studded funeral in West Los Angeles. The Rev. Jesse Jackson presided over what he called "an hour of sadness and celebration" attended by more than 2,000, including Red Buttons, Dodgers manager Tommy Lasorda, Raiders owner Al Davis, Motown Records founder Berry Gordy, singer Lou Rawls, heavyweight champ Mike Tyson, Don King and Archie Moore.

Associated Press

OLYMPIC ICON JESSE OWENS DID A LITTLE RUNNING FOR OHIO STATE, TOO.

OH, WHAT A DAY

Everybody remembers Jesse Owens for spoiling Adolf Hitler's little party with those four gold medals at the Berlin Olympics in 1936, but check out his itinerary for the afternoon of May 25, 1935, when the Ohio State track team came to Ann Arbor for a meet against Michigan:

2:45: Owens tied the 100-yard dash record with a time of 9.4 seconds.

3:25: He broke the long-jump mark (26 feet, 8¼ inches).

3:34: He set the 220 record (20.3).

4:00: He set the 220 low hurdles record with a 22.6.

And that's how Owens, then a sophomore, set three world records and tied another in less than an hour and a half, and became the most beloved Buckeye in Ann Arbor.

"That was a great day, a historic day," said Red Simmons, a former Eastern Michigan Olympian who worked the long jump pit that day. "He was from Ohio State, but even the Michigan fans cheered him on that day. He was incredible, but you expected it from Owens. He was so good.

"Jesse was a great athlete and a great man. I don't know that anyone else could have done what he did, in running or in standing up for his race. I'm proud that I knew him and raced against him."

CHAPTER 4

TWO DYNASTIES
1948-1962

TWO DYNASTIES,
1948-1962

By Nicholas J. Cotsonika

When sports fans wanted to see the best of hockey and football in the 1950s, they turned their attention to Detroit. Nowhere else. With Gordie Howe smashing records and smashing opponents for the Red Wings, with Bobby Layne passing to teammates and passing out in bars for the Lions, no other city in North America came close.

Howe, a slope-shouldered forward from Canada, developed into the greatest all-around hockey player in history, and the Wings developed into the undisputed class of the NHL. From the 1948-49 season to 1954-55, the Wings continued their Ice Age by winning seven straight regular-season championships and four Stanley Cups — giving them seven Cups total, more than any other American franchise. Only their hated rivals, the Toronto Maple

Gordie Howe and the Red Wings. Bobby Layne and the Lions. The '50s were a time for legends.

Leafs, had won as many.

Layne, a brash and boozing quarterback from Texas, led the Lions so well that they competed with the Cleveland Browns for the distinction as the NFL's dominant team. From 1951 to '57, the Lions won or shared four division titles and beat the Browns in three NFL championship games, winning five of the six playoff games in which they appeared. Fans packed Briggs Stadium to see them play, elevating professional football's popularity to that of the college game.

There were other local teams to watch. The Tigers bid farewell to third baseman George Kell, who beat Boston's Ted Williams for the American League batting title in 1949, .3429 to .3427. They also introduced outfielder Al Kaline, who won the batting title in '55 with a .340 average — at age 20. The football programs at Michigan and Michigan State made news, and in '57, a professional basketball team nicknamed the Pistons arrived from Ft. Wayne, Ind., thanks to NBA owner Fred Zollner.

Nevertheless, the Lions and Wings were kings. Life was good.

But if the story of Detroit in the fabulous '50s were a Shakespearean play, it would have been a tragicomedy. The people who built the city and its two dominant sports teams enjoyed postwar prosperity — in the factories, on the field and on the ice

PRECEDING PAGE: COACH BUDDY PARKER GOT CARRIED AWAY AFTER THE LIONS WON THEIR SECOND STRAIGHT NFL CHAMPIONSHIP, IN 1953.

Photograph from the Richard Bak Collection

No one lit up a room like Ted Lindsay, Gordie Howe and Alex Delvecchio. From 1948-49 through 1954-55, the Red Wings won seven straight NHL regular-season championships and four Stanley Cups.

Jan. 1, 1948: A 49-0 victory over Southern Cal in the Rose Bowl
capped Michigan's first 10-0 season and first, although disputed, national title since 1933.

deepening a racial divide that one day would explode in destructive violence.

The Wings and Lions kept winning, and the City of Champions label had not yet worn off. But as the teams' management meddled, their rosters disintegrated, stars went off to other teams, and those who were left behind became bitter. Losses started to pile up, and Detroit, which always held the highest standard of success, spent many of the coming years in want of winners.

AND HOWE!

In Detroit, the legend of humble Howe was known well by all: He never should have become known as Mr. Hockey with the Wings. He should have been a New Yorker. Should have died, too.

In 1942, at the age of 14, Howe attended a New York Rangers tryout in Winnipeg, Manitoba. He was homesick for Floral, Saskatchewan, a prairie town nine miles east of Saskatoon, where he lived a life of deprivation and poverty as one of nine children. He didn't play well at all. In a few brief whirls on the ice, he did nothing exceptional, and the Rangers blew a golden opportunity. They sent him back to Saskatchewan. Unsigned.

A year later, Wings scout Fred Pinckney invited Howe to a tryout in Windsor, Ontario, and even bought him his first suit of clothes for the trip. Already 6-feet and nearly 200 pounds at age 15, Howe displayed his extraordinary skills. He was ambidextrous, and that caught the eye of coach and general manager Jack Adams. "Who's the big kid?" asked Adams, who didn't make the same mistake the Rangers did.

Impressed, Adams arranged for Howe to work out with a junior team in Galt, Ontario. As part of the deal, he promised him a Wings jacket. "I wanted that jacket so bad all the time I was in Galt," Howe said. "I remember that quite a few times I walked down to the railroad station by myself. I knew when the Red Wings' train would be coming through town, traveling to games. I'd just wait there for them. I figured that if they stopped for anything, I'd go aboard and see if I could ask Adams about my jacket. But the train never stopped. They went rolling through every time. I'd just walk back home."

In 1945, Howe was invited to training camp with the Wings, bunking in Olympia Stadium because of the wartime housing shortage. He amused himself by killing rats with his stick. After scoring two goals in an exhibition in Akron, Ohio, he signed his first contract to play for the Wings' farm club in Omaha, Neb. He scored 22 goals there. In '46, he made the big-league team

Detroit Free Press

GORDIE HOWE, WHO JOINED THE RED WINGS IN 1946 AS AN 18-YEAR-OLD FROM FLORAL, SASKATCHEWAN, WORE THE WINGED WHEEL FOR 25 SEASONS.

— but then made terrible mistakes, laying the groundwork for decades of hard times to come.

The auto industry kept humming, and the Motor City remained one of the nation's sparkling centers of manufacturing might. But as technology advanced, the industry decentralized, fought with labor unions and cut jobs. Affluent whites began branching out, riding away on the new superhighways in the cars they had built, slowly sprawling to the suburbs and

JAN. 15, 1948: A SYNDICATE HEADED BY EDWIN J. ANDERSON BOUGHT THE LIONS FOR $165,000.

WHEN GORDIE HOWE RETIRED IN 1980, HIS NHL STATS WERE 1,767 GAMES, 801 GOALS, 1,049 ASSISTS AND 1,685 PENALTY MINUTES.

COACH TOMMY IVAN HAD A WINNING COMBINATION WITH TED LINDSAY ON LEFT WING AND GORDIE HOWE ON THE RIGHT.

for good — and approached Adams about some unfinished business.

"Mr. Adams," he said, "it has been two years now, and I haven't got my jacket yet." Adams sent Howe, along with forwards Ted Lindsay and Marty Pavelich, to a sporting goods store downtown and told him to sign for it. "It was smooth, like satin on the outside, with leather sleeves and an alpaca lining," Howe said. "It had a big 'D' with 'Red Wings' written on it. It looked like the most beautiful jacket in the world."

Had an incident in 1950 turned out for the worse, Howe wouldn't have been able to enjoy his prized jacket for very long.

In the playoff opener at Olympia, the Wings trailed Toronto in the second period, 3-0. Howe charged toward Leafs captain Ted (Teeder) Kennedy but, as he lunged to hit him, Kennedy pulled up. Howe missed him and went hurtling headfirst into the boards, right in front of the Detroit bench. Paramedics placed him on a stretcher as the crowd watched in stunned silence, then rushed him to Harper Hospital. He had broken his nose, shattered his cheekbone and seriously scratched his right eye. And his brain was hemorrhaging. He was in critical condition. His mother was flown in.

At 1 a.m., neurosurgeon Fredric Shreiber saved Howe and a hockey town's hopes. He drilled an opening in Howe's skull and drained fluid to relieve pressure on his brain. Afterward, he put

JUNE 15, 1948: THE TIGERS BEAT PHILADELPHIA, 4-1, IN THE FIRST NIGHT GAME AT BRIGGS STADIUM,
WHICH WAS THE LAST AMERICAN LEAGUE PARK TO INSTALL LIGHTS.

Howe in an oxygen tent. By morning, Howe's condition had improved. He pulled through, the only lingering effects of the operation being a facial tick, which earned him the nickname Blinky. As the story goes, while he lay on the hospital gurney, he even apologized to coach Tommy Ivan, who had replaced Adams in 1947, for not playing better.

Howe went on to complete a spectacular 26-season NHL career in which he played 1,767 games, scored 801 goals, tallied 1,850 points, won six scoring titles, and took home six Hart Trophies as the league MVP. He played in 23 All-Star Games from 1948 to '80, when he skated at age 52 with the Hartford Whalers, still strong, playing with sons Marty and Mark.

No stupid boards would get the best of him. Nothing and nobody ever did. Howe was harder than them all.

THE BEST

In time, hockey would understand that Howe was above little things like head injuries. Like the Tigers' Ty Cobb, Howe was arguably the best ever to play his sport. Period. As great as Bobby Orr and Wayne Gretzky were, neither matched Howe's combination of scoring, toughness, intimidation and longevity. Howe was neither artist nor innovator. He played raw hockey, old-time hockey, Detroit hockey, ripping wrist shots and exploding elbows like atom bombs. To him, a hat trick wasn't three goals. It was a goal, an assist and a fight.

Howe never needed the help of enforcers. He was his own policeman, one of the best in the game. He once skated past a heckler in the crowd and nicked the offender's nose with the blade of his stick, shutting him up. He often did much more than nick opponents when they dared challenge him. In '59, Howe engaged in perhaps his most famous fight.

The Rangers that year promoted defenseman Lou Fontinato as the toughest player in hockey. New York-based Look magazine even presented a six-page picture spread on him, showing him flexing his muscles and looking mean. Whenever the Rangers played the Wings, Fontinato was on the ice with Howe. "The

Detroit Free Press

WHO NEEDED HELMETS? GORDIE HOWE NEARLY LOST HIS LIFE AFTER HE PLUNGED HEADFIRST INTO THE BOARDS DURING THE 1950 PLAYOFFS.

JIMMY TAFOYA/Detroit Free Press

CENTER NORM ULLMAN, WHO PLAYED WITH THE WINGS FROM 1955 TO 1968, WAS A FEROCIOUS FORECHECKER WHO THRIVED IN THE PLAYOFFS.

idea was to distract me," Howe said. After a few altercations one night at Madison Square Garden, Howe got even.

"Red Kelly and Eddie Shack were in a fight behind our net, and I'm leaning on the net, watching it," Howe said. "Then I remembered a bit of advice from Lindsay: Always be aware of who's out on the ice with you. I took a peek and sure enough, there was Louie with his gloves off about 10 feet away and coming my way. I truly thought he was going to sucker-punch me. If he had, I'd have been over. I pretended I didn't see him, and when he swung, I just pulled my head aside and that honker of his was right there, and I drilled it. That first punch was what did it. It broke his nose a little bit."

A little bit? With one punch, Howe made a mess of Fontinato's face and further solidified his reputation as the league's only one-man team. Even rival Maurice (Rocket) Richard, whom Howe felled with one punch in his first visit to the Montreal Forum in '46, eventually admitted Howe's overall superiority. "Sincerely, I have never seen a greater hockey player — I mean, a more complete player," Richard said. "Gordie Howe does everything and does it well." Chicago star Bobby Hull was just as blunt: "I wish I was half the player Gordie was."

Athletically, there was little Howe couldn't do.

He was so strong from the waist up, he could out-muscle almost anyone. In any sport. He was a wicked golfer, booming balls off the tee. He once played with 1954 PGA Championship winner Chick Harbert and outdrove him on every hole. Cleveland Indians manager Lou Boudreau invited Howe to take batting practice at Briggs Stadium. After seeing two pitches, Howe drove the third into the leftfield seats.

Howe spent some of his finest seasons playing with Lindsay and veteran captain Sid Abel as part of the Production Line, a scoring machine with a name that meshed well with Detroit's manufacturing image. The three were marvels to watch, taking long shifts of up to three minutes, crossing and criss-crossing in

SEPT. 25, 1948: BENNIE OOSTERBAAN COACHED HIS FIRST GAME FOR MICHIGAN, A 13-7 VICTORY OVER MICHIGAN STATE THAT STARTED THE WOLVERINES TO A 9-0 SEASON.

"I wish I was half the player Gordie was."

BOBBY HULL

Richard Bak Collection

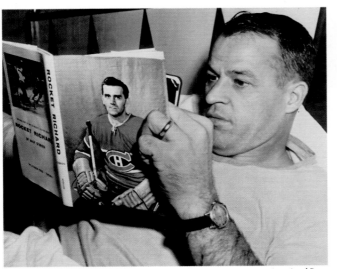

Associated Press

No, Gordie Howe wasn't showing a new magic trick. He was posing after a hat trick in the 1955 Stanley Cup playoffs. During a 1961 visit to Montreal, Mr. Hockey read all about Monsieur Hockey, Maurice Richard, the Canadiens' Rocket who retired in 1960. Howe passed the Rocket's record of 544 goals in 1964.

June 6, 1949: Jake LaMotta knocked out middleweight champ Marcel Cerdan
in the 10th round at Detroit.

front of each other, banging the puck off a special spot on Olympia's boards to create scoring chances.

"Gordie would lead the charge down the right wing, and just after he crossed center ice, he'd fire the puck between the defensemen," center Murray Costello said. "If he hit the spot just right — and he was uncanny about hitting it — the puck came right out to the top of the left circle, and Lindsay would scoot in behind the defensemen and get a point-blank shot on goal."

The members of the Production Line were unselfish and unstoppable. In the 1949-50 season, Lindsay, Abel and Howe finished 1-2-3 in league scoring. "Those boys could score in their sleep," Adams said. All were stars, and Howe was just glad to be a part of the group, as he was just glad to wear that Wings jacket as a rookie.

CUP AFTER CUP

Talent surrounded and supported Howe.

Lindsay was only 5-8, 163, but he was among the most aggressive players of his time. He racked up 1,808 career penalty minutes and became known as Scarface, in tribute to the snaking stitches that held his features together. "I had the idea that I had to beat up everybody in the league," Lindsay said. "I'm still not convinced it wasn't a good idea." Lindsay was more than a brawler, of course. He could score. He could defend. He also took care of Howe, his best friend, who lived with him even after Lindsay got married.

Abel became Chicago's player-coach in 1952, making way for Alex Delvecchio, who moved from left wing to play center on the Production Line. Fluid in his skating and precise in his passing, Delvecchio established himself as one of the best forwards ever to play in Detroit. He spent 24 seasons with the Wings, 11-plus as captain, and won the Lady Byng Trophy for sportsmanship and gentlemanly conduct three times.

Kelly and Marcel Pronovost were on defense. Kelly later helped build a dynasty as a center in Toronto, but as a Wing, he was the most dynamic defender in the game. He could rush the puck into the offensive zone like no one before Orr, yet rarely was beaten behind his own blue line. Pronovost played through pain as well as Howe, gutting through the '61 Cup finals with a broken ankle. At once a rugged player and a smooth skater, he continually put his body at risk for the team, as did Jack (Black Jack) Stewart.

Harry Lumley was steady in net early in Howe's career, winning the Cup in '50. But Adams traded him to Chicago to make room for Terry Sawchuk, who would become perhaps the best goaltender in history. Famously moody, Sawchuk battled opponents, referees and even fans on his way to four Vezina trophies and 103 shutouts, a league record. "Each day, I would say good morning to him in French and English," Pronovost said. "If he answered, I knew we would at least talk a little that day. But if he didn't, which was most days, we didn't speak the entire day."

COACH JIMMY SKINNER AND GORDIE HOWE HAD SOME FUN WITH THE STANLEY CUP IN 1955. THE WINGS WOULDN'T HOLD IT AGAIN FOR 42 YEARS.

TOMMY IVAN — PICTURED WITH GOALIE HARRY LUMLEY — WON THREE STANLEY CUPS WITH THE RED WINGS. BUT IVAN BECAME FED UP WITH GENERAL MANAGER JACK ADAMS' BACKSEAT COACHING AND IN 1954 LEFT DETROIT TO BECOME GENERAL MANAGER OF THE CHICAGO BLACK HAWKS.

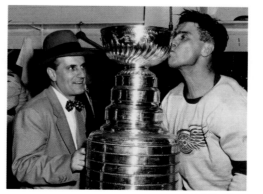

IN HAPPIER TIMES, TOMMY IVAN LOOKED ON AS TONY LESWICK PUCKERED UP WITH HOCKEY'S PRIZED POSSESSION.

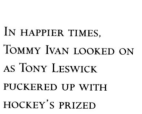

APRIL 23, 1950: THE WINGS CLINCHED THE STANLEY CUP WITH A 4-3 VICTORY OVER THE RANGERS IN GAME 7 AT HOME. PETE BABANDO SCORED THE WINNER AT 8:31 OF THE SECOND OVERTIME.

WITH OR WITHOUT A MASK, TERRY SAWCHUK GUARDED THE WINGS' NETS FOR 14 SEASONS. HE HAD 103 SHUTOUTS DURING A 21-YEAR NHL CAREER.

There were others throughout the years who never received their due, such as center Norm Ullman, a ferocious forechecker who thrived in the playoffs but, because he wasn't flashy, found himself overshadowed. But no one disliked Howe and his bashful, goofy grin. No one was jealous. Howe never acted like a superstar. "We had great unity," center Glen Skov said. "We did a lot of things together off the ice. On the ice, we defied anybody to beat us."

All of the Wings — and all of Detroit — came together for Howe after his head injury in 1950. The Wings brawled brutally with the Maple Leafs the next night, advanced to the Stanley Cup finals, and beat the Rangers in seven games when reserve left wing Pete Babando scored in double overtime. Olympia shook with excitement as fans chanted, "WE WANT HOWE! WE WANT HOWE!" until Gordie appeared in street clothes. Then the fans laughed when Lindsay pulled off Howe's hat — revealing the bald spot where Howe had been shaved for surgery — and threw it into the stands.

The next season, Howe won his first scoring title, Sawchuk was in the net, and the Wings became the first team to surpass 100 points,

OCT. 8, 1950: TED LINDSAY SCORED THE FIRST HAT TRICK IN ALL-STAR GAME HISTORY
AS THE RED WINGS BEAT THE NHL STARS, 7-1. HE ALSO ASSISTED ON GORDIE HOWE'S FIRST ALL-STAR GAME GOAL.

posting 101. Montreal upset them in the first round of the playoffs, but that only served as motivation for 1952, perhaps the best Detroit hockey season of the century. The tradition of the octopus was unveiled as the Wings became the first team to sweep through the playoffs, beating Toronto and Montreal. Sawchuk stood out with four shutouts and an 0.63 goals-against average.

More fun with Montreal was to come.

The Canadiens owned the Cup when the Wings returned to the finals in '54. In Game 7, 4:29 into overtime, Wings forward Tony Leswick lifted a shot toward the net. Defenseman Doug Harvey raised a hand to bat away the puck — but it glanced off his glove and past goaltender Gerry McNeil, giving Detroit a 2-1 victory. The Canadiens were so steamed, they stormed off the ice and spurned the traditional post-series handshakes. "I wouldn't have meant it," Canadiens coach Dick Irvin said. "I refuse to be a hypocrite."

In '55, Montreal and Detroit met again. But this time, the Canadiens were without Richard, who had been suspended for the final three games of the regular season and the playoffs for striking linesman Cliff Thompson. Again, the series went to seven games. Again, the Wings won. This time, Delvecchio was their hero, scoring two goals in the clincher and igniting a celebration some thought never would stop.

Writers became fond of comparing the Wings to the New York Yankees — an idea to which Adams responded by saying: "We are not the Yankees of hockey; the Yankees are the Red Wings of baseball." The Hockey News wrote that the Wings appeared primed to "imprison the Cup for all time." These were heady times. Montreal couldn't stop the Wings. Toronto couldn't stop the Wings.

In fact, only the Wings could stop the Wings.

Adams interrupted the '55 Cup victory party at the Book-Cadillac Hotel to give a speech on the intoxicating state of the team. He ticked off names. Howe. Lindsay. Delvecchio. Kelly. Then he told the crowd that some good young players were coming up. Ullman. John Bucyk. Larry Hillman. "If all of them come through," he said, "we'll be all right for the next few years."

The dynasty lasted but five more weeks.

Remembering the Wings' failures after winning a second straight Cup in '37, Adams quickly broke up the team as he once

Detroit Free Press

TWICE TRADED BY THE WINGS, TERRY SAWCHUK HAD THREE TOURS OF DUTY IN DETROIT.

promised he would, shipping out eight players and receiving no one of note in return. Skov, defenseman Benny Woit and left wings Leswick and Johnny Wilson went to Chicago for three lesser players. Sawchuk went to Boston in a nine-player deal to make room for up-and-coming Glenn Hall, then returned in '57 in a trade for Bucyk, who would become a Hall of Famer. "Jack Adams had this theory that if you were standing pat, you actually were losing ground," Howe said.

And so the greatest sports machine the Motor City had

DEC. 3, 1950: CLOYCE BOX CAUGHT 12 PASSES FOR A LIONS' RECORD 302 YARDS IN A 45-21 VICTORY OVER THE BALTIMORE COLTS.

"Sincerely, I have never seen a greater hockey player — I mean, a more complete player."

MAURICE (ROCKET) RICHARD

Detroit Free Press

SID ABEL DID IT ALL FOR THE RED WINGS — HIS PLAYING DAYS STRETCHED FROM 1938 TO 1952; HE BEGAN COACHING THE TEAM IN 1958; AND HE SERVED AS COACH AND GENERAL MANAGER THROUGH MOST OF THE 1960S. HIS DUTIES INCLUDED GETTING GORDIE HOWE TO SIGN ON THE DOTTED LINE.

APRIL 15, 1952: THE WINGS COMPLETED A CUP FINALS SWEEP WITH TERRY SAWCHUK'S 3-0 SHUTOUT OF MONTREAL AT HOME.
IT ALSO WAS THE NIGHT THE FIRST OCTOPUS WAS THROWN, COURTESY OF PETE AND JERRY CUSIMANO.

produced was dismantled, piece by piece, by the very man who built it. Some smelled the influence of the Norris family, grousing that the NHL actually stood for the Norris House League. James (Pops) Norris Sr. died in '52. Daughter Marguerite and son Bruce then ran the Wings; son James Jr. was chairman of the board of the Black Hawks; and the family owned a controlling interest in Madison Square Garden, which operated the Rangers. Trades to the Norrises' native Chicago seemed suspicious to agonized Detroiters.

In '57, Adams traded Lindsay — who had been making unwelcome noise about a union — to the Black Hawks with Hall as part of a six-player deal that brought back Wilson. Lindsay played with Chicago for three seasons, was retired in 1960-64, then came out of retirement in '64 to play one final season with the Red Wings. More puzzling moves led to more puzzling moves, leaving Howe, in the prime of his career, destined never to win another Cup. During one of his spurts as the Wings' coach, Abel told Howe to think positively. Howe replied: "Yeah, I'm positive Montreal has a damn fine team."

With Toe Blake as coach, Jacques Plante in goal and an array of sharpshooters up front, the despised Canadiens supplanted the Wings as the league's best. They won five consecutive Cups in 1956-60, then four out of five in 1965-69. The Wings returned to the finals in 1961, '63, '64 and '66 but didn't win another Cup until the New Ice Age, decades later, leaving the city forlorn. Adams was out in '62; he took over the Central Hockey League. He ended up a controversial figure, loved for his laughter and success, hated for his deviously demanding leadership style and miserable miscues.

"It was pathetic how Adams destroyed that team," Lindsay said. "Of course, there was an uproar about it. But Adams generally was respected for what he had done for the Wings in other years. And then he thought he was God anyway and could do no wrong."

The Lions' glory days ended much the same way.

FOLLOW THE LEADER

As Howe helped reinforce Detroit's status as a hockey town, Bobby Layne made sure the fans spent the fall watching football. The blond, slightly pudgy product of Texas' hard-scrabble gridirons loved to lead men, in the backfield or in the barroom, and almost single-handedly pulled his fellow Lions together as a championship team. None of his teammates crossed him. No matter where. No matter when. "There's no question," said Russ Thomas, then a scout and assistant coach, "that he was a legendary figure. No one ever led a team as he did."

On the field, Layne tolerated nothing but honest effort. "Bobby had an affinity for chewing your rear end out," tackle Lou Creekmur said in a book by Richard Bak. "If you ever missed a block, not only did you know about it, but all the other guys on the offensive team and everybody on the bench

MAYBE "FATHER HOCKEY" WOULD HAVE BEEN A MORE APT MONIKER. TWO OF GORDIE AND COLLEEN HOWE'S BOYS, MARK AND MARTY, GREW UP TO PLAY IN THE NHL.

Detroit Free Press

MARY SCHROEDER/Detroit Free Press

THE PRODUCTION LINE — LEFT WING TED LINDSAY, CENTER SID ABEL, RIGHT WING GORDIE HOWE — REUNITED WHEN ABEL'S NO. 12 WAS RETIRED IN 1995.

Quarterback Bobby Layne —
leader of the Lions teams
that dominated the NFL during
the 1950s — was at his best
when rallying the team
to victory in the fading
moments of a game.

Associated Press

knew about it. On top of that, the 50,000 fans up in the stadium all knew about it, too, because he told you right then, out there in front of the whole crowd. It was so embarrassing, we all made a pact that we would never miss a block that would ever disturb Bobby Layne."

Off the field, Layne tolerated nothing but team togetherness. Every Monday, he led a Lions ritual: He would buy his teammates drinks at the Stadium Bar, across the street from Briggs Stadium. They would goof off, joke around, laugh a lot and talk a little, and Layne, between shots of scotch, would belt out the lyrics of his favorite song: "Ida Red." Although a few players didn't drink — most notably halfback Doak Walker — the entire team had to attend.

Or else.

"The biggest thing about our success was the tightness of the group," Layne said. "You showed up whether you drank or not. We had 100 percent attendance. The worst thing that could happen was if a couple of players went somewhere, and two others went somewhere else. Pretty soon, those two are blaming the other two for something that went wrong. We'd meet, go over Sunday's game, and iron out any differences we had. We all left there as friends and if we had a loss, by Tuesday we'd have it behind us and be ready for the next game. Nobody was blamin' anybody else."

Legends of Layne's shenanigans piled up over the years — that he never played a game without a hangover, that he never even played a game sober. "He always got more credit than he deserved for some of the off-field escapades," linebacker Joe Schmidt said. "Not to say some of them didn't happen."

In '57, he was arrested on a charge of drunken driving early in the season and acquitted — because of his thick drawl. In court, he made the arresting officer admit that his slow Texas drawl might have sounded like the slurred speech of a man in his cups. Afterward, the Lions' team trainer celebrated the verdict by making a sign that he hung above Layne's locker. It read: "I'M NOT DRUNK. I'M JUST FROM TEXAS."

Layne loved to break in rookies. Before the '58 season, he got hold of defensive tackle Alex Karras — and wouldn't let him go, barking at him in his trademark twang.

"Listen, rookie," Layne said. "You think you're hot stuff. You're nothin' but a rookie who don't know *enathang*."

"Yes, sir, Mr. Layne," Karras said.

"From now on, you just follow me around like a puppy," Layne said. "You understand? You're my puppy."

"Yes, sir," Karras said.

Layne gave Karras the nickname Puppy, then changed it to Tippy, which became Tippy Toes. Day after day, after practice, Layne made Karras go out drinking with him into

JERRY HEIMAN/Detroit Free Press

BOBBY LAYNE KEPT GENERAL MANAGER NICK KERBAWY SMILING WITH THREE CHAMPIONSHIPS IN SIX SEASONS.

Detroit Free Press

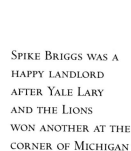

SPIKE BRIGGS WAS A HAPPY LANDLORD AFTER YALE LARY AND THE LIONS WON ANOTHER AT THE CORNER OF MICHIGAN AND TRUMBULL.

NOV. 22, 1952: MICHIGAN STATE BEAT MARQUETTE, 62-13, AND POSTED A SECOND STRAIGHT UNDEFEATED AND UNTIED FOOTBALL SEASON. THE SPARTANS FINISHED NO. 1 IN BOTH MAJOR POLLS.

Detroit Free Press

THE LIONS DAZZLED OPPONENTS AND WON A CHAMPIONSHIP IN 1957 WITH A BACKFIELD (FROM LEFT) OF HALFBACK GENE GEDMAN, FULLBACK JOHN HENRY JOHNSON, HALFBACK HOWARD CASSADY AND QUARTERBACK BOBBY LAYNE. IN 1953, DOAK WALKER (BELOW) SCORED A TD, KICKED A FIELD GOAL AND BOOTED TWO EXTRA POINTS AS THE LIONS BEAT CLEVELAND, 17-16, IN THE TITLE GAME.

Detroit Lions

SEPT. 26, 1953: MICHIGAN STATE PLAYED ITS FIRST BIG TEN
FOOTBALL GAME, A 21-7 VICTORY AT IOWA.

Detroit Free Press

THAT'S FUNNY: ON A WEST COAST SWING IN 1956, LIONS (FROM LEFT) YALE LARY, DAVE
MIDDLETON AND GIL MAINS FOUND THEMSELVES BEHIND BARS AT DISNEYLAND.

the wee hours of the night, sometimes despite Karras' wholehearted efforts to get out of it — by hiding under the bed. To bar after bar they went, scarfing down scotch and bribing bands with $100 bills to keep them playing after hours.

"We'd sit there and drink and get drunk and get sick," Karras said. "There were many nights when Layne and I'd get so darned sick, I couldn't drive, and he'd drive back to training camp. He used to tell me, 'I don't like the dark. I'm scared of the dark. I don't want to go to sleep.' He never required sleep. It'd be daylight when we rolled into camp, and while I'd try to sneak in an hour's sleep, he'd be in the shower, still singing."

In time, Karras became worried about his health — worried about making the team with his veins so full of alcohol. But he also became another of Layne's loyal disciples.

"I liked him," Karras said. "Layne to me was sort of a pacifier, my blanket. When things went wrong, I'd say, 'Well, Bob will take care of it.' The whole club felt that way about him. Layne threw big parties, win or lose. We just had a ball, drinking and singing. There was never a team so close-knit."

Detroit Free Press

NOT SO FUNNY: PARTY ANIMAL BOBBY LAYNE, WITH HIS
TEXAS DRAWL, FOUND HIMSELF EXPLAINING AWAY A
DRUNKEN DRIVING ARREST IN 1957.

LAYNE'S LIONS

Layne loved his teammates, a rambunctious bunch not unlike the Oakland Raiders of later years. "Every son of a bitch on that team," Layne said, "was all football." Creekmur was a physical force who perfected the practice of the leg whip. Defensive back Jimmy (The Hatchet) David loved to rub the noses of opponents into the Briggs Stadium turf.

Jack Christiansen was one of the best pass defenders and kick returners in league history. Les Bingaman, a 349-pound middle guard, anchored the defense until the arrival of Schmidt, the first of the NFL's great middle linebackers. Yale Lary was among the league's best safeties and punters.

But Layne loved Walker the most — despite Walker's clean living. "He didn't do what I did," Layne said. Layne and Walker were high school teammates in Dallas, went their separate ways in college, joined the Merchant Marines together, then ended up as teammates with the Lions. Together, they made up an electric backfield. Walker, who became a Texas folk hero by winning the Heisman Trophy at Southern Methodist, was the

OCT. 8, 1953: RED WINGS CENTER DUTCH REIBEL ASSISTED ON ALL FOUR GOALS IN HIS NHL DEBUT,
A 4-1 VICTORY OVER THE NEW YORK RANGERS.

THE MOST FAMOUS PHOTOGRAPH IN DETROIT LIONS HISTORY: PACKERS QUARTERBACK BART STARR GOT STUFFED BY A PRIDE OF LIONS ON THANKSGIVING DAY 1962 — THE ONLY GAME GREEN BAY LOST THAT YEAR. THE LIONS FINISHED SECOND TO GREEN BAY IN 1960, '61 AND '62.

NFL's leading scorer in 1950, his rookie season, and again in '55. Although he played only six seasons, ending his career early in an attempt to save his first marriage, he left a lasting legacy.

"He wasn't the fastest guy in the world," said end Leon Hart, who won the Heisman at Notre Dame the season after Walker. "But he had quickness and a change of pace and change of direction. He had football savvy." And a sense of timing.

"He was the greatest clutch player I ever saw," Layne said. "I'll tell ya, if we were ahead, 28-0, or something, you might not notice Doak on the field. But if it was a close game, everybody knew he was there, and he would be the difference."

The Lions needed clutch players like Layne and Walker and Schmidt and Christiansen. Rarely did they blow away teams, even in their best years. Their coach, Raymond (Buddy) Parker, didn't seem to want them to. Parker was a sad enigma, a man nobody understood or really knew. He was strangely different — friendly but distant, as if he were constantly preoccupied. He was properly intense, as coaches were supposed to be, but always seemed lonely, humorless.

"I never figured him out," said Nick Kerbawy, then the Lions' general manager and as close a confidant as Parker would allow. "He was the kind of guy who might say hello on the first day of the season and good-bye on the last — except some years, he might forget to say good-bye. He was outrageously superstitious, and he had a temper. But nobody ever said he was cruel."

Somewhere in Parker's odd mind was football genius. Although Cleveland's Paul Brown was widely acknowledged as the league's leading coach, Parker beat him in four of their five meetings while Parker was Lions coach. And Parker, not Brown, originated the concept of the two-minute offense. "I noticed how so many teams let down the last two minutes," Parker said. "It seemed you could get things done then that you couldn't in the other 56 minutes of play. So we drilled on it every day."

Under Parker, the Lions were amazingly deceptive, rarely performing well in the first half. Crowds often called for Parker to replace Layne, whose throws always wobbled and often missed their early targets. They needed Parker's patience. He knew the game plan. He knew how to make adjustments so that, as Kerbawy said, "in the second half the Lions always seemed to be a different team." He knew Layne.

"Nobody knew quarterbacking like Layne," Karras said. "The great thing about him was that he could break down a rival team, dissect it, in three quarters. They said he was a great two-minute man, but the reason was that he knew where he could go to get his

Detroit Lions

Courtesy Betty Steen

Detroit Free Press

UNSUNG HEROES (CLOCKWISE FROM TOP): JACK CHRISTIANSEN (1951-58) WAS ONE OF THE BEST PASS DEFENDERS AND KICK RETURNERS IN THE LEAGUE; LOU CREEKMUR (1950-59) WAS A TACKLE WHOSE PRIMARY JOB WAS PROTECTING BOBBY LAYNE; LES BINGAMAN (1948-54) WAS A 349-POUND MIDDLE GUARD WHO DOMINATED THE LINE OF SCRIMMAGE. CHRISTIANSEN AND CREEKMUR MADE THE PRO FOOTBALL HALL OF FAME.

NOV. 14, 1953: MSU WON ITS FIRST BIG TEN MEETING WITH MICHIGAN, 14-6, AND THE FIRST PAUL BUNYAN TROPHY. THE 9-1 SPARTANS LATER BEAT UCLA IN THEIR FIRST ROSE BOWL, 28-20, IN BIGGIE MUNN'S FINAL GAME AS COACH.

Detroit Free Press

DICK TRIPP/Detroit Free Press

JOE SCHMIDT, THE LIONS' MIDDLE LINEBACKER IN 1953-65, WAS A 10-TIME ALL-PRO AND CAPTAIN WHO SPARKED A DEFENSE THAT CONSISTENTLY WAS RATED AMONG THE BEST IN THE NFL.

points when he absolutely had to. Often, he would throw to one side or the other with short passes, not really caring whether he completed the pass or not, just to see the defensive reaction. That's why he looked so bad at times. And then, when he needed, he knew just where to strike."

Layne's Lions were more than tight-knit; they often were the most dramatic team in sports.

TWIN TITLES

Walker was the hero of the '52 title game, a 17-7 victory that gave the Lions their first NFL championship since '35. He missed five games that season with a hamstring injury. But he came back to throw a 24-yard touchdown pass to Hart as the Lions beat Los Angeles in a divisional playoff, 31-21. He then baffled the Browns with a sensational run the next week.

After Layne scored on a second-quarter sneak to give the Lions a 7-0 halftime lead, Walker made the crowd at Cleveland Stadium gasp. He took a handoff from Layne, shook off a tackle by Bert Rechichar and eluded the rest of the Browns on his way to a 67-yard touchdown. It was his first TD of the season.

"He literally ran through the whole Cleveland team," Thomas said. "I don't know how 11 guys missed him, but he was like that. He made things happen. He had uncanny field vision, but I was always amazed how he survived. He wasn't particularly big."

No. Walker weighed 167 pounds. But he was huge for Detroit that day, the best of his career. "That Cleveland game was my biggest thrill in football, because it was a great climax to a great Lions season," Walker said. "To take the championship back to Detroit, to have the kind of year we had, the way we were treated by the fans, well, nothing could match it."

DEC. 27, 1953: QUARTERBACK BOBBY LAYNE DROVE THE LIONS 80 YARDS FOR THE WINNING SCORE, A 33-YARD PASS TO JIM DORAN WITH 2:08 LEFT, AND DETROIT BEAT CLEVELAND, 17-16, FOR ITS SECOND STRAIGHT NFL TITLE.

GEORGE GELLATLY/NFL Photos

DOAK WALKER, A HEISMAN TROPHY WINNER FROM SOUTHERN METHODIST, WON TWO NFL TITLES DURING HIS SIX SEASONS WITH THE LIONS. HE DID IT ALL — RUN, CATCH, PASS, KICK AND PLAY DEFENSE. WITH BOBBY LAYNE HOLDING, WALKER KICKED THE EXTRA POINT THAT WON THE 1953 TITLE GAME.

Well, nothing but the '53 title game, one of the century's classics, a 17-16 victory that gave the Lions their second straight title. This time, Walker watched as Layne showed the nation his two-minute-drill skills.

The Browns finished that regular season 11-1. They had a potent passing combination of Otto Graham to Dante Lavelli. They were so feared, the wives of the defending champions wore green-dyed jockstraps on their heads for good luck. "Here possibly are the two best teams to meet for the championship," NFL commissioner Bert Bell said.

On a cool Sunday afternoon at Briggs Stadium, Lou Groza kicked a 43-yard field goal to give Cleveland a 16-10 lead in the fourth quarter. The Lions took over on their 20-yard line with 4:10 to play. Layne stepped into the huddle. "Awright, fellas," he said. "Y'all block, and ol' Bobby'll pass you *raht* to the championship."

The Browns were expecting Layne to pass to Walker or end Dorne Dibble, because defensive end Jim Doran, subbing for the injured Hart, had caught only six passes all season. So sure enough, Layne went to Doran. Three times. His last pass to Doran was a 33-yard floater over Warren Lahr for a touchdown with 2:08 remaining. "Bobby never lost a game in his life," Walker said. "Time just ran out on him."

Two minutes. Two titles.

Soon, Layne was a national story. He even became the first professional football player to make the cover of Time. But the Lions' bid for what would have been a record three consecutive championships died in '54, when Cleveland wreaked revenge on them by winning the title game, 56-10, intercepting Layne six times. And then things started to go sour. Injuries to Layne caused the Lions to drop to last place in '55 and to lose a season-ending showdown with Chicago for the division crown in '56.

Only the breathtaking '57 season interrupted the Lions' free fall, which would ground them in the NFL's gutter for decades.

Detroit Free Press

APRIL 16, 1954: TONY LESWICK'S WINNER AT 4:29 OF OVERTIME IN GAME 7 BEAT MONTREAL, 2-1, AND BROUGHT THE STANLEY CUP HOME TO DETROIT AFTER A YEAR'S ABSENCE.

Burton Historical Collection

STRANGE DAYS

Parker might have been the most tolerant coach the NFL ever had seen. As Layne led the Lions in and out of watering holes, they broke all sorts of team rules. But Parker looked the other way. "Once at training camp," Kerbawy said, "an assistant coach came to Parker with a list of players who had missed bed check the night before. Parker was really upset. He told the coach to mind his own business: 'When I want a bed check, I'll take it.'"

Eventually, however, everything caught up with him. During training camp in '57, Parker sparked perhaps the team's best season of the century by announcing his resignation at a "Meet the Lions" banquet at the Statler Hotel. "I have a situation here I cannot handle," Parker told the stunned audience. "This is the worst team in training camp I have ever seen. The material is all right, but the team is dead. I don't want to get involved in another losing season, so I'm leaving Detroit football. I'm leaving tonight."

With that, Parker stepped down from the podium and disappeared. The Lions had one big strike against them, and quite a few fans figured the second strike immediately followed when the club named assistant coach George Wilson as Parker's replacement. Wilson was a nice guy, an end on the Chicago Bears' championship teams of the early '40s. But he never had been more than a part-time coach for the Lions, helping the ends and backs during the season, selling mill supplies and playing golf the rest of the year. He was a big man, quiet, gentle. Most people liked him, but few thought he could lead a team to a title.

Which was just what Wilson did, of course.

When the regular season began, Layne shared his starting duties with Tobin Rote, acquired as insurance against Layne's history of injuries. The Lions lost their opener in Baltimore, then rebounded to win their next two games. Week 4 featured a wild rematch with the Colts. Johnny Unitas threw four touchdown passes as Baltimore amassed a 27-3 lead on a gray, overcast day at Briggs Stadium. Time for Layne to go to work. He threw three touchdown passes to Howard (Hopalong) Cassady, including one in the final seconds, to give the Lions a 31-27 victory. The Lions split their next six games, and in their final home game, Layne suffered a broken right ankle against Cleveland.

Rote took over, and the Lions never weakened. He finished off a 20-7 victory over the Browns, beat the Bears with three touchdown passes the next week, then led

Detroit Lions

AT TOP: JOE SCHMIDT (NO. 56) AND LIONS TEAMMATES POUNCE ON CLEVELAND'S LEW CARPENTER, A FORMER LION, DURING THE 1957 TITLE GAME, WHICH THE LIONS WON, 59-14. ANOTHER CHAMPIONSHIP MOMENT CAME IN 1953 WHEN FANS TORE DOWN THE GOALPOSTS AFTER BOBBY LAYNE RALLIED THE LIONS IN THE CLOSING MINUTES FOR A 17-16 VICTORY OVER THE BROWNS.

Detroit Free Press

BOBBY LAYNE, PICTURED WITH TEAM PRESIDENT EDWIN ANDERSON, PICKED UP HIS SHARE OF HARDWARE DURING EIGHT-PLUS SEASONS WITH THE LIONS.

MARCH 17, 1955: THE WINGS WON BY FORFEIT IN MONTREAL. THE GAME WAS STOPPED AFTER ONE PERIOD
BECAUSE OF RIOTING FANS PROTESTING ROCKET RICHARD'S SUSPENSION FOR THE END OF THE REGULAR SEASON AND THE PLAYOFFS.

the Lions to their most thrilling comeback victory ever — just as Layne might have. In a special playoff to determine the Western Division crown, the Lions trailed San Francisco on the road early in the third quarter, 27-7. At halftime, the 49ers already had been celebrating, their chortles passing through thin walls into the Lions' den. "All we could do was sit and listen," Rote said. The Lions stormed back in anger and won, 31-27.

"I don't believe it," said Karras, standing as a guest on the sidelines, just a fresh-faced draft pick out of Iowa.

"You better!" shouted Layne, on crutches. "You better believe it!"

No comebacks were needed in the title game against Cleveland. Wilson outcoached Brown, and the Lions played with the tough insouciance that was their trademark. They destroyed the Browns at Briggs Stadium, 59-14. The men Parker had deserted weren't so bad, after all. Schmidt, leader of the bloody-nosed defenders, was waltzed around the field on the shoulders of fans. All the while, he clutched the game ball desperately to his chest. "They weren't after me," he said of the fans. "They wanted that ball."

Detroit Free Press

BUDDY PARKER MADE A SURPRISE EXIT AS LIONS COACH. "I'M LEAVING TONIGHT," HE TOLD A STUNNED AUDIENCE AT A PRESEASON BANQUET IN 1957. BEFORE LONG, PARKER WAS THE COACH OF THE PITTSBURGH STEELERS, WHERE HE WAS 51-47-6 IN EIGHT SEASONS. IN FIVE OF THOSE YEARS, HIS QUARTERBACK WAS ROBERT LAWRENCE LAYNE.

For reasons that never were explained fully, they traded Layne to the Pittsburgh Steelers and limped to a 4-7-1 finish. Immediately, the team's chemistry went from steady to volatile. "When Bobby was traded, the ballplayers in Detroit changed," Jimmy David said. "I just went ahead and retired a year later in 1959. The fun of playing was gone. The concept of all for one and one for all was gone."

After that, if fans wanted to watch several years' worth of winning football, they would have to look to a man named Bo instead of one named Bobby. If they wanted to see success at the corner of Michigan and Trumbull, they would have to buy Tigers tickets. The Lions, who moved into the Pontiac Silverdome in '75, didn't host another playoff game for more than three decades. Once, after president Edwin Anderson allowed their first three draft picks to sign with a rival league, the players filled an old uniform with smelly socks and dirty underwear, painted Anderson's face on the effigy, and hung it from the goalposts at Briggs Stadium in protest.

On Thanksgiving Day in '62, at renamed Tiger Stadium, the Lions sprinted out to a 26-0 lead and earned

Wilson was pleased. "The big thing about them is that they never quit," he said slowly, after bathing his face in cold water afterward. "I guess this is the fightingest team I ever saw." Somewhere else in the locker room, end Steve Junker smiled and said: "It couldn't be much better, could it?"

He had no idea how right he was.

The next season, the Lions made like the Wings, beginning a rapid decline because of ill-advised moves by management.

an emotional 26-14 victory over the Green Bay Packers, who were defending their first NFL championship for coach Vince Lombardi. Never again would a Lombardi team be so humbled. "It was a day when the Lions could have beaten any team they played," Wilson said. But it also was a day when the Lions tasted true triumph for the last time. At century's end, despite featuring a smattering of stars, they still were without a fifth NFL championship. ◆

APRIL 14, 1955: ALEX DELVECCHIO SCORED TWICE AS THE WINGS WON THEIR SEVENTH STANLEY CUP WITH A 3-1 VICTORY OVER MONTREAL IN GAME 7 AT HOME.

Tobin Rote got a lift after he took over for injured quarterback Bobby Layne and lifted the Lions to their fourth NFL championship in 1957. Rote completed 12 of 19 passes for 280 yards and four touchdowns and ran for a touchdown in the 59-14 whipping of the Browns.

Richard Bak Collection

Jan. 2, 1956: Michigan State scored a 17-14 Rose Bowl victory over UCLA when Dave Kaiser kicked the winning 41-yard field goal with seven seconds left.

Win some, dispute some

Mad magicians

Bentley Historical Library

THERE WAS NO STOPPING MICHIGAN'S 1947 BACKFIELD OF (FROM LEFT) BUMP ELLIOTT, JACK WEISENBURGER, HOWARD YERGES AND BOB CHAPPUIS, BECAUSE THE WOLVERINES RAN THE SINGLE WING TO PERFECTION.

BY MICHAEL ROSENBERG

As Michigan's Board in Control of Intercollegiate Athletics met to determine who would succeed Harry Kipke as football coach for the 1938 season, there were two candidates. One was Navy coach Tom Hamilton, the favorite of athletic director Fielding H. Yost.

The other was a reserved, private coach from Princeton named Herbert Orrin (Fritz) Crisler. Yost pushed for Hamilton, but Crisler got the job, with the promise that he would someday replace Yost as athletic director. It was one of the best hirings Michigan ever made. In Ann Arbor, Crisler changed more than the college football landscape. He changed the game.

Crisler was not just Michigan's most innovative coach ever. He was one of the most creative coaches in football history. The winged helmet? He designed it. Two-platoon football? He invented it. The single-wing offense? He perfected it.

OCT. 6, 1956: MICHIGAN STADIUM'S CAPACITY HIT SIX FIGURES FOR THE FIRST TIME, AND 101,001 WATCHED MICHIGAN STATE BEAT THE WOLVERINES, 9-0.

And the greatest team of all time? He might have coached it.

The 1947 Wolverines went 10-0 and outscored their opponents, 394-53. They are always mentioned as one of the best teams in Big Ten history, and some argue they were *the* best. Almost 50 years later, Sports Illustrated wrote a story on what the magazine determined was the finest team of all time, a squad that dominated everybody in 1947.

Sports Illustrated picked Notre Dame.

A few folks who spent that year in Ann Arbor would argue with that. They're backed up by the Associated Press voters from that season, who concluded — belatedly, after much waffling — that the Wolverines were better than the Irish.

The two teams see-sawed at No. 1 all season, with the Wolverines grabbing the top spot after their eighth game of the season, a 40-6 waxing of Wisconsin in Madison. The next week, U-M beat its biggest rival, Ohio State, 21-0 — and dropped to No. 2.

That's because Notre Dame finished its season with an even bigger thumping of *its* biggest rival, Southern Cal. The Fighting Irish beat the Trojans, 38-7, and since USC was more highly regarded than Ohio State, Notre Dame went to No. 1 in the AP poll.

That was supposed to be it. The AP had held its final poll. Notre Dame was No. 1, and as was their custom, the Irish were not going to a bowl that season. But U-M was. The Wolverines were headed to Pasadena, Calif., for the Rose Bowl against Southern Cal, determined to prove, if only to themselves, that they composed the best team in the land.

U-M, a 15-point favorite, scored on a Jack Weisenburger one-yard plunge in the first quarter, then scored again in the second quarter on another Weisenburger one-yard run. Then Bob Chappuis threw an 11-yard touchdown pass to Bump Elliott. And then Chappuis hit Howard Yerges for 18 yards and another score. It was 28-0, and the game was not even three quarters old.

Weisenburger ran for his third one-yard touchdown early in the fourth quarter, and Michigan completed two more touchdown passes to make it a 49-0 final. Forty-six years earlier, in its only previous bowl, U-M had beaten Stanford in the first Rose Bowl, also by a 49-0 score. (Sports writer Braven Dyer of the Los Angeles Times wryly noted that U-M showed "no improvement.")

U-M had gained 491 yards and held Southern Cal to 133.

Bentley Historical Library

INNOVATIVE FRITZ CRISLER CAPPED 10 YEARS AS MICHIGAN'S COACH WITH A 10-0 SEASON IN 1947. HIS FINAL RECORD WAS 71-16-3.

Notre Dame had swiped the top ranking after beating the Trojans by 31, and now the Wolverines had responded by beating the same team by 49. The AP voters, stunned by how thoroughly Michigan dominated the Trojans, held a special poll after the Rose Bowl. The Wolverines jumped to the top of the poll, earning 226 votes to Notre Dame's 119, but the AP said that its first "final" poll, which had Notre Dame on top, was the one that counted.

Forget about polls being split. This was a single poll that was split. To this day, both schools claim the 1947 national title.

Regardless of whether U-M was better than Notre Dame, there was little question the Wolverines had begun to redefine the game. Crisler's single-wing offense was as difficult to defend as any in history to that point.

"We did a lot of fakes, spinning and handing off," Chappuis recalled 50 years later. "The ball kept exchanging hands. The defense had trouble figuring out who had the ball."

Chappuis finished second in the Heisman Trophy balloting that year, behind Johnny Lujack of — who else? — Notre Dame. But Chappuis wasn't even the most valuable player on his own team. Bump Elliott was, and Elliott was Big Ten MVP as well. Apparently nobody could definitively decide on anything in 1947.

There was no such problem in 1948. Crisler had retired as coach, Chappuis and Elliott had graduated, but U-M was almost as dominant as it was in 1947. Bennie Oosterbaan, a former three-time All-America at U-M, took over for Crisler, and Oosterbaan proved to be as adept on the sideline as he was on the field.

Michigan couldn't go to the Rose Bowl that year because Big Ten rules prohibited back-to-back appearances, but the Wolverines won all nine of their games and claimed the national title. Pete Elliott took over for Chappuis at quarterback and made All-America. Alvin Wistert, a 32-year-old U.S. Marine Corps veteran, was an All-America at tackle, the third of the Wistert brothers to receive such recognition. U-M end Richard Rifenburg also made All-America that year.

"The difference is that the '48 team didn't have as much depth as the '47 team," Bump Elliott said. "The '47 team was two- or three-deep at every position. A lot of the key players changed, but the performance was still very good."

APRIL 17, 1957: THE NBA BOARD OF GOVERNORS
APPROVED THE FT. WAYNE PISTONS' MOVE TO DETROIT.

Bentley Historical Library

IN THE 1948 ROSE BOWL, FRITZ
CRISLER'S WOLVERINES MAULED
SOUTHERN CAL, 49-0. HALFBACK BOB
CHAPPUIS, WHO GRACED THE COVER OF
TIME AND FINISHED SECOND IN VOTING
FOR THE HEISMAN, RUSHED FOR 91
YARDS AND PASSED FOR ANOTHER 139
YARDS, INCLUDING TWO TOUCHDOWNS.

Although the '48 team was coached by Oosterbaan, it owed a great debt to Crisler. It solidified the return of U-M football to preeminence.

None of Kipke's final four teams had winning records. Crisler quickly turned things around, but championships were tough to come by. In Crisler's first eight seasons, U-M never finished worse than 7-3, but the Wolverines failed to win a Big Ten title outright. That was mostly a function of the conference's high quality. In 1940, the year Tom Harmon won the Heisman, the Wolverines were second in the Big Ten — and third in the country. From 1941 to 1946, they never finished lower than ninth in the AP poll, but their co-Big Ten title with Purdue in 1943 was the best they could do in the conference.

By the time the national title teams took the field, Crisler already had earned respect as one of the country's best coaches. He had secured his legacy in 1945, as his team prepared for top-ranked Army. In the week leading up to the game, Crisler made a decision that changed football so dramatically, it's difficult to understand now why nobody else thought of it.

Traditionally, players competed for the entire game; for most of the early part of the century, that was the rule. But because so many potential college football players were serving in World War II, rules were changed in 1941 to allow for liberal substitution. The change was designed to help short-stocked teams compete. Crisler was the first to recognize that by resting players, they would have more energy and their weaknesses wouldn't hurt the team. The Wolverines lost to Army that day, 28-7, at Yankee Stadium, but a revolution was afoot.

Together with the single wing, the two-platoon system would be pivotal in U-M's unbeaten 1947 season. With their best offensive players concentrating on offense, the Wolverines led the nation in total offense (412.7 yards a game) and passing (173.9).

Crisler, a former premed student at the University of Chicago, was held in awe by his players. They called him "The Lord." Time magazine, which featured Chappuis on its cover in 1947, wrote: "The boys say that it never rains in Ann Arbor before 6 p.m. when football practice is over; Crisler won't let it."

Crisler's guarded nature made him more imposing. Few people got to know him. But his players formed bonds that were unusually close, and as time went on, the 1947 team held reunions every five years. In 1992, at their 45-year reunion, they decided to do something special for their 50-year reunion. They went back to Pasadena for the Rose Bowl, to the same stadium where they had dominated Southern Cal 50 years earlier.

"Almost every game was a highlight for me because I just loved being able to play with those guys," Weisenburger said at the reunion. "But scoring three touchdowns in the Rose Bowl certainly was a thrill."

Weisenburger and his contemporaries were in for another thrill in Pasadena: The 1997 U-M team joined them there and captured their school's first national title since 1948. Well, half a national title. Nebraska beat Tennessee in the Orange Bowl, 42-17, and jumped to No. 1 in the coaches' poll. But as Weisenburger and Co. could tell you, that doesn't matter much. In time, poll controversies fade and champions are remembered as champions. ◆

Bentley Historical Library

FILM STAR MARLENE DIETRICH MADE A PASS AT SOME MICHIGAN MEN BEFORE THE 1948 GAME; FROM LEFT, BUMP ELLIOTT, BOB CHAPPUIS AND BRUCE HILKENE.

JULIAN H. GONZALEZ/Detroit Free Press

FIFTY YEARS LATER, TEAMMATES FROM 1947 — JOHN GHINDIA (NO. 23), THEN A SOPHOMORE QUARTERBACK, AND QUENTIN SICKELS (NO. 62), A JUNIOR GUARD — WERE BACK AT THEIR FIELD OF DREAMS TO WATCH THE WOLVERINES OF 1997 CAP ANOTHER PERFECT SEASON AT THE ROSE BOWL.

AUG. 12, 1957: BUDDY PARKER — THE LIONS' MOST SUCCESSFUL COACH WITH A .671 WINNING PERCENTAGE AND TWO CHAMPIONSHIPS — RESIGNED AND WAS REPLACED BY GEORGE WILSON.

Roses that bloomed in the snow

Frozen tundra

By George Puscas

As Tony Momsen recalled, there was no reason to expect that Nov. 25, 1950, would become a historic day in college football.

"We'd stayed overnight in Toledo," Momsen said, "and we walked around downtown in the morning, waiting for the train to leave. The weather was fine."

Within a few hours, though, Momsen and the Wolverines would play and win one of the most extraordinary games in the history of college football.

At the time, it was said that no football game was played under worse conditions. But there was more . . .

Poets of the sports pages called it the day that roses bloomed in the snow. Football students remember the game because:

Michigan beat Ohio State, 9-3, without gaining a first down.

Or a yard passing.

Or completing a pass.

The Wolverines gained only 27 yards.

And punted 24 times.

All of it brought Michigan a fourth straight Big Ten championship and sent the Wolverines to the Rose Bowl, where they beat California and proved themselves truly the champions of the West.

It was a remarkable day in football for many reasons, most of them springing from the worst snowstorm to hit the Ohio State campus since 1913.

Little did Momsen, a senior center, or his U-M teammates wandering the Toledo streets that morning realize what awaited them in Columbus.

Already it was snowing so heavily that Richard Larkins, the OSU athletic director, called Fritz Crisler, the U-M athletic director, and offered to postpone the game.

Eventually, they decided to play simply because they

Ohio State University Archives

The "Snow Bowl" pitted Michigan against Ohio State at Columbus on Nov. 25, 1950.

couldn't remember a conference game being postponed.

"I suppose you have to mention the circumstances to appreciate all that happened that day," Momsen said 40 years later. "We'd been beaten several times, so we weren't considered in the running for anything. We certainly weren't thinking about going to the Rose Bowl."

Entering the game, Michigan was 4-3-1 overall, 3-1-1 in the conference.

To get to Pasadena, the Wolverines needed to beat OSU, a 13-point favorite, and get a great boost in Evanston, Ill. Northwestern had to upset second-place Illinois, a 17-point favorite. All in all, it was an improbable parlay.

"It was bitter cold in Columbus, about 15 degrees, with the wind about 25 miles per hour," Momsen said. "Our game was about 45 minutes late starting because they had trouble getting the tarp off the field. Somebody later said a foot of snow fell during the game. But I'll never forget the cold, or how, at times, you couldn't even see the people in the stands.

"The only signals anybody ever got from our bench were reminders to just hang onto the ball."

The Wolverines lost only one fumble. But Chuck Ortmann's first punt was an omen for both teams — it was blocked.

Ohio State tackle Bob Momsen, Tony's younger brother, smacked down Ortmann's kick at the Wolverines' 8. Shortly, the Buckeyes had a 3-0 lead on a field goal by Vic Janowicz.

"I don't think it was tough for the coaches to decide what our strategy would be in that game," Tony Momsen said. "It was so cold and windy you couldn't throw the ball or go anywhere with it. It was enough to hang onto it.

"So we just ran the ball a play or two and punted. When we got it back, we'd run it once or twice and kick it away again. What else could you do?"

Late in the first quarter, the Wolverines retaliated when Al Wahl blocked Janowicz's punt back through the end zone for

Oct. 23, 1957: The Pistons played their first game in Detroit, a 105-94 loss to Boston at Olympia Stadium.

MICHIGAN'S VICTORY OVER THE BUCKEYES AND THE ELEMENTS SENT U-M TO SUNNY PASADENA, WHERE THEY ICED CALIFORNIA, 14-6, IN THE ROSE BOWL.

a safety. Ohio State led, 3-2.

Then, in the final minute of the first half . . .

"They were punting from about their 20-yard line and I came from the right side," Tony Momsen said. "I had a clear shot at him — Vic Janowicz.

"I just busted through; I don't know that anybody touched me. The ball hit me and bounced back into their end zone, and I dived and missed it and dived again. Dick McWilliams jumped on top of me and I said, 'Hey, Dick, I've got it, I've got the ball!' He'd buried me in about two feet of snow.

"At halftime, we didn't figure anything; we were just glad to get in the locker room and warm up. I don't think it stopped snowing until Monday."

More than 30,000 ticket-holders never showed up to watch. And when the teams came out to play the second half, only a small portion of the original 50,000 spectators remained.

"Well, it wasn't only that it was so cold and impossible to enjoy," Momsen said. "But most of the time, you couldn't see anything or anybody."

Neither team scored or threatened in the second half. For Michigan, the strategy was simple: punt and pray.

The teams combined for 45 punts and 68 total yards.

Before the Wolverines left Columbus, they knew their next trip would be to the Rose Bowl.

A sleet storm and bitter cold in Evanston grounded the Illini, and Northwestern completed a golden double for U-M with a 14-7 upset.

"We heard about it in the locker room," Momsen said, "and there was a lot of screaming and hollering. We never expected to be going to the Rose Bowl that year.

"I never really thought the game might go down in history. There always was some talk about it, but it just seemed to get bigger and bigger as years went by."

DEC. 29, 1957: THE LIONS WON THEIR FOURTH NFL TITLE, 59-14,
OVER CLEVELAND IN BRIGGS STADIUM.

A grand experiment

Biggie & Duffy

BY DREW SHARP

John Hannah, president at Michigan State College, had the dream of joining the hallowed Big Ten Conference in the late 1940s and changing the way we all see football. Most people laughed off the land-grant school: Stick to your agricultural studies, your cattle experiments and your formulas for homogenizing milk, Aggies. Leave the big-time athletics to the big-timers.

But Hannah was unbowed, determined to see his dream come true. Through Hannah's sheer will, Michigan State constructed the facilities necessary to join the conference. And then the president hired a football coach he thought shared his vision of greatness — Biggie Munn.

Hannah and Munn became a marriage made in green-and-white heaven.

Against Michigan's wishes, Michigan State finally was admitted to the Big Ten in 1949 and played its first conference football game in 1953. A rivalry was born.

Hannah is regarded as the father of Michigan State University, which Michigan State College became in 1955. More athletic than academic icon, Hannah became one of the few university presidents to have his "number" retired for his contributions to the athletic department. He used sports as a springboard to gain attention for his institution. He also believed in innovation, daring to blaze new trails that others were hesitant to tread.

Hannah wanted the Spartans to dominate as soon as they joined the Big Ten, and winning meant placing no boundaries on procuring the finest players available. Hannah insisted that East Lansing embrace athletes unwanted elsewhere.

Michigan State's football legacy of the 1950s extends far beyond a 28-game winning streak, a national championship in 1952, Rose Bowl victories in 1954 and 1956, and a growing reputation as one of the nation's finest college programs. The

Michigan State University

BIGGIE MUNN (RIGHT) COACHED THE SPARTANS FOR SEVEN SEASONS. IN 1954, DUFFY DAUGHERTY TOOK THE BALL AND RAN WITH IT FOR ANOTHER 19 SEASONS.

Spartans were at the forefront of the burgeoning civil rights movement, becoming a visible symbol of desegregation.

Black players that other schools shunned, Michigan State welcomed with open arms.

As a 19-year-old Army private, Clarence Underwood assumed he could pursue a college degree only in his native South. After all, that's where the black schools were in this illusory separate-but-equal America of the 1950s.

Little did Underwood know that the window to a new world would be a football game. During a break from guard duty at Ft. Bragg, N.C., in January 1954, Underwood watched the Rose Bowl on television. The Alabamian's jaw dropped as he watched Michigan State play UCLA. Blacks and whites were playing on the same team, hugging each other and working together.

"As soon as I saw that, I knew that Michigan State was the place for me," said Underwood, who eventually would become a longtime MSU athletic administrator. "Knowing that such a seemingly amiable climate existed was foreign to most blacks at that time, especially from the South. You have to wonder how many other black athletes and students were positively influenced about Michigan State by watching that game."

The Spartans developed tackle Gideon Smith (1913-15), possibly the first black professional football player, and in 1934 were the first major team to have at least three black players. That came when the vast majority of schools had none. The first black NFL quarterback — Willie Thrower, with the Chicago Bears in 1953 — played for Michigan State during its 1952 national championship season.

"No school was more receptive to black players at that time than Michigan State," said Henry Bullough, a Spartans guard in 1952-54 and an assistant to Duffy Daugherty in 1959-69. "You look at other teams in the Big Ten in the early '50s

MARCH 27, 1958: THE PISTONS FINISHED THEIR FIRST SEASON IN DETROIT WITH A 120-96 LOSS TO ST. LOUIS, DROPPING THE WESTERN FINALS, 4-1. GEORGE YARDLEY WON THE NBA SCORING TITLE WITH 2,001 POINTS (28.7 PER GAME).

THE SPARTANS OF 1953 RODE THE PONY BACKFIELD (FROM LEFT) OF HALFBACK BILLY WELLS, FULLBACK EVAN SLONAC, HALFBACK LEROY BOLDEN AND QUARTERBACK TOM YEWCIC ALL THE WAY TO A ROSE BOWL VICTORY OVER UCLA.

Michigan State University

and they probably averaged four or five blacks on their entire team. We'd have five or six starting alone. We wanted to provide an opportunity to those who were denied one."

Munn and Minnesota coach Murray Warmath were considered the primary architects in this bold experiment. Their teams were the first in the '50s to develop a strong recruiting base among Southern blacks.

"We changed the rules, changed the game and changed some attitudes," said tackle Don Coleman, who became the Spartans' first black football All-America in 1951. "What we did at Michigan State helped everyone take a step closer to better understanding those who before that had no prior contact with one another."

It wasn't easy for Coleman and his black teammates. Some endured vicious verbal assaults, even from home fans. The abuse got so bad once that one white player reportedly told an MSU fan that if he didn't shut his mouth, he would shut it for him. Some schools refused to play the Spartans because of their black players.

"Biggie was really the first coach to get Michigan State actively involved in bringing in black players," said Larry Bielat, an MSU quarterback in 1957-59, an assistant coach in 1983-89 and later a radio analyst. "Biggie opened the door, but it was Duffy who blew it wide open."

Daugherty was Munn's line coach. And when Munn surprisingly retired after the Spartans' Rose Bowl victory over UCLA in 1954, Daugherty was promoted to head coach. He remained for 19 years, becoming one of college football's national treasures, winning a school-record 109 games, two conference titles and one national championship.

Daugherty, the smooth-talking, sweet-smiling politician, cultivated alliances with many black high school coaches in the South. When Daugherty replaced Munn, blacks were excluded from national coaching conventions and seminars. Daugherty saw an opening.

Five years later, he began his own seminars for black coaches and dispatched Bullough and fellow assistants Dan Boisture and Cal Stoll to Texas, Alabama, Mississippi,

JUNE 6, 1958: ELEVEN YEARS AFTER JACKIE ROBINSON BROKE BASEBALL'S COLOR LINE WITH BROOKLYN, THE TIGERS CALLED UP OZZIE VIRGIL, LEAVING THE BOSTON RED SOX AS BASEBALL'S ONLY ALL-WHITE TEAM.

ONE OF THE MOST FAMOUS PLAYS IN MICHIGAN STATE HISTORY: THE SPARTANS SCORED 21 UNANSWERED POINTS AFTER ELLIS DUCKETT BLOCKED A UCLA PUNT IN THE 1954 ROSE BOWL. THE SPARTANS TURNED A 14-0 DEFICIT INTO A 28-20 VICTORY.

Georgia and South Carolina to share their expertise with black high school and small-college coaches.

That segregationist hard-liner in the houndstooth hat, Bear Bryant, tried to band the Southern schools together in a boycott of Michigan State. After the Spartans played Texas Christian in 1953, they couldn't get another Southern team on the schedule until Texas A&M in 1959.

"Some will argue that Duffy's sole motivation in courting the black coaches was only to win games, and that wasn't true," Bullough said. "This was also a very compassionate man who saw something that was wrong. A door was closed to many people, and he helped open it."

Michigan State was instrumental in finally opening those doors at Southern schools.

"You better believe we had a lot to do with that," Underwood said. "Alabama and those other schools down there got to the point where if they didn't accept blacks, they would get beaten by them on the field. I guess the threat of losing makes you swallow your prejudices."

Michigan State's pipeline to the South lasted well into the '60s. It helped the Spartans land perhaps their two greatest players — Bubba Smith and George Webster.

"Michigan State played a big, big role in helping everyone accept integration in the sport," Webster said. "Back in the '50s, a black kid down South probably thought he wouldn't have that opportunity to play at a big school like that. It helped open the door."

ROSES AND THE STREAK

Considering the way the Spartans introduced themselves to the Big Ten in the early '50s, the rest of the conference

JUNE 23, 1958: BILLY CASPER WON THE INAUGURAL BUICK OPEN AT WARWICK HILLS COUNTRY CLUB AND COLLECTED $9,000 FROM THE $52,000 PURSE.

probably wished it never answered that door when Hannah came knocking.

Although the Spartans weren't eligible for the Big Ten championship until 1953, they nonetheless dominated the conference. Michigan State was a combined 26-1 for 1950-52 — far and away the best record in the Big Ten. MSU won its first national championship in '52 after completing back-to-back unbeaten seasons.

Munn revolutionized college offense with the Spartans' overall speed in 1952, including its agile, fluid linemen. Coleman personified that speed; the ripple effect was that coaches everywhere started looking for more quickness at the line. "That team was ahead of its time," Coleman said.

The Spartans finally were eligible for the Big Ten championship in 1953, and shared it with Illinois. Their first Rose Bowl appearance was their second bowl. The first was the Orange Bowl against Auburn after the 1937 season.

Notre Dame may have had the Four Horsemen, but Michigan State had the Pony Backfield — quarterback Tom Yewcic, halfbacks LeRoy Bolden and Billy Wells, and fullback Evan Slonac.

In six conference games in 1953, the Spartans outscored their opponents, 131-50. That team set many school offensive records that stood for 25 years, until the 1978 team of Eddie Smith and Kirk Gibson shared the Big Ten title with Michigan.

When Munn arrived in East Lansing in 1947, he began posting winning seasons immediately. The Spartans, 6-2-2 in '48, were ranked in the final Associated Press poll for the first time, at 14th. Munn's breakthrough year was 1950, with the school's first victory over Michigan since 1937 and Notre Dame since 1918. The AP ranked the 8-1 Spartans eighth — one place higher than Michigan.

The only loss had been in the third game, Oct. 7, 1950, at East Lansing — a 34-7 wipeout by Maryland, which confounded the Spartans with a newfangled option. Michigan State would not lose again for three years, until Oct. 24, 1953, to Purdue, 6-0.

Thrilling rallies saved the streak time and again. In the third game of '51, the Spartans overcame a 10-point deficit at Ohio State in the final six minutes and won, 24-20. The Spartans were ranked second that season, behind Tennessee.

The Spartans were ranked first heading into 1952. In the second game, Gene Lekenta missed a game-winning field goal attempt from the 12 against Oregon State. But the Beavers were offside and Lekenta made good on his second chance in the closing moments, 17-14. (Munn refused a photographer's request to kiss Lekenta's foot.)

The next week, Michigan State — which had lost its No. 1 ranking to Wisconsin in one poll — returned to No. 1 in all the polls after whipping Texas A&M, 48-6.

Michigan State won its final six games by an average of 28.2 points and won the national championship, finishing ahead of, in order, Georgia Tech, Notre Dame, Oklahoma and Southern California.

The winning streak at 24, Michigan State made its official Big Ten debut to open the 1953 season, beating Iowa, 21-7, in Iowa City. Victories followed over Minnesota, TCU and Indiana.

The streak had reached 28, and the next opponent was Purdue,

Associated Press

HAPPY NEW YEAR! EVERYTHING WAS ROSY FOR BIGGIE MUNN AND THE SPARTANS ON THE FIRST DAY OF 1954.

Michigan State University

LEROY BOLDEN, A HALFBACK FROM FLINT NORTHERN, JOINED THE SPARTANS IN 1951 AND DID NOT PLAY IN A LOSS UNTIL MIDWAY THROUGH HIS JUNIOR SEASON.

which had lost its four games and would finish with seven losses. But the Boilermakers intercepted five passes and stunned the visiting Spartans and themselves with a 6-0 victory.

Michigan State won its final four games, shared the conference title with Illinois at 5-1 (the schools hadn't played), and won the vote of athletic directors to play in its first Rose Bowl — the one that Clarence Underwood and so many others remembered so vividly having watched on TV, watching blacks and whites work together.

The Spartans were trailing UCLA, 14-0, in the second quarter when end Ellis Duckett made one of the biggest plays in school history.

With the ball at the UCLA 25, he blocked a punt by Paul Cameron. The ball hit at the UCLA 7, bounced like a basketball into Duckett's arms, and he ran six yards for a touchdown. Momentum had changed.

Bolden scored after a 14-play drive midway through the third quarter, and Slonac's extra point tied the score. Wells scored after an 11-play drive late in the quarter, and Slonac's extra point gave MSU a 21-14 lead.

UCLA scored early in the fourth quarter, missed the point, and MSU's lead was 21-20. Wells then returned Cameron's punt 92 yards for a touchdown at 10:09 of the fourth quarter, and Slonac's extra point completed the scoring, 28-20. Wells was voted the bowl's outstanding player.

ALL-AMERICA QUARTERBACK EARL MORRALL, A PREP LEGEND IN MUSKEGON, LED MICHIGAN STATE TO THE 1956 ROSE BOWL, WHERE THE SPARTANS BEAT UCLA, 17-14.

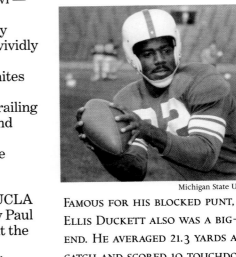

Michigan State University

FAMOUS FOR HIS BLOCKED PUNT, ELLIS DUCKETT ALSO WAS A BIG-PLAY END. HE AVERAGED 21.3 YARDS A CATCH AND SCORED 10 TOUCHDOWNS.

Michigan State University

AS BOB HOPE MIGHT HAVE SAID: THANKS FOR THE MEMORIES, BIGGIE.

A POX ON ANN ARBOR

The Spartans, now coached by Daugherty, didn't win another Big Ten title in the decade. They were second, though, in 1955, '57 and '59.

Michigan State got the Rose Bowl invitation following the '55 season because league policy prohibited consecutive appearances in Pasadena. Two-time Big Ten champion Ohio State had won the previous Rose Bowl against Southern Cal. The Spartans beat UCLA, 17-14, on Dave Kaiser's 41-yard field goal with seven

BIGGIE MUNN WAS THE MAN IN THE MIDDLE IN THIS COLLECTION OF COACHES. AMONG HIS MICHIGAN STATE ASSISTANTS WERE (FROM LEFT) LOU ZARZA, KIP TAYLOR, FOREST EVASHEVSKI AND DUFFY DAUGHERTY, HIS EVENTUAL SUCCESSOR.

seconds left.

The Spartans did exact a measure of revenge against the school that didn't want them in the Big Ten. Michigan, the conference's dominant school at the end of the 1940s, handed Michigan State a humiliating 55-0 loss in Munn's debut in 1947 — a game Munn used as a motivating tool for years.

Munn finally beat the Wolverines, 14-7, at Ann Arbor in 1950, and beat them again in his final three seasons. From 1950 to '67, the Spartans were 13-3-2 against the Wolverines. As the '50s faded into the '60s, the Spartans were the superior program — an advantage they carried until the end of the '60s, when a fellow named Bo first went to Ann Arbor.

Michigan State raised the bar in the Big Ten. Teams more aggressively recruited talented players. Coaches were more willing to experiment with innovative ideas. Sports became a tool for social enlightenment.

Change, culturally and competitively, wasn't a bad thing after all. Sounds like John Hannah got the last laugh.

IT'S GOOD! DAVE KAISER'S 41-YARD FIELD GOAL WITH SEVEN SECONDS LEFT GAVE MICHIGAN STATE A 17-14 VICTORY OVER UCLA IN THE '56 ROSE BOWL.

OCT. 15, 1960: MICHIGAN STATE BEAT NOTRE DAME, 21-0, AND BECAME THE FIRST TEAM TO WIN FIVE STRAIGHT OVER THE IRISH.

North Carolina 74, Michigan State 70 (3 OT)

Forgotten classic

Michigan State University

SPARTANS COACH FORDDY ANDERSON LINED UP HIS TROOPS —
(FROM LEFT) DAVE SCOTT, LARRY HEDDEN, ALL-AMERICA
JOHNNY GREEN, BOB ANDEREGG AND JACK QUIGGLE.

Michigan State University

JOHNNY GREEN — AN ALL-AMERICA IN 1959 AND ALL-BIG TEN FIRST
TEAM IN 1958 AND '59 — WATCHED AS ATHLETIC DIRECTOR MERRITT
NORVELL RETIRED HIS NO. 24 IN 1995.

BY JACK SAYLOR

In NCAA basketball tournament lore, the game still stands alone. It started when North Carolina coach Frank McGuire sent a 5-foot-11 guard to jump against (and psych out) Kansas 7-footer Wilt Chamberlain. It ended with North Carolina winning the NCAA title in three overtimes.

This historic game was played March 23, 1957, at Municipal Auditorium in Kansas City, Mo. Hoops history, however, has pretty much overlooked the remarkable game that made the classic final possible. In the national semifinals, unbeaten North Carolina needed three overtimes to beat unheralded Michigan State.

The Spartans weren't supposed to be anything special in the 1956-57 season. They lost seven of their first 11 games after finishing 13-9 the previous year. In coach Forrest (Forddy) Anderson's third season, Michigan State had Jumpin' Johnny Green, a 6-foot-6 sophomore who seemingly could jump through the roof, and not a whole lot else.

But the Spartans then won 10 straight games. When they lost their regular-season finale at Michigan, they were tied with Indiana for the Big Ten title at 10-4, but MSU received the NCAA bid because it had never played in the tournament.

In 1957, only one conference team was allowed to play in the NCAA tournament.

For the first time, MSU fans got truly excited about basketball.

Michigan State was assigned to the Mideast Regional at Lexington, Ky., and barely slipped past Notre Dame in the opening game, 85-83. Anderson said: "We set basketball back 10 years."

The Spartans were given no chance in their next game, against Kentucky on its home floor. The gloom thickened even more as MSU fell behind at halftime, 47-35.

Green, who had four fouls at the break, got his fifth. But Michigan State fought back. Backup center Chuck Bencie filled in admirably, and MSU upset the Wildcats, 80-68.

Spartans fans were euphoric. A crowd estimated at 7,000 greeted the plane returning the team to Lansing. People poured onto the runways, forcing the plane to park far from the terminal. Athletic director Biggie Munn, who observed the scene with amazement from the plane, declared: "This many people never showed up for any of our football teams."

Michigan State was the underdog to North Carolina. But the Spartans played the Tar Heels to a standstill, gaining confidence through a game with 31 lead changes and 21 ties.

Finally, as time expired in regulation with the score tied at 58,

JAN. 23, 1961: WILLIAM CLAY FORD, A MEMBER OF THE LIONS' HIERARCHY SINCE 1956,
WAS NAMED TEAM PRESIDENT.

Green got a rebound and passed to guard Jack Quiggle, who unleashed a shot from near center court. It swished. But before bedlam could break out, there were groans. Quiggle's shot was a split-second late. No good.

In the first overtime, the Spartans came close again. With MSU leading, 64-62, Green was fouled with 11 seconds left. Never too accurate from the free-throw line (he was 56 percent for his career), Green missed. Carolina's Pete Brennan got the rebound, dribbled downcourt, and hit a 20-footer with three seconds left to force a second overtime.

"I knew at the end of that first overtime that Michigan State was done," McGuire said. "Lady Luck was with us then."

The Spartans were running out of gas, but they held on for another tie, at 66, forcing a third overtime. The final points came on Green's tip-in of a missed shot with 56 seconds left.

All-America Lennie Rosenbluth scored four of the Tar Heels' eight points in the third overtime. Final score: North Carolina 74, Michigan State 70.

Green scored only 11 points but grabbed 19 rebounds. Larry Hedden had 14 points and 15 rebounds; George Ferguson scored 10 points. The fifth MSU starter was playmaker Pat Wilson, later a university trustee. Quiggle led the Spartans (16-10) with 20 points.

Rosenbluth scored 29 for the Tar Heels.

Back in Lansing, a serious problem had developed. So many fans refused to be pried from their TV sets that during breaks in the game, thousands of toilets were flushed almost simultaneously. The city couldn't maintain adequate water pressure.

Michigan State University

IN 1957, JUMPIN' JOHNNY GREEN LED THE SPARTANS TO THE FINAL FOUR, WHERE THEY RAN INTO ALL-AMERICA LENNIE ROSENBLUTH AND A NORTH CAROLINA TEAM THAT FINISHED 32-0.

APRIL 26, 1961: PAUL FOYTACK GAVE UP THE FIRST
OF ROGER MARIS' RECORD-BREAKING 61 HOME RUNS THAT SEASON.

Old Blue ice

By DOUG CHURCH

Vic Heyliger not only built Michigan's great hockey dynasty of the late 1940s and early 1950s, he was the father of the NCAA hockey tournament, an event that flourished and grew into today's Frozen Four.

Heyliger played for Michigan before winning a Stanley Cup with the Chicago Black Hawks in 1938. He played again with the Hawks in 1943-44, and in between coached at Illinois. After his last NHL season, he became Michigan's coach in 1944. Heyliger had built a strong Wolverines program by 1948. He had the vision for the sport to start a national championship playoff tournament and to help build a league for the teams in the western part of the country.

But while that vision was historically significant, his legacy on the ice remains what is truly remarkable: six national titles in the first nine years of the NCAA tournament, a second-place finish in the 10th year, three thirds and an overall record of 228-61-13 (.777).

"College hockey wouldn't be what it is today if it wasn't for Vic Heyliger, and I'm sure things would be much different at Michigan," said Al Renfrew, captain of the 1948-49 team. "He was the first guy in hockey to recruit. He was the Fielding H. Yost of hockey."

When Heyliger left Michigan in 1958 for Colorado Springs, Colo., to ease his severe asthma (he eventually started a hockey program at Air Force), Renfrew took over the program. He won its seventh national title in 1964 by defeating Denver. One of Renfrew's star players before that title was Red Berenson, who, two decades later, would return to Michigan and lead the Wolverines to their eighth and ninth titles in 1996 and 1998.

It all seems to stay in the hockey family with the maize and blue.

And it was Heyliger who got the puck rolling upon his arrival in Ann Arbor, shortly after athletic director Fritz

Bentley Historical Library

GOALIE HAL DOWNES WATCHED AS THE WOLVERINES TRIED TO CLEAR THE PUCK AGAINST BROWN IN THE 1951 CHAMPIONSHIP GAME. MICHIGAN WON, 7-1.

Crisler saved the program. The school considered dropping hockey because of a limited number of opponents.

Heyliger immediately started to seek support for a national championship playoff. He wrote to all the coaches in the country and received an overwhelmingly positive response. At a meeting in Minnesota, the idea was approved and plans were drawn up.

The only thing the coaches needed was an arena. Heyliger tried and failed to secure Boston Garden or Madison Square Garden. The coaches eventually decided on — of all places — the Broadmoor World Arena in Colorado Springs. The decision turned out to be a smart one. The town enthusiastically supported the event in its early years. The tournament began moving to neutral sites around the country in 1958.

In 1948, the first tournament was staged; Boston College and Dartmouth represented the East, Michigan and Colorado College represented the West.

Michigan beat Boston College in overtime, 6-4, and took on Dartmouth in the final. Wally Gacek scored a hat trick and added three assists for the Wolverines, who scored four goals in the third period in an 8-4 victory.

Dartmouth got its revenge in the 1949 semifinals, beating Michigan, 4-2. And Boston University eliminated Michigan in the 1950 semifinals, 4-3. But the Wolverines had the last laugh on everybody the next few years:

■ In 1951, goalie Hal Downes didn't have to make a save in the first 15 minutes against Brown. Neil Celley and John McKennell each scored two goals as Michigan beat Brown, 7-1, for its second title.

■ In 1952, the Wolverines got first-period goals from captain Earl Keyes and Doug Philpott within one minute and went on to beat Colorado College, 4-1.

■ In 1953, Michigan beat Minnesota, 7-3, for its third straight

JUNE 11, 1961: NORM CASH BECAME THE FIRST TIGER TO HIT A HOME RUN OUT OF BRIGGS STADIUM.
HE DID IT A RECORD FOUR TIMES IN HIS CAREER, ALL TO RIGHTFIELD.

Bentley Historical Library

MICHIGAN WON THE NCAA'S FIRST HOCKEY NATIONAL CHAMPIONSHIP IN 1948 WITH AN 8-4 VICTORY OVER DARTMOUTH.

title. That feat never was achieved again in the 20th Century. Denver (1960-61 and '68-69) and Boston University (1971-72) are the only other schools to win two straight titles.

■ In 1955, goalie Lorne Howes made 47 saves, including 21 in the final period, as U-M beat Colorado College, 5-3, in the title game.

■ In 1956, U-M won its sixth and final NCAA title under Heyliger. Ed Switzer had a hat trick in a 7-5 victory over Michigan Tech.

Each of Heyliger's title teams featured the three things a coach dreams about: an explosive offense, a tight defense and strong goaltending. But only two times was a Wolverine selected as the tournament's most outstanding player (John Matchefts in 1953 and Howes in 1956).

"All of our teams were extremely well-balanced during that time," Heyliger said. "I was very fortunate to have some tremendous talent on those squads."

Heyliger took the Wolverines back to the finals in 1957, but they lost, 13-6, to Colorado College. That was the legend's last game behind the Michigan bench.

◆

NOV. 14, 1961: JOHN FETZER ASSUMED FULL OWNERSHIP OF THE TIGERS
AND RENAMED THEIR PARK TIGER STADIUM.

The greatest round ever

The Monster

BY GENE MYERS

He finished only three under par, but all things considered, his round often is considered golf's greatest. After he holed out, the silent man with the steely demeanor delivered the line that, all things considered, might be golf's greatest.

"I am glad," Ben Hogan said, "I brought this course, this monster, to its knees."

Even without his final-round 67 to win the 1951 U.S. Open at Oakland Hills Country Club, Hogan still would be one of golf's greatest pros. His round only added to his legend. But without his round, and his famous quote, Oakland Hills certainly would not have as prominent a place in golf laurels.

Six times, the Birmingham, Mich., course, designed by Donald Ross in 1918 and updated by Robert Trent Jones for the '51 Open, held the national tournament in the 20th Century. Only in 1951 did a true giant of the sport capture the prize. In 1924, Cyril Walker edged Bobby Jones by three shots; in 1937, Ralph Guldahl edged Sam Snead by two; in 1961, Gene Littler beat a field with Arnold Palmer and Jack Nicklaus; in 1985, Andy North beat a bunch of no-names; and in 1996, Steve Jones beat Tom Lehman and Davis Love III by one shot.

They called him "Bantam Ben" because he was slight and trim. In Scotland, he was "The Wee Ice Mon" because of his intensity and calm under fire. To players, he was "The Hawk" because of the way he studied a course.

When he went to Oakland Hills in 1951, he was the defending Open champ.

Hogan always considered the '50 Open at Merion his favorite tournament, because it came 16 months after a car crash shattered his legs so badly that he never walked without pain again. At Oakland Hills, he would create his classic round.

Associated Press

BEN HOGAN GAVE HIS CADDY, DAVE PRESS, A HUG AND $350. "AFTER THAT, I WAS MAKING MORE MONEY THAN MY FATHER," SAID PRESS, WHO AT 13 HITCHHIKED FROM HAZEL PARK EACH DAY AND DREW HOGAN'S NAME FROM A HAT.

For the first 18 holes, Hogan carded a six-over 76, five shots behind Snead. Hogan followed that with a 73 for a nine-over 149 that left him five shots behind Bobby Locke. "I'd have to be a Houdini to shoot 140 Saturday," Hogan said, "and that's what it will take to lead."

He shot 71-67—138 for the final two rounds, both played on Saturday. Because of his accident, Hogan suffered immensely playing back-to-back rounds, but on this day he kept improving as he kept playing. His 67 consisted of five birdies, two bogeys, 11 pars and a back-nine 32. He missed only two fairways. Five times he put irons within five feet of the pin.

His 67 was the first subpar round of the tournament, which he finished at seven-over 287, two shots ahead of Clayton Heafner (whose final-round 69 was the other subpar round). Snead finished 15 over, Jimmy Demaret 16 over and Gene Sarazen 23 over.

Hogan immediately proclaimed his 67 as his best round ever — a claim he never recanted for the last 46 years of his life. At the time, golf officials, golf pros and the golf press immediately realized that Hogan's 67 deserved a treasured place in the sport's trophy case.

At the 1969 Masters, Hogan relived his glorious round:

"That's a good as I ever shot. I was a little lucky that day — I had to be on that kind of course — but I believe I made more outstanding shots in that one round than I ever had before or since. At the time, Oakland Hills was the hardest course in the country . . . or anywhere. They just didn't give you any room to shoot. They had sand all over the place. You had to be almost perfect with every shot, and nobody can really make perfect shots."

Then a smile crossed his face. "But I came pretty close to making 'em."

TWO DYNASTIES

147

Ozzie does it

By Gene Myers

Ozzie Virgil always said he didn't think of himself in terms of black or white.

That made him the only one.

In Michigan's sports century, Virgil played a bit part — only 131 games with the Tigers — but in many ways, his role couldn't have been more historically significant.

On June 6, 1958, he became the Tigers' first black player.

Eleven years had passed since Jackie Robinson had broken baseball's color line. By 1958, Robinson had been retired from the Brooklyn Dodgers for two seasons. Henry Aaron had hit 110 home runs en route to his record of 755. Willie Mays had won a batting title at .345, hit 51 homers in a season and made a historic catch in the World Series.

By 1958, only the Tigers and Boston Red Sox had not integrated their teams. Detroit historically had been a city divided along racial lines, and the Tigers did their part to keep the lines distinct. Black fans in the '40s and '50s were regularly banished to the leftfield seats. People of color who wanted to love baseball found it hard, if not impossible, to love the Tigers. On the field, the talent-starved Tigers missed out on the initial wave of black stars.

The call went out for Ozzie Virgil on June 5, 1958. Why Virgil? The Tigers, after all, had 19 black players under contract in the minors. Virgil, a 25-year-old third baseman, had been playing well for the top farm team, Charleston, hitting .292 with a league-leading 34 RBIs. The Tigers intended to bench slumping third sacker Reno Bertoia. But Virgil had bombed in his big call-up with the New York Giants in 1957.

Why Virgil? Why then? General manager John McHale Sr. said pressure from black groups did not influence the decision. "A look at the standings tells the reason," McHale said. "We need help at third base. Virgil is the best third baseman and has more experience than anyone else we have in our system."

Virgil played the next night in Washington. The Tigers won easily, 11-2. He got a hit, a ground-rule double, but made a horrible base-running mistake. He handled three routine

chances in the field.

After the road trip came the night Virgil would never forget. A crowd of 29,794 came out to Briggs Stadium for his Detroit debut on June 17. He batted five times and had five hits — a double and four singles — in a 9-2 victory over the Senators. He received a standing ovation.

"I remember Pedro Ramos started for the Senators that day," Virgil recalled a quarter-century later. "I had no idea what to expect when I got to Detroit, but the people were supportive of me. I remember, after I got that fifth hit, they gave me a standing ovation. I had never had a standing ovation before."

His career in Detroit went downhill from there. At the time, he had hit in 10 of his 12 games for a .327 average. He played only 37 more games and hit only .244 with three homers and 19 RBIs. After another year in the minors, he did worse in 1960 (.227 in 62 games) and 1961 (.133 in 20 games).

Also, he hadn't exactly been embraced for his place in Tigers history.

"The only thing I didn't like was that the black people in Detroit didn't accept me," he said. "The blacks in Detroit wanted an Afro-American. I had Latin ancestry, and they wanted one of their own. I could understand that. The problems they had were foreign to me. They wanted a Larry Doby, a player they could identify with."

Virgil was born in the Dominican Republic to Puerto Rican parents and grew up in the Bronx.

The Tigers traded him to Kansas City in 1961, and he then bounced around the game. He played his final major league game — only his 324th — for his first team, the Giants (now in San Francisco), in 1969. He played professionally for 26 seasons and developed a nice career as a major league coach and winter-league manager. Virgil didn't return to Detroit until the 1984 World Series, when he was third base coach for the San Diego Padres. He returned again in '97 to be honored for his part in Tigers history.

"I don't believe the Tigers called me up because I was black," Virgil said. "They called me up because I was a player."

If only the Tigers had made more such calls and many years earlier . . .

Detroit Free Press

OZZIE VIRGIL WENT 5-FOR-5 WITH A STANDING OVATION IN HIS BRIGGS STADIUM DEBUT.

Our scrapbook

BEST NICKNAMES

Terrible Ted Lindsay

The Fearsome Foursome, below — The Lions' defensive front four of ends Sam Williams and Darris McCord and tackles Alex Karras and Roger Brown. (Yes, there was a Los Angeles Rams quartet that used the same nickname, but the Lions got there first.)

Detroit Lions

MUSICAL COACHES	
Out	In
Fritz Crisler	Bennie Oosterbaan
Gus Dorais	Bo McMillin
Steve O'Neill	Red Rolfe
Ozzie Cowles	Ernie McCoy
Benjamin VanAlstyne	Alton Kircher
Bo McMillin	Buddy Parker
Alton Kircher	Pete Newell
Red Rolfe	Fred Hutchinson
Ernie McCoy	Bill Perigo
Biggie Munn	Duffy Daugherty
Tommy Ivan	Jimmy Skinner
Pete Newell	Forddy Anderson
Fred Hutchinson	Bucky Harris
Buddy Parker	George Wilson
Jimmy Skinner	Sid Abel
Charley Eckman	Red Rocha
Bennie Oosterbaan	Bump Elliott
Bucky Harris	Jack Tighe
Jack Tighe	Bill Norman
Red Rocha	Dick McGuire
Bill Norman	Jimmy Dykes
Bill Perigo	Dave Strack
Jimmy Dykes	Joe Gordon
Joe Gordon	Bob Scheffing

FANTASTIC FINISH

It went into the books as perhaps the most stunning finish to a Lions game ever, with two lead changes in the last 15 seconds. And all Jim Gibbons wanted to do was give them a chance at a field goal as time ticked away.

It was Dec. 4, 1960, at Baltimore's Memorial Stadium, and the Colts' Lenny Moore — seemingly covered by Night Train Lane — had just made a diving catch in the end zone for a 15-13 lead.

"People went crazy," Lions linebacker Joe Schmidt said. "Thousands ran onto the field and a big fight broke out. I was standing next to Alex Karras. Some fan hit him over the head with a rosary. Alex had these beads hanging down over his forehead and he started chasing the guy; he was going to

crack him over the head with his helmet.

"After the field was cleared, we took the kickoff and had the ball at our 35. There was time for just the one play."

Hail Mary time, right? Send all the fleet receivers deep and toss the ball as far as you can? Wrong. Lions quarterback Earl Morrall ignored the receivers running deep routes and hit Gibbons, the tight end, on a crossing pattern.

"To this day, I can't understand why Morrall didn't throw the ball to Gail Cogdill, who was running deep downfield and was one of the fastest receivers in the league," said Jim Ninowski, who had started at quarterback. "Instead, he threw it to Gibbons, our slowest receiver. Gibbons

caught the ball on about our 40, and by the time he reached the Colts' 40, time had run out."

And by that time, Gibbons had more on his mind than field-goal position. "When I reached the 50-yard line, I saw the field ahead was open down the whole right side — there was nobody there!" said Gibbons, who just kept running. "Time ran out as I was running for the goal line. The guys always razz me about that."

Gibbons' score gave the Lions a 20-15 victory.

"It was phenomenal," Schmidt said. "One second the crowd was in a tremendous roar, and the next there was this instant eerie silence."

BONUS BABY

Mom, Dad and a baby-faced Al Kaline celebrated his signing with the Tigers in 1953. The 18-year-old — who got a bonus of $35,000 — went straight from high school in Baltimore to the big leagues that year.

Associated Press

WHEN HE WAS GOOD ...

Right-hander Virgil (Fire) Trucks, right, had a lousy year for the Tigers in '52, a 5-19 record and 3.97 ERA. It would have been a total waste if it hadn't been for those two no-hitters.

Yes, Trucks — who gave up 190 hits in the 179 other innings he pitched that season — tossed two no-no's and won them both, 1-0. He did it to the Washington Senators on May 15 at Briggs Stadium and to the New York Yankees on Aug. 25 in their own ballpark.

As it turned out, the no-hitters were more indicative of Trucks' talent: He pitched 17 seasons in the majors with a 177-135 record.

Detroit Free Press

HEROES

George Mason didn't live long enough to make his dream come true. But his good friend George Griffith did. The two were standing on the banks of the Au Sable River near Grayling on a summer day in the mid-1950s when Mason remarked that trout needed an advocacy organization like Ducks Unlimited to protect the valuable resource. But Mason, the president of Nash-Kelvinator Corp., which eventually became American Motors, died in 1954.

On a hot July 18, 1959, a group of anglers gathered at Griffith's retreat, dubbed the Barbless Hook, outside Grayling on the Au Sable mainstream, and listened to him outline plans for Trout Unlimited. Its motto was "Limit your kill, don't kill your limit." Its purpose was to preserve and improve fishing nationwide by protecting and enhancing cold-water habitats where trout

swam, and it grew to 100,000 members and 450 chapters nationwide.

"If it hadn't been for George Griffith, there might not have been a Trout Unlimited," said Glen Sheppard, editor of the North Woods Call newspaper in Charlevoix.

When Griffith was on the old Michigan Conservation Commission, Sheppard said, "He almost single-handedly pushed through the idea of flies-only waters on some streams, no-kill sections on trout streams, ending hatchery stocking, and improving streams so that they would have natural reproduction of trout."

When Mason died, he bequeathed a 13-mile wild stretch of the Au Sable South Branch, now known as the Mason Tract, to anglers. And Griffith, who died April 7, 1998, at the age of 97, willed the Barbless Hook to Trout Unlimited.

Detroit Free Press

COLLEGE HOOPS PIONEERS

Charlie Primas, above, who starred at Wayne State and went on to play with the Harlem Globetrotters, recalled the racial climate when he came out of Miller High in Detroit.

"Black athletes weren't recruited by colleges then," Primas said. "But Joel Mason, the coach at Wayne State, helped change that. He brought in black players and gave them a chance to play."

Even then, Primas said, black players had to endure hardships like hostile crowds.

"I remember a tournament in Indiana in 1952 where the fans were giving us a particularly rough time," he said. "With about three minutes to go, Coach called time out and sent all five black players on the floor at the same time. I believe that was the first time a university had five black players on the floor at once."

Our scrapbook

Detroit Free Press

WINGS CAPTAIN SID ABEL ACCEPTS
THE CUP FROM CLARENCE CAMPBELL.

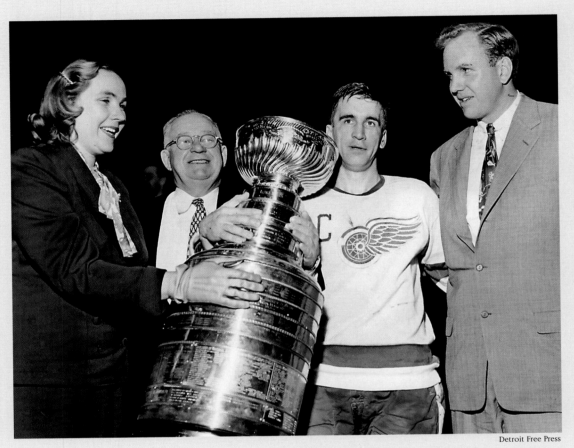

Detroit Free Press

THE RED WINGS WERE NEARING THE END OF A DYNASTY WHEN MARGUERITE NORRIS, JACK ADAMS,
TED LINDSAY AND BRUCE NORRIS HELD THE STANLEY CUP IN 1954.

WOMEN IN SPORTS

Marguerite Norris, who was Red Wings president in 1952-55, was the first woman to have her name inscribed on the Stanley Cup. And she was the only woman on the Cup until 1989, when Calgary Flames co-owner Sonia Scurfield joined the club. The Cup now includes the names of Marian and other Ilitch women.

DUMB AND DUMBER

First dumb thing: Montreal Canadiens star Rocket Richard struck linesman Cliff Thompson in the last week of the 1954-55 season, and NHL president Clarence Campbell suspended him for the final three games of the season and the playoffs.

Second dumb thing: Campbell attended the Canadiens' next game at Montreal, four nights later against the Red Wings. The teams were tied for the league lead with two games left.

Third dumb thing: One fan sucker-punched Campbell in the Forum and others pelted him with eggs, tomatoes and garbage. Police arrived to whisk him to safety, and used tear gas to quell the rebellion. Outside, a mob gathered and rioted on Rue Ste. Catherine.

The Habs lost by forfeit after one period, and two nights later the Wings clinched the league title with a 6-0 victory over Montreal at Detroit. Richard lost the scoring title to teammate Bernie Geoffrion by one point, 75-74.

Of course, the two teams would meet again in the Stanley Cup finals, and the Wings won in seven games.

ICON

April 15, 1952: That's the night the Red Wings completed a Stanley Cup finals sweep of Montreal with Terry Sawchuk's 3-0 shutout at Olympia. It also was the night the first octopus was thrown on the ice by fish dealer Pete Cusimano, who said its eight legs represented the eight victories it took to win the Cup in the old six-team NHL.

ICONOCLAST

Another take on octopus-tossing: "Too bad. Those guys started a tradition that always made us officials a little uneasy during Detroit games. That damn thing would come flying out of the stands sometime during the first five minutes of play. I'd have one eye on the game and the other eye on the stands, wondering when those little buggers were going to throw that ugly thing. As a result, I seldom called any penalties early in the game. I was on octopus watch.

"Pick the damn thing up? Not me. I never went near them. Somehow, Marcel Pronovost always got to be the picker-upper. It didn't bother him at all to scoop one of those weird-looking things off the ice and toss it in the nearest garbage bin."
— former referee Red Storey, quoted in "The Red Wings," by Brian McFarlane.

GORDIE THE FIGHTER

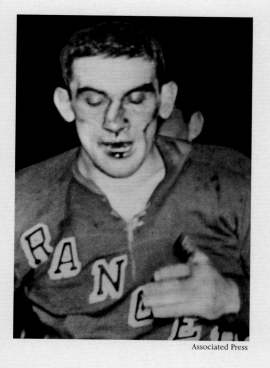

Associated Press

Old-time hockey fans will tell you it was the most one-sided fight ever: Gordie Howe vs. Lou Fontinato, Feb. 1, 1959, in Madison Square Garden.

Fontinato, left, a New York Rangers defenseman, was known as one of the NHL's toughest guys. Now he's remembered mostly as the guy Howe beat up.

Trouble had been brewing between the two for several games when the Red Wings came to town that night. Lots of bad blood and stitches.

Howe was leaning on his net, watching a fight between Red Kelly and Eddie Shack, when he remembered a bit of sage advice from Ted Lindsay: Always be aware of who's out on the ice with you.

"I took a peek and sure enough, there was Louie with his gloves off about 10 feet away and coming my way," Howe said. "I truly thought he was going to sucker-punch me. If he had, I'd have been over. I pretended I didn't see him, and when he swung, I just pulled my head aside and that honker of his was right there, and I drilled it."

Accounts of the incident say Howe grasped Fontinato's shirt with his left hand, pulling it half off and restricting the Ranger's movement, then hammered him with uppercuts.

Fontinato sagged to the ice, his nose broken and jaw dislocated. His reputation as an enforcer was destroyed — especially after photos of his mangled face were published — and the Rangers traded him to Montreal, where his career ended in 1963.

"He tried to ram Vic Hadfield in a game there," Howe said, "but Hadfield ducked him, and Louie went headfirst into the boards and broke his neck. That was the end of his hockey."

GORDIE THE LOVER

Not only did the Red Wings rule the NHL in the '50s, they were pretty good bowlers, too. Management encouraged the players to take up bowling, figuring it would keep them too busy for dalliances with the opposite sex.

The plan backfired in the case of Gordie Howe. Because in 1950, that's where he met Colleen, a recent Detroit Mackenzie graduate. As Howe remembers it, ". . . When I saw Colleen, I almost jumped over the bowling racks to get over there to meet her."

The couple married in '53, and Gordie wasn't just gaining a wife who became mother to their four children, he was gaining a business manager. Colleen ran — even in retirement — the Howes' financial affairs.

"It's been a mutual agreement, a partnership," Gordie said. "I married a strong lady who has been very, very good for me because there are a lot of departments where I know I lack. . . .

"She was telling me every day, 'You're not getting the money you should be getting.' She said: 'Stand up to them, ask for more money.' I said: 'I couldn't. It's not in my nature.' "

Colleen wasn't a favorite of Wings management, who preferred Gordie's nature when it came to contract negotiations. Longtime Wings executive Jimmy Skinner once admitted that when he saw Colleen coming down the hall, he would hide in the men's room.

"I am not a sports Barbie doll," Colleen said. "It's hard for me to accept things like the players having to be so subservient. I am not a subservient person."

Detroit Free Press

GORDIE HOWE MET HIS PERFECT MRS. HOCKEY IN COLLEEN BACK IN THE '50S.

THE WINNER IS . . .

JIM MCFADDEN: NHL's Calder Trophy in 1948.

SID ABEL: NHL's Hart Trophy in 1949.

BILL QUACKENBUSH: NHL's Lady Byng Trophy in 1949.

TED LINDSAY: NHL's Art Ross Trophy in 1950.

GORDIE HOWE: NHL's Art Ross Trophy in 1951, '52, '53, '54 and '57; Hart Trophy in '52, '53, '57, '58, '60 and '63.

RED KELLY: NHL's Lady Byng Trophy in 1951, '53 '54; Norris Trophy in 1954.

TERRY SAWCHUK: NHL's Calder Trophy in 1951; Vezina Trophy in '52, '53 and '55.

HARVEY KUENN: American League rookie of the year in 1953.

DUTCH REIBEL: NHL's Lady Byng Trophy in 1956.

ALEX DELVECCHIO: NHL's Lady Byng Trophy in 1959.

JOE SCHMIDT: NFL co-most valuable player with Philadelphia quarterback Norm Van Brocklin in 1960.

1948-1962
Our scrapbook

WHITEY   OX   MOOSE

NBA PIONEERS

Former Pistons player and coach Earl Lloyd was the first black to play in an NBA game. He was among three blacks drafted in 1950 — Chuck Cooper by Boston, Lloyd by the now-defunct Washington Capitols, and former Harlem Globetrotter Nat (Sweetwater) Clifton by the New York Knicks — but because Washington opened one day before the others, Lloyd was the first to play in a game. Cooper was the first to be drafted, Clifton was the first to sign a contract.

Lloyd, left, recalls his first game as "uneventful," a 78-70 loss at Rochester. "I think I took about six shots, made three, got a couple of free throws and about 10 rebounds," he said. "For a rookie, that was good."

After his rookie season, Lloyd was drafted by the Army and served two years during the Korean War. When he returned, he played six seasons with Syracuse and his final two with the Pistons.

In Detroit, he eventually became the first black assistant coach, under Dick McGuire in 1960, and the first black non-playing head coach in 1971. Lloyd, who stayed in the area, compiled a 22-55 record as Pistons coach.

SLIPPERY WHEN WET

The Pistons, fresh in town from Ft. Wayne, Ind., played their first game in Detroit and lost to the Boston Celtics, 105-94, in the second game of an Oct. 23, 1957, twin bill at Olympia. The St. Louis Hawks beat the New York Knickerbockers in the opener, 112-95.

But the main topic of conversation was the new floor, which got slippery when laid over the Olympia ice.

THE WISTERTS

Alvin (Moose) Wistert decided he would be the one to break the mold. After serving four years in the Marines during World War II, he enrolled at Boston University. But it lasted only a year; the Wistert brothers from Chicago were all destined to play for Michigan, wear No. 11 and earn All-America recognition at tackle.

Alvin accomplished all that in 1947-49, when he played on two national-champion teams for Fritz Crisler and then Bennie Oosterbaan. At 32, he was the oldest ever to play football at Michigan.

Francis (Whitey) Wistert, who also starred in baseball for U-M, set the pattern in the early '30s, played on the Wolverines' 1933 championship team for Harry Kipke, and made All-America the same year. Albert (Ox) Wistert was an All-America for Crisler in '42, then went on to play nine years in the NFL, first for a combined Pittsburgh/Philadelphia team and then with the Eagles.

Michigan retired the No. 11 jersey in honor of all three Wistert brothers.

OLYMPIC CHAMPIONS

London, Summer, '48
ROBERT BORG, Oxford, equestrian: silver in team dressage.
LELAND MERRILL, Michigan State, free-style wrestling: bronze in welterweight class.
NORB SCHEMANSKY, Dearborn, weight lifting: silver in heavyweight class.
BOB SOHL, Michigan, swimming: bronze in 220 breaststroke.
LORENZO WRIGHT, Wayne State, track and field: gold for 400 relay.

Helsinki, Summer, '52
JOHN DAVIES, Michigan, swimming: gold in 200 breaststroke.
BUMPY JONES, Michigan, swimming: gold in 800 freestyle relay.
NORB SCHEMANSKY, Dearborn, weight lifting: gold in heavyweight class.
CLARKE SCHOLES, Grosse Pointe Park, swimming: gold in 100 freestyle.

Cortina D'Ampezzo, Winter, '56
WILLIAM IKOLA AND JOHN MATCHEFTS, Michigan, hockey: silver.
CAROL HEISS JENKINS, Michigan State, figure skating: silver.

WELDON HOWARD OLSON, Marquette, hockey: silver.

Melbourne, Summer, '56
BERNARD COSTELLO, Bloomfield Hills, AND JAMES GARDINER, Wayne State, rowing: silver in double sculls.
DICK HANLEY, Michigan, swimming: silver in 800 freestyle relay.
ARMIN KURT SEIFFERT, Detroit, rowing: gold in pairs with cox.
GARY TOBIAN, Detroit, diving: silver in 10-meter platform.
JOHN WELCHLI, Grosse Pointe Farms, rowing: silver in fours without cox.
HERB WILLIAMS, Macatawa, sailing: bronze in Star class.

Squaw Valley, Winter, '60
EUGENE GRAZIA, Michigan State, hockey: gold.
CAROL HEISS JENKINS, Michigan State, figure skating: gold.
WELDON HOWARD OLSON, Marquette, hockey: gold.
RODNEY PAAVOLA, Hancock, hockey: gold.

Rome, Summer, '60
EDWARD CROOK JR., Detroit, boxing: gold in middleweight class.
WILLIAM DARNTON, Michigan, swimming: gold in 800 freestyle relay.
FELIX JEFFREY FARRELL, Detroit, swimming: gold in 400 relay and 800 relay.
DAVID GILLANDERS, Michigan, swimming: bronze in 200 butterfly, gold in 400 medley relay.
HAYES JONES, Pontiac, track and field: bronze in 110 hurdles.
EELES LANDSTROM, Michigan, track and field: bronze in pole vault (for Finland).
NORB SCHEMANSKY, Dearborn, weight lifting: bronze in heavyweight class.
JOAN SPILLANE, Michigan, swimming: gold in 400 freestyle relay.
GARY TOBIAN, Detroit, diving: silver in 10-meter platform, gold in three-meter springboard.
ROBERT WEBSTER, Michigan, diving: gold in platform.

CHAPTER 5

SOCK IT TO 'EM
1963-1968

SOCK IT TO 'EM,
1963-1968

By Nicholas J. Cotsonika

Never was Detroit in need of a champion as much as it was in the summer of 1968. Sadly segregating itself in the face of fear, the city was splitting apart at its seams, suffering so much damage, its leaders would spend the rest of the century trying — and failing — to figure out how to repair it.

On a hot July night in 1967, the predominantly white police department raided an illegal after-hours gambling establishment on 12th Street. The bust drew a crowd of angry black onlookers, and when police tried to force their way through it to get to their wagons, no one budged. Pushes and shouts were exchanged, along with a few punches and slaps. Then someone threw a rock, and the city exploded in flame and fury.

The crowd quickly grew into an angry mob, fueled by the rev-

Detroit was racially torn after the '67 riots. What could possibly unite the city again? The '68 Tigers.

olutionary air of the period, primed to make mayhem. Businesses were attacked. Houses began burning. John Conyers, a popular African-American congressman, mounted a flatbed truck and pleaded for calm. But he was too late. Shooed away by rock-hurling hooligans, he retreated and immediately sped out of the area, which soon became unrecognizable.

Violent reactions to racism injured many American cities in the late '60s. Washington. Chicago. Newark. But they might have hurt Detroit the most. Then the nation's fifth-largest city, home to 1.6 million people, its population already was shrinking rapidly. After World War II, the auto industry decentralized and cut jobs, and whites began an exodus to the suburbs. The disorder only accelerated the process because of its staggering horror. In the end, police made 7,231 arrests and counted 2,509 buildings as being looted or burned. More than 1,000 people were injured. Forty-three were killed.

Tiger Stadium, with its highly stacked stands acting as a shield to the outside world, seemed like a sanctuary, the safest place in the city. Only those seated in the far reaches of its upper deck could see the ominous clouds of rising smoke, as the Tigers played a doubleheader on the first day of the disturbance. But troubled times made their way to the corner of

PRECEDING PAGE: WHEN BILL FREEHAN TAGGED OUT LOU BROCK IN GAME 5, THE TIDE OF THE 1968 WORLD SERIES TURNED.

Photograph by TONY SPINA/Detroit Free Press

AL KALINE WAS A WORLD SERIES HERO WITH A .379 MARK. BUT DURING THE REGULAR SEASON — HIS 16TH OF 22 WITH THE TIGERS — HE WAS INJURED, LOST HIS SPOT IN THE LINEUP AND BATTED ONLY .287.

JAN. 10, 1964: WILLIAM CLAY FORD TOOK OVER AS SOLE OWNER OF THE LIONS
AFTER PURCHASING THE TEAM FOR $4.5 MILLION.

Michigan and Trumbull, too.

As attendance sharply fell, the Tigers battled Boston for the pennant. They thought their talent would be the difference down the stretch, but it wasn't. They blew leads late in games, making mistakes behind a bad bullpen, and stumbled. Everything came down to one final cold October day, a doubleheader against California.

The Tigers won the first game, giving themselves a chance to force a one-game playoff with the Red Sox by winning the nightcap. But victory wasn't meant to be. Scrappy Dick McAuliffe, who had grounded into one double play all season and would ground into none in all of the next, batted in the ninth inning representing the trying run with one out and two runners aboard. As surely as Detroit was cursed that summer, he hit a sharp grounder to second.

Double play. Season over.

No pennant. No nothing.

Hours afterward, catcher Bill Freehan sat somberly in the clubhouse and moaned: "I can't believe it. Now there's no tomorrow." He was right, of course. There was no tomorrow for the Tigers. But there would be a next year, a most scintillating '68.

When the Vietnam War reached its terrible peak. When Martin Luther King Jr. and Robert Kennedy were blindsided by assassins' bullets. When antiwar protesters ransacked the Democratic National Convention in Chicago. When the Tigers won the World Series mercifully, allowing their beloved, bruised and battered city a respite from its chaos and pain.

A TIGHT TEAM

The '68 Tigers, in many ways, were the last of their kind. They won the American League's last pure pennant; baseball expanded, introduced divisions and instituted playoffs in 1969. They were a tight-knit group of men who had known one another for years; nearly half had come up together via the Tigers' Triple-A affiliate in Syracuse, N.Y. They had a deep identification with Detroit; Freehan, Willie Horton, Jim Northrup and Mickey Stanley were Michigan natives, and several others were from the Midwest.

After games, most of them enjoyed liquid refreshment

JERRY HEIMAN/Detroit Free Press

WILLIE HORTON — WITH LOU D'ANNUNZIO, THE SCOUT WHO SIGNED HIM — JOINED THE TIGERS IN 1963 AS A TEENAGER OUT OF DETROIT'S NORTHWESTERN HIGH.

Detroit Free Press

CAB DRIVER JOE MARTIN WOUND UP WITH THIS BALL, ONE OF FOUR NORM CASH SOCKED OVER THE RIGHTFIELD ROOF IN 1961 AND 1962.

together. On the road, team pictures could be taken at the hotel bar. At home, they could be taken at the downtown Lindell A.C. All kinds of capers arose from the boys-will-be-boys atmosphere. One night in Anaheim, Calif., the team stayed in the same hotel as an aviation convention and became fond of a large model plane in the lobby. In the morning, the plane was at the bottom of the pool. General manager Jim Campbell had to pay the damages quietly, so the press wouldn't find out.

First baseman Norm Cash was the most popular of the group, never without a sense of humor. Once, knowing he was a dead duck during a pickoff, he signaled hopefully for a time-out as the ball was in mid-air. Once, having been on second base when a rain delay was called, he ran out to third when play resumed, telling the umpire he had stolen the base while no one was watching. Famously, in a game against a hot Nolan Ryan, he brought a table leg to the plate instead of a bat.

Horton, an outfielder, was the fan favorite, the only Tiger immune to catcalls and booing. He was a symbol of hope, because he came from the city — one of the roughest parts of the city — and fulfilled every Detroit kid's dream. He attended Northwestern High, a brutal place in the early '60s, and suffered the loss of his parents months before his first full season with the Tigers. In '68, he combined power and average better than anyone else in the league, finishing with a career-high 36 homers and a .285 average.

Gates Brown was perhaps one of the last players on the roster, but he embodied a season in which the Tigers always seemed to be coming from behind. He batted .462 as a pinch-hitter, and half of his 18 pinch hits were for extra bases. Three were homers. Only once did he strike out. On Aug. 11, he hit a pinch-hit, game-winning homer in the bottom of the ninth inning in Game 1 of a doubleheader against Boston, then started in leftfield and drove in the winning run in the ninth of the nightcap. "That's my job," he said.

The Tigers were full of gritty players willing to do just that — their jobs. Freehan was a rock behind the plate. McAuliffe blossomed into a solid second baseman. Northrup become known for his power, hitting grand slams. Hall of Famer Eddie Mathews, the former Braves great, didn't play

JAN. 1, 1965: MICHIGAN BEAT OREGON STATE, 34-7, FOR AN 8-1 RECORD.
IT WAS THE BEST SEASON AND ONLY BIG TEN FOOTBALL TITLE OF BUMP ELLIOTT'S TENURE.

By the late '60s, injuries started to nag Al Kaline. In 1968, he went down with a fractured forearm and missed five weeks.

much but provided leadership. The city related to its team so well, people began pasting bumper stickers on their cars that read: "Sock It to 'Em, Tigers!" A corny song on the radio became the soundtrack of the summer:

We're all behind our baseball team.
Go get 'em, Tigers.
World Series bound and pickin' up steam.
Go get 'em, Tigers.

TWO RIVALS

But inside the Tigers' happy clubhouse, a rift festered between their top pitchers, both of whom rose to national prominence in the end. Denny McLain and Mickey Lolich did not like each other, and it only pushed them to become better.

McLain was more colorful than Cash. An eccentric at best, a weirdo at worst, he was so enraptured with playing the organ, he thought he was a musician who happened to play baseball, not the other way around. He was a pilot, too, and had his own plane,

Come October, Kaline keyed the Tigers' World Series comeback and was feted with his wife by their neighbors in the suburb of Franklin.

March 11, 1965: Boston's Bill Russell grabbed 49 rebounds, most ever by a Pistons opponent.

WITH SUCCESS CAME CELEBRITY. THE DENNY MCLAIN QUINTET
FEATURED THE TIGERS' 31-GAME WINNER ON THE ORGAN. MCLAIN
CUT A RECORD IN EARLY AUGUST OF '68.

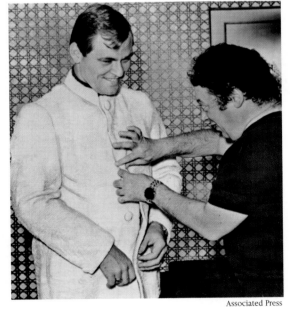

AFTER THE WORLD SERIES, MCLAIN TOOK HIS ACT
TO LAS VEGAS, WHERE COMEDIAN MARTY ALLEN
PROVED TO BE A STAND-UP GUY BY HELPING
MCLAIN INTO HIS NEHRU JACKET.

which he would use to get to gigs, even in midseason. His confidence often crossed the border of good sense into arrogance, and his antics usually went unpunished.

Lolich despised how McLain didn't abide by the rules; McLain despised how Lolich always seemed to brood. Unlike McLain, Lolich was not loud or brash or cocky. He liked motorcycles, but that was about as wild as he got. Long before the suburbs stretched far from the city, he lived in rural Washington Township, about an hour from the ballpark. He loved the long ride. It cleared his mind — a mind McLain thought always was plotting against him.

"We just went our separate ways," McLain wrote in his autobiography. "Lolich had a great arm, but he also had a personality that rubbed people the wrong way, especially me. What bothered me was his petty jealousy. He couldn't stand to see other guys succeed. I think that he secretly wished the Tigers would lose every game but the ones he pitched."

Glory met McLain first. He stormed through the season, shutting down lineup after lineup all the way to Sept. 14, when he became the first pitcher since Dizzy Dean in 1934 — and the last pitcher of the century — to win 30 games. Dean was there to see it. So was Sandy Koufax. So was a capacity Tiger Stadium crowd, although the pennant race was all but decided.

When the game was over, the Tigers celebrated on the field, and the crowd did something odd: It didn't leave after the Tigers disappeared into the dugout. The fans chanted McLain's name, forcing him to return and acknowledge the applause. McLain walked slowly around the perimeter of the infield, waving his cap. It was one of the first curtain calls in sports.

A few months before, McLain had said Tigers fans were the worst in the world. Thirty victories had absolved him.

McLain finished 31-6, with a 1.96 ERA and the first of two straight Cy Young Awards. His accomplishment would become the highlight of his life: After baseball, he spent time in jail because of drug problems and his involvement in a business scam.

Lolich, a pot-bellied man who ran a local doughnut shop after retiring, had a difficult regular season. He struggled early, was banished to the bullpen and needed a strong stretch run to finish with a 17-9 record and 3.19 ERA.

The most remarkable part of Lolich's season occurred off the field: A member of the National Guard, he was mobilized at one point because of lingering civic unrest, as he had been right after pitching on the first day of the '67 disturbance.

In October, he indeed helped heal his city while in uniform — but while carrying a glove instead of a rifle.

NO. 6

The most peculiar story of '68 centered on outfielder Al Kaline. He was in the midst of a 22-year career with Detroit in which he collected 3,007 hits, 399 homers and 10 Gold Gloves. He was on his way to becoming the 10th player to be inducted into the Hall of Fame in his first year of eligibility, and his No. 6 was destined to be the first uniform retired by the Tigers. But for much of the season, he was left out of the starting lineup.

After being hit by a pitch during the season, Kaline suffered a

TONY SPINA/Detroit Free Press

IN A FEW SHORT YEARS WITH THE TIGERS, DENNY MCLAIN WON 117 GAMES AND WALKED OFF WITH TWO CY YOUNG AWARDS.

APRIL 11, 1965: NORM ULLMAN SET AN NHL PLAYOFF RECORD WITH TWO GOALS FIVE SECONDS APART
IN THE RED WINGS' 4-2 VICTORY. BUT CHICAGO WON THE FIRST-ROUND SERIES IN SEVEN GAMES.

Richard Bak Collection

THE FIREWORKS WERE READY AND THE TIGERS LIT THE FUSE. BY SCORING A RUN IN THE BOTTOM OF THE NINTH ON SEPT. 17, THEY BEAT THE YANKEES, 2-1, AND CLINCHED THE PENNANT — DETROIT'S FIRST IN 23 YEARS AND THE LAST PURE PENNANT BEFORE BASEBALL INTRODUCED DIVISIONS AND PLAYOFFS IN 1969.

fractured forearm and missed five weeks. When he returned, the Tigers were in the thick of the pennant race, and manager Mayo Smith didn't want to break up his outfield of Horton, Stanley and Northrup. So Kaline, a 33-year-old veteran who never spent a day in the minor leagues, sat on the bench for the first time in his life, pinch-hitting when he could. He played in only 102 games, hitting .287 with 10 homers and 53 RBIs.

But Kaline simply couldn't come off the bench during the World Series; the Tigers wouldn't allow it. It wouldn't have been right. Kaline was their biggest star, the soul of the franchise, a player who once turned down a salary offer of $100,000, telling Campbell that he didn't think he was playing well enough to deserve so much money.

At a time when sculpted bodies were becoming the norm in clubhouses, Kaline was a throwback. He didn't succeed because of his body; he succeeded in spite of it. He made his living on guts and drive and gall, overcoming injuries and physical limitations unfathomable to lesser men.

He always had osteomyelitis, a persistent bone disease. When he was 8 years old growing up in Baltimore, doctors removed two inches of bone out of his left foot, leaving jagged scars and permanent deformity. To compensate, he developed a special running style: on the heel and toes of his right foot and on the side of his left foot.

Pain always bothered him, but he never said so, and he never let on while playing. In fact, he made everything look effortless. Defensively, his range was so good, the Tigers had to remove a section of seats in Tiger Stadium's rightfield corner — hence dubbed "Kaline's Corner" — to keep him from hurting himself. Offensively, the biggest mistake he made was winning the batting title at age 20 and having Boston great Ted Williams call him "the greatest right-handed hitter in the league." Afterward, the fans expected him to win the batting title every year, and because he never did it again, he endured heavy criticism and suffered frequent depression.

MAY 9, 1965: STEVE YZERMAN WAS BORN IN CRANBROOK, BRITISH COLUMBIA.

IT WAS OCT. 3, 1968, AND THE FREE PRESS DESCRIBED A ONCE-IN-A-LIFETIME MOMENT THIS WAY: "IF YOU'VE BEEN TO THE ZOO BUT NEVER SEEN A TIGER GRIN, LOOK AT THIS CAT. HE'S MICKEY LOLICH, FLITTING AROUND THE BASES THURSDAY AFTER HITTING HIS FIRST MAJOR LEAGUE HOME RUN, WHICH, ALONG WITH HIS POWERFUL PITCHING, HELPED THE TIGERS CHEW UP THE ST. LOUIS CARDINALS." EVENTUALLY, THE SIGNS POINTED TO DETROIT'S NEWEST BASEBALL HERO.

TONY SPINA/Detroit Free Press

THE TIGERS WON GAME 7 IN ST. LOUIS, BUT THAT DIDN'T STOP FANS — WHITE AND BLACK — FROM DANCING IN THE STREETS OF MOTOWN.

"The start I had in the big leagues put pressure on me," Kaline said. "Everybody said, 'This guy's another Ty Cobb, another Joe DiMaggio.' How much pressure can you take? Imagine how hard it feels to be compared to Cobb. He was the greatest ballplayer that ever lived. To say that I'm like him is the most foolish thing that anybody can make a comparison on."

People did compare, however, and Tigers brass did demand that he play like Cobb in the Series. To get him in the lineup, Smith made a bold move. Stanley hadn't made an error in centerfield all season, and he won a Gold Glove because of it. But he also was the team's best athlete and had been known to take infield for fun infrequently. So with the pennant clinched and six games left in the regular season, which the Tigers finished 103-59 (12 games ahead of Baltimore), Smith replaced good-glove, no-hit shortstop Ray Oyler with Stanley to open a spot in the outfield.

MARCH 10, 1966: ALL-PRO JOE SCHMIDT ANNOUNCED HIS RETIREMENT
AFTER 13 SEASONS TO BECOME THE LIONS' LINEBACKERS COACH.

Stanley was shocked. "To be taken out of that situation and put at shortstop," he said, "it was like landing in alien territory." He wasn't afraid. In fact, he felt flattered that the organization thought so highly of his abilities, and he performed valiantly, giving Kaline a chance to shine in the Series and add to his legend before a national audience.

But the move came at a high cost. Stanley played so well at shortstop, he worked out there for Smith the next spring and, not knowing how to warm up properly as an infielder, hurt his arm badly. He played after that, but he never was the same. "It was horrible," he said. "It was a terrible experience. It was no fun for me at all."

AN IMPROBABLE HERO

McLain's mouth kicked off the Series with an in-your-face challenge to the Cardinals, the defending World Series champions. "I'm sick of hearing about what a great team the Cardinals are," he said. "I don't want to just beat them, I want to demolish them." To his chagrin, his arm couldn't back up the bluster.

But Lolich's could.

Game 1 in St. Louis was an eagerly anticipated battle between McLain and Bob Gibson, whose 22-9 record and 1.12 ERA were as fearsome as his glare off the mound. But it was no contest. Gibson struck out a Series-record 17 and easily beat McLain, 4-0.

That left Lolich to pick up the pieces in Game 2. In the first inning, Lolich needed help: Racing recklessly around the outfield, Kaline had to make two spectacular catches to keep him out of trouble. But Lolich was brilliant afterward. He hit the only homer of his career high and long to left in the third inning, and he went the distance for an 8-1 victory that sent the city into hysterics.

Detroit hadn't seen a Series in 23 years, and although it still limped because of what had happened the year before, it put on its best face. Washington Boulevard was renamed Tiger Drive, and orange stripes ran down the center of it. Banners and bunting draped every building. Downtown was alive again.

But the real celebration had to wait. The Tigers still had five games to play.

Three steals by Lou Brock and three-run homers by Tim McCarver and Orlando Cepeda gave Game 3 to the Cardinals, 7-3. Then 10 strikeouts by Gibson on a rain-soaked afternoon beat McLain in Game 4, 10-1. Things looked very dismal for Detroit, and they continued to seem so early in Game 5, as the Tigers trailed, 3-0.

But then the Tigers turned things around. They were trailing with one out in the fifth inning, 3-2, when Horton — the home-grown hero of the scarred city — threw to Freehan at the plate and nailed Brock, who chose not to slide. Kaline, who hit .379 with two homers and eight RBIs in the Series, gave the Tigers a 5-3 victory with a bases-loaded single in the seventh.

McLain won Game 6 in St. Louis, 13-1, thanks to a Northrup grand slam and four Kaline RBIs. But McLain couldn't overshadow Lolich, who beat Gibson, 4-1, in an incredible Game 7. It was scoreless through six, when Lolich picked off Brock and Curt Flood at first base. In the seventh, Flood misjudged Northrup's

Detroit Free Press

THE SIDEWALKS OF DETROIT WERE PURRING DURING THE HAPPY DAYS OF 1968. . . .

JIIMMY TAFOYA/*Detroit Free Press*

TIGERS MANAGER MAYO SMITH (LEFT) AND OWNER JOHN FETZER GLADLY ACCEPTED THE WORLD SERIES TROPHY. . . .

CRAIG PORTER/*Detroit Free Press*

AND THEY WERE STILL SMILING WHEN (FROM LEFT) PAT DOBSON, WILLIE HORTON, JOHN HILLER AND EARL WILSON REUNITED IN 1978 AT THE CORNER.

MAY 11, 1966: THE PISTONS TOOK SYRACUSE GUARD DAVE BING IN THE FIRST ROUND OF THE NBA DRAFT.

drive to center, fell, and allowed a triple that helped make the Tigers the third team ever to come back from a 3-1 Series deficit and win.

"You all thought I was an improbable hero, but I came sneaking through," said Lolich, whose 3-0 record and 1.67 ERA made him the Series' most valuable player. "There's always been somebody ahead of me. A hitter like Al Kaline. A pitcher like Denny. It was always somebody else — never Mickey Lolich.

"But now, my day has finally come."

Detroit's, too.

Healed — albeit momentarily — by the Tigers' first World Series title since 1945, whites and blacks together poured onto the streets in celebration. Fans flooded Metro Airport to greet the team in such numbers, the plane had to be rerouted to Willow Run for safety reasons.

This was a different kind of disturbance. This was better than anything the upcoming years would offer, as bitter and intense as the Michigan-Ohio State rivalry would become. This was pure goodness.

For a moment, July '67 was forgotten. For a moment, what the Tigers had done was bigger than baseball. Much bigger.

"I believe," Horton said, "the '68 Tigers were put here by God to heal this city."

It was that divine.

MARY SCHROEDER/Detroit Free Press

"Freehan never tagged me," Lou Brock insisted when they recreated The Play before an old-timers game in 1988. "No, no," Bill Freehan said. "You never touched the plate."

IRA ROSENBERG/Detroit Free Press

We're all behind our baseball team — go get 'em, Tigers.

Game of the Century

BY DREW SHARP

The chant of "Kill, Bubba, kill!" inside Spartan Stadium would ignite a flame inside defensive end Bubba Smith that would rise to the surface, turning his eyes red, creating the look of a monster turned loose.

Even 30 years later a similar response could be elicited from the College Football Hall of Famer.

Just mention 1966 and Notre Dame.

"It doesn't matter how old and beaten up we've all gotten," Smith said while attending the 1997 Michigan State football bust. "If somebody told us today that we've been given another quarter to finally decide that game, we'd all take that field in a second."

This was the first "Game of the Century." And as the century concluded, it remained, perhaps, the only sporting event truly worthy of that designation.

All you need to say is "10-10" and anyone with the slightest knowledge of college football history will know what you're talking about.

College football in the 1960s was defined that cloudy, crisp November afternoon in East Lansing. No. 1- and No. 2-ranked teams had played before, but not so late in the season and not when the No. 1 team was the nationally revered Fighting Irish and the No. 2 team was the defending national champion — Michigan State.

"WE DIDN'T TIE THEM," MICHIGAN STATE COACH DUFFY DAUGHERTY SAID AFTER NOTRE DAME RAN OUT THE CLOCK RATHER THAN RISK A TURNOVER. "THEY TIED US."

Michigan State University

Roverback George Webster remembered everyone pointing to the Notre Dame game all season. With all the buildup, Webster figured there was no way the game could live up to the hype. He was wrong.

Notre Dame linebacker and captain Jim Lynch later won Super Bowl IV with the Kansas City Chiefs, but he insisted that game "was not as big as that Michigan State-Notre Dame game."

Notre Dame (8-0) had the name, but Michigan State (9-0) had the numbers. The Spartans had one losing season through the decade's first seven years. Coach Duffy Daugherty was quickly becoming one of the game's legendary figures.

Notre Dame had hired Ara Parseghian away from Northwestern in 1964 to revive the echoes.

The 1965 and '66 Spartans were considered among the best college football teams ever. Smith and Webster were consensus selections on most all-century college teams. They were products of the Southern talent pipeline that Daugherty mined with expert skill, providing opportunities to black players shunned by schools in their home states.

Daugherty strongly courted the coaches at black high schools, creating coaching seminars specifically for them. The move was unprecedented and probably wouldn't have succeeded if not for Daugherty's natural ease and likability in ➤

Michigan State University

THE SPARTANS BOASTED A SLEW OF PLAYERS NAMED TO ALL-AMERICA TEAMS. AMONG THEM WERE (FROM LEFT) FULLBACK BOB APISA, HALFBACK CLINTON JONES, DEFENSIVE END BUBBA SMITH, END GENE WASHINGTON AND ROVERBACK GEORGE WEBSTER.

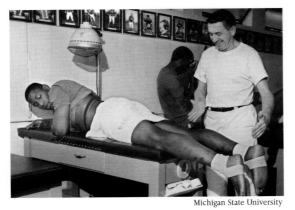

Michigan State University

BUBBA SMITH, AT 6-FEET-8 AND 280 POUNDS, WAS A BIG MAN ON CAMPUS AND THE TRAINING TABLE.

any situation. The black coaches developed a trust in him and passed that along to their players.

Free of today's more restrictive NCAA recruiting rules, Michigan State even paid to bring some coaches to East Lansing to learn in surroundings more elaborate than they had at home.

Willie Ray Smith, coach at Pollard High in Beaumont, Texas, visited East Lansing and left richer, not only in coaching knowledge but in boxes of basic classroom supplies such as notebooks and pencils. Impressed with his treatment, Smith convinced his son, Charles, to play football for the Spartans.

You might know Charles Smith by his more menacing nickname — Bubba.

The coach from Westside High in Anderson, S.C., also was impressed with the Michigan State coaches and the racial climate of tolerance on campus. The best player to come from Westside

JUNE 15, 1967: FIVE DAYS BEFORE BEING FOUND GUILTY OF DRAFT EVASION, HEAVYWEIGHT CHAMP CASSIUS CLAY (MUHAMMAD ALI) FOUGHT TWO EXHIBITIONS IN DETROIT, HIS LAST KNOWN PUBLIC FIGHTS UNTIL HIS 1970 COMEBACK.

had wanted to go to Clemson, 15 miles away, but couldn't because of his skin color.

Instead, Webster went to Michigan State, where he became the greatest player ever to wear the green and white. As a freshman, Webster wrote on his student questionnaire how he was "amazed" that the races could attend classes together without the slightest provocation.

THE DOOMSDAY DEFENSE

In 1965, the Spartans surrendered points and rushing yards as through an eyedropper — 6.2 points and 45.6 rushing yards a game, both tops in the nation. Three opponents scored in double digits — Illinois 12, Purdue 10 and Indiana 13. On consecutive Saturdays, the Spartans held Michigan to minus-51 yards rushing and Ohio State to minus-22 yards. They closed a 10-0 regular season with a 12-3 victory in South Bend, Ind., holding the Irish to 24 yards passing and minus-12 yards rushing.

In the United Press International poll, the Spartans were awarded the national championship, the second in school history. The Associated Press poll would come out after the bowls, and MSU was headed to Pasadena, Calif., for the third time. For the third time, UCLA was the opponent. UCLA and MSU also had played in East Lansing in September in their openers. MSU won, 13-3.

In the Rose Bowl, the Bruins, 7-2-1 in the regular season, took a 14-0 lead early in the second quarter. Quarterback Gary Beban scored on a pair of one-yard sneaks, sandwiched between a successful onside kick.

MSU finally scored midway through the fourth quarter on a 38-yard run by Bob Apisa, which had followed a 42-yard pass from Steve Juday to Gene Washington. MSU attempted a fake kick on the conversion and Juday's pass failed. But the Spartans weren't finished. They drove 51 yards in 15 plays and scored on Juday's one-yard sneak with 31 seconds left. On the two-point attempt to tie, UCLA defensive back Bob Stiles stopped Apisa's run.

"Duffy always told us we didn't lose, the clock ran out on us," linebacker Charles Thornhill said. "If we'd had five more minutes we would have won."

The final AP poll listed Alabama first and MSU second. UCLA was fourth.

BACK FOR BLOOD

When Smith and Webster approached their senior seasons in 1966, their goals were clear. The Spartans couldn't return to the Rose Bowl because the Big Ten prohibited consecutive appearances. And the Rose Bowl was the only postseason option for conference members.

The goal was another national championship, this one undisputed. But that would mean beating Notre Dame on the final weekend.

The Spartans controlled the showdown for the first half. In the first quarter, Smith, 6-feet-8 and 280 pounds, hit star quarterback Terry Hanratty so hard that his shoulder was separated. The Irish

Michigan State University

Detroit Free Press

FULLBACK REGIS CAVENDER PUT THE SPARTANS ON THE BOARD FIRST WITH A FIRST-QUARTER TOUCHDOWN. BUBBA SMITH CAME TO EAST LANSING FROM BEAUMONT, TEXAS. AFTER BACK-TO-BACK ALL-AMERICA SEASONS, HE WAS THE NO. 1 PICK IN THE 1967 DRAFT BY BALTIMORE AND PLAYED NINE NFL SEASONS FOR THE COLTS, RAIDERS AND OILERS.

SEPT. 28, 1967: DETROIT DEVELOPER LARRY LOPATIN BROKE GROUND ON MICHIGAN SPEEDWAY NEAR BROOKLYN IN THE IRISH HILLS.

JIMMY RAYE QUARTERBACKED MICHIGAN STATE FOR THREE SEASONS, STARTING IN 1965, "THANKS TO THE COURAGE OF DUFFY DAUGHERTY," RAYE SAID YEARS LATER. "IT WAS UNPRECEDENTED IN THE '60S FOR A MAJOR COLLEGE TO HAVE A BLACK PLAY QUARTERBACK. I'LL NEVER FORGET WHAT HE DID."

AND FEW WILL FORGET WHAT NOTRE DAME DID. A SPORTS ILLUSTRATED COVER STORY SCOLDED THE FIGHTING IRISH FOR RUNNING OUT THE CLOCK, CAUSING A FUROR OVER NO. 1.

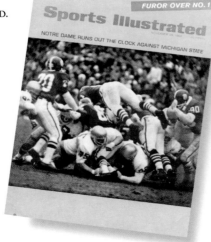

lost their center, George Goeddeke, to an ankle injury in another battle with Smith.

The epic confrontation between the No. 1 and No. 2 teams — ABC-TV had promoted it as "the greatest battle since Hector fought Achilles" — had started as a brutal, violent classic, and it would end that way.

Late in the first quarter, a 42-yard pass from Jimmy Raye to Washington put the ball on the Irish 31. Nine running plays later, fullback Regis Cavender ran into the end zone.

When the Irish couldn't move the ball again, the Spartans drove 51 yards to the Notre Dame 30. The drive stalled, and Dick Kenney kicked a 47-yard field goal.

MSU had its 10 points.

The Irish finally started to stir. Tom Quinn returned the kickoff 38 yards. Then came sophomore quarterback Coley O'Brien, who had been diagnosed with diabetes two weeks earlier and still was adjusting to insulin shots. After an incomplete pass, O'Brien hit Bob Gladieux for 11 yards, Rocky Bleier for nine, and Gladieux again for 34 and a touchdown. Four plays, 54 yards, 10-7 with 4:30 left in the half.

"Worst thing we did was knock Hanratty out," Smith said.

DEC. 2, 1967: MICHIGAN PLAYED ITS FIRST BASKETBALL GAME IN CRISLER ARENA AND LOST, 96-79, TO KENTUCKY.

"They brought O'Brien in, and we didn't know anything about O'Brien."

Momentum had changed. In the second half, the Spartans wouldn't gain a rushing yard. Sixteen times the Irish stopped them for no gain or a loss. But MSU kept the lead until Joe Azzaro kicked a 28-yard field goal on the first play of the fourth quarter.

Notre Dame had its 10 points.

The Spartans and Irish wrestled for field position until, with five minutes left, Raye threw a pass that was intercepted by safety Tom Schoen and returned to the MSU 18.

Smith remembered what happened next as one of the biggest defensive stops during his days in East Lansing. Three plays, minus-six yards for the Irish left them with a 42-yard field goal attempt that sailed wide right.

But the Spartans still couldn't generate any offense. They gave the ball back to the Irish with 1:24 remaining, at their 30. What followed remains one of college football's most controversial finishes.

Parseghian knew that a tie on the road against the undefeated national champion would keep him No. 1 in the polls. Ara ran out the clock.

The Spartans couldn't believe it. Smith wagged his finger at the Irish. "Be a man! Come at us!" he shouted. Six straight running plays exhausted the clock.

"We didn't tie them. They tied us," Daugherty said. "Make no mistake about that."

Parseghian offered this defense: "We'd fought hard to come back and tie it up. After all that, I didn't want to risk giving it to them cheap. They get reckless and it could cost them the game. I wasn't going to do a jackass thing like that at this point."

The national press reflected the frustration of the fans and players. The Associated Press called the tie "galling." The New York Daily News said Notre Dame played "with the tenacity of a has-been trying to hold onto her millionaire lover." Dan Jenkins wrote in Sports Illustrated: "Old Notre Dame will tie over

Michigan State University

DUFFY DAUGHERTY, NAMED TO THE COLLEGE FOOTBALL HALL OF FAME IN 1984, COACHED SOME OF MSU'S GREATEST TEAMS. HIS SPARTANS OF 1965-66 COMPILED A 19-1-1 MARK.

Michigan State University

GEORGE WEBSTER, FLANKED BY AD BIGGIE MUNN AND DAUGHERTY, WORE THE GREEN AND WHITE WITH SUCH DISTINCTION THAT THE SPARTANS RETIRED HIS NUMBER.

all." Another expression became popular: "Tie one for the Gipper."

But Parseghian's strategy eventually worked. In that week's polls, which were close, Notre Dame remained atop the AP poll, conducted by sports writers, and MSU took over No. 1 in the UPI poll, conducted by coaches. The Irish then throttled Southern Cal, 51-0, and was ranked first in both polls. Because Notre Dame didn't participate in bowls — and because Michigan State couldn't — the season was over in November and the Irish's eighth national championship was secured.

The two programs met at a crossroads that historic afternoon, headed in opposite directions. Parseghian brought the Irish back to national prominence. But that classic game was the last the nation heard of the Spartans. Smith, Webster, Washington and Clinton Jones were first-round selections in the next NFL draft. The Southern pipeline dried up after the old-line segregationists like Alabama coach Bear Bryant decided to open their doors to black players.

Michigan State was instrumental in bringing about such social change, but the Spartans weren't prepared for its aftermath. Duffy thought he still could attract talent with a smile and a joke, but it was tough to sway an Alabama kid who suddenly could attend Alabama.

The talent drop-off was significant. The Spartans ended the '60s in nondescript fashion — 3-7 in 1967, 5-5 in 1968 and 4-6 in 1969. They beat Michigan twice and Notre Dame once in those three years, and most fans assumed that Duffy would regain the magic that took Michigan State to such previous heights.

He didn't.

Michigan hired Bo Schembechler after the 1968 season to revive a moribund program. And as the Wolverines thrived, the Spartans languished. Not once since that time has Michigan State come close to reaching the pinnacle it enjoyed in the middle '60s. And not once since that time have the Spartans come close to matching the drama of Nov. 19, 1966.

JULY 16, 1968: FUTURE LIONS RUNNING BACK BARRY SANDERS WAS BORN IN WICHITA, KAN.

Jazzie Cazzie

Special to the Detroit Free Press

Associated Press

OFFICIALLY, IT'S CRISLER ARENA. UNOFFICIALLY, IT'S "THE HOUSE THAT CAZZIE BUILT," THOUGH RUSSELL NEVER PLAYED THERE.

BY BILL L. ROOSE

Once asked why he chose Michigan over many of the nation's top college basketball schools, Cazzie Russell, in his usually calm, casual way, answered, "I watched Michigan on TV and they were so bad I thought they needed help."

Egotistical, maybe, but the young man was right: As a basketball school, U-M was awful.

As it turned out, Russell delivered on his promise, lifting the Wolverines out of the shadows of their football brethren and into national roundball prominence.

In three seasons, 1963-64 to 1965-66, Russell took the basketball world by storm, leading U-M to the NCAA Final Four for the first time in 1964,

SEPT. 14, 1968: REGGIE JACKSON HOMERED TWICE, BUT THE TIGERS RALLIED FOR TWO IN THE NINTH AT TIGER STADIUM AND DENNY MCLAIN BEAT OAKLAND, 5-4, FOR HIS 30TH VICTORY.

and to the national championship game in '65.

To this day, he's considered the best shooter in U-M history. A three-time consensus All-America, two-time Big Ten MVP, and the '66 college player of the year. Russell's school-record 30.8-point average in his senior season was approached only once, by Rudy Tomjanovich (30.1) in 1969-70.

Michigan lost a 91-80 shoot-out to UCLA and Gail Goodrich's 42 points in that 1965 final, but Russell was up to the challenge with 28 points.

What Russell accomplished at Michigan will be treasured forever. He was a hugely exciting and entertaining guard, capable of heights that others could only hope to scale.

He pursued victory as if everything that mattered to him was confined to that court.

"That's what I'm out there for," said Russell, who averaged 15.1 points in 12 NBA seasons with New York, Golden State, the Los Angeles Lakers and Chicago. "That's the job to be done and I'll do it to the best of my ability. If I get my thoughts sidetracked, then I'm in big trouble."

Russell's legacy lives on through the maize-and-blue walls of Crisler Arena, revered as "The House That Cazzie Built" since it opened in 1967.

Russell's passion was baseball; he didn't try basketball until, as a 14-year-old freshman, he was urged to do so by his teacher and coach at Chicago's Carver High, Larry Hawkins.

Hawkins told him, "You're not going to get a scholarship playing baseball. Let's try basketball."

Which quickly evolved into a compulsion.

It wasn't uncommon to visit Yost Field House on a Sunday afternoon and see Russell, by himself, bouncing a ball. He would say, "I sometimes stop on my way home from church. I don't feel I practice enough."

His combination of flamboyance and modesty earned him the nickname "Jazzie Cazzie" and brought U-M basketball recognition reserved for such powerhouses of the era as UCLA and Kentucky.

Before Russell, basketball in Ann Arbor was bleak. It was so dreadful that women worked on their needlepoint in the

Detroit Free Press

CAZZIE RUSSELL COULD SLASH TO THE BASKET OR KNOCK DOWN A JUMPER. HE AVERAGED 30.8 POINTS AS A SENIOR.

stands during games.

But by Russell's senior season, he was dazzling standing-room-only crowds from Madison Square Garden in New York to Detroit's Cobo Arena, from Chicago Stadium to Los Angeles.

His muscular 6-foot-6, 220-pound frame made him a focus of opposing defenses. An incredible outside shooter, Russell never shied away from contact in the lane, and he never disappeared when the game was on the line.

Despite an injured ankle, Russell, a sophomore, played in the 1964 NCAA semifinals. In obvious pain, he still led both teams with 31 points in a 91-80 loss to Duke.

The following year, U-M held the No. 1 ranking for much of the season and reached the NCAA championship game for the first time in the tournament's 27 years. The Wolverines, behind Russell's 28 points, handled Princeton and All-America Bill Bradley, who scored 29 points, in the national semifinals, 93-76. But they couldn't stop UCLA and All-America guard Goodrich.

The most anticipated matchup of the 1964-65 season did not occur in the NCAA tournament. Instead, it was the showdown between Russell and Bradley in their first meeting, at the Holiday Festival in Madison Square Garden on Dec. 30.

"When the newspapers heard that we were going to meet in the Garden, it was predictable what some of the reaction would sound like," Russell said.

Bradley scored 41 points, but fouled out with five minutes left and his Tigers leading by 12 points. U-M steamed back for an 80-78 victory on Russell's jumper with three seconds remaining — the last of his 27 points.

"A lot of the publicity made it sound like a personal duel between us," Russell said, "and that was anything but."

Russell averaged 25.1 points in nine career NCAA tournament games. Only Bradley, Oscar Robertson, Jerry West, Elvin Hayes and Lew Alcindor averaged more points in the same number of games.

But in Ann Arbor, Russell will always be in a class by himself.

◆

SOCK IT TO 'EM, 1963-1968

A decade of change

Cup runneth empty

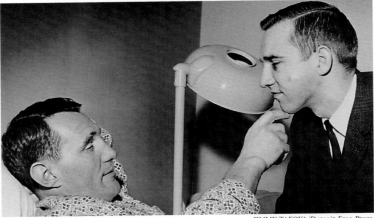

JIMMY TAFOYA/Detroit Free Press

WHY HOCKEY IS A ROUGH SPORT: DEFENSEMAN BILL GADSBY, HOSPITALIZED WITH A BUM BACK, CHECKED OUT ROGER CROZIER'S BRUISED FACE, THE RESULT OF A FRANK MAHOVLICH SHOT.

BY BERNIE CZARNIECKI

In America, the 1960s will be remembered as the decade of war protests, civil rights demonstrations, political upheaval, free love, rock 'n' roll and drug experimentation.

In the NHL, the decade began with six teams, barefaced goalies and bareheaded players . . . and ended with 12 teams, widespread use of goalie masks, and helmets regarded as acceptable equipment.

For the Red Wings, the '60s meant change for the worst. The decade marked the beginning of a free fall for a once-proud franchise that lasted until the middle '80s.

The '60s weren't all bad. With Sid Abel as coach and general manager, the Wings had winning records and were Stanley Cup finalists in 1963, '64 and '66. But like the Wings of the early and middle '90s, they couldn't hoist that Cup.

Abel inherited quite a mess when Jack Adams retired as GM after the 1961-62 season. Adams had triggered the franchise's decline by trading away the past — Terry Sawchuk, Ted Lindsay and Red Kelly — and the future — Glenn Hall, Bronco Horvath and Johnny Bucyk — while getting little in return.

In the summer of '62, Abel acquired bruising rookie defenseman Doug Barkley from Chicago. Barkley, Marcel Pronovost and Bill Gadsby anchored the defense, and Gordie Howe, Alex Delvecchio and Norm Ullman provided the offensive leadership as the Wings posted their first winning season since 1957. Although the Wings, with Sawchuk back in goal, lost to Toronto in the finals in five close games, Detroit appeared poised for another Cup.

Abel's next step in 1963 was acquiring Roger Crozier, an acrobatic young goalie with Chicago. In the 1963-64 season,

the Wings finished over .500 (30-29-11), Gordie Howe broke Rocket Richard's record of 544 goals, and Detroit pushed Toronto to seven games in the Cup finals. Johnny Bower outdueled Sawchuk, 4-0, in Game 7.

When Crozier replaced Sawchuk in 1964-65, Abel thought the Wings finally were approaching the right blend of youth and experience, especially with young guns like Paul Henderson, Bruce MacGregor and Gary Bergman.

Even Lindsay, now 39, could sense something special happening. Retired from Chicago since 1960, Terrible Ted was coaxed back, scored 14 goals, and helped Detroit finish first (40-23-7) for the first time since 1956-57.

But in the semifinals against Chicago with Bobby Hull and Stan Mikita, the Wings were eliminated in seven hotly contested games. Crozier won the Calder Trophy as the league's top rookie.

Would 1966 finally be the year? Lindsay re-retired. So Abel got left wing help by trading for Toronto's Andy Bathgate, a future Hall of Famer, but had to part with Pronovost to get him.

A nine-game unbeaten streak in January put Detroit in first place. Then, suddenly, having lost Pronovost via trade became crucial.

On Jan. 30 against Chicago, Barkley collided with Doug Mohns, whose stick struck Barkley's face, detaching the retina of his right eye — an injury that forced him to retire.

"Barkley, in my opinion, was the best defenseman in the league at the time," Lindsay said.

With Barkley, Detroit was 23-13-6 and in first place. Without Barkley, the Wings struggled at 8-14-6 and dropped to fourth.

Still, the Wings stunned the Blackhawks in six games in

OCT. 10, 1968: MICKEY LOLICH OUTDUELED BOB GIBSON FOR HIS THIRD VICTORY, AND THE TIGERS BEAT THE ST. LOUIS CARDINALS, 4-1, IN GAME 7 OF THE WORLD SERIES.

GORDIE HOWE ENJOYED A LIGHT MOMENT WITH BILLY MCNEILL AFTER SCORING HIS 545TH GOAL, BREAKING MAURICE RICHARD'S RECORD.

the semifinals and met the first-place Canadiens in the finals.

Detroit won Games 1 and 2 in the Forum, and the Wings were giddy on the train ride home. Too giddy?

Gadsby, in his 20th and final season, said: "We didn't think it was a lock for damn sure." Bruce Martyn, then in his second season as radio announcer, recalled: "Andy Bathgate was telling me as we left the Forum after the second game that the team was going to throw me in the shower when they won the Cup. There was some celebrating after they took two from Montreal."

But not after Montreal won twice in Detroit and Game 5 back at the Forum. Habs goalie Gump Worsley declared: "Detroit has simply lost its speed. It is not their fault and there is nothing they can do about it. It's just the age has taken its toll."

Game 6 was at Olympia Stadium in Detroit, where the temperature was an unhockey-like 81 degrees. Down, 2-0, midway through the second period, Detroit forced overtime with goals from Ullman and Floyd Smith.

It would be an overtime that would haunt the Wings for three decades.

Carrying the puck toward Crozier, Montreal's Henri Richard was hooked off balance from behind by Bergman. The fallen Richard slid into the crease with the puck against his body, and his momentum carried him into Crozier. The puck somehow found its way into the net at 2:20.

Abel and the Wings argued that the puck was purposely guided in by Richard's arm. "I had taken down Richard, and I had his stick pinned and he slipped it past Crozier just inside the post," Bergman said. "I was right in the middle of that tainted goal."

Ullman searched for referee Frank Udvari. "We tried to talk to him right away," Ullman said. "He took off. It was very disappointing for sure, especially on a goal like that."

Montreal captain Jean Beliveau was handed the Stanley Cup by NHL president Clarence Campbell amid a barrage of programs, peanut bags and other debris hurled by angry fans.

Crozier was awarded the Conn Smythe Trophy as most valuable player of the playoffs. His heroics in defeat made him a folk hero.

But 1966 was the end of the line for a generation of Wings fans. Detroit made the playoffs only twice in the next 17 years and didn't reach the finals again until 1995.

To Red Wings loyalists, those years seemed like forever. ◆

OCT. 13, 1968: RONNIE BUCHMAN GOT $20,000 FOR WINNING THE INAUGURAL RACE AT MICHIGAN SPEEDWAY, A 250-MILE CHAMP CAR RACE.

Bowhunter for the ages

Straight arrow

By Eric Sharp

When Fred Bear was about 20, he got a good, reliable job setting up machinery at a small factory in his hometown of Waynesboro, Pa. One day he heard a "Caw!," looked out a window and saw a crow sitting in a tree. Minutes later, Bear was out the door and on the way home to get his gun — fired, but content, as he headed for the woods where he always had been happiest.

The man who almost single-handedly created the modern archery-hunting industry never made any bones that all he really wanted to do was hunt and fish during an adventurous, globe-trotting life that ended in 1988 at age 86.

"My legs are way too long for my desk," he said. "I am happy I was able to have the opportunity to work at what I enjoyed doing most — hunting and fishing."

Born in 1902 in a part of western Pennsylvania where hunting and fishing were as much a way of life as they are in Michigan, Bear's lessons in woodsmanship came from his dad, Harry, a superb rifle shot who on any weekend could be expected to come home with prizes from a competition or game for the table.

Harry Bear instilled a love not of killing, but of the chase. Decades later, his son remembered those lessons. "I have always tempered my killing with respect for the game pursued," he said. "I see the animal not only as a target, but as a living creature with more freedom than I will ever have. I take that life, if I can, with regret as well as joy, and with the sure knowledge that nature's ways of

Fred Bear Museum

Fred Bear used a bow, from 20 yards, to bag this 1,000-pound Kodiak. The bear received a place of honor at his museum, formerly in Grayling.

Detroit Free Press

In the '60s, Fred Bear spent a good deal of time in cold climes hunting polar bear. "I have always tempered my killing with respect for the game pursued," he said.

fang and claw or exposure and starvation are a far crueler fate than I bestow."

Although he dropped out at 16, Bear always had confidence that he could succeed in business. He had family in Michigan and saw the auto industry of the 1920s as the place for a smart young man. So in 1923 he moved to Detroit. The move led to a series of jobs with Packard and Chrysler, but he complained that the regular hours kept him away from the woods and waters.

About 1925, Bear saw a movie at the Adams Theatre featuring the trick shooting and hunting exploits of archer Arthur Young. Bear began making traditional longbows for target shooting. A few months later, he met Young and his hunting partner, Saxton Pope (now memorialized in the Pope & Young Club for trophy bow kills), and the meeting encouraged Bear to continue making bows and arrows.

In 1933, Bear became a partner in a silk-screening company and made archery gear on the side. That part of the business grew so well that two years later he sold the silk-screen plant to his partner and started Bear Archery Tackle in an old auto plant on West Philadelphia.

The company enjoyed modest sales and growth for 20 years, but things really took off when Bear started photographing and publicizing the exploits of himself and other early bowhunters in the 1950s. By the '60s, Bear was appearing on television with Arthur Godfrey, another archery aficionado. A trip to Africa with Godfrey and a Life magazine picture spread of Bear killing a world-record

ALAN R. KAMUDA/Detroit Free Press

EVEN IN HIS EARLY 70S, FRED BEAR STILL LOOKED THE PART OF AN EXPERT WOODSMAN.
HE HUNTED INTO HIS 80S. HE DIED AT 86 IN 1988 AFTER A LIFETIME OF ADVENTURE.

Kodiak bear at 20 yards catapulted him to fame and made his name synonymous with bowhunting.

His hunting exploits also coincided with the growth of America's whitetail deer herds, a growth that made archery hunting feasible. At the turn of the 20th Century, hunters can see dozens of deer a day, but in 1920 there probably were fewer than 500,000 deer in all of the lower 48 states. In 1999, the deer numbered about 25 million. When Bear killed his first whitetail with a bow in the Upper Peninsula in 1935, whitetail numbers were a fraction of Michigan's 1999 herd of 1.8 million.

In 1947, Bear moved his plant to Grayling, mostly because of the hunting and fishing opportunities virtually outside his office door. He married a widow named Henrietta, who became an integral part of his hunting and fishing trips, and the business continued to prosper. Bear eventually sold it to a group of investors but continued to run it and promote it, largely because his partners realized that Bear Archery and Fred Bear were inseparable.

Bear's business sense usually was acute, but he did make some mistakes. One was turning down an offer of virtually exclusive rights to a gadget that the inventor called a compound bow. Bear examined the pulleys and cables on the contraption, said it looked like "the Mackinac Bridge" and dismissed it as a flash in the pan that would disappear while his beautiful recurves and longbows would prosper. He couldn't have been more wrong.

Much easier to shoot and requiring far less practice, compound bows make up about 90 percent of the archery market and allowed Michigan's archery-license sales to boom to about 400,000.

In 1977, the United Auto Workers who organized Bear Archery called a strike, a bitter dispute that alienated Bear from employees who also had been close friends. By then the plant was a subsidiary of a large corporation, and the parent company responded to the strike by moving the firm to Gainesville, Fla.

Bear hunted into his 80s and used his bows to kill record-book grizzly and Kodiak bears, moose, tiger, lion, cape buffalo and even an elephant. But the animal that fascinated him the most, and which he loved and respected the most, was one that was so much a part of his life in Michigan.

In an essay called "Thoughts on Hunting," written near the end of a long and productive life, Bear concluded that "the wariest, craftiest and hardest game of all to hunt is the whitetail deer of North America."

And all true hunters said, "Amen."

NOV. 23, 1968: BUMP ELLIOTT COACHED HIS LAST GAME AT MICHIGAN, A 50-14 LOSS TO OHIO STATE
THAT COST THE WOLVERINES A BIG TEN TITLE.

Our scrapbook

1963-1968

OH, SAY CAN YOU SEE?

All sorts of musical acts have played Tiger Stadium, from the Beatles to the Three Tenors. But none was more memorable than Jose Feliciano's love-it-or-hate-it rendition of the national anthem before Game 5 of the Detroit-St. Louis World Series in 1968.

Feliciano's highly personalized, guitar-accompanied interpretation sounded more like his hit "Light My Fire" than it did the traditional rendition of "The Star-Spangled Banner."

There wasn't much of a reaction at the stadium, where fans were more interested in getting the game started, but it launched a nationwide furor and debate.

"In my mind, I didn't just want to sing it the regular way because I was kind of tired of hearing how everybody wants to rush through the anthem and get to the game," said Feliciano, who was invited to sing the anthem by Tigers announcer Ernie Harwell. "I thought people weren't as proud of our national anthem as I was. It was my way of really doing something for America in the sense that America has done a lot for me. I never knew that my patriotism was going to be misconstrued.

"It really took me by surprise. I was sitting there and all of a sudden Tony Kubek comes up to me and says, 'Well, we're with Jose Feliciano' — I didn't even know we were live on TV — he said, 'Listen, do you know you have just caused a national thing?'

"And I said, 'Why? What happened?' He said, 'With your version of the anthem, a lot of vets who were watching threw their shoes at the

Detroit Free Press

JOSE FELICIANO CAUSED A FLAP WITH HIS PERSONALIZED RENDITION OF THE NATIONAL ANTHEM IN 1968.

television, they were so furious.'

"I'm not bitter about it. I have no regrets. I am so grateful that I have a friend like Ernie Harwell who stood by me all the time."

Harwell said he thought the furor came about "because we were in the '60s and people were very skeptical of rebellion. He played a guitar, which was considered an instrument of rebellion then."

But when Feliciano suggested a return performance in the 1984 Series, the Tigers told him all the slots had been filled.

The winner in all of this? Until his death in 1995, WJR personality Fat Bob Taylor, the Singing Plumber, had pretty much a standing gig at Tiger Stadium.

"Jim Campbell got letters threatening his life if this ever happened again," Taylor said. "So Jim went to his publicity guy and said: 'From now on in any big games out here, I want Bob Taylor for our anthem singer.'"

LOVE COUPLE

Denny and Sharon Boudreau McLain

LOUNGE LIZARD

In '68, Tigers fans knew Denny McLain had two passions besides baseball. One was Pepsi, which he swigged by the case. The other was his Hammond organ, and he tried to parlay his baseball fame into an entertainment career.

A week after the Tigers won the World Series, McLain opened at the Tropicana Hotel in Las Vegas, decked out in white tails with

No. 17 on the back. He appeared on television with Ed Sullivan, the Smothers Brothers and Steve Allen, and in 1969 released an album called "Denny McLain at the Organ."

A couple of cuts from that disc — "The Girl from Ipanema" and "Laura" — are on "Organs in Orbit," Volume 11 of Capitol Records' Ultra-Lounge Series.

ALBERT WILLIAM KALINE
DETROIT A.L., 1955 - 1974
TWELFTH PLAYER TO REACH ELITE 3,000-HIT
PLATEAU. SOCKED 399 HOMERS AND ATTAINED
.297 CAREER AVERAGE, WITH NINE YEARS IN
.300 CLASS. FINISHED IN ALL-TIME TOP 15
WITH 2,834 GAMES, 3,007 HITS, 1,583 RUNS
BATTED IN AND 4,852 TOTAL BASES. PLAYED
100 OR MORE GAMES 20 YEARS AND HAD 242
CONSECUTIVE ERRORLESS GAMES IN OUTFIELD,
1970-1972, FOR A.L. RECORDS. LED IN HITS
AND WON BATTING TITLE IN 1955 AT AGE 20.

AL KALINE BY THE NUMBERS

It just seems like Al Kaline has been a part of the Tigers forever. Actually, it has been only about half of the century.

Kaline was 18 when he signed with the Tigers off the sandlots of Baltimore, and he never played an inning in the minors. In his second full season, Kaline hit .340; at age 20, he became the youngest batting champion in major league history.

For fans who have known him only as a broadcaster, here are the numbers for his 22-year career — all, of course, with the Tigers:

YEAR	G	AB	R	H	2B	3B	HR	RBI	BB	SO	SB	AVG
1953	30	28	9	7	0	0	1	2	1	5	1	.250
1954	138	504	42	139	18	3	4	43	22	45	9	.276
1955	152	588	121	200	24	8	27	102	82	57	6	.340
1956	153	617	96	194	32	10	27	128	70	55	7	.314
1957	149	577	83	170	29	4	23	90	43	38	11	.295
1958	146	543	84	170	34	7	16	85	54	47	7	.313
1959	136	511	86	167	19	2	27	94	72	42	10	.327
1960	147	551	77	153	29	4	15	68	65	47	19	.278
1961	153	586	116	190	41	7	19	82	66	42	14	.324
1962	100	398	78	121	16	6	29	94	47	39	4	.304
1963	145	551	89	172	24	3	27	101	54	48	6	.312
1964	146	525	77	154	31	5	17	68	75	51	4	.293
1965	125	399	72	112	18	2	18	72	72	49	6	.281
1966	142	479	85	138	29	1	29	88	81	66	5	.288
1967	131	458	94	141	28	2	25	78	83	47	8	.308
1968	102	327	49	94	14	1	10	53	55	39	6	.287
1969	131	456	74	124	17	0	21	69	54	61	1	.272
1970	131	467	64	130	24	4	16	71	77	49	2	.278
1971	133	405	69	119	19	2	15	54	82	57	4	.294
1972	106	278	46	87	11	2	10	32	28	33	1	.313
1973	91	310	40	79	13	0	10	45	29	28	4	.255
1974	147	558	71	146	28	2	13	64	65	75	2	.262
TOTAL	**2834**	**10116**	**1622**	**3007**	**498**	**75**	**399**	**1583**	**1277**	**1020**	**137**	**.297**

Detroit Free Press

SWEET-SWINGING AL KALINE MADE IT TO 3,000 HITS WITH SEVEN TO SPARE WHEN HE RETIRED IN 1974. IN HONOR OF THIS ACCOMPLISHMENT, KALINE RECEIVED A HANDSHAKE FROM TIGERS OWNER JOHN FETZER AND 3,000 SILVER DOLLARS. IN 1980, KALINE WAS ELECTED TO THE BASEBALL HALL OF FAME. HE WAS THE 10TH PLAYER ELECTED IN HIS FIRST YEAR OF ELIGIBILITY.

JIMMY TAFOYA/Detroit Free Press

1963-1968
1963-1968
Our scrapbook

BEST MARKETING CAMPAIGNS

Go Get 'Em, Tigers

Sock It to 'Em, Tigers

DETROIT'S PAPER LION

George Plimpton had this great idea in 1963. Why not go to training camp with a real NFL team — as a player, maybe even a quarterback — and then write a book about the experience?

Green Bay Packers coach Vince Lombardi said no thanks, so Plimpton tried the Lions. "I came to training camp," Plimpton said, "and told coach George Wilson what I wanted to do. He thought about it for 10 seconds, then handed me a playbook."

So Plimpton went to camp at Cranbrook as one of the boys, albeit a skinny boy. He worked out with the Lions, showered with them, engaged in good-natured horseplay, all with the hopes of getting into an exhibition game against Cleveland.

This was a simpler time, but NFL commissioner Pete Rozelle still nixed that idea. So Plimpton's big chance was limited to a few plays in a big intrasquad scrimmage.

On the first play, Plimpton got tangled up with pulling guard John Gordy and fumbled before he could hand off. On the second, he dropped back to pass but fell, untouched. On the third play, his handoff was too slow, so Plimpton kept the ball and

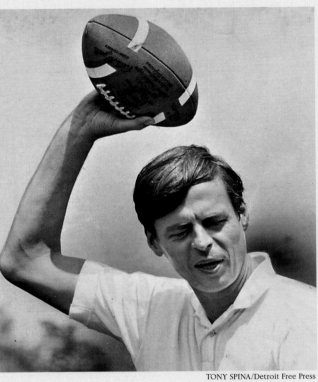

TONY SPINA/Detroit Free Press

AS A QUARTERBACK FOR THE LIONS, GEORGE PLIMPTON MADE A PRETTY GOOD WRITER.

followed running back Danny Lewis into the line, where he was tackled and given the rag-doll treatment by Roger Brown. After an incomplete pass, Plimpton pitched to Nick Pietrosante, who was tackled for a loss at his 1.

So Plimpton's drive started at his 30 and lost 29 yards. Not bad for a Lions quarterback.

BEST NUMBER CRUNCHING

"We won three games, lost none and were upset in seven." — Michigan State football coach Duffy Daugherty, explaining the Spartans' 3-7 record in 1967.

BY THE NUMBERS

225
Mickey Lolich's playing weight.

185
Denny McLain's playing weight.

1
Number of homers Al Kaline needed for 400.

0
Number of roof shots Kaline hit at Tiger Stadium.

FASHION STATEMENTS

Turtlenecks, Nehru jackets, neck chains and sideburns.

Detroit Free Press

FREE PRESS COLUMNIST SHIRLEY EDER GOT THE LOWDOWN FROM DAPPER DENNY MCLAIN AND KEN (HAWK) HARRELSON.

RUB IT IN

Just another salvo in the Michigan-Michigan State football war:

In 1965, the Spartans won, 24-7, but the score didn't have to be that lopsided.

"We played 'em down there and the game was a war, an absolute war," MSU middle guard Tony Conti said. "We get ahead and there's maybe 35 seconds or so left, so we're gonna run one more play to run out the clock. Duffy Daugherty puts Bob Apisa in the game so he'll have two backs to block in front of Steve Juday kneeling down with the ball.

"But Apisa runs into the huddle and says, 'Give it to me and I'll fall down, Steve.' Instead, he runs over everybody for a 39-yard touchdown. Duffy was furious. I'm sure his relationship with Bump Elliott was good enough he could explain it, but, boy, was he mad."

MAIN EVENTS

Alex Karras, the Lions' All-Pro defensive tackle, went on hiatus in 1963 at the request of NFL commissioner Pete Rozelle.

The commish didn't approve of Karras' betting, even if it was on his own team (Green Bay golden boy Paul Hornung met the same fate that season).

To keep himself busy, Karras bought into the Lindell AC in downtown Detroit, where he tended bar, and did some wrestling on the side.

Toss a little Dick the Bruiser — a Packer-turned-wrestler named Richard Afflis, not some radio funny man — into that mix, and you got trouble.

Karras and the Bruiser had an upcoming bout at Olympia, so the Bruiser showed up at the Lindell one night to stir up trouble, and presumably some publicity. Since they're still talking about what went down, it worked.

The Bruiser came in and bellowed that he wanted "that fat, four-eyed bartender to serve me." A shouting match turned into a fight, Karras went down, and two of the eight policemen needed to drag Bruiser away were seriously injured. (They later sued and got a settlement from the Bruiser.)

Still, it was no better than a draw. "They used pool cues, billy clubs, everything," said

DICK THE BRUISER HANDLED ALEX KARRAS IN THE RING, BUT DETROIT POLICEMEN LEFT THEIR MARK ON HIM.

the Bruiser, who died in 1991. "My eye was hanging out of the socket. I spent the night in jail. It was ugly."

A week after the main event, Karras and the Bruiser met for their anticlimactic bout at Olympia, and the Bruiser pinned him in 11 minutes, 21 seconds. Karras was paid $17,000 for the night's work, or $4,000 more than his season's pay from the Lions.

Rozelle didn't care for Karras' wrestling or affiliation with the Lindell. Karras sold his interest in the bar and was reinstated for the '64 season.

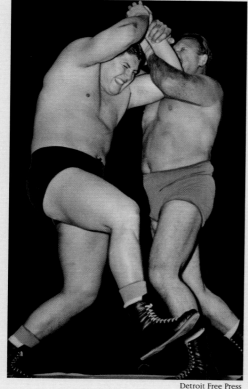

AS HE GRAPPLED WITH HIS SUSPENSION IN 1963, LIONS DEFENSIVE TACKLE ALEX KARRAS TURNED TO PRO WRESTLING.

FIRST STEPS

Ed Kozloff hadn't had much experience with long-distance running when he joined 22 other runners on Belle Isle to try a marathon on Thanksgiving Day, 1963. He ran for Wayne State, but the collegiate cross-country distance was four miles, and his longest training run was 10.

So he attacked that Motor City Marathon, 4-plus laps around the 5.4-mile park, staged by the Michigan Road Runners.

"I ran the first 10 miles in one hour flat," Kozloff said. "I was doing six-minute miles, and I completed 20 miles in two hours and eight minutes, which was still good."

And then, "I guess I found out what hitting the wall meant, from not training," said Kozloff, who finished in a respectable three hours and 13 minutes despite suffering a slightly twisted ankle. "The finish was very lonely. There were about three people at the finish line, and we all had one of those classical-type feelings like we may never run again. I finished sixth, and trophies went to the top five."

Kozloff ran his second — and last — marathon the next year, with similar results. "I remember going to the movies the next

day and sitting through two double features, and I could barely make it up the aisle. I have not run a marathon since."

But many others have, with Kozloff's help. In 1972 he assumed administrative duties, and in '75 became president of the organization, by now named the Motor City Striders. The state's largest running club continued to stage the marathon at Belle Isle through 1977, when it had a field of 400.

That's when the race became the Detroit Free Press International Marathon.

"Marathons were peaking in popularity in 1978, and the Free Press was looking for an event to promote the newspaper when someone suggested we talk with the Striders," then-managing editor Neal Shine said. "Our sports editor at the time, Ladd Neumann, had the crazy idea of starting the race in Detroit, running through the Detroit-Windsor tunnel, and coming back across the Ambassador Bridge and finishing in Detroit.

"The bridge company turned us down, so

when we met with the tunnel corporation, I told everyone not to leave unless we got an OK or a maybe. The tunnel representative told us the tunnel had never been shut down for any reason, ever. We just kept talking and talking, and he finally gave in."

Kozloff developed the route that went from the tunnel out to the Grosse Pointes and back to the finish on Belle Isle. Bob McOmber of Bowling Green, Ohio, and Erma Tranter of Chicago were the men's and women's winners of the first Freep Marathon.

The course has changed over the years, the finish moved to Hart Plaza, and wheelchair racers and racewalkers joined the fun.

Six-time champion Doug Kurtis was named director of the last Freep Marathon of the century, and he announced a dramatic route change similar to Neumann's vision: The race would start at Tiger Stadium, go to Windsor over the bridge, return through the tunnel, tour Belle Isle, and eventually finish back at the stadium.

Our scrapbook

1963-1968

CRAIG PORTER/Detroit Free Press

Detroit Free Press

NORB SCHEMANSKY OF DEARBORN
FLEXED HIS WAY TO FOUR
WEIGHTLIFTING MEDALS IN FOUR
OLYMPICS — 1948, '52, '60 AND '64.

OLYMPIC CHAMPIONS

Innsbruck, Winter, '64
TERRY McDERMOTT, Essexville, speedskating: gold in 500 meters.

Tokyo, Summer, '64
KENT BERNARD, Michigan, track and field: bronze in 400 relay (for Trinidad and Tobago).
HENRY CARR, Detroit, track and field: gold in 200 meters and 1,600 relay.
WARREN (REX) CAWLEY, Highland Park, track: gold in 400 hurdles.
EMORY WENDELL CLARK, Metamora, rowing: gold in eights with coxswain.
GARY DILLEY, Michigan State, swimming: silver in 200 backstroke.
HAYES JONES, Pontiac, track and field: gold in 110 hurdles.
CYNTHIA GOYETTE McCULLOCH, Detroit, swimming: gold in 400 medley relay.
NORB SCHEMANSKY, Dearborn, weight lifting: bronze in heavyweight.
MARCIA JONES SMOKE, Michigan, kayak: bronze in 500 singles.
CARL ROBIE, Michigan, swimming: silver in 200 butterfly.
BOB WEBSTER, Michigan, diving: gold in platform.

Grenoble, Winter, '68
TERRY McDERMOTT, Essexville, speedskating: silver in 500 meters.
TIM WOOD, Detroit, figure skating: silver.

Mexico City, Summer, '68
DON BEHN, East Lansing, freestyle wrestling: 57-kilogram class, silver.
JOHN CLAWSON, Michigan, basketball: gold.
ALVARO GAXIOLA, Michigan, diving: silver in platform (for Mexico).
SPENCER HAYWOOD, Detroit, basketball: gold.
ALFRED JONES, Detroit, boxing: bronze in middleweight class.
SHARON WICHMAN JONES, Detroit, swimming: bronze in 100 breaststroke, gold in 200 breaststroke.
CARL ROBIE, Michigan, swimming: gold in 200 butterfly.
KEN WALSH, Michigan State, swimming: gold in 400 medley relay.

JIMMY TAFOYA/Detroit Free Press

DETROIT'S HENRY CARR
TWICE STRUCK GOLD AT
THE TOKYO GAMES.

MUSICAL COACHES

Out	In
Dick McGuire	Charles Wolf
Bob Scheffing	Chuck Dressen
Charles Wolf	Dave DeBusschere
Chuck Dressen	Bob Swift
George Wilson	Harry Gilmer
Forddy Anderson	John Benington
Bob Swift	Frank Skaff
Frank Skaff	Mayo Smith
Harry Gilmer	Joe Schmidt
Dave DeBusschere	Donnis Butcher
Dave Strack	Johnny Orr
Donnis Butcher	Paul Seymour
Sid Abel	Bill Gadsby

THE WINNER IS ...

GORDIE HOWE: NHL's Art Ross and Hart trophies in 1963 and Lester Patrick Trophy in 1967.

DAVE BING: NBA rookie of the year in 1967.

LEM BARNEY: NFL defensive rookie of the year in 1967.

ROGER CROZIER: NHL's Calder Trophy in 1965 and Conn Smythe Trophy in 1966.

JACK ADAMS: NHL's Lester Patrick Trophy in 1966.

ALEX DELVECCHIO: NHL's Lady Byng Trophy in 1966.

DENNY McLAIN: American League MVP and Cy Young awards in 1968.

PLAYING WITH PAIN

Toronto defenseman Bobby Baun was taken from the ice on a stretcher after he was felled by a Gordie Howe slap shot in Game 6 of the 1964 Stanley Cup finals. With the help of painkillers, he came back and scored the winner at 1:43 of overtime for the Maple Leafs, 4-3. After two days on crutches, Baun played in the Leafs' Cup-clinching, 4-0 victory. Then he consented to X rays, which revealed his ankle was broken. But it hurt Wings fans more than it hurt Baun.

CHAPTER 6

BO & WOODY
1969-1978

BO & WOODY,
1969-1978

BY NICHOLAS J. COTSONIKA

Upon replacing Fritz Crisler as Michigan's athletic director in 1968, Don Canham had no idea that he would change the face of football so greatly that the effect on the state's sports landscape would be felt for the rest of the century. He had no idea he would hire a gruff grunt of a coach he never had heard of, a man with a long German name that was difficult to pronounce, let alone spell. He had no idea his decision would spark an era of epic battles with his school's chief rival, Ohio State, for Big Ten and national supremacy. He just knew he had to make some changes.

Michigan did not have a stranglehold on the hearts and wallets of fans, local or far-flung. After cruising to undefeated seasons in 1947 and '48, winning a disputed national championship

They were the last of the one-name coaches. Bo. Woody. Their rivalry became legendary.

the first time and an undisputed one the second, the Wolverines won consecutive Big Ten titles. But then they went into decline, winning the conference just once more, in 1964. Sadly, Michigan Stadium sat half-empty most Saturdays, filling only when Michigan State, the true glamour program of the period, invaded every other year or so. The Wolverines weren't all over the radio; the Spartans were. The Wolverines didn't get newspapers to buy ink by the bucket; the Spartans did.

Canham was a Michigan man, all maize-and-blue, having coached track at his alma mater for nearly 20 years. But he was green-and-white with envy. So after sitting down with coach Bump Elliott during the summer and securing a mutual agreement that 1968 would be Elliott's final season, he went looking for a new coach. Canham didn't want to hire an assistant. He wanted a head man, someone who knew how a program purred, someone who would win on the job, not learn.

The first person Canham pursued was Penn State's Joe Paterno, in 1968 three years into what would be his legendary tenure in Happy Valley. Early in December, Canham met with Paterno at a hotel in Pittsburgh and came away thinking he had at least a 50 percent chance of landing him. A week later, Paterno called Canham and said he didn't think he could make

PRECEDING PAGE: FOR 10 SEASONS, COACHING LEGENDS WENT HEAD-TO-HEAD: MICHIGAN'S BO SCHEMBECHLER AND OHIO STATE'S WOODY HAYES.

Photograph by Associated Press

Detroit Free Press

BO SCHEMBECHLER CAME TO MICHIGAN IN 1969 WITH A SCARLET-AND-GRAY BACKGROUND,
BUT HE REMAINED TRUE BLUE FOR TWO DECADES.

a firm decision until after the Nittany Lions played in the Orange Bowl.

"Joe," said Canham, eager to proceed, "I can't wait a month."

"Well," Paterno replied, "I don't think, really, I should leave Penn State anyhow."

Canham said he was sorry to hear the bad news and asked Paterno to keep the job offer a secret, which Paterno did. Canham then moved on to the next name on his short list: Glenn E. Schembechler of Miami (Ohio). Quite a few football insiders had mentioned him as a hot prospect, most of them referring to him by his simple nickname, Bo, because Schembechler always seemed to come off their twisted tongues as "Shlum-beck-er" or "Shem-bleh-ker" or worse. So Canham summoned him to Ann Arbor for an interview, checking him into the Ambassador Hotel under an assumed name: Mr. Shems.

Fifteen minutes into their meeting, Canham was impressed. Schembechler was self-assured, undeniably tough. More important, he had the right resume. He had played for the prominent Woody Hayes at Miami and also had served on Hayes' staff at Ohio State before coaching Miami to a 40-17-3 record in 1963-68. Although Canham knew that some Michigan true-bluebloods would see scarlet because of that, he didn't mind the Buckeyes background at all.

"With that history, he had to know what the Big Ten was all about," Canham said. "It was a plus with me."

Canham called Schembechler on Christmas Eve to offer him the job, and he asked him when he wanted to meet again and go over the details. "Right now!" barked Schembechler, who arrived in Ann Arbor on Christmas Day, providing the Wolverines with a most priceless present. Bo became the last of the one-name coaches, a titan who made the Wolverines the state's main attraction.

SEPT. 20, 1969: BO SCHEMBECHLER COACHED HIS FIRST GAME AT MICHIGAN,
A 42-14 VICTORY OVER VANDERBILT.

DON CANHAM FILLED THE STADIUM AND RESTORED MICHIGAN'S REPUTATION AS VICTORS VALIANT DURING HIS TENURE AS AD, 1968-88.

THE OLD FOOTBALL COACH (WOODY HAYES) AND THE OLD TRACK COACH (DON CANHAM) SHARED COFFEE, CONVERSATION AND A HEALTHY DISTASTE FOR THE OTHER'S SCHOOL.

RULES AND RULERS

Schembechler didn't begin his legacy smoothly. His first day on the job, he drove down the wrong street, got lost, and had to call the football office from a pay phone. "Uh, this is Bo Schembechler, the new coach?" he said to a rather confused secretary. "Where the heck are you?" His first practice, he filled his lungs with fall air, blew into a whistle and . . . nothing. The whistle was broken, so he filled his lungs again and yelled: "Gather 'round!" But in time, a very short time, he was the one giving directions, and just about everything he touched performed its function without error.

Right from the start, Schembechler made one thing clear: At Michigan, things would be done one way. His way. Always his way. He planned to run, run, run; critics could choke on his three yards and a cloud of dust. He upgraded what were then lousy facilities; Michigan Stadium was indeed a jewel in the rough. He mandated that his program would be forever clean; agents and boosters and bad guys were not welcome. And he made a famous promise to his players: "Those who stay will be champions." It meant that, no matter what, if a kid had the guts and stamina to take on the Michigan program and not quit, when he graduated, he would be a man, walking away wearing a ring.

MARCH 30, 1970: THE PISTONS TOOK ST. BONAVENTURE CENTER BOB LANIER
WITH THE FIRST PICK OF THE NBA DRAFT.

The Wolverines were stunned. Elliott had been lax, a players' coach, a positive coach. Schembechler was a field marshal. He became known for storming around the practice field with a yardstick in his right hand, prowling behind the offensive line, especially. Bo loved his linemen. He related to them best, and to show it, he was tougher on them than on anyone else. If he didn't like the way his right guard lined up ... WHAP! He would smack him on the back of the legs with the yardstick. If he didn't like the stance of his left tackle ... SMACK! Same thing. The equipment manager always kept his supply of yardsticks well-stocked. Three broken yardsticks usually meant a good day of practice.

Some players couldn't handle Schembechler and quit. Most didn't. Sore, they swore to themselves and kicked themselves and wondered why they were putting themselves through such torture. Then they realized that what Schembechler was teaching them was that football wasn't about themselves at all. It was about the team. It was about Michigan. It was an old-school idea they bought into, despite the atmosphere of the rebellious '60s. Those who didn't learn to love him at least learned to respect him. Years later, team reunions were packed with past players, all still faithful disciples of Bo.

"You see all these grown men with a look of total admiration in their eyes," said Dan Dierdorf, an offensive lineman in 1968-70 who went on to a Hall of Fame NFL career. "They'd still do anything for the man. It's the essence of what he's tried to accomplish. Anyone who's ever known him is the better for it."

DICK TRIPP/Detroit Free Press

BO SCHEMBECHLER, NOT QUITE 40, ON THE DAY HE WAS ANNOUNCED AS BUMP ELLIOTT'S SUCCESSOR.

Associated Press

IN THE BEGINNING, DUFFY DAUGHERTY'S SPARTANS HAD THE UPPER HAND — A 23-12 VICTORY OVER MICHIGAN IN BO'S FIRST GAME AGAINST MSU, IN 1969.

THE UPSET

As the Wolverines marched toward their annual regular-season finale against Ohio State in 1969 — the game that would make Bo a hero — much was made of Schembechler's relationship with Hayes. "Bo and I are a lot alike," Hayes said. "We're both left-handed, and we both have such wonderful dispositions."

Schembechler's first team was playing well at 7-2, ranked No. 12 after having won four straight games since a loss at Michigan State. But he seemed primed to learn a few more things from his mentor, whose team was being hailed by some members of the press as one of history's best. Ohio State, packed with power, was ranked No. 1 and riding a 22-game winning streak, averaging 46 points and 512 yards for the season.

The Buckeyes were 17-point favorites. No one thought Bo had a chance.

Except Bo, of course.

Schembechler knew how to rile his troops. Although part of him deeply loved Hayes, another part of him knew Hayes could be a

NICK UT/Associated Press

IN THE END, AS BO CONTINUED TO WIELD A PURPOSEFUL STICK, SCHEMBECHLER HAD COMPILED 194 VICTORIES AT MICHIGAN — AND A 17-4 RECORD AGAINST MSU.

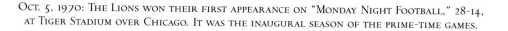

OCT. 5, 1970: THE LIONS WON THEIR FIRST APPEARANCE ON "MONDAY NIGHT FOOTBALL," 28-14, AT TIGER STADIUM OVER CHICAGO. IT WAS THE INAUGURAL SEASON OF THE PRIME-TIME GAMES.

WOODY HAYES USED ALL THE FIELD TO DELIVER SIGNALS IN 1969, BUT HIS DREAM TEAM GOT STEAMROLLED IN ANN ARBOR, 24-12.

bully. Unfair, too. Once, in the early '50s, Hayes had promised him a job. When he went to Columbus to inquire about it, Hayes drove him down to the unemployment bureau. Hayes' actions stung him — as badly as Hayes' actions stung Michigan in the 1968 game at Columbus. With the score 50-14 in his favor, Hayes attempted a two-point conversion. He didn't get it, but that didn't matter. The Wolverines were livid that Hayes had tried to embarrass them, and Schembechler made sure to remind them of that on that cold, gray November day in '69.

The Wolverines took the field at Michigan Stadium a determined bunch, spurred by Schembechler and the crowd of 103,588, the biggest Ann Arbor ever had seen. Immediately, the Buckeyes knew they weren't in for a walkover. Ohio State advanced to the Michigan 10-yard line on the game's opening drive, but the Wolverines held. Ohio State took a 6-0 lead, but the Wolverines responded with a Garvie Craw touchdown to pull ahead, 7-6. Ohio State took a 12-7 lead, but the Wolverines bottled up the Buckeyes afterward.

Craw scored again with 11:54 remaining in the second quarter, putting Michigan ahead, 14-12. Less than two minutes later, quar-

DEC. 26, 1970: THE LIONS, IN THE PLAYOFFS FOR THE FIRST TIME SINCE 1957, LOST TO THE DALLAS COWBOYS, 5-0.

terback Don Moorhead scored, extending Michigan's lead to 21-12. The Buckeyes were looking less and less invincible. Michigan Stadium was rocking. Then the Wolverines scored again on a 25-yard field goal by Tim Killian. With 1:15 remaining in the first half, the score was Michigan 24, Ohio State 12, and that's the way it ended.

Schembechler had been preaching defense since his arrival, and now he looked like a genius. The Wolverines forced seven Ohio State turnovers, with Barry Pierson intercepting three passes and Tom Curtis two. Pupil had defeated teacher. Michigan had won. Michigan had clinched a share of the Big Ten title with OSU and, even better, a Rose Bowl berth. Michigan was back. Schembechler's players carried him off the field on their shoulders on national television, as fans jammed the field, staying there long after the teams had left for the locker room.

Hayes was furious.

"Bo," he grumbled later, "you'll never win a bigger game."

Schembechler, the big block of granite that he was, just smiled. The victory was the beginning of a beautiful 10-year era, in which nearly every Michigan-Ohio State game decided the Big Ten title, in which both teams hardly budged from the Top 10, in which Schembechler went 5-4-1 against Hayes, in which the Wolverines became glamorous again.

MARKETING MICHIGAN

The next morning, Michigan alumni all over the nation were celebrating one of the greatest upsets in college football history.

Canham was celebrating much more than that. The Wolverines had received huge gate receipts and a bonanza of positive publicity, two things they had been without for a long, long while. An accomplished businessman, Canham saw opportunity. Soon, Michigan not only overtook Michigan State in attendance and exposure, it took over every other college in the nation.

When Canham assumed control of the athletic department, he also assumed control of its $250,000 deficit for the coming academic year and its sunken public image. Horrified, he went to work right away, and the first item on his agenda was selling football tickets. He knew enough arithmetic to figure that a stadium seating more than 100,000 fans, if filled six times a season, could support a first-class football program and have enough cash left over for everything else. He knew enough about marketing to make it happen.

First, he had to put fannies in the seats to create demand. As big as the '69 game against Ohio State was, about 25,000 tickets remained unsold a month beforehand. So Canham did something commonplace among businesses but rare among universities at the time: He

Detroit Free Press

BO COULD BE A TEDDY BEAR WHEN HE HAD TO BE. IN EARLY 1970, WIFE MILLIE ADMINISTERED SOME TLC AFTER HE SUFFERED A HEART ATTACK ON THE EVE OF THE ROSE BOWL AGAINST SOUTHERN CALIFORNIA.

ANDY EDMONDS/Detroit Free Press

BUT HE WAS BETTER KNOWN FOR GROWLING AND PROWLING THE SIDELINES. "IF HE DIDN'T HAVE AN ALL-AMERICAN, HE'D GET A GUY TO PLAY LIKE ONE," RECALLED ALL-AMERICA WIDE RECEIVER ANTHONY CARTER. "HE IS A FUN GUY, A GOOD GUY, A GUY YOU DIDN'T MIND PLAYING FOR."

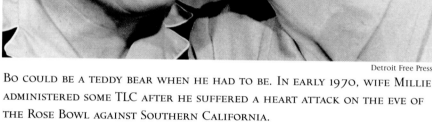

JULY 13, 1971: REGGIE JACKSON'S BLAST OFF THE RIGHTFIELD LIGHTS WAS AMONG SIX HOME RUNS IN THE LAST ALL-STAR GAME AT TIGER STADIUM, WON BY THE AMERICAN LEAGUE, 6-4.

SOME SAID MICHIGAN'S FIELD GENERAL REMINDED THEM OF ANOTHER MILITARY MAN, GEN. GEORGE PATTON. OTHERS SAID THE SAME THING OF OHIO STATE'S FIELD GENERAL, INCLUDING PRESIDENT REAGAN.

advertised. He placed ads in every major Ohio newspaper, highlighting Hayes' so-called "Team of the Century." In three weeks, he had a sellout. Later, he sold $2 tickets to special groups and invited high school marching bands to games, creating the illusion of a full stadium until he could fill it at full price.

Canham also instituted a direct-mail campaign. In the beginning, the athletic department mailed fewer than 100,000 ticket applications. The envelopes were full of brightly colored cards, one for each game, one for parking, others for other things. "When you opened the envelope, it was like confetti falling out on the desk," Canham said. That wasn't going to work. So Canham switched to a full-color self-mailer, sending out 400,000 for the same money. He purchased mailing lists of high-income families and people who had bought new cars recently. "We figured they had transportation and probably enough money for tickets, programs and hot dogs," he said. Eventually, more than 1.7 million ticket applications were mailed annually.

But Canham wasn't done. He developed Michigan logos of all kinds, then plastered them on anything and everything: coffee cups, lamps, key chains, rugs — even underwear. He sold his products in the mailers, too. "We figured if people

IN 1973, THE TEAMS TIED, 10-10, AND THERE WAS NO JOY IN ANN ARBOR AS BIG TEN ATHLETIC DIRECTORS VOTED TO SEND OHIO STATE TO PASADENA.

didn't buy football tickets, they might buy coffee cups," he said. Using advice received from NFL commissioner Pete Rozelle, Canham pioneered the licensing of collegiate sports logos. Michigan merchandise became popular from Maine to Malibu, and Canham started raking in money.

In addition, Canham encouraged fans to make the most out of football games, to bring food and drink and grills and friends to the parking lot for tailgate parties long before kickoff. Instead of simply promoting the team's record, he promoted the spectacle of a football Saturday itself. On posters. On placards. On anything anyone would look at. "I thought making a family day of a football game might encourage more women to become interested in coming to Ann Arbor," he said. "We understood that women controlled the weekend."

The aggressive strategy worked, riding the wild success of Schembechler's teams. Gradually, Michigan Stadium began to fill —and fill with people draped in Wolverines paraphernalia. Scores of schools from all over the nation noticed and started calling, asking for advice. Canham began holding a series of seminars coast-to-coast on marketing and fundraising, earning a reputation as the father of prime-time collegiate athletics.

Photos by Associated Press

WOODY HAYES RANG UP THE
NUMBERS IN 28 YEARS AT
OHIO STATE: 205 VICTORIES,
13 BIG TEN CHAMPIONSHIPS,
THREE NATIONAL TITLES. HAYES
TOOK A JOY RIDE IN 1972 AFTER
OHIO STATE BEAT MICHIGAN,
14-11, EARNING A TRIP TO THE
ROSE BOWL.

OCT. 30, 1971: ERIC ALLEN GAINED A MICHIGAN STATE-RECORD 350 YARDS
IN A 43-10 VICTORY OVER PURDUE.

United Press International

THOSE WERE TEMPESTUOUS TIMES. BEFORE THEY WERE RIVALS, SCHEMBECHLER PLAYED FOR HAYES AT MIAMI (OHIO) AND SERVED ON HIS STAFF AT OHIO STATE. WOODY OBVIOUSLY SCHOOLED BO WELL IN THE PROPER USE OF A CAP.

MARY SCHROEDER/Detroit Free Press

NOV. 25, 1972: WITH ONLY ONE WINNING SEASON IN SIX YEARS, DUFFY DAUGHERTY
FINISHED HIS MICHIGAN STATE CAREER WITH A 24-14 VICTORY OVER NORTHWESTERN AND A 5-5-1 SEASON.

And the best part? "All those people we drew saw some pretty good Michigan football," Canham said.

HEART ATTACK, THEN HEARTBREAK

After the 1969 upset, the Wolverines prepared for the Rose Bowl against Southern Cal energized by excitement. Too much excitement. For Bo, anyway. The night before the game, Schembechler suffered a mild heart attack and had to be hospitalized. He told doctors, "Hey, I've got a game to coach." But they not only wouldn't let him out of bed, they wouldn't let him listen to the game on the radio. The team went numb, devastated. No one could believe the iron man had melted. With defensive coordinator Jim Young at the helm, the Wolverines lost, 10-3.

But Bo would be back, bad heart be damned.

In 1970, he had the Wolverines playing like a powerhouse. They rolled through their schedule, winning their first nine games and shutting out three opponents. But then they met a very ornery Ohio State team. Hayes had his undefeated Buckeyes fuming over old injustices, and they won their revenge with a 20-9 victory at Ohio Stadium that clinched a Rose Bowl berth. The Wolverines finished 9-1, but they went nowhere for New Year's Day. At the time, only the Big Ten champion could play in a bowl — and only in Pasadena, Calif.

"This was our biggest victory," Hayes said. "It was the biggest, because it makes up for what happened to us last year. The players were hurt. They promised me all along they were going to play their greatest game today, and they did. Going to the Rose Bowl wasn't the main thought on their minds. It was avenging last year's loss."

A real rivalry was born. Hayes' players continued to fuel it. Guard Jim Stillwagon said: "We had a little debt to pay before we left Ohio State." Cornerback Jack Tatum said: "It feels better beating Michigan than going to the Rose Bowl." Linebacker Doug Adams said: "I've been thinking about Michigan every morning for a whole year." No longer was the Michigan-Ohio State game just an annual regular-season finale. It was its own one-game season, its own bad-will, bad-blood bowl.

Each of the next five seasons, the Wolverines again entered the Ohio State game undefeated. Only once did they leave it as winners. In 1971, tailback Billy Taylor used a big block by Fritz Seyferth to score on a 21-yard run with 2:07 remaining, giving Michigan a 10-7 home victory that threw Hayes into hysterics. Ohio State attempted a desperation pass with 1:25 remaining, but Michigan's Thom Darden intercepted it. Hayes thought Darden had

Detroit Free Press

FOR YEARS, SCHEMBECHLER LIVED BY THE AXIOM THAT THREE THINGS CAN HAPPEN WHEN YOU PASS THE FOOTBALL, AND TWO OF THEM ARE BAD. BUT ANTHONY CARTER TOOK THE PASSING GAME TO NEW HEIGHTS DURING HIS STAY FROM 1979 TO 1982.

Detroit Free Press

SCHEMBECHLER SHOWED THEM HOW IT WAS DONE FOR 21 SEASONS AT MICHIGAN. "ANYONE WHO'S EVER KNOWN HIM IS THE BETTER FOR IT," SAID A FORMER OFFENSIVE LINEMAN, DAN DIERDORF.

JAN. 12, 1973: JOE SCHMIDT RESIGNED AFTER GOING 43-34-7 AS LIONS COACH. THE NEXT SIX — DON MCCAFFERTY, RICK FORZANO, TOMMY HUDSPETH, MONTE CLARK, DARRYL ROGERS AND WAYNE FONTES — ALL FINISHED WITH LOSING RECORDS.

DOUG MARTIN/Associated Press

MAN IN THE MIDDLE: BO SCHEMBECHLER WAS THERE IN '79 WHEN FORMER OHIO STATE PLAYERS AND COACHES HONORED WOODY HAYES. EARLE BRUCE (RIGHT) TOOK OVER AFTER HAYES' FIRING.

CRAIG PORTER/Detroit Free Press

MICHIGAN MEN: SCHEMBECHLER ENTERTAINED GERALD FORD, WHO WOUND UP WITH A JOB IN WASHINGTON AFTER HE PLAYED FOOTBALL FOR THE WOLVERINES IN 1932-34.

DAVID C. TURNLEY/Detroit Free Press

FAMILY MAN: MILLIE, BO AND SON SHEMY HAD ROSY SMILES BEFORE ANOTHER TRIP TO PASADENA, EVEN THOUGH BO WENT 2-8 IN THE RUN FOR THE ROSES.

gone up the back of the intended receiver, Dick Wakefield, and let everyone know it, charging onto the field, bumping officials, scattering yard markers, screaming at the top of his lungs.

Hayes seemed ready to make like Schembechler and have a heart attack, but he didn't, and he was much happier afterward. In 1972, his Buckeyes beat Michigan at home, 14-11, and in 1973, they elevated the rivalry to an even uglier level. Ranked No. 1, they faced No. 4 Michigan in Ann Arbor for the right to go to the Rose Bowl. The game ended in a 10-10 tie, and most observers expected the Big Ten's athletic directors to send the Wolverines to Pasadena in a telephone vote the next day. Even Hayes thought so, because Ohio State had gone the year before.

"I can't imagine anyone going against Michigan," Canham said. "Frankly, I think the vote will be 9-1 in our favor."

It wasn't. It was 6-4, Buckeyes. It was home for the holidays for the Wolverines. Since their quarterback, Dennis Franklin, had suffered a broken collarbone with little more than two minutes remaining against Ohio State, the ADs thought the Buckeyes had a better chance of winning out west. Bo was white-hot mad, especially with Michigan State, which went with the Buckeyes. He tore apart his office. He screamed to the press. He swore revenge, which he didn't get for a long while.

In 1974, the Wolverines trailed Ohio State by two points in Columbus with 18 seconds remaining, and Mike Lantry set up at the 23 to kick a field goal. A Vietnam veteran, Lantry knew real pressure, but this was as close as football could come to it. A good kick meant victory, a perfect season, an undisputed conference championship, a Rose Bowl berth and a chance at the national championship. A bad kick meant nothing, nothing and more nothing. The snap came back, the kick went up, and the Wolverines' heads went down. Wide left. The Buckeyes won, 12-10.

A few days before the 1975 game, Hayes fanned the flames with this comment about how Michigan fans loathed him: "It doesn't hurt my feelings at all. It's the greatest compliment I could have. They couldn't beat me with two Michigan coaches, so they had to come down here and take a coach that I trained — and they haven't beaten me with him yet." Hayes' oversight of the 1969 and '71 games infuriated the Wolverines, but they did little about it. A late interception and touchdown beat them, 21-14, as Ohio State tailback Archie Griffin clinched his second straight Heisman Trophy.

All of Ann Arbor was crushed. Except Canham. He hated the losses to Ohio State as much as any Michigan man, and he wanted to winter in Pasadena as much as anyone. But the success, the bitterness, they were moneymakers, seat-fillers. In November of '75, the Wolverines drew 102,415 fans for a game against Purdue. They wouldn't draw fewer than 100,000 fans for a home game for the rest of the century.

MARCH 27, 1973: MICKEY REDMOND BECAME THE RED WINGS' FIRST 50-GOAL SCORER, BEATING TORONTO'S RON LOW IN AN 8-1 VICTORY. REDMOND FINISHED WITH 52.

CRAIG PORTER/Detroit Free Press

ASSISTANT BILL McCARTNEY, WHO WENT ON TO COACH COLORADO, LEARNED FROM THE MASTER HOW TO EXCHANGE PLEASANTRIES WITH GAME OFFICIALS.

WILLIAM DeKAY/Detroit Free Press

BO SCHEMBECHLER
QUARTERBACKED
MICHIGAN TO 17
BOWL APPEARANCES.
HE ONLY WON FIVE
OF THEM, BUT NEVER
WHINED ABOUT IT.

JULY 15, 1973: CALIFORNIA'S NOLAN RYAN TOSSED A 6-0 NO-HITTER AT TIGER STADIUM,
HIS SECOND OF THE SEASON AND SECOND OF HIS RECORD SEVEN.

Bo Schembechler didn't win a Rose Bowl until his sixth try, but he got the ride of his life after U-M walloped Washington, 23-6, in 1981.

"Those who stay will be champions."
BO SCHEMBECHLER'S PROMISE TO HIS PLAYERS

MARY SCHROEDER/Detroit Free Press

JULY 28, 1974: LIONS COACH DON MCCAFFERTY DIED OF A HEART ATTACK ON THE EVE
OF TRAINING CAMP. RICK FORZANO WAS SELECTED TO REPLACE HIM.

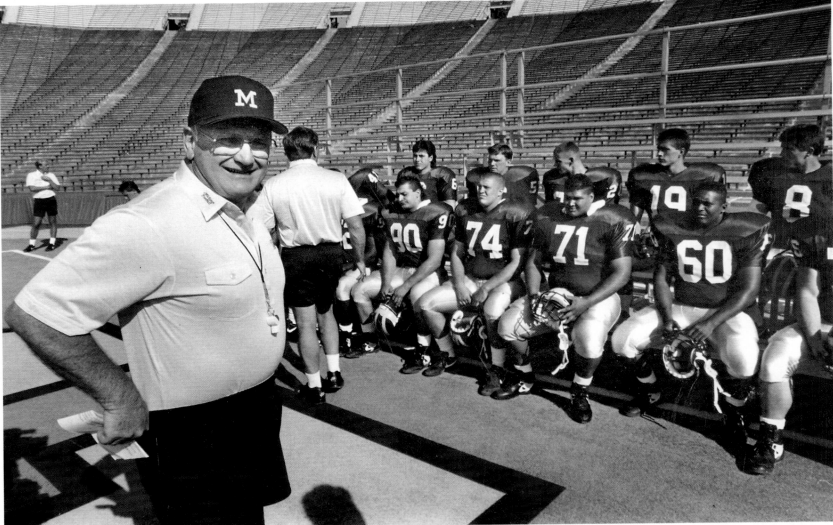

ALAN R. KAMUDA/Detroit Free Press

WHEN BO SCHEMBECHLER POSED IN
AUGUST '89, NO ONE KNEW THIS WOULD BE
HIS FINAL TEAM. HE GAVE UP COLLEGE LIFE
FOR A DESK JOB IN JANUARY 1990, WHEN HE
BECAME PRESIDENT OF THE DETROIT TIGERS.
"IT'S TRUE, I'M NOT USED TO PAYING PLAYERS
$3 MILLION A YEAR," HE SAID. "BUT I'VE BEEN
DEALING WITH BUDGETS, ADMINISTRATIONS,
TICKETS, ALL THAT STUFF FOR A LONG TIME AT
MICHIGAN. THAT'S WHAT A PRESIDENT DOES."

ALAN R. KAMUDA/Detroit Free Press

JULY 29, 1974: A GROUP HEADED BY BILL DAVIDSON BOUGHT THE PISTONS
FROM TEAM FOUNDER FRED ZOLLNER FOR $8.1 MILLION.

BO'S REVENGE

Hard times were hard on Schembechler's heart. In the spring of '76, he underwent quadruple-bypass surgery, and his top assistant, Gary Moeller, conducted drills in his absence. But with running back Rob Lytle and quarterback Rick Leach rising to stardom, times changed for the better for him — and for the worse for Hayes.

The Wolverines didn't enter the 1976 Ohio State game undefeated. They had lost to Purdue early in November. Perhaps that released some pressure and helped break the curse, because they romped around Ohio Stadium for a 22-0 victory that clinched their first trip to the Rose Bowl since the '71 season. In 1977, they won again, 14-6, and returned to the Rose Bowl. In 1978, it was the same story, a 14-3 victory this time. Bo was the best. And then, the era ended.

Ohio State played in the Gator Bowl that season. Late in the game, the Buckeyes trailed, 17-15, and were driving for victory. But Clemson middle guard Charlie Bauman intercepted a pass just beyond the line of scrimmage and ran to his left, toward the Buckeyes' bench. As he was forced out of bounds, he encountered Hayes, who — in full view of television cameras — took a swing at him. Hayes, winner of three national and 13 Big Ten titles in his 28 angry years in Columbus, was fired the next morning.

Schembechler was upset. He wanted to help his old coach and mentor, so he arranged a meeting with him at the home of former Bowling Green coach Doyt Perry and drove through a blinding snowstorm to get there. Bo spoke to Woody for hours, trying to convince him to apologize. Hayes promised he would. But he never did, hurting Schembechler's feelings for a final time.

Life went on without Woody. Although it wasn't nearly the same, ushering an era of hoop dreams for the state, it was still triumphant for Bo. On New Year's Day '81, Schembechler finally won the Rose Bowl, beating Washington, 23-6, after five losses in Pasadena. In '82, Schembechler rejected an offer from Texas A&M worth $3 million over 10 years, the richest contract in the history of college athletics. He announced he was staying by saying: "Frankly, I've come to the conclusion that there are things more important in this world than money." Things like winning. Things like team. Things like loyalty.

When Schembechler retired in December '89, two years after his second quadruple-bypass surgery, he wrapped up an incredible run. He had coached All-Americas such as Dierdorf, Darden, Lytle, Leach, Bubba Paris, Anthony Carter, Jumbo Elliott, Jim Harbaugh and Mark Messner. Bo had won more games than any other Michigan coach, compiling a 194-48-5 record — marred only by his 5-12 mark in bowls — and winning 13 Big Ten titles to match his mentor. He had raised money to build a new football facility, Schembechler Hall. He even had served as athletic director, as Fielding H. Yost did.

He had become a legend, and like every legend, he had accumulated a canon of anecdotes about his ability. One perhaps summed up his reign best: One day in practice, the Wolverines ran a pass play. A lineman came running past, Schembechler couldn't get out of his way, and ... BOOM! Down he went. He was hurting. The pain was killing him. But he couldn't just lie there. His players were watching.

So he hopped up.

"Well," he said, "that probably would have killed an ordinary man."

No one said a word.

TIMOTHY E. BLACK/Associated Press

A FITTING TRIBUTE: BO SCHEMBECHLER RECEIVED THE COLUMBUS TOUCHDOWN CLUB'S WOODY HAYES AWARD, AS THE COUNTRY'S TOP COLLEGE COACH, FROM HIS FORMER COACH AND BOSS IN 1986. HAYES DIED ON MARCH 12, 1987.

ALAN R. KAMUDA/Detroit Free Press

"I WILL NEVER BE FAR AWAY FROM MICHIGAN," SCHEMBECHLER SAID WHEN HE LEFT THE WOLVERINES IN 1990. "I WILL ALWAYS BE AVAILABLE FOR CONSULTATION. I WILL FOREVER BE A MICHIGAN MAN."

SEPT. 24, 1974: AL KALINE DOUBLED DOWN THE RIGHTFIELD LINE OFF DAVE MCNALLY OF BALTIMORE FOR HIS 3,000TH CAREER HIT.

A final title for the '68 gang

Last hurrah

By Brian Murphy

They were the rusted remnants of a championship team that brought a smoldering city together at the height of an unpopular war and hung around long enough to unite it again during the beginnings of a national scandal.

The 1972 Tigers were nothing like their more talented 1968 counterparts, whose seven-game World Series victory over St. Louis salved the wounds of a riot-torn city in the throes of racial and political unrest.

They were grayer in the beard, creakier in the leg and saltier in the tongue — a patchwork blend of veterans and castoffs led by hard-talking and hard-drinking manager Billy Martin. They eked out a division title on the season's next-to-last day because a players strike at the beginning of the season cost the Boston Red Sox one more game than the Tigers (156-155).

The Tigers hit only .237 and stole only 17 bases, but were carried by pitching and defense. They made up for their lack of speed and grace with spit and grit. They captured the Eastern Division and took on Charlie Finley's grumpy Oakland A's in a classic playoff series that foreshadowed the end of a Detroit era and launched a Bay Area dynasty.

Most of the faces were familiar from '68 — Kaline, Freehan, Horton, Stanley, McAuliffe, Cash, Northrup, Brown and Lolich. Also on the roster in '72 were 19-game winner Joe Coleman, power-hitting Frank Howard, smooth-fielding Eddie Brinkman and game-saving John Hiller.

In cash deals in August, general manager Jim Campbell acquired Howard from Texas, catcher-turned-outfielder

TONY SPINA/Detroit Free Press

THE TIGERS LOST GAME 5 TO THE ATHLETICS, THEN THE TIGER STADIUM FANS LOST ALL SENSE OF REASON.

Duke Sims from Los Angeles, and pitcher Woodie Fryman from Philadelphia.

Fryman, a portly 32-year-old left-hander, was trudging through a 4-10 season. He went 10-3 the rest of the way and pitched a four-hitter to win the clincher.

"I remember walking off the mound in the eighth with a 3-1 lead, and the Tiger Stadium fans gave me a standing ovation," Fryman said. "It was the greatest moment of my career."

The late-season pickups became key foot soldiers in Martin's brigade. "Billy Martin thought he had a chance to win with that club," Campbell had said. "And anytime you have that chance, you go for it. Fortunately, it worked out for us."

When the Tigers squared off with the A's in the best-of-five league championship series, playoff baseball was in its fourth year and the break-in at a Washington office complex called Watergate was sowing the seeds of political upheaval.

Finley loaded his club with rebellious players who wore their hair long and their dislike for their colorful owner on their sleeves. Reggie Jackson and Joe Rudi were roaming the outfield; Vida Blue, Catfish Hunter and Blue Moon Odom were stalking the mound; and Dick Green, Sal Bando and Bert Campaneris patrolled the infield.

In the opener in Oakland, Lolich pitched into the 11th inning for the Tigers and Hunter left after eight with the score tied, 1-1. Kaline gave Detroit a 2-1 lead with a homer in the top of the 11th, but his errant throw allowed the winning run to score after obscure sub Gonzalo Marquez drove in the

In Game 2, Bert Campaneris of the Oakland Athletics didn't take kindly to getting hit in the ankle by Tigers pitcher Lerrin LaGrow.

LaGrow ducked for cover when Campaneris sent his lumber into a low Earth orbit.

With the bat out of Campaneris' hands, LaGrow prepared for hand-to-hand combat.

A melee eventually ensued and LaGrow and Campaneris were ejected by umpire Nestor Chylak.

tying run with a single in the bottom of the inning.

The next day, Odom three-hit the Tigers en route to a 5-0 victory. But Game 2 and the series were forever marred by a vicious brawl in the seventh inning. Detroit reliever Lerrin LaGrow hit Campaneris in the ankle with a pitch, prompting the spindly shortstop to hurl his bat toward the right-hander, who ducked just in time as the Louisville Slugger sailed over his head.

Both dugouts emptied, the Tigers' assault led by the fiery Martin. As the Oakland Coliseum crowd hooted, plate umpire Nestor Chylak (a 1999 Hall of Fame inductee) ejected

Campaneris and LaGrow, sending Martin and Horton into such a rage that the other umpires had to physically restrain them.

"I didn't want to have any mayhem or riot out there," Chylak later said of his decision to boot LaGrow. "I had to even things out. I had to keep the fans in their seats."

Martin wasn't as diplomatic.

"That's the dirtiest thing I ever saw in my whole life in baseball," he said after the A's shoved Detroit into an elimination corner. "He could have killed my man. Campaneris is as gutless as any player who ever put on a

Nov. 28, 1974: The Lions lost their last game at Tiger Stadium, 31-27, to the Denver Broncos.

uniform in this game. It was like using a gun and then running away. The next time he'll probably use a knife. Or does he fight with his feet?"

American League president Joe Cronin suspended Campaneris for the rest of the series, but a bitter tone had been set as the teams traveled to Tiger Stadium for Game 3.

Trailing in the series, 2-0, the Tigers faced elimination on their home field, just as they did when they trailed the Cardinals, 3-1, four years earlier in the World Series.

Coleman — whom the Tigers had acquired from Washington after the 1970 season in a trade that included '68 poster boy Denny McLain — struck out 14 in a 3-0 victory.

Game 4 pitted the workhorse Lolich against Hunter again. And again the teams battled to a 1-1 tie through nine innings. Oakland scored two runs in the 10th, and the silver American League trophy was waiting for the A's in the clubhouse. So were a few dozen cases of iced champagne. The A's needed three outs and it was all theirs.

They never got one.

Northrup, whose Game 7 triple over Curt Flood's head blew open the '68 Series, donned the hero's cape again, singling in Gates Brown with the bases loaded in a wild finish, 4-3, that sent the 37,615 shivering fans home Wednesday evening with a reason to wish for Thursday.

It was Blue Moon vs. Woodie in a winner-take-all Game 5 at The Corner.

But controversy stole the show again on this blustery afternoon.

Detroit lost, 2-1, on Gene Tenace's first hit of the series, a fourth-inning, two-out single that scored George Hendrick from second base. But it was how Hendrick got on that left the Tigers fuming all winter. Hendrick grounded to McAuliffe deep behind second, and Cash had to stretch as far as he could to take the throw. Too far, according to first-base umpire John Rice, who said Cash's foot came off the bag and called Hendrick safe.

Three batters later, Tenace singled to left and Hendrick beat Sims' throw to Freehan.

The scoring was over. Odom and Blue combined to five-hit the Tigers, and the A's were on their way to a World Series date with Cincinnati.

"We had him beat by a step and a half," Cash moaned in an empty locker room, near where champagne bottles sat unopened. "Sure, I've cheated. But I don't cheat on plays that

aren't close. And that one wasn't close, and we lose the game on a little ol' technicality."

Things weren't exactly rosy in the A's clubhouse, though.

Jackson sobbed about a pulled hamstring that kept him from finishing the game and also kept him out of the World Series.

Odom sulked after teammates accused him of choking under the pressure of starting a clincher after he lasted only five innings.

And Blue refused to shake hands with Finley, revealing leftover bitterness from a preseason contract dispute.

The A's used their disdain for Finley as fuel to beat the Reds in seven games, and then roll through the Mets and Dodgers the next two years to capture three straight World Series titles.

Meanwhile, the magic of '72 quickly wore off the Tigers. The old gang faded simultaneously.

By 1974, that third-rate burglary forced Richard Nixon out of the White House, Kaline retired, and Fryman and his 6-9 record were traded to Montreal.

Detroit lost 90 games that season and 102 in 1975.

It would be several years before the Tigers were respectable again, but it was a risk Campbell was willing to take, just as his successor, Bill Lajoie, did in August 1987 when he traded minor-leaguer John Smoltz to Atlanta for Doyle Alexander, whose 9-0 finish lifted Detroit to the East title that year.

TONY SPINA/Detroit Free Press

BILLY MARTIN WAS A HARD-DRIVING, HARD-DRINKING MANAGER, BUT HE ALSO LIKED GOOD HORSEPLAY, ESPECIALLY WITH VETERANS SUCH AS AL KALINE AND NORM CASH.

"I came very close to breaking up that team earlier than I did," Campbell said. "I probably delayed our development by one or even two years by bringing in more veterans. But anytime you win, you've made the right move.

"This isn't an 'I' business. It's a 'we' business, right from the front office to the scouts to the players and everyone else. You win as a team, and you lose as a team. We won that thing as an organization."

Perhaps Eddie Brinkman best personified that. The skinny shortstop — a quiet, workmanlike performer who led the AL in fielding in '72 (.990) while playing every Tigers game — found himself staring into a TV camera in a delirious clubhouse after the division clincher.

"These are the greatest (bleeping) bunch of guys I ever played with!" Brinkman screamed during a live interview.

Brinkman later admitted that he never lived it down.

"The guys got on me for that for a long time," he said. "But at least I was telling the truth."

Spirit of '76

BY GEORGE SIPPLE

They were maize-and-blue collar.

And they took Michigan to the NCAA basketball finals for the second time in school history.

In the 1975-76 season, the Wolverines were small for a Big Ten team, and they didn't boast a lineup of high school All-Americas. But they outhustled opponents and made up for their size with incredible speed. They made NCAA history — setting up the first championship game between schools from the same conference.

That Indiana was their opponent that March night in Philadelphia was almost preordained. The Hoosiers had lost once the previous season — to Kentucky in the NCAA tournament. In 1975-76, they beat Michigan twice in the Big Ten season and were unbeaten conference champions at 18-0. Coached by irascible Bobby Knight, their stars were Kent Benson, Quinn Buckner, Scott May, Tom Abernethy and Bobby Wilkerson.

Associated Press

U-M COACH JOHNNY ORR HAD A THING OR TWO TO SAY AFTER ONE OF HIS PLAYERS WAS KNOCKED DOWN IN THE NCAA FINAL.

victory. Against Notre Dame, Grote hit four free throws in the final 27 seconds to hold off the Irish, 80-76. Against Missouri, Michigan won, 95-88, after trailing with 7:30 left.

In the national semifinals, the Wolverines finally coasted to victory. A 13-2 first-half run erased Rutgers' 31-game unbeaten streak, 86-70.

Then came the third showdown with Indiana.

Michigan actually led at halftime, 35-29. But Benson and May controlled the boards in the second half and snuffed U-M's fast break. No Hoosier committed a turnover for 16½ minutes. The Wolverines couldn't tire out or outhustle the Hoosiers, who went up by four, 47-43, with 12 minutes left and used a 10-0 run to make it 73-59 with 3:50 to play. Indiana won, 86-68 — the last team of the millennium to win the NCAA title without losing a game.

"Indiana had the best team here," Orr declared. "Hell's fire, anybody who believes anything else is an imbecile. Indiana is the best . . . and we're the second-best."

Michigan coach Johnny Orr gave his players a role each played to perfection. Junior guard Rickey Green, a junior college transfer, was the scorer. Center Phil Hubbard, a freshman, conquered the boards. Forward Wayman Britt, the captain and only senior, shut down the opposition's top scorer. Guard Steve Grote outworked players with his hustle and determination. Forward John Robinson provided the right mix of scoring and rebounding. Dave Baxter and Joel Thompson provided points off the bench.

In its first three tournament games, Michigan had to overcome deficits with eight minutes left. Against Wichita State, Green made a jumper with six seconds left for a 74-73

Michigan won the Big Ten championship the next season, but lost in the Mideast Regional final, 75-68, to North Carolina-Charlotte.

Green and Hubbard went on to long careers in the NBA. Orr, whose 209 victories led all other Michigan basketball coaches, left for Iowa State and a lucrative offer after the 1979-80 season.

Two unsung heroes also got their rewards: Michigan named its Defensive Player Award for Britt and its Hustler Award for Grote.

◆

NOV. 22, 1975: MICHIGAN STATE FLANKER KIRK GIBSON FINISHED HIS FRESHMAN SEASON WITH NINE CATCHES FOR 262 YARDS AND FOUR TOUCHDOWNS IN A 27-23 VICTORY OVER IOWA.

Birdmania

By Tom Panzenhagen

Detroit, once the City of Champions, was the City of Chumps in the summer of 1976. Consider:

■ The Lions were coming off a 7-7 season — typical of the '70s — and hadn't won a championship since 1957. The Super Bowl? Forget about it.

■ The Red Wings had missed the playoffs in nine of the previous 10 seasons and hadn't won a championship since 1955. Little Stevie Yzerman, the captain-to-be, was 11 years old.

■ The Pistons had logged 19 mostly uneventful seasons in Motown and were 13 years from their first title.

■ The Tigers lost 102 games in 1975. Al Kaline, Norm Cash, Denny McLain and Mickey Lolich — stalwarts of the 1968 championship squad — were gone from the team.

Detroit, itself beset by economic and social woes, needed hope. Detroit needed a hero.

And along came The Bird.

Mark Fidrych, a 21-year-old rookie pitcher, rose from obscurity in a few short weeks during the summer of 1976, capturing the imagination of the city and the nation.

The Tigers came north that year with a starting rotation of Joe Coleman, Dave Roberts, Vern Ruhle and Dave Lemanczyk. Fidrych, less than two years removed from high school, started the season in the bullpen. "I don't think I even pitched in the month of April," he said. "Then Joe Coleman came up sick, and I got my first start."

And what a start it was — a two-hitter against Cleveland. Fidrych possessed a natural sinker that he placed with pinpoint precision. But just as remarkable was his demeanor on the mound.

Fidrych talked to the ball between pitches. "Stay low, ball," he would say, "stay

ALAN R. KAMUDA/Detroit Free Press

CURTAIN CALLS WERE COMMON WHEN MARK FIDRYCH PITCHED AT TIGER STADIUM. FANS FLOCKED TO SEE THE BIRD IN THE SUMMER OF 1976.

low," and usually the ball obliged. Then he would drop to one knee to smooth the dirt on the pitcher's mound, making sure the landing area was just right for his front foot.

After a play was made, he would vociferously congratulate the players behind him. At the start of an inning, he would dash to the mound. After an inning, dash back to the dugout.

Fidrych, a gawky 6-feet-3 and 175 pounds, sported long, curly blond hair, which, along with his mound mannerisms, earned him the nickname The Bird, after a Sesame Street character, Big Bird.

He also earned the ardor of the fans, who would chant "Go, Bird, Go!" and demand curtain calls of their hero.

"I've never seen a city turned on like this," said Rusty Staub, a veteran teammate who had spent summers in Houston, Montreal and New York before coming to Detroit in 1976.

Crowds of 40,000 — more than double the average attendance — were common when Fidrych pitched. But he was unaffected by all the commotion. Fidrych owned a Dodge Colt, dressed casually — usually in jeans and T-shirt, much to the chagrin of general manager Jim Campbell — lived in an unfurnished apartment and never complained about his meager $16,500 salary.

Fidrych's defining moment came in a nationally televised Monday night game against New York on June 28 when he mowed down the first-place Yankees, 5-1, running his record to 8-1. Afterward, Tiger Stadium rocked with chants of "We Want Bird!" as he was interviewed by ABC sportscaster Bob Uecker.

Fidrych went on to start the All-Star Game and finished the year with a 19-9 record, a league-high 24 complete games in

JAN. 1, 1976: MICHIGAN MADE ITS FIRST APPEARANCE IN A BOWL OTHER THAN THE ROSE
AND LOST THE ORANGE TO OKLAHOMA, 14-6.

ALAN R. KAMUDA/Detroit Free Press

MARK FIDRYCH, WHO
RETURNED TO
MASSACHUSETTS AND TOOK
UP FARMING FOLLOWING HIS
PLAYING DAYS, TOILED IN
THE SOIL AS A BIG LEAGUER,
TOO. BETWEEN PITCHES HE
WOULD SMOOTH THE DIRT
ON THE PITCHERS MOUND,
AND BEFORE DELIVERING
THE BALL HE WOULD TELL
IT WHAT TO DO.

ALAN R. KAMUDA/Detroit Free Press

29 starts, and a 2.34 ERA, best in the majors. Unfortunately, his rise had little impact on the Tigers, who finished fifth in the American League East, 24 games behind the Yankees.

And, alas, it was a meteoric rise. Like Joe Hardy, the aging Senators fan in "Damn Yankees" who barters with the devil for a season in the sun, or the mythic Roy Hobbs from "The Natural," who steps from the shadows and saves the franchise, Fidrych's days were numbered.

The following spring, he injured his left knee and underwent an operation. The injury affected his pitching motion and ultimately ruined his arm. He won only 10 games during the next four seasons before drifting to the minors and then out of baseball.

But the fans didn't forget him. In 1984, when the Free Press asked readers to name their favorite Tigers, Fidrych finished second to Al Kaline while outpointing such legends as Charlie Gehringer and Hank Greenberg.

"That summer was a happy time," Fidrych said years later. "It was a year when you didn't want anything to change. You just wanted to pitch and play baseball and leave all the other stuff.

"I'll always be grateful to Detroit and to the Tiger fans. They were great to me."

NOV. 25, 1976: BUFFALO'S O. J. SIMPSON RUSHED FOR 273 YARDS
IN A 27-14 THANKSGIVING LOSS, MOST EVER BY A LIONS OPPONENT.

BO & WOODY, 1969-1978

At Grand River and McGraw

Old Red Barn

BERNIE CZARNIECKI (top) and MARY SCHROEDER (above)/Detroit Free Press

OLYMPIA STADIUM MAJESTICALLY STOOD ITS GROUND AT GRAND RIVER AND MCGRAW FROM 1927 TO 1986 — FROM HOCKEY TO HOOPS TO HOOVER.

By Bernie Czarniecki

If the Red Wings were your religion before 1980, Olympia Stadium was your shrine, a balconied basilica at the corner of Grand River and McGraw in Detroit.

Its intimacy captivated you. Its acoustics energized you. Its history consumed you. Its closing haunted you.

Olympia Stadium was a majestic, ornate, rectangular red brick edifice known as the "Old Red Barn," hardly the nickname expected of a design by C. Howard Crane. He was an internationally known theater designer based in Detroit. Among his gems were the Fox Theatre, State Theater and United Artists Theater.

Olympia opened Oct. 15, 1927, with a rodeo. The formal opening came two days later with a polo match for high society. Hockey, the sport that would bring the arena its biggest fame, followed Nov. 22, when the Cougars, Detroit's NHL entry, lost to the Ottawa Senators, 2-1.

The opening festivities included the mayor's presentation of a floral wreath to general manager Jack Adams, a "fancy skating" exhibition by Gladys Lamb and Norval Baptie, and the University of Michigan band as it paraded across the ice.

The Free Press account of the game started this way: "Ottawa's collection of systematic hockey players provided

APRIL 9, 1978: DENVER'S DAVID THOMPSON SCORED 73 POINTS,
MOST EVER BY A PISTONS OPPONENT, AT COBO ARENA. THE PISTONS WON, 139-137.

the only wet blanket on the hockey inaugural at the new Olympia last night."

Olympia played host to just about every type of sporting event, concert and political gathering. Its events included ice shows (Sonja Henie, Dorothy Hamill), concerts (Elvis Presley, the Beatles), boxing matches (Sugar Ray Robinson, Jake LaMotta, Thomas Hearns), circus performances (Flying Wallendas), wrestling matches (Alex Karras vs. Dick the Bruiser), pro and college basketball (early Pistons, U-D and Wayne State doubleheaders), Junior Wings hockey (Mark and Marty Howe), political rallies (Herbert Hoover, Black Muslims) and countless other special events (cycling, roller derby, lacrosse).

But Olympia was foremost a Red Wings mecca. Its ice was considered the league's fastest, and its boards the trickiest. For fans and players, the Old Red Barn had character with a capital C.

The seats were close to the action. The crowds were loud. And the fans and players were face-to-face between periods.

Players traveled to and from their dressing rooms in the lower concourse amid fans visiting concession stands, separated only by wooden barricades.

A trip around the red-and-white-tiled lower concourse included a trophy case for team awards, a glass-enclosed Red Wings Hall of Fame with oil paintings of its members, a display of Larry Aurie's retired jersey No. 6, and an area in the back where the Zamboni and spare nets were kept.

The stadium seats — lower and upper arena and mezzanine — were wide and well-cushioned, unlike most modern buildings. Any arena seat treated you to wonderful sight lines and the crisp sounds of the game interrupted only by energetic organ music.

In pre-Plexiglas days, when fans at the rink's ends were protected only by fencing, they could easily exchange pleasantries and not-so-pleasantries with players and officials. During a game in the 1954-55 season, Ted Lindsay scaled the fence, with Terry Sawchuk close behind, to introduce his right fist to a fan who had questioned Lindsay's heritage once too often.

Upper-arena end sections were often sold in blocks to busloads of opposing fans, which led to occasional fistic crowd chemistry during close games. Wings announcer Budd Lynch referred to these seats whenever a deflected shot ended up in the crowd. The fastest row counter in hockey history, Lynch instantly reported the final resting place for an errant puck, as in "Unger over the New York line, he shoots!!! . . . 38 rows up."

And then there was the mezzanine, reached by an escalator in the rear of the building (added in the 1960s) or by braving long, steep, winding stairwells. Seating there was especially intimate in the first dozen rows, where you felt as if you could touch the game.

Standing room was anywhere you could see the ice without the benefit of a seat — upstairs or downstairs. The wide upper-arena steps were a favorite perch, especially

ALAN R. KAMUDA/Detroit Free Press

OLYMPIA CLOSED WITH A SPECIAL HOCKEY GAME — 1979-80 RED WINGS VS. WINGS OLD-TIMERS. LINED UP FOR THE OLD DUDES ARE TED LINDSAY, SID ABEL AND GORDIE HOWE.

behind the nets. All that was needed was a cardboard hot dog tray to sit upon and a friendly usher to leave you alone.

Olympia's end came slowly and painfully. In the Wings' final NHL game there, Dec. 15, 1979, they rallied from a 4-0 deficit to tie the Quebec Nordiques, 4-4. Defenseman Greg Joly scored the tying goal with a little more than a minute left, prompting a deafening ovation from 16,000-plus.

The final game came Feb. 21, 1980, when the Red Wings defeated the Wings Old-Timers, 6-2. The 14,364 fans pulled for the old men, such as the famed Production Line of Lindsay, Sid Abel and Gordie Howe, standing for rousing ovations again and again and booing when the current Wings scored. Howe, in the midst of his final NHL season with the Hartford Whalers, wore his Whalers gloves and Red Wings uniform for the Old-Timers and appropriately enough scored the game's, and stadium's, last goal.

Howe said: "It was a fitting way to see the Old Barn close." Lindsay added: "The fans have showed what a tremendous city, and a hockey city, this is."

For six more years Olympia stood its ground at Grand River and McGraw, unused but at least intact. On July 9, 1986, the wrecking crew went to work. All morning people showed up at the lot next to the building. Some wore Wings caps and T-shirts. Some took pictures. Most left carrying bricks or chunks of masonry.

A giant wrecking machine pulled at the red brick wall near the spot somebody had chalked a farewell to Olympia Stadium. It read: "Later, Big Red Barn."

In a few weeks Olympia would be dust, surviving only in the bits and pieces its fans scavenged — and in those many treasured memories.

◆

OCT. 14, 1978: A 24-15 VICTORY AT ANN ARBOR BROKE AN EIGHT-GAME LOSING STREAK TO MICHIGAN FOR THIRD-YEAR COACH DARRYL ROGERS' MICHIGAN STATE. ONE SEASON LATER, ROGERS LEFT FOR ARIZONA STATE.

Our scrapbook

Associated Press

BILLY MARTIN AND FORMER TEAMMATE MICKEY MANTLE LIKED THE HIGH LIFE.

MUSICAL COACHES

Out	In
Bump Elliott	Bo Schembechler
Paul Seymour	Butch van Breda Kolff
John Benington	Gus Ganakas
Bill Gadsby	Sid Abel
Sid Abel	Ned Harkness
Mayo Smith	Billy Martin
Ned Harkness	Doug Barkley
Doug Barkley	Johnny Wilson
Joe Schmidt	Don McCafferty
Butch van Breda Kolff	Terry Dischinger
Terry Dischinger	Earl Lloyd
Duffy Daugherty	Denny Stolz
Don McCafferty	Rick Forzano
Johnny Wilson	Ted Garvin
Earl Lloyd	Ray Scott
Billy Martin	Joe Schultz
Joe Schultz	Ralph Houk
Ted Garvin	Alex Delvecchio
Alex Delvecchio	Doug Barkley
Doug Barkley	Alex Delvecchio
Denny Stolz	Darryl Rogers
Alex Delvecchio	Billy Dea
Ray Scott	Herb Brown
Gus Ganakas	Jud Heathcote
Rick Forzano	Tommy Hudspeth
Tommy Hudspeth	Monte Clark
Billy Dea	Larry Wilson
Larry Wilson	Bobby Kromm
Herb Brown	Bob Kauffman
Bob Kauffman	Dick Vitale

BILLY BRAWL

Billy Martin fought teammates, opponents, fans, writers, even marshmallow salesmen. But one of his earliest publicized bouts happened in 1969 in Detroit, before he managed the Tigers.

Martin, then the Minnesota manager, flattened Twins pitcher Dave Boswell outside the Lindell AC in downtown Detroit after Boswell reportedly sucker-punched teammate Bob Allison.

"It was one of the greatest street fights I'd seen in a long time," Lindell owner Jimmy Butsicaris said. "Boswell got in one punch, above Billy's temple. Then Billy got inside and really took care of him. He looked like Jake LaMotta."

Boswell needed 20 stitches, Martin seven.

WHAT A SHOT

Having lost the lead with only three holes left in the 1972 PGA Championship at Oakland Hills Country Club, Gary Player needed desperately to make something happen when he reached the par-four, 409-yard 16th. He tried to shorten the hole with a drive down the right side, but the ball drifted far right, into rough behind willow trees that border the green-guarding lake.

"I couldn't even see the green, only the flag," Player said. "I had to gamble — it would either be there or in the water."

Although 150 yards away, with the lake in the way, Player needed nine-iron loft to clear the willows. He jumped on it and the ball soared high and true, stopping four feet from the cup. The ensuing birdie was the impetus for a two-stroke victory.

In 1991, when Oakland Hills hosted the Senior Open, a commemorative plaque was placed at the site, and Player was asked whether he remembered the shot.

"It's like asking, 'Do you remember the day you got married?' " Player said. "I remember hitting a lousy drive. The branches on the tree were lower and you couldn't see the green. But a lady got up and left her stick-seat. That's what I aimed at, the empty stick-seat.

"Today, I kissed the green, because I still don't see how I did it."

Detroit Free Press

OH, BABY!

There was a guy named Dick Vitale who coached for the University of Detroit and the Pistons in the 1970s. Anybody heard from him lately?

COMEBACK

Associated Press

GORDIE, MARK AND MARTY HOWE TWICE BROUGHT THE AVCO CUP TO HOUSTON.

The Wings retired Gordie Howe after the 1970-71 season. The next year, they retired his famed No. 9 and he was inducted into the Hockey Hall of Fame.

But after two years as a vice president in charge of nothing, getting what he called the "mushroom treatment" — he was kept in the dark, he said, and periodically covered with manure — he quit the Wings and followed a cherished dream to the World Hockey Association.

Howe signed with the Houston Aeros to play on a line with his sons, Mark and Marty, something he had always dreamed of. The three Howes signed a four-year, $2.5-million deal negotiated by Colleen, the ultimate hockey mom.

It was no mere publicity stunt orchestrated by the upstart league. Gordie played in 419 WHA games in 1973-79, scoring 508 points. He was league MVP in 1974 at the age of 46, and helped the Aeros win two Avco Cups as WHA champions.

In 1977, Colleen tried to negotiate a return to the Wings for Howe and sons. But that fell through and they signed with the New England Whalers of the WHA. "We were extremely happy in Hartford," Colleen said. "We would have been happier in Detroit."

The WHA folded after the 1978-79 season, Howe's sixth in the WHA. But his team, now the Hartford Whalers, was one of four absorbed by the NHL. So Howe got to take a farewell tour of his old league before retiring at age 52.

And that meant that Detroit fans got another chance to cheer No. 9, even if it was adorning the back of an unfamiliar jersey. In addition to the Whalers' regular-season visits, Howe also played in the NHL All-Star Game in Joe Louis Arena and an old-timers game that closed Olympia.

GORDIE'S NUMBERS

YEAR		GP	G	A	PTS
1946-47	Red Wings	58	7	15	22
1947-48	Red Wings	60	16	28	44
1948-49	Red Wings	40	12	25	37
1949-50	Red Wings	70	35	33	68
1950-51	Red Wings-y	70	43	43	86
1951-52	Red Wings-xy	70	47	39	86
1952-53	Red Wings-xy	70	49	46	95
1953-54	Red Wings-y	70	33	48	81
1954-55	Red Wings	64	29	33	62
1955-56	Red Wings	70	38	41	79
1956-57	Red Wings-xy	70	44	45	89
1957-58	Red Wings-x	64	33	44	77
1958-59	Red Wings	70	32	46	78
1959-60	Red Wings-x	70	28	45	73
1960-61	Red Wings	64	23	49	72
1961-62	Red Wings	70	33	44	77
1962-63	Red Wings-xy	70	38	48	86
1963-64	Red Wings	69	26	47	73
1964-65	Red Wings	70	29	47	76
1965-66	Red Wings	70	29	46	75
1966-67	Red Wings	69	25	40	65
1967-68	Red Wings	74	39	43	82
1968-69	Red Wings	76	44	59	103
1969-70	Red Wings	76	31	40	71
1970-71	Red Wings	63	23	29	52
1973-74	Houston-z	70	31	69	100
1974-75	Houston-z	75	34	65	99
1975-76	Houston-z	78	32	70	102
1976-77	Houston-z	62	24	44	68
1977-78	New England-z	76	34	62	96
1978-79	New England-z	58	19	24	43
1979-80	Hartford	80	15	26	41
NHL totals		**1767**	**801**	**1049**	**1850**
WHA totals		**419**	**174**	**334**	**508**
32-year totals		**2186**	**975**	**1383**	**2358**

x-won Hart Trophy as league's most valuable player
y-won Art Ross Trophy as league's leading scorer
z-World Hockey Association

VILLAINS

CRAIG PORTER/Detroit Free Press

■ Colorado Rockies forward Wilf Paiement, who clubbed the Red Wings' Dennis Polonich during a game on Oct. 25, 1978. Polonich later sued and was awarded $850,000.

■ Oakland A's shortstop Bert Campaneris, who threw a bat at the Tigers' Lerrin LaGrow after he was hit in the ankle by a pitch in Game 2 of the best-of-five 1972 playoff series. The bat

missed, but a brawl ensued. Tigers manager Billy Martin tried to fight Campaneris, who was suspended for the rest of the playoffs. But the A's won in five.

■ Denny Stolz, left, whose recruiting tactics got Michigan State three years of NCAA probation and cost Darryl Rogers' '78 Spartans a trip to the Rose Bowl.

Our scrapbook

Detroit Free Press

LIONS TRAGEDIES

CHUCK
HUGHES

It was one of the most chilling moments in Detroit sports history. On Oct. 24, 1971, more than 54,000 people saw Lions receiver Chuck Hughes topple onto the Tiger Stadium grass and die as Chicago linebacker Dick Butkus waved frantically for help.

Hughes died when a blood clot lodged in an already clogged artery with 62 seconds left in the Lions' 28-23 loss to the Chicago Bears. He had just run a pass pattern, but Greg Landry instead threw an incompletion to Charlie Sanders. Hughes turned toward the Lions' huddle, took a couple of steps, threw both hands to his chest, and fell face-first at the 25-yard line.

The Lions had to deal with another tragedy in 1974. Looking for a capable replacement for coach Joe Schmidt, they hired Don McCafferty, who had coached the Baltimore Colts to a 16-13 victory over Dallas in Super Bowl V. But after a 6-7-1 season with Detroit, McCafferty collapsed and died of a heart attack just before the start of training camp in '74.

IRON MOUNTAIN MEN

They were best friends and teammates at Iron Mountain High in the early '70s — Steve Mariucci was the quarterback and Tom Izzo was the center on the football team, and they played side-by-side in the backcourt of the basketball team. Both went on to Northern Michigan, where Izzo was the basketball team's MVP his senior year in '77.

Mariucci completed five of 14 passes for 133 yards, including a 49-yard TD toss to Maurice Mitchell, as the Wildcats beat Western Kentucky, 16-14, in the 1975 NCAA Division II title game.

And both boys shared similar dreams.

"We'd spend hours every night talking and dreaming about what we were going to do and how we were going to become big-time head coaches somewhere," Izzo said. "I'm sure most people there probably thought we were crazy.

"I mean, you're in Iron Mountain. How is anybody going to find you up there? That one of us would be able to live the dream would be incredible. But that both of us are doing what we dreamed about is sometimes beyond belief."

They realized their dreams — Izzo as Michigan State's basketball coach, Mariucci as coach of the San Francisco 49ers — and remained tight friends through it all.

"We may only see each other once a year now because of our schedules," Mariucci said, "but we talk so much on the phone, it's almost like we're roommates at Northern Michigan again. Ours is a very special relationship."

THE WINNER IS . . .

ALEX DELVECCHIO: NHL's Lady Byng Trophy in 1969.

DENNY MCLAIN: American League Cy Young Award in 1969.

ALEX DELVECCHIO: NHL's Lester Patrick Trophy in 1974.

RAY SCOTT: NBA coach of the year in 1974.

MARCEL DIONNE: NHL's Lady Byng Trophy in 1975.

BRUCE NORRIS: NHL's Lester Patrick Trophy in 1976.

MARK FIDRYCH: American League rookie of the year in 1976.

BOB LANIER: J. Walter Kennedy Citizenship award in 1978.

LOU WHITAKER: American League rookie of the year in 1978.

BOBBY KROMM: Jack Adams Award as NHL's top coach in 1978.

OLYMPIC CHAMPIONS

Sapporo, Winter, '72

MARK HOWE, Detroit, hockey: silver.

Munich, Summer, '72

MICKI KING, Pontiac, diving: gold in three-meter springboard.

BILL MALONEY AND BILL KENNEDY, Michigan, swimming: bronze in 400 medley relay (for Canada).

DICK RYDZE, Michigan, diving: silver in platform.

Innsbruck, Winter, '76

SHEILA YOUNG-OCHOWICZ, Detroit, speedskating: gold in 500 meters, bronze in 1,000, silver in 1,500.

Montreal, Summer, '76

PHIL BOGGS, Michigan, diving: gold in three-meter springboard.

GORDON DOWNEY AND ALAN MCCLATCHEY, Michigan, swimming: gold in 800 freestyle relay (for Great Britain).

PHIL HUBBARD, Michigan, basketball: gold.

TOM LAGARDE, Detroit, basketball: gold.

TRISH ROBERTS, Michigan, basketball: silver.

Associated Press

TRADED TO THE BLUES, A SHOELESS GARRY
UNGER LET HIS HAIR DOWN ON THE LINKS.

FASHION STATEMENTS

■ Garry Unger's golden locks (which helped get him traded to St. Louis for Red Berenson).

■ Big collars and plaid, plaid, plaid.

Detroit Free Press

LIONS LEM BARNEY AND WAYNE WALKER
DISPLAYED THE FASHIONABLE LOOKS OF THEIR DAY.

REGGIE ROOFS IT

In an article leading up to the 1971 All-Star Game at Tiger Stadium, the Free Press asked, "Can Any of the Stars Clear Roof?"

Oakland's 25-year-old Reggie Jackson provided the answer in the bottom of the third inning.

With a runner on first, Jackson pinch-hit for Vida Blue. Pittsburgh's Dock Ellis, firing fastballs, built a 1-2 count on Jackson. Then he came in with another.

Jackson wrapped his bat around the pitch, then watched as it rocketed to right. The ball rose . . . and rose . . . before crashing into the light tower atop the roof.

It was one of six homers — three by each league — in the AL's 6-4 victory.

"The game was memorable in many ways," observed the next day's Free Press, "mostly because it was the last of these classics that will be played in Tiger Stadium. We should have our new stadium in another 20 years or so."

PITCHMEN

Special to the Detroit Free Press

BUBBA SMITH — BACK ROW, FAR RIGHT — WAS A CHARTER MEMBER OF THE TASTES-GREAT, LESS-
FILLING CROWD. HIS CO-STAR IN THE MILLER LITE ADS WAS DICK BUTKUS (AT LEFT IN STRIPED SHIRT).

BARNEY'S BIG DAY

Yes, No. 20 was ripping off big plays for the Lions before Barry Sanders or even Billy Sims. On Dec. 20, 1970, at Tiger Stadium, defensive back Lem Barney, left, had a 74-yard kickoff return that set up an Errol Mann field goal; a 65-yard punt return that set up a Greg Landry-to-Charlie Sanders TD pass; and a 49-yard interception return for a touchdown that sealed a 20-0 victory over Bart Starr's Green Bay Packers.

When he scored his TD, Barney said, "The place just went wild. The fans tore the goalposts down, and I had never seen that before. It reminded me of the '68 Tigers."

The fans were excited because the season-ending victory clinched the 10-4 Lions' first trip to the playoffs since their 1957 NFL championship. They lost in the first round to the Dallas Cowboys, 5-0.

BUMPER CROP

The good ol' boys got their first look at that little ol' track in the Irish Hills on June 15, 1969, when Cale Yarborough won the first NASCAR race on the 2½-mile D-shaped oval at Michigan International Speedway in Brooklyn.

Yarborough won the Motor State 500 in a door-to-door battle with Lee Roy Yarbrough, who spun and crashed just 300 yards from the finish of the 500-mile race.

That was the longest NASCAR race ever held at the track; the Yankee 600 later in '69 was shortened to 330 miles because of rain and darkness, and every other NASCAR race there was a 400-miler.

The original MIS grandstand held 25,000. By 1999 the seating capacity had grown to 125,445, and crowds approaching 160,000 jammed into Michigan Speedway — "International" was dropped from the name in '96 — for each of the summer's two NASCAR races.

The Roger Penske-owned track also held a couple of Indy-car races every summer, including a 250-mile race that opened the track Oct. 13, 1968, and the first U.S. 500 in '96.

1969-1978
Our scrapbook

BEST MARKETING CAMPAIGN

Aggressive Hockey is Back in Town

SUGGESTED (BY FANS) MARKETING CAMPAIGN

Darkness with Harkness

A STAR IS BORN

Funny thing, Lions defensive tackle Alex Karras wasn't around when George Plimpton was doing his "Paper Lion" thing in 1963 — that was the year Karras was serving a league suspension for betting on his team.

But when the book was made into a movie — starring a pre-"M*A*S*H" Alan Alda as Plimpton — it was updated to fit the current cast of Lions. Joe Schmidt was now the coach, "Plimpton" now got to play in an exhibition against the St. Louis Cardinals, and Karras played a major role in the film — as himself, of course — and got rave reviews for his acting and comedic touch.

So the colorful Karras went Hollywood and found a lucrative career as an actor after his football days ended in 1970. He even did a three-year stint on "Monday Night Football" with Frank Gifford and Howard Cosell.

Special to the Detroit Free Press

Special to the Detroit Free Press

FAVORITE ALEX KARRAS ROLES

■ As Mongo, above, in Mel Brooks' "Blazing Saddles" — a classic cinema moment when he punched out the horse.

■ As a lovable wrestler in "The 500 Pound Jerk" — where's Dick the Bruiser when you need him?

■ As a lovable wrestler in "Babe" — no talking pig here, he played George Zaharias to future wife Susan Clark's Babe Didriksen.

■ As a crooked sheriff in "Porky's" — no talking pig here either, just the top-grossing Canadian flick of all time.

■ As the adoptive dad (with Clark again) in "Webster," left — a tender portrayal, yet more macho than Conrad Bain in "Diff'rent Strokes."

Associated Press

ICONS

Bob Lanier's size-22 shoes

BY THE NUMBERS

93,857
The attendance for Michigan's 55-7 homecoming victory over Indiana on Oct. 25, 1975 — the last time Michigan Stadium failed to draw 100,000.

133
Laps in the rain-shortened 1973 Indianapolis 500, won by Gordon Johncock of Hastings.

$236,023
The prize money for Johncock's victory.

$100,000
The contract Al Kaline signed after the '71 season that made him the first Tiger to reach that plateau.

41
Michigan State's average points for Big Ten games in 1978, led by quarterback Ed Smith and flanker Kirk Gibson. It was a conference record until 1994.

Michigan State University

KIRK GIBSON, NOT PLAYING FOOTBALL.

CHAPTER 7

HOOP DREAMS
1979-1993

By Nicholas J. Cotsonika

The morning of April 22, 1977, was a magical one for the sport of basketball in the state of Michigan. At about 9 o'clock, a teenager with a big hairdo and an even bigger smile walked into a room at his high school, Lansing Everett, and sat down at a table to make a major announcement. The place was jam-packed. Reporters clutched notebooks. Photographers popped flashbulbs. Television crews rolled cameras. Students, teachers, coaches and even a few rabid local fans were there, too, waiting breathlessly to hear what young Earvin Johnson had to say.

Until that point in the century, basketball really hadn't blossomed in the area. The state wasn't a hoops haven, as Indiana and North Carolina and Kansas were reputed to be. Not at all.

The Pistons were a team without a history, and Michigan and MSU had no NCAA titles. Until now.

Its autumns were for football, its winters for hockey. The Pistons had been mostly mediocre since moving to Detroit in 1957 from Ft. Wayne, Ind., despite featuring a few accomplished players such as George Yardley, Bailey Howell, Dave DeBusschere, Bob Lanier and Dave Bing. Michigan had come close to NCAA national championships in the 1960s and 1970s, starring sweet guards Cazzie Russell and Rickey Green, but hadn't captured the full imagination of sports fans. Michigan State had been short on glory, although Johnny Green, Julius McCoy and Horace Walker had brought pride to their school.

So the fact that Johnson's announcement was big news was, in a certain sense, big news itself. Finally, basketball was a big deal. A huge deal. A deal so enormous, Johnson actually had to hold a press conference to accommodate the interest, a rare circumstance for a prep athlete at the time. Everyone wanted to know whether Johnson would choose to play for Michigan or Michigan State. He had attended Spartans games since he was 10 years old and was loyal to Lansing, his hometown. Everyone knew that. But the Wolverines were the runners-up in the NCAA tournament in '76, were considered perhaps the nation's best team in '77, and were certainly a seductive option, because the Spartans' program was in turmoil. Everyone knew that, too.

The room quieted. Johnson, charismatic and comfortable in

Michigan State University

IN THEIR TWO SEASONS TOGETHER, MAGIC JOHNSON AND GREG KELSER RACKED UP VICTORIES AND
HARDWARE. IMAGINE IF THEY COULD HAVE ADDED THE BIG, ROCK-SOLID GUY TO THE LINEUP.

The crowd chuckled, uneasy.

Again, he leaned toward the microphone slowly.

"Next fall," he said, "I will be attending Michigan . . . State University."

With that, all of Everett erupted in applause and cheering. Those who weren't in the room heard the news over the public-address system — or from the word-of-mouth bulletins that spread all over the state in seconds. Suddenly, football didn't matter quite as much. Hockey, either. A new era was beginning, one of national championships for Michigan State and Michigan, one of back-to-back NBA titles for the Pistons.

It was Magic.

FROM GUS TO JUD

Hopes were so high for Johnson, because they had been so low for Michigan State so recently. An ugly incident in January 1975 helped cost coach Gus Ganakas his job and put the program's reputation in peril. Ten black players, already upset with what they thought was the athletic department's preference toward football, were angered by a lineup that consistently started a white freshman, Jeff Tropf, over more experienced blacks. They challenged Ganakas at a pregame meeting on the very morning they were to face top-ranked Indiana. Ganakas reminded them that he was the coach: He made all lineup decisions, alone.

And then, they walked out on him.

Stunned, sickened and sunken, Ganakas spent the afternoon advising his bosses of the situation and rounding up junior varsity players to fill in against the best team in the land. When he got to Jenison Field House, he found the 10 players sitting in front of their lockers. They asked what he would do; he told them he would suspend them. No way would they play. The Spartans lost that night, 107-55, in a game that was sheer comedy. But worse, the press descended upon campus from all over. The mutiny had become national news. Soon afterward, the rebellious players apologized to Ganakas, and he reinstated them immediately, smiling to reporters and calling

the spotlight even at age 17, leaned toward the microphone slowly, building the suspense to its breaking point. He always was at his best under pressure, colorful in tense moments, when everyone was watching.

"Are there any questions?" he asked, straight-faced.

MARCH 26, 1979: LARRY BIRD SCORED 19 POINTS FOR INDIANA STATE, BUT MAGIC JOHNSON GOT 24
TO LEAD MICHIGAN STATE TO A 75-64 VICTORY IN THE NCAA CHAMPIONSHIP GAME.

AFTER DIRECTING THE SPARTANS TO THE NCAA TITLE, COACH JUD HEATHCOTE TIGHTENED THE BOLTS ON A SIGN OF THE TIMES. HE CAME TO MSU FROM MONTANA IN 1976 – WITHOUT VISITING THE EAST LANSING CAMPUS.

SPARTANS HEROES GREG KELSER, TERRY DONNELLY AND MAGIC JOHNSON, WITH A SOUVENIR, TOOK QUESTIONS AFTER TAKING DOWN INDIANA STATE IN THE BIG GAME.

the spat a "lovers' quarrel."

But there was no question that severe damage was done. Ganakas received all kinds of negative responses, from blacks who thought he had been unfair in the first place, from a mostly white community that didn't want to welcome back a bunch of ingrates so easily. For the rest of the season, the crowd greeted the Spartans quite coolly, although their 17-9 record was their best since 1967. When summer arrived, the scars were still there. Tropf transferred to Central Michigan, convinced he could not progress in that environment. A year later, after enduring more controversy, the athletic department dumped Ganakas as coach and reassigned him.

The Spartans were in trouble. They needed a sense of stability, direction and discipline. After interviewing several candidates for the coaching job in Chicago, they found it. Jud Heathcote of Montana, when asked what he would do if his team walked out on him, said simply: "I'd resign." Then, he backed up his shocking statement by saying that a walkout would mean that he had lost control, that he no longer had any hope of regaining the respect he needed as a leader. The athletic department was impressed. He was hired.

Heathcote never had seen East Lansing, but he jumped at the chance to coach in the Big Ten. In rebuilding the program, he worried less about race and more about apathy and talent. Michigan State needed excitement. It needed to root for itself again. It needed to pack in more than the 5,000 lonely souls who showed up at Jenison on most nights. In the fall of '76, he began appearing at student dorms, begging for green-and-white, grassroots support. He also began recruiting Johnson and Lansing Eastern's Jay Vincent, whose prep battles were overshadowing anything the Spartans did, anyway. He had no idea how soon the bad old days would be over.

LIKE MAGIC

Johnson's parents, Earvin Sr. and Christine, called him Junior. The rest of the adults in his neighborhood called him June Bug. His buddies called him E. J. or simply E. But during his sophomore year in high school, he earned a new nickname, one that erased all the others.

After Johnson scored 36 points, pulled down 18 rebounds and dished out 16 assists to lead Everett to a hocus-pocus victory over conference favorite Jackson Parkside seven games into the season, Fred Stabley Jr. of the Lansing State Journal walked into the Vikings' locker room, his mind whirring. He approached Johnson with an idea. All great ones need a nickname, don't they?

"How about if I call you Magic?" he asked.

Johnson smiled.

"Yeah," he said. "Fine. Whatever you like."

Magic. Perfect. It stuck to Johnson's identity like the ball stuck to his hand during a dribble. Everything he did seemed touched by a mysterious, unknowable force. Bused cross-district against his wishes to Everett, Johnson took over the school at a turbulent time. Racism never was a problem there, as at other schools, because Johnson wouldn't allow it. On the

EARVIN JOHNSON COMMITTED TO MICHIGAN STATE AS A 17-YEAR-OLD FROM LANSING EVERETT, WHERE HE WON A CLASS A STATE TITLE.

MAGIC JOHNSON AND THE SPARTANS CAME UP BIG IN THE 1979 NATIONAL SEMIFINALS, ELIMINATING PENNSYLVANIA, 101-67. LARRY BIRD'S UNBEATEN SYCAMORES WERE NEXT. THE PROMOS: MAGIC MAN VS. BIRD MAN.

court, a lack of flash on offense was never a problem, as at other schools, because Johnson wouldn't allow that, either.

The Spartans had to have him, the hometown kid. One of seven children, Johnson learned the value of a strong work ethic at 814 Middle Street from his father, who balanced two jobs. In his spare time, E. J. learned to love hoops — Michigan State hoops. When he wasn't playing against his friend Vincent, he was at Main Street School, pretending to be Wilt Chamberlain, or competing against older players on street courts. He rarely missed a game at Jenison. He knew

Ganakas and said he "saw him as a friend."

But nothing was assured. With Ganakas gone, Johnson began to waver. "The coaching change kind of threw me for a loop," he said. "The problem was still not knowing about Jud." Heathcote had decided to leave Johnson alone during the recruiting process. He didn't want to try too hard, knowing that someone as sharp as Johnson would find out the facts for himself. Michigan, meanwhile, was going all-out. Coach Johnny Orr and top assistant Bill Frieder spoke to Johnson almost daily, repeatedly sent him letters, and visited him at

DEC. 11, 1979: INDIANA PACERS ASSISTANT COACH JACK MCCLOSKEY
APPOINTED PISTONS GENERAL MANAGER.

school.

Johnson became very interested in Ann Arbor. He saw a lot of games at Crisler Arena, got to know the guys, and felt comfortable. The catchy fight song bounced around in his head, even as he lay in bed, minutes from Michigan State's campus. By the time Everett beat Birmingham Brother Rice to win the 1977 Class A state title — at Crisler, of all places — he was still uncertain. He traveled to Germany with an all-star team, and when he returned, he leaned toward Michigan, which had convinced him that his 6-foot-8 height would force him to be a center if he became a Spartan.

But then, Michigan State stopped being passive. Vern Payne, who had been recruiting Johnson as a Heathcote assistant, had been hired as Wayne State's head coach. But he did one last favor for his old school. The day before Johnson's press conference, he drove over to Everett, pulled Johnson out of class, and explained to him why he needed to stick with Michigan State. *Heathcote was a good, smart coach. Screamed a lot, yes, but knew the game. Center was not an option. Roots — and staying faithful to them — were important.* Johnson nodded through the lecture, thanked Payne, and told him he would sign the next morning.

Not good enough.

"No," Payne said, taking a risk, "I want you to sign now."

Johnson had been convinced.

"OK, Coach," he said.

And that was that.

Magic for Michigan State.

Johnson later said he always had loved the Spartans, but if Payne had not come there that day, he probably would have signed with Michigan. "He spoke from the heart," Johnson said. "I'm so glad he did. He was right." A friend of Johnson's, Kenny Turner, had purchased an assortment of Michigan gear for Johnson to wear at his press conference. A jacket. A cap. A T-shirt. Some shorts.

He threw everything away. Gladly.

SO CLOSE

Johnson's style of basketball electrified the Spartans, because it was anything but, well, Spartan. He revolutionized the guard position. At his height, he should have been playing the low post. But he controlled the ball with the quickness and sure-handedness of a skilled small man — and with the flair and creativity of a genius, of an artist. He knew the game and demonstrated uncommon court awareness, often thinking like, or ahead of, Heathcote. He didn't have a classic jump shot, but that didn't matter. He found ways to get the ball in the basket, or he found ways to get it to someone else.

The first day he dressed in green and white, no one viewed him as a freshman. He was more than just precocious. He was someone the team could follow. Even Greg Kelser — a junior at the time and a star with his own nickname, Special K — couldn't deny what Johnson brought to the team. After all, Johnson gave him the ball, and with the dunk having been reinstated in college basketball, that meant alley-oops and all kinds of fun. There was no question

Michigan State University

SLEIGHT OF HAND: JUD HEATHCOTE WAS IN HIS FOURTH SEASON AS MICHIGAN STATE'S COACH AND MAGIC JOHNSON WAS A SUPER SOPHOMORE WHEN THE SPARTANS WENT ALL THE WAY IN 1978-79.

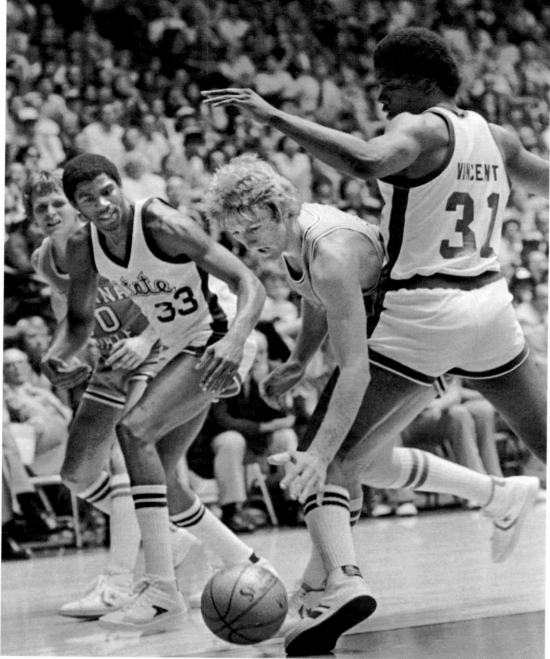

LARRY BIRD RARELY HAD THE UPPER
HAND ON MAGIC JOHNSON AND THE
SPARTANS, WHO PUT THE SQUEEZE ON
HIM AND INDIANA STATE, WINNING
THE FINAL, 75-64.

in 1977-78 that Magic was putting Michigan State on the map.
The Spartans, 12-15 the previous season, set a school record
for victories by going 25-5.

Heathcote allowed Johnson a player's dream: freedom.
Johnson could post up, lead the fast break, shoot from outside, anything. Turnovers were a problem for a while. That
was to be expected. What no one expected were all the victories. The Spartans won 14 of their first 15 games, losing only
to Syracuse at the Carrier Dome. They beat the best Detroit
team in years. They beat their first seven Big Ten opponents.

Better yet, Johnson appeared to be doing what great players
do: He made his teammates better. Kelser, ever acrobatic in
midair, came into his own, benefiting from Johnson's up-
tempo ball movement. Vincent settled in at center, his soft
hands and stunning grace making up for his girth. The sup-
porting cast kept up well.

Suddenly, Jenison started selling out. Television loved the
Spartans for drawing high ratings. Johnson was the preemi-
nent freshman in the nation, so confident that he could do to
Heathcote comfortably what 10 players had done so uncom-

fortably to Ganakas a few years before: rebel. Heathcote would yell and stomp his feet and pump his fists and bang his head. Sometimes, he would be a little too assertive about what he wanted done on the court. Johnson, with an ambassador's tact, would wave his hand subtly and say, "Back off." And Heathcote, never feeling his authority was being threatened, would.

After a mid-season mini-slump, the Spartans won eight of their final nine games, captured the Big Ten title, then dispatched Providence and Western Kentucky in the first two rounds of the NCAA tournament. Heathcote's only complaints were with the media, which he thought were unfairly critical of a program that had risen so high so quickly. But then came Kentucky, which Michigan State led by five at halftime in the third round. The Spartans stepped out of char-

acter in the second half, playing a conservative rather than freewheeling style, and the Wildcats hunkered down into a zone. In the end, they beat Michigan State, 52-49, and went on to win the whole darn thing.

Johnson had brought the Spartans to the brink almost overnight. They had lost to no less than the national champion — and barely. So naturally, what came next was considered nothing but destiny.

SPARTY TIME

At the 1977-78 team banquet, Johnson rose to a standing ovation and stepped to the podium to speak. When he touched the microphone it fell, causing a cacophony of sound to clatter through the eardrums of everyone in the audience. Johnson handled the situation with his usual ease, class and good humor. "We win the Big Ten championship," he said, "and all they give us is a cheap, old microphone." Johnson couldn't stop smiling. He had lost to Kentucky, but that was a learning experience. Nothing like that would happen again.

The 1978-79 Spartans were the best team Michigan State ever had and one of the best teams ever to play college basketball. They set another school record for victories, going 26-6 and sharing the Big Ten title with Purdue and Iowa. Outside the holy trinity of Johnson, Kelser and Vincent were forward Ron Charles, shooter Mike Brkovich and guard Terry Donnelly, all solid support players. The only regular who didn't return from the previous season's team was guard Bob Chapman. Talented, experienced and hungry, Michigan State was primed for excellence.

After a draining training trip to Brazil, the Spartans struggled early. Their only loss in the seven games that preceded the Big Ten schedule was a 70-69 defeat at North Carolina, but things were much worse than that, and it soon showed. They went 4-4 to open the Big Ten season, losing to lowly Northwestern at the tail end of the streak, 83-65. Heathcote was furious. He called a team meeting, in which coaches and players aired grievances. It made a big difference, and most important, no one felt the need to stage a walkout. "There was a renaissance," Kelser said.

The next game was a classic. With their season on the line, the

Associated Press

MAGIC JOHNSON LET THE SALT LAKE CITY CROWD — AND THE LARGEST TV AUDIENCE TO WATCH AN NCAA TITLE GAME — KNOW WHO WAS NO. 1 ON MICHIGAN STATE'S BANNER NIGHT.

APRIL 29, 1980: THE LIONS TOOK RUNNING BACK BILLY SIMS, A HEISMAN TROPHY WINNER FROM OKLAHOMA, WITH THE FIRST OVERALL PICK IN THE DRAFT.

MAGIC JOHNSON, WHO HAD WON A HIGH SCHOOL STATE CHAMPIONSHIP, ADDED AN NCAA TITLE. NEXT WOULD COME AN NBA TITLE AS A ROOKIE.

Spartans faced first-place Ohio State in an exhibition of toughness at Jenison. Johnson sustained an ankle injury with 2:23 left until halftime. Doctors told him to quit, that he would be out for two more games at least. But Johnson would have none of it. He yelled, "Wrap me up!" And, with his bum ankle mummified, he marched defiantly down from the training room to the bench before the crazy crowd, pushing through a bone-rattling roar of a magnitude that Jenison had never seen. "You couldn't hear anything," Johnson said. "It was like your eardrums had popped." The Spartans won, 84-79, in overtime, and their season was back on track.

From that day forward, the Spartans lost just one game, their regular-season finale at Wisconsin. They humbled Kansas, 85-61, in a nationally televised game. They avenged their Northwestern loss. They thoroughly dismantled Michigan, which also had beaten them earlier. They were on a Magic mission, destined for greater things. They opened the NCAA tournament with victories over a loud-mouthed Lamar team and Louisiana State, setting up a third-round game against Notre Dame, another classic.

The Fighting Irish were loaded with talented future professionals such as Kelly Tripucka, Bill Laimbeer and Orlando

JAN. 1, 1981: BO SCHEMBECHLER GOT HIS FIRST ROSE BOWL VICTORY AFTER FIVE LOSSES
AS MICHIGAN BEAT WASHINGTON, 23-6. BUTCH WOOLFOLK RUSHED FOR 182 YARDS.

Woolridge. Heathcote made no pregame pep talk. He simply wrote on the blackboard: "LET'S KICK SOME ASS." And his players responded. Angry that Notre Dame pulled rank as the No. 1 seed in the Mideast Regional and forced them to wear green and not their lucky white, the second-seeded Spartans played with fire, beginning with a slam off the opening tip-off by Brkovich. Kelser and Johnson never played better. Kelser had 34 points and 13 rebounds; Johnson had 19 points and 13 assists. The Spartans won, 80-68.

Heathcote was perhaps as happy as he ever was, shaking his fists over his head in triumph. But after the game, he was calm with perspective. He told his players, "Now we're on to something bigger." Yes. The Final Four. The Spartans routed Pennsylvania in the semifinals, 101-67. Johnson then met up with the man who would become his foil in the NBA, Larry Bird, who led 33-0 Indiana State into the final the same way Johnson had led the Spartans there: using an extraordinary offensive touch to uplift a group of guys from home.

Played in Salt Lake City before one of the largest television audiences in history, the game helped launch the NCAA tournament into March Madness. Bird couldn't solve Heathcote's matchup zone and double-teaming. He made just seven of his 21 shots and scored 19 points, eight below his average, and sat crying on the bench afterward, his head hidden by a towel. Johnson fared better. He scored a game-high 24 points in the Spartans' 75-64 victory, won the Final Four outstanding player award, and squeezed Kelser in a famous embrace.

Johnson and his home state had their first big-time basketball championship. Both would get more in the years to come, although the Spartans, despite great players such as Scott Skiles and Steve Smith and Shawn Respert and Eric Snow, wouldn't rise to such heights again until the late '90s.

After the season, Johnson went to visit the Los Angeles Lakers, who by trade had the No. 1 pick in the NBA draft. They wanted him. He wanted them. Magic in Tinseltown. Perfect.

So he left school early, with no hard feelings from his fellow Michigan natives, to whom he would return — as the enemy of what became their new favorite basketball team, the Pistons.

NO DOUBTING THOMAS

Isiah Thomas grew to be a close friend of Johnson's as the years progressed. They even kissed on the court before games. But despite his cherubic face and angelic grin, Thomas didn't share Johnson's universal popularity and charisma. He was a complex sort, raised in a Chicago neighborhood so rough, a reporter who once tried to visit it couldn't convince his cab driver to stop long enough to let him out. He was his mother Mary's son, a proud man who had been taught to know what he wanted and not be afraid of what anyone thought. He was definitely likable at his best. In time, he became one of the most beloved celebrities in Detroit history, a magnet for children, especially. But he could be definitely prickly at his worst. He could ruffle feathers and tick off enemies and friends alike. And he did. Right from the start.

Before the Pistons made Thomas their No. 1 pick (second overall) in the 1981 draft, he said he didn't want to play for Detroit, a sad-sack franchise that had lost 61 games in 1980-81 and averaged fewer than 100 points a night. He was young, just a 20-year-old kid with a bright smile and suction cups for hands, a cocky 6-foot-1 point guard fresh off winning a national championship in his sophomore season at Indiana.

"My job is to get the ball to somebody who can score," he said. "In Detroit, who would I pass to?"

After the draft, embarrassed, he scrambled to change his tune. But that didn't work well, either, although he praised the savvy management group that had selected him, of course. Having already insulted his new team's forwards, he now insulted its guards.

"I want to clear something up that I said before," he said. Assistant coach Don Chaney "has informed me that maybe the players we have here just didn't have anybody to get them the ball. Hopefully, I'll be able to get them the ball."

Pistons veterans, not to mention sensitive Detroiters, weren't thrilled with Thomas — until he made his NBA debut, in which he had 31 points, 11 assists and three rebounds in a 118-113 victory over Milwaukee before 9,182 at the Pontiac Silverdome. Zeke, as he was known, had set the tone. He showed he was the real deal, that success was all that he wanted. Prickly or not, he would get his teammates the ball, all right.

And a couple of titles, too.

LONA O'CONNOR/Detroit Free Press

IT STARTED WITH THE SMILE. ONLY 20, ISIAH THOMAS WAS INTRODUCED AS THE PISTONS' TOP DRAFT CHOICE IN 1981. HE COMPLIMENTED MANAGEMENT: "THEY'RE NOT SIT-BACK-AND-WAIT PEOPLE. THEY WANT TO WIN, AND I'LL DO ANYTHING POSSIBLE TO WIN, TOO."

PAULINE LUBENS/Detroit Free Press

ALWAYS THE SMILE. THOMAS VISITED A COMMUNITY CENTER IN 1986 ON NO CRIME DAY, A CAMPAIGN HE STARTED. A CROWD OF 15,000 ATTENDED HIS RALLY AT HART PLAZA IN DOWNTOWN DETROIT.

FACING PAGE: DESPITE ROLANDO BLACKMAN, RALPH SAMPSON AND KAREEM ABDUL-JABBAR, THOMAS WON HIS SECOND ALL-STAR GAME MVP AWARD, IN 1986.

GROWING UP

During the '80s, Thomas and his team-mates slowly built momentum and a foundation for future joy. Each little milestone they crossed, each little sign of progress, was cause for celebration. In December '83, they set a new standard for points scored in wretched excess, playing a prodigious and preposterous game against Denver that ended with them on top, 186-184, after three overtimes. Later that season, they set a new standard for themselves.

They finished 49-33. That meant they had completed their first winning season since 1976-77. They were finally back in the playoffs. Although they bowed out to New York in the first round, they showed grit and proud promise. Especially Thomas. Refusing to lose with a whimper, Thomas scored 16 points in the final 94 seconds of regulation in Game 5, the deciding game, drawing gasps from fans and praise from opponents.

"With all sincerity," Knicks coach Hubie Brown said, "it's too bad someone had to lose. Isiah Thomas' effort in the fourth quarter was a staggering punch to us. I've been around a long time, and I've never been in a game like that."

Thomas' reputation continued to improve. He made the All-Star Game every season, winning its MVP award in '84 and '86. He came to be respected around the league as a top-notch competitor, although some saw him as selfish and overly bold. His team followed him on his rise, despite considerable obstacles. Bill Laimbeer, the suburban conservative, and Rick Mahorn, the product of the city, maintained a close friendship and an intimidating physical presence inside. Joe Dumars and Adrian Dantley were solid and smart and steady with the ball outside. James (Buddha) Edwards, Dennis (The Worm) Rodman, John (Spider) Salley and Vinnie (The Microwave) Johnson were eclectic personalities and valuable spark plugs who played a variety of roles.

But everyone still had a lot of maturing to do. Especially Thomas. In 1986-87, the Pistons advanced to the conference finals for the first time in their history and, after a series of bitter moments, suffered a

CRAIG PORTER/Detroit Free Press

IN GAME 6 OF THE 1988 NBA FINALS — WITH THE PISTONS LEADING THE LAKERS, THREE GAMES TO TWO — ISIAH THOMAS CRUMBLED UNDER A TWISTED ANKLE. HE PLAYED WITH PAIN THE REST OF THE WAY, DESPITE TREATMENT FROM TRAINER MIKE ABDENOUR. HE EVEN SCORED 25 POINTS IN THE THIRD QUARTER, BUT THE PISTONS LOST THE GAME AND THE SERIES.

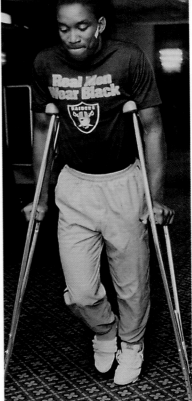

PAULINE LUBENS/Detroit Free Press   PAULINE LUBENS/Detroit Free Press

FEB. 16, 1982: THE PISTONS ACQUIRED BILL LAIMBEER
IN A FOUR-PLAYER DEAL WITH CLEVELAND.

LOSING NEVER CAME EASY. PISTONS VINNIE JOHNSON AND ADRIAN DANTLEY CLUNKED HEADS IN GAME 7 OF THE 1987 EASTERN CONFERENCE FINALS.

haunting defeat against Boston. Thomas learned more in that series perhaps than he did at any other time because of an ill-advised statement he made to reporters.

Thomas said Bird, the white Celtics sharpshooter whom some considered one of the greatest players of all time, would have been thought of as "just another good guy" if he were black. Some people, whites in particular, wondered whether Thomas was a closet racist. Some people, blacks in particular, wondered whether Thomas, when asked to explain himself, had failed to hammer home the real point he had been trying to make: that the media tended to characterize white athletes as dedicated and smart but blacks as physically gifted.

Since he couldn't win, Thomas turned inward. Once as open and accessible as any superstar, he became more of a closed book, especially when discussions centered on his family. The public was madly in love with him, but he kept everyone at a distance. He wanted one focus, basketball, because the Pistons were oh, so

JOHNSON RETURNED AFTER APPLYING AN ICE PACK, BUT THE BOSTON CELTICS STOPPED THE PISTONS, 117-114, IN THE GARDEN.

MAY 30, 1982: HASTING'S GORDON JOHNCOCK, 45, WON HIS SECOND INDIANAPOLIS 500, FINISHING .16 SECOND AHEAD OF RICK MEARS.

THE PISTONS HAD A NEW LOOK IN 1988-89, THANKS IN PART TO A TRADE MANY SAID ISIAH THOMAS ENGINEERED. DETROIT GOT MARK AGUIRRE FROM THE DALLAS MAVERICKS IN EXCHANGE FOR ADRIAN DANTLEY.

close to accomplishing something special.

The Celtics took the first two games, the Pistons the next two. In Game 5, with the Pistons five seconds from ending a 16-game Boston Garden losing streak, Bird stole an inbounds pass from Thomas and fed Dennis Johnson for the winner. The Pistons tied the series again, then strapped in for a Game 7 that was so remarkable it defied simple description. It was incredible and stirring and even frightening at times. It was a classic well before it was over.

In the third quarter, Dantley and Johnson collided, banging heads while diving on Boston Garden's parquet floor after a loose ball. Dantley spent the night in the hospital with a concussion. Johnson missed the final 7:21 because of an injured neck.

That collision killed the Pistons.

In the fourth quarter, the Celtics put the game away by dominating the boards and sinking second- and third-chance shots in the suffocating afternoon heat, eventually winning, 117-114.

The loss hurt. Bad. Really bad. "I don't know what else we could have done," Rodman said. "That's more than a kick in the stomach. That's like trying to have a baby."

In the 1987-88 season, the Pistons beat Boston in the conference finals, winning a soothing dose of revenge. In the NBA Finals, they met none other than the state's old friend from Lansing Everett and Michigan State, Magic, and his powerful Lakers.

WITH DANTLEY A MAV AND AGUIRRE IN A PISTONS UNIFORM, DETROIT WON 31 OF ITS LAST 37 REGULAR-SEASON GAMES.

Again, the Pistons pushed their opponent to a heartbreaking, heart-stopping final show, a Game 7. They fought off defeat like some Atlas in sneakers, the weight of the world on their shoulders, until finally, at the very end, their shoulders buckled and the world caved in.

The final score was 108-105. With two seconds left, A. C. Green beat the Detroit defense for a lay-up that drove the Forum into frenzy and the Pistons back home on their charter plane. So close. Afterward, coach Chuck Daly mumbled: "We came within a hair's breadth . . . a hair's breadth."

Someone asked whether that gave him any consolation.

He gave a simple answer.

No.

JUNE 22, 1982: LITTLE CAESARS PIZZA MAGNATE MIKE ILITCH BOUGHT THE WINGS
FROM THE NORRIS FAMILY FOR A REPORTED $10 MILLION.

THE TRADE

The 1987-88 Pistons might have been the best team that didn't win it all. They stayed with glamorous LA purely on guts, on effort, on desire. And on courage. Thomas played the final game in incredible pain, after spraining his right ankle two days before. But all of that was not enough. A piece of the puzzle was missing. A change needed to be made for 1988-89.

Dantley was traded to Dallas in February for Mark Aguirre, the only player taken ahead of Thomas in the '81 draft. The way management saw things, Dantley, a veteran with a face that always seemed halfway between amusement and anger, had peaked. His best years were behind him. His moves were being anticipated by opposing teams and referees alike. But of course, for the organization to part with Dantley, who had done so much, there was more to it than that.

Personality conflicts were eating away at the team like a cancer. Daly said of Dantley: "We got along fine." Everyone knew they didn't. Daly found Dantley selfish and greedy and infatuated with money. Even Aguirre, who had a reputation as a me-first and moody player, seemed to be an improvement. But the real conflict perhaps was between Dantley and Thomas. After the trade, Dantley's mother, Virginia, railed against the team captain.

"You shouldn't blame (general manager) Jack McCloskey," she said. "He's not the one. It's that little con artist you've got up there. When his royal highness wants something, he gets it."

Thomas denied he had any involvement, although he was distant to Dantley and close to Aguirre. No matter. Bitterness lingered anyway. Most fans were as displeased as Dantley, who failed to report to Dallas for several days and whispered a rebuke in Thomas' ear the first time they met on the court. When Aguirre debuted by scoring eight points on 3-for-11 shooting in 29 minutes, the situation worsened like a rubbed rash.

But everything settled down eventually. The Pistons scratched and clawed their way down the stretch, fighting Cleveland for the Central Division title. On April 18, they beat the Cavaliers, 118-102, to clinch the division and went on to the league's best record, an impressive 63-19. They were peaking at the right time. They had their prized identity back. They were on their way to a championship.

BAD BOYS

Throughout their tumultuous maturation process, the Pistons had gained a most valuable weapon: attitude. They were downright mean, nasty, cold people when they needed to be, smashing elbows in faces, throwing punches below the belt, forcing NBA vice president of operations Rod Thorn to levy as many fines as they did forearms. They were unruly, intimidating. They came to be known affectionately — in Detroit, at least — as the Bad Boys.

And everyone in the NBA was scared.

Everyone.

"I think as the media, as the public, as the fans say 'They're the Bad Boys,' the Pistons are going to live up to it," said His Airness, Chicago guard Michael Jordan. "That's something they take pride

Detroit Free Press

A NEW ATTITUDE JOINED THE NEW LOOK, AND THE PISTONS, LED BY BILL LAIMBEER AND RICK MAHORN, WERE DUBBED THE BAD BOYS.

PAULINE LUBENS/Detroit Free Press

SOON THEY RAISED A CHAMPIONSHIP BANNER, AND THE PUBLIC PROCLAIMED: "NOT BAD, BOYS."

STEVEN R. NICKERSON/Detroit Free Press

JAMES EDWARDS AND THE PISTONS SOARED OVER JACK SIKMA AND THE MILWAUKEE BUCKS IN THE SECOND ROUND OF THE 1989 PLAYOFFS.

PATRICIA BECK/Detroit Free Press

THE HIGH-FLYING PISTONS HAD A SECRET WEAPON — A PRIVATE JET CALLED ROUNDBALL ONE. THE PLANE, WITH LUXURY SEATING FOR 24, EVEN HAD ITS OWN FLIGHT CREW.

in now, especially with the success they've had being the Bad Boys. We've created a monster, and now nobody knows what to do."

The Pistons assumed their persona officially on Jan. 18, 1988. Thomas was upset about a fine and suspension handed down to Mahorn, and he made a declaration. "If they want to make us out to be a Raiders-type of basketball team," he said, "then we can become a very, very aggressive type of team and let people know that, hey, this is the game we play." Not long after that, Los Angeles Raiders owner Al Davis sent the Pistons a package of Raiders paraphernalia, which they happily wore before coming up with Bad Boys T-shirts of their own.

For a while, the Pistons were announced as the Bad Boys during pregame introductions. McCloskey said that promoting such an image was a mistake but that nothing would change — "not as long as we're in first place." Thorn didn't appreciate that. He fined the Pistons $29,000 because of altercations during the 1988-89 season, more than three times more than Portland, which was ranked second in fines at $9,500.

Why? "We can't have people punching other people in the face," Thorn said. The Pistons just thumbed their noses at Thorn. "He's the sheriff, we're all wearing black, and all our posters are on his wall," Salley said. Mahorn, who along with Laimbeer was among Thorn's favorite thugs, was more blunt. "As far as I'm concerned," he said, "Rod Thorn can kiss my ass."

Hey. When they called themselves the Bad Boys, they meant it.

JOE DUUUU-MARS!

While Laimbeer and Mahorn were the baddest of the boys, Dumars was the nicest. Quiet. Polite. Reserved. Not big on words. "I guess I don't have much to say," he

MAY 17, 1983: THE PISTONS SELECT CHUCK DALY AS COACH.
HE HAD BEEN WORKING ON THE PHILADELPHIA 76ERS' BROADCASTING TEAM.

PAULINE LUBENS/Detroit Free Press

ROBERT KOZLOFF/Associated Press

MAGIC JOHNSON HAD TWO YEARS ON ISIAH THOMAS
AND FIVE NBA CHAMPIONSHIPS UNDER HIS BELT
BEFORE THE PISTONS WON THEIR FIRST. BUT THE TWO
WERE FRIENDLY RIVALS FROM THE TIME THOMAS
ENTERED THE LEAGUE IN 1981, AND A SMOOCH BEFORE
GAMES BECAME THEIR TRADEMARK.

JUNE 12, 1983: THE G-MEN RETURNED TO SEE THEIR NUMBERS — CHARLIE GEHRINGER'S NO. 2
AND HANK GREENBERG'S NO. 5 — RETIRED IN A CEREMONY AT TIGER STADIUM.

CRAIG PORTER/Detroit Free Press

THE BUBBLY FLOWED AS THE
PISTONS BROUGHT HOME
BACK-TO-BACK NBA TITLES,
THEIR FIRST AFTER 32 SEASONS
IN DETROIT. AND THE PHRASE
WORLD CHAMPIONS HAD A
REALLY NICE RING TO IT.

said. He grew up in a little town called Natchitoches, La., as one of seven children, playing basketball with a sawed-off door for a backboard. His parents called him Boopie. He loved to read. But he was a Bad Boy just the same, a man of strength and moxie. This was a guy who as a kid, if he lost a one-on-one game to his older brother Mark, would immediately challenge him to a fight. No. Joe D fit right in.

Recognition was hard to come by in Detroit. Thomas and Dumars were known as the Palace Guards when the team moved from the Silverdome to a sparkling new building in 1988, but there was no question that Thomas owned the town. About the only time anyone paid attention to plain, old Joe was when he scored, and the Pistons' public-address announcer, Ken Calvert, called his name in a great, guttural groan: "Joe DUUUU-mars!" Although obscurity was fine with Dumars, it probably was unfair. He was a much better player than that. He gained a reputation as one of the few players — possibly the *only* player — capable of shutting down Jordan. But that was the extent of what people knew about him.

Then came the 1989 NBA Finals, in which Dumars blew his cover for good. The Pistons had marched back through the playoffs, beating Boston again for fun, sweeping Milwaukee, shutting down Chicago, on their way to another Magic moment, a rematch with the Lakers. Magic's men were rolling on an 11-0 run — three series sweeps. But the Pistons swept them, thanks to Joe.

Dumars showed he could be known for torrid scoring as well as defensive dirty work. He scored 22 points in Game 1 and another 33 in Game 2 — 26 in the first half. In Game 3, he started innocently, then exploded for 21 third-quarter points and finished with 31. Reporters used to gather around Thomas' locker. Or Laimbeer's. Or Mahorn's. "Now," Dumars said, "they're crowding around mine." Dumars still didn't say much, despite his performance. About the most egotistical thing that came out of his mouth was this: "It's like people are just finding out, 'Oh! Hey. He can play.' "

As hot as he had been, Dumars approached Game 4 with some anxiety. His mind was consumed by the game, the

FACING PAGE: JOE DUMARS, THE MOST VALUABLE PLAYER OF THE 1989 FINALS, PLAYED 14 SEASONS WITH THE PISTONS BEFORE RETIRING IN 1999.

Photograph by WILLIAM DeKAY/Detroit Free Press

game, the game. How would everything turn out? He tossed and turned the night before, waking up at 3 a.m. and not returning to sleep. His stomach rolled around. So many people were discussing him and the most valuable player award in the same sentence, he approached a reporter and whispered: "Do you really think I've got it?" Was he kidding? He added another 23 points in the finale. He had it, all right.

After it was over, Dumars walked through the locker room, carrying his trophy and listening to his teammates chant his name. Ten years after the Spartans had won the state of Michigan's first national championship, the Pistons had won its first NBA championship.

Bad Boys?

Not bad, boys.

"Anonymity," Dumars said. "I just lost it."

Champagne soaked the locker room, and the players wrung out bad memories from their heads. The '87 series against Boston. The '88 series against Los Angeles. The days when the struggles looked pointless, when Thomas thought the Pistons' effort seemed destined to culminate in fruitless misery.

JOHN A. STANO/Detroit Free Press

"IT'S A HARD, HARD, HARD, LONG PROCESS," ISIAH THOMAS SAID OF THE CHAMPIONSHIP CLIMB. BUT IT WAS WORTH IT. THE ADORING FANS THAT GREETED ROUNDBALL ONE CERTAINLY AGREED.

"When I think back, it seems the mental and physical pressure has been so great," Thomas said. "It's a hard, hard, hard, long process. It wears on you, because you get knocked off so many times and the hardest part is picking yourself back up and starting the climb all over again."

Thomas once had said there were a lot of times when he wanted to quit, to never obsess about anything so much ever again. But holding the gold trophy, kissing it, tasting the champagne spray that beaded on it, Thomas appreciated for the first time the weariness and the wait.

"I could never understand the secret," he said. "I understand now."

DADDY RICH

As long as the road had been for Thomas, it was longer for Daly. Nearly 60, he was the oldest coach in the NBA. He had spent seven years in high school coaching, eight as a college head coach, four as an NBA assistant. He had been hired, fired, worked as a furniture loader, a construction worker and a bouncer in a Tokyo bar. He joined the Pistons in 1983, wondering whether he would last one season. He did, then endured a lot more: a short stretch in Joe Louis Arena, a busted roof at the Silverdome, the brand-

CRAIG PORTER/Detroit Free Press

HAMMER TIME WAS ONE OF THE PISTONS' MOTTOS. JOHN SALLEY AND FRIENDS HAMMERED THEIR PLAYOFF OPPONENTS, COMPILING A 15-2 MARK EN ROUTE TO THEIR FIRST TITLE.

OCT. 5, 1983: STEVE YZERMAN SCORED HIS FIRST NHL GOAL AND ASSIST IN THE WINGS' SEASON-OPENING 6-6 TIE AT WINNIPEG.

JOHN LUKE/Detroit Free Press

AS CHAMPIONS, THE PISTONS RUBBED SHOULDERS WITH CELEBRITIES, AND JOHN SALLEY, THE BIGGEST HAM
OF THE BUNCH, SCHMOOZED WITH DETROITER CAROLE GIST, WHO WORE THE MISS USA CROWN.

new Palace, the purchase of a luxurious team plane, a record crowd of 60,000, rumors of his imminent firing, Thomas' coming to his rescue, bitter trades, and gut-wrenching losses.

Through it all, he not only stayed standing, he stayed standing with style. Known as Daddy Rich, he always was dapper, dressed in well-tailored suits, neatly coiffed. He looked like he should have been carrying an investment portfolio instead of a clipboard.

"I still have my hair," he said. "I'm glad about that. It helps fool people about my age. Of course, that's the only good thing, right? I mean, look at this nose, this chin, these teeth. I mean, the hair's the only good thing, right?"

No. Not at all. But that was Daly, always knocking himself, always settling for less credit than he deserved. Although he molded a team of diverse, ornery personalities into a unit, with a 6-1 guard as his only true superstar, he won championships but not coach of the year awards. In the beginning, he was obscure. In the end, he was overlooked. He moved so fast in achieving success, he went right past appreciated. "He's getting taken for granted," Lakers coach Pat Riley said.

Daly didn't seem to mind. He had plenty of distractions to deal with, as usual, after the 1988-89 title. The Pistons lost Mahorn, the muscle around their heart, in the expansion draft. Business. The city shrieked. The team deflated. How would they repeat? Well, they were champions, right? So their coach pushed them to play like it in 1989-90.

In one glorious stretch of the regular season, they held the NBA hostage, putting together a 25-1 run. It began in January. The Pistons lost to Los Angeles at the Palace, and their sense of security was rattled. They thought they needed to prove they were still the league's best team. So they

OCT. 10, 1983: DOMINO'S PIZZA MAGNATE TOM MONAGHAN PURCHASED THE TIGERS
FROM JOHN FETZER FOR A REPORTED $53 MILLION.

STEVEN R. NICKERSON/Detroit Free Press

CHUCK DALY WORKED THE SIDELINES FOR NINE PISTONS SEASONS. HE KNEW WHEN TO IGNORE JOHN SALLEY AND WHEN TO YELL.

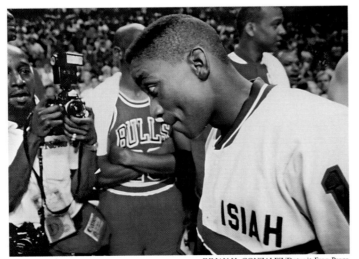

JULIAN H. GONZALEZ/Detroit Free Press

ISIAH THOMAS DIDN'T WISH MICHAEL JORDAN WELL AFTER THE BULLS ENDED THE PISTONS' RUN IN THE 1991 EASTERN FINALS.

did. They beat Chicago two days later, won 12 in a row, lost at Atlanta, then won 12 more. "We'll remember it as the time that we came together as a team," Rodman said.

When the playoffs began, the Pistons were humming, well-oiled. Everyone was cruising. Rodman even had been voted defensive player of the year. After finishing the regular season with a 59-23 record, they swept Indiana, eliminated New York, squeaked past Chicago in seven, then smoked Portland, 4-1, in the Finals. The Microwave scorched a jumper at 0:00.7 to win Game 5, 92-90. Dumars soldiered on, although his father died hours before Game 3, in which he scored 33 points. This time, Thomas was selected most valuable player. Asked whether twice was nicer, he smiled, thought about all he had been through, and said: "It was."

Back to back, baby.

A Daly double.

FOLLOWING PAGE: AFTER THE CHAMPIONSHIP YEARS, CHUCK DALY STAYED ON AS PISTONS COACH FOR TWO MORE SEASONS. IN 1994, HE ENTERED THE BASKETBALL HALL OF FAME.

Photograph by Detroit Free Press

STEVEN R. NICKERSON/Detroit Free Press

THE FISHER FAMILY WHOOPED IT UP AFTER THE WOLVERINES WON THE NCAA CHAMPIONSHIP IN 1989 IN SEATTLE.

ALAN R. KAMUDA/Detroit Free Press

BILL FRIEDER HAD PLENTY TO SAY — TO ANYONE
WHO WOULD LISTEN — AFTER ATHLETIC DIRECTOR
BO SCHEMBECHLER REFUSED FRIEDER'S REQUEST TO
COACH IN THE NCAA TOURNAMENT.

FROM FRIEDER TO FISHER

While the Pistons made their run, Michigan made a run of its own. Only the Wolverines' run culminated in one of the most bizarre, unlikely and utterly awesome stories in the history of college athletics.

For much of the '80s, the Wolverines were quite competitive under Bill Frieder, who succeeded Johnny Orr as coach in 1980-81. In the 1983-84 season, they won the National Invitation Tournament, smashing Notre Dame, 83-63, at Madison Square Garden. "I think this team of ours would have done very well in the NCAA," Frieder said. In 1984-85, Frieder was selected national coach of the year as his team finished 26-4. In 1985-86, Michigan finished the regular season 27-4 and captured its second straight outright Big Ten championship. Since the middle '60s, only Indiana had managed back-to-back outright titles. "These kids have risen to the occasion," Frieder said.

But Frieder's eyes were elsewhere. Despite his regular-season success, he had been haunted by the NCAA tournament, advancing past the second round just once, and he wasn't beloved in Ann Arbor. Arizona State repeatedly pursued him, dangling dollar signs before his face. At the end of the 1988-89 season, although the Wolverines were preparing for the NCAA tournament, Arizona State gave him a take-it-or-leave-it offer and a 24-hour deadline for a decision. Frieder took it. After conducting a practice March 14, he told his top assistant, Steve Fisher, what he was going to do, then caught a plane for Phoenix.

The next day was nuts. At 10 a.m., Frieder was introduced as Arizona State's new coach. At 11 a.m., Frieder called Michigan football coach and athletic director Bo Schembechler to tell him the news and work out a plan for the tournament — and he didn't like what he heard in response. At 12:30 p.m., Fisher was introduced as Michigan's new interim coach.

"I told him I preferred Steve Fisher coach the team," Schembechler said. "Things always turn out for the best. I'm disappointed by the timing. I'm sure he will say he wanted to coach the team, but I did not want an Arizona State man coaching Michigan.

"I wanted a Michigan man."

Fisher, a mild-mannered man markedly different from the frenetic Frieder, began his first press conference by saying: "For the benefit of most of you, I'm Steve Fisher." He later added: "I've gone from the guy most of the media used to shove away to get to the stars — to this."

Strange as it was, change became a theme. Schembechler wanted to wipe away the stain he thought Frieder had left behind. He spoke to the team. "Bo told us we were not second to anyone, and we believed him," guard Sean Higgins said. Schembechler established a dress code, too. The Wolverines left for the first round in Atlanta with a 24-7 record while wearing beige sweaters, which displayed a basketball logo over the heart and this prophetic message: *Michigan on the road to the Final Four.*

Frieder stayed at the same hotel as his former players in Atlanta and watched their 92-87 victory over Xavier (Ohio). "It's a big stadium," Schembechler said. "It's a free country." Fisher even allowed him a quick, secret meeting with the team.

"I know people are going to be negative," Frieder said. "But I didn't have any choice. Bo said he could not understand why we couldn't hold off until the end of the tournament to announce it. But what if I'd taken the job and not announced it? There would have been tremendous pressures on the kids. There would have been questions all the time."

After Frieder said what he had to say, he was gone for good. And so were Michigan's troubles in the NCAA tournament.

DRIBBLE, SHOOT, SWISH

Fisher inherited some pretty good players, and having been an assistant at Michigan since 1982, he knew them all intimately. The star was Glen Rice, a forward with a sweet

ALAN R. KAMUDA/Detroit Free Press

WITH VICTORIES OVER XAVIER (OHIO), SOUTH ALABAMA AND NORTH CAROLINA UNDER THEIR BELTS, SEAN HIGGINS AND GLEN RICE LED THE CHEERS AS THE WOLVERINES ROUTED VIRGINIA BY 37 POINTS.

STEPHEN R. NICKERSON/Detroit Free Press

NEXT CAME CONFERENCE RIVAL ILLINOIS, AND SEAN HIGGINS' BUZZER-BEATING, PUT-BACK GAVE MICHIGAN A TWO-POINT VICTORY AND A DATE WITH SETON HALL IN THE FINAL.

STEPHEN R. NICKERSON/Detroit Free Press

He looked like the loneliest man in the world — Michigan's Rumeal Robinson, who went to the free-throw line with the Wolverines trailing Seton Hall by one with time running out in overtime. First shot, swish . . .

STEPHEN R. NICKERSON/Detroit Free Press

ALAN R. KAMUDA/Detroit Free Press

He turned away briefly as teammates stood by, then Robinson returned to the line with the season on the line. Second shot, swish — the Wolverines led, 80-79, and Robinson was mobbed by teammates after a last-second shot by Seton Hall missed.

jumper, clutch ability on the boards and quickness on the break. Rumeal Robinson was the general, a whirlwind of a point guard whose weakness was free-throw shooting. Terry Mills and Loy Vaught were fierce and rugged up front. Mike Griffin was a calming force in the backcourt. Higgins and Mark Hughes provided quality minutes off the bench. All Fisher had to do was keep them confident, focused on the future, not the past. Himself, too.

Before the Wolverines faced Xavier, Fisher fretted. A lot. "I was worried that I might become the only winless coach in the history of college basketball," he said. "I was scared over the fact that I was now *the* guy. As an assistant, very few eyes are on you. When I walked out there, I felt everyone was watching me. There was a sense of relief when we won. They couldn't blame anyone and couldn't say, 'Fisher's not really that good.' "

In a few days, no one would doubt Fisher's value. The Wolverines defeated South Alabama, then faced North Carolina in the third round. Late in the game, Robinson turned over the ball. "Some of the players were chirpin' on Rumeal," assistant coach Mike Boyd said. "Steve called a quick time-out and jumped in the huddle. He said, 'Let's go back. Has anyone here made a mistake today?' All the kids nodded yes. I believe that was the big turnaround in the game. The reason he got it across was because he was calm, rather than nervous or hyper." Nobody mentioned a certain coach at Arizona State. Nobody had to.

The Wolverines beat North Carolina, then routed Virginia. But things were still a bit confusing. After his team clinched its spot in the Final Four, Fisher did an interview with CBS-TV in which Tim Brant referred to him as Steve Frieder. Ah, well. All smiles. On to Seattle. The Wolverines faced an old nemesis in the semifinals, Illinois, which had beaten them twice during the season. The NCAA rematch ended in a most unlikely manner — but then, that was just in keeping with the theme.

Rice, Michigan's top scorer, set a screen for Mills, who took a shot from the right baseline that missed. Higgins, known for nailing rainbows much more than second-chance shots, had the angle on the left for the rebound. He grabbed the ball and wasted no time depositing a six-footer with two seconds left. "It didn't happen picture-perfect," Vaught said, "but it worked." The play had been designed for Rice to shoot behind a double screen set by Mills and Hughes. But Rice couldn't get open, and Robinson improvised, giving the ball to Mills and giving Higgins

JUNE 18, 1985: THE PISTONS TOOK MCNEESE STATE GUARD JOE DUMARS
WITH THE 18TH PICK IN THE NBA DRAFT.

GLEN RICE AVERAGED 30.7 POINTS IN SIX TOURNAMENT GAMES AND NETTED THE MOST OUTSTANDING PLAYER AWARD.

STEPHEN R. NICKERSON/Detroit Free Press

Bo Schembechler, Michigan's athletic director, removed the
interim from coach Steve Fisher's title soon after the
Wolverines won the championship.

Chris Webber, who acted
so tough on the court,
broke down with emotion
after the Wolverines beat
Ohio State for a berth in
the 1992 Final Four.

JULIAN H. GONZALEZ/Detroit Free Press

the chance to be a hero.

By winning, the Wolverines set a school standard for victories,
raising their record to 29-7, and broke Illinois' 10-game winning
streak. They were in the final for the first time since 1976. They
weren't going to be denied now. No matter what. Against Seton
Hall, they found themselves on center stage of wonderful theater,
gripping drama, that again came down to a few sweat-soaked seconds.

In overtime, Robinson drove to the basket and was fouled by the
Pirates' Gerald Greene. He stepped to the line. Three ticks
remained on the clock. His team trailed by one. Life came to a
standstill. A school and a nation and a glorious destiny held their
breath for Robinson, who made less than two-thirds of his foul
shots in his career.

Dribble. Shoot. Swish.

Tie game.

One more shot. Everything riding on it, the whole Frieder thing,
Fisher's future, the hopes and dreams of all of his teammates.
Everything. Robinson licked his lips.

Dribble. Shoot. Swish.

Champions.

Moments later, Robinson and Rice, the tournament's most valuable player, locked themselves together in a huge hug. The
Wolverines had won, 80-79. Higgins scolded the world by saying
"nobody believed in us," and the world nodded back, sheepishly.
Who would have believed it but Bo and the boys in blue? Michigan
had its first national championship; college basketball had perhaps its story of the century.

FAB FIVE

Days later, Schembechler gave Fisher the permanent job, beginning the second part of his improbable story. In 1989-90, Fisher's
team finished 23-8. In 1990-91, his team finished 14-15. In 1991-92,
his team shocked the world.

Fisher brought the Best Class Ever Assembled to Michigan.
The Fab Five. Two kids from Detroit, one from Chicago, two from
Texas. By the time Michigan played Notre Dame on national television midway through their first season, all were starters.
Although they never won a national title — or even a Big Ten title
— they came close enough to captivate the nation. Their swagger
and baggy shorts earned them attention. Their talent earned them
respect.

Forward Chris Webber and guard Jalen Rose, the Detroit kids,
were best friends. Webber went to high school at suburban
Birmingham Detroit Country Day. Remarkably talented, he was
widely recognized as the best prep player in the nation. Rose
stayed near home and played at Detroit Southwestern. He earned
All-America honors himself, but he didn't gain fame until college.

Center Juwan Howard, the Chicago kid, had known Webber and
Rose since their early high school years. Paths crossed at summer
camps. Competitions escalated. Another extension of friendship
emerged. "We were tight right away," Howard said. "I don't know
how it happened." He was the first to pick Michigan, starting the
happy chain reaction of commitments.

Dec. 1, 1986: Hall of Famer Bobby Layne, who quarterbacked the Lions
to their last championship in 1957, died at age 59.

> **"We're freshmen in school.
> We aren't freshmen when it comes to playing basketball."**
>
> **CHRIS WEBBER**

ALAN R. KAMUDA/Detroit Free Press

THE FAB FIVE — RAY JACKSON, CHRIS WEBBER, JUWAN HOWARD, JALEN ROSE AND JIMMY KING — WAS TOGETHER FOR TWO FAB SEASONS.

OCT. 12, 1987: TIGERS RIGHT-HANDER DOYLE ALEXANDER, 9-0 DOWN THE STRETCH, WAS THE LOSING PITCHER
AS MINNESOTA GAINED THE WORLD SERIES WITH A 9-5 VICTORY IN GAME 5 OF THEIR PLAYOFF SERIES.

JULIAN H. GONZALEZ/*Detroit Free Press*

FIVE FOR ONE AND ONE FOR FIVE! THE FABULOUS FRESHMEN HUDDLED
TOGETHER IN THE NCAA TOURNAMENT TO BEAT TEMPLE, EAST
TENNESSEE STATE, OKLAHOMA STATE, OHIO STATE AND CINCINNATI
BEFORE LOSING TO DUKE, 71-51.

Forward Ray Jackson and guard Jimmy King, the Texas kids, didn't know each other, and they didn't know the other three very well. They were less heralded, had less pro potential. But they rounded out the class, gave it balance, and were confident and comfortable with their teammates by the time they began their first season. "It's like I've known them all my life," Jackson said.

Before the Fab Five ever played a game, Rose declared: "I know there's nothing we're afraid of." There was a reason for that, Webber explained: "We're freshmen in school. We aren't freshmen when it comes to playing basketball." In time, both proved their points. They finished their first season at 25-9, advancing through the NCAA tournament without losing any of their bravado. Even when they lost the championship game to Duke, 71-51, they were cocky, promising to come back the next year.

MARY SCHROEDER/*Detroit Free Press*

DESPITE JUWAN HOWARD'S
QUICK CHANGE IN THE 1994,
ARKANSAS WON THE REGIONAL
FINAL AND ENDED AN ERA.
SOON AFTER, HOWARD AND
JALEN ROSE TURNED PRO.

Which they did. In 1992-93, the Fab Five improved. They were scary sophomores, ripping off a 31-5 season and roaring through the tournament to the final, this time against North Carolina. But then, their campaign of domination fell apart because of a youthful mistake. Trailing by two points with 11 seconds left, Webber dribbled down the court, got caught on the sideline in front of his bench, and put his hands together.

Time-out. Era over.

Since Michigan already had used its final time-out, a technical foul was called. The Tar Heels ended up with a 77-71 victory, and the Wolverines ended up feeling as if they had eaten raw eggs on a roller coaster. They were just sick. In agony. Teammates and coaches tried to soothe Webber. "It cost us a chance," Fisher said. "It didn't cost us the game." But Webber was downcast, blaming himself. It wasn't the way he wanted to go out.

Soon afterward, Webber left for the NBA. He was the first player drafted, by the Orlando Magic, who that same night traded his rights to Golden State. That reduced the Best Class Ever Assembled to the Fab Four. Rose and Howard bolted to the NBA a year later, although Howard still completed his degree on time, keeping the promise he had made to his dying grandmother.

Basketball was still a strong sport in Michigan, but it wasn't the same after that. It wasn't as hot. It cooled dramatically, as a new ice age descended on the state. ◆

NOV. 14, 1987: LORENZO WHITE GAINED 292 YARDS ON A SCHOOL-RECORD 56 CARRIES AS MICHIGAN STATE
CLINCHED THE BIG TEN WITH A 27-3 VICTORY OVER INDIANA AT SPARTAN STADIUM.

SUSAN RAGAN/Associated Press

TIME RAN OUT ON CHRIS WEBBER IN THE 1993 FINAL. AND IT WAS TIME TO CELEBRATE FOR NORTH CAROLINA'S ERIC MONTROSS. TWICE THE FAB FIVE WENT TO THE BIG DANCE AND TWICE THE WOLVERINES FAILED.

JAN. 1, 1988: MICHIGAN STATE BEAT SOUTHERN CAL IN THE ROSE BOWL, 20-17, AND FINISHED 9-2-1, ITS BEST SEASON SINCE 1966.

Roar of '84

By Bill McGraw

The start. In 1984 and for a while thereafter, that's all you had to say. People immediately understood you were talking about how that year's Tigers had begun the season with a bang. It was a start that was unique in baseball history.

Leaving the warmth of mid-Florida for chilly Minnesota, the Tigers won their first nine games, 16 of their first 17, and 35 of their first 40.

Those amazing weeks transformed Michigan and Trumbull into the epicenter of baseball and turned the Tigers into the biggest story in sports. The national media descended like june bugs, giving springtime games a postseason ambience. The Tigers always seemed to be on national TV.

Fans fell in love with the team with an intensity that the Pistons, Lions and even Red Wings have never known. This was crazy — head-over-heels love.

College students introduced "The Wave" to Tiger Stadium, giving the rippling cheer some of its first widespread publicity. There were songs dedicated to the Tigers, and huge pep rallies. TV sportscaster Al Ackerman recruited celebrities to tape a nightly benediction, "Bless You, Boys." The bleachers were a nightly party. Otherwise normal people walked down Trumbull with their bodies painted in tiger stripes. The Tigers would set their all-time attendance record for Tiger Stadium, 2.7 million. Nearly 5 million eventually would see the Tigers play at home and away.

Like the Tigers of 1935, 1945 and 1968, the Tigers of 1984 were good news with no strings attached, and their

Detroit Free Press

THE SAN DIEGO PADRES COULDN'T CONTAIN KIRK GIBSON. THE SLUGGER — WHO HOMERED TWICE FOR THE TIGERS IN THE FINAL GAME — COULDN'T CONTAIN HIMSELF DURING THE 1984 WORLD SERIES.

championship season happened when metropolitan Detroit needed a lift. A monstrous recession was hammering the Detroit region, throwing even comfortable, middle-class people out of work.

In 1982, Detroit Mayor Coleman Young declared a hunger emergency. In 1983, J. L. Hudson's downtown department store closed, and Germans sent care packages after the city became the symbol in western Europe of the failure of U.S. social and economic policy. In 1984, Detroit again was scorned as "Murder City" after recording the nation's highest homicide rate.

The big picture had been mostly bad since the last baseball championship in 1968. With white flight and economic change, Detroit in the 1970s lost 21 percent of its population and 30 percent of its jobs. Despite the best efforts of many to make things better, the rich, talented Tigers from California, Cuba, Puerto Rico and points between were one of the best things Detroit had going in 1984.

The '84 Tigers were so good that Howard Cosell proclaimed to the nation that the team's success was a symbol of Detroit's renaissance. But sadly, the city's image again would deteriorate literally minutes after the World Series victory, when a mob burned an overturned Detroit police car. That ugly scene soon became the face of Detroit on national TV.

THE NEW GUYS

There was a special buzz about the team from the first day of spring training amid the palm trees of Lakeland, Fla.

THEY LOOKED LIKE CUBS, BUT THEY WERE THE HEART OF THE TIGERS UP THE MIDDLE — (CLOCKWISE FROM TOP LEFT) SECOND BASEMAN LOU WHITAKER, SHORTSTOP ALAN TRAMMELL, CENTERFIELDER CHET LEMON AND CATCHER LANCE PARRISH.

NOV. 5, 1988: THE PISTONS RAISED THEIR CENTRAL DIVISION AND EASTERN CONFERENCE BANNERS
AND THEN WON THEIR DEBUT GAME AT THE PALACE, 94-85 OVER CHARLOTTE.

It was the Tigers' first spring under new owner Tom Monaghan, a little-known Ann Arborite who founded Domino's Pizza. Monaghan was 46 and curly-haired and had an aw-shucks manner unusual for a corporate boss. He donned a Tigers uniform and played catch with his hero, Al Kaline, and he hung around the stadium with another visiting hero, Bo Schembechler.

Gushing about his lifelong dream of playing shortstop for the Tigers, the guileless Monaghan, a devout Roman Catholic and an architecture buff, spent huge amounts of time doing interviews. It wasn't long before much of Michigan knew that his three favorite people were Jesus, Mary and Frank Lloyd Wright.

On paper, the Tigers showed enormous promise, especially after having signed their first major free agent, veteran power hitter Darrell Evans. General manager Bill Lajoie also swung a deal that further pumped up fans. He traded outfielder Glenn Wilson and catcher John Wockenfuss to Philadelphia for left-handed relief pitcher Willie Hernandez and pinch-hitter/first baseman Dave Bergman.

Arriving in Lakeland the next day, Hernandez, a tall man who exuded the kind of arrogance that pitchers use to intimidate hitters, announced, "I put my uniform on and I sent a message to the big man: 'What inning am I pitching?' I wanted to show people I have my attitude together."

Even popular culture seemingly conspired to build a baseball-intensive climate. One of the year's film hits was "The Natural," which starred Robert Redford and dealt with good and evil, heroes and legends, and love and corruption among major league players. Hollywood changed the sad and cynical mood of Bernard Malamud's novel to happy and

TONY SPINA/Detroit Free Press

TIGERS RELIEF ACE WILLIE HERNANDEZ PUT OUT THE FIRE 32 TIMES DURING THE 1984 SEASON. HE SAVED ANOTHER GAME IN THE AL PLAYOFFS, TWO MORE IN THE WORLD SERIES AND WON THE CY YOUNG AWARD AND MVP AWARD THAT YEAR.

MARY SCHROEDER/Detroit Free Press

optimistic. Many Tigers gave the film thumbs-up reviews.

"There was one scene where Redford is talking to the girl, and he ended by saying, 'God, I love baseball,' " recalled third baseman Tom Brookens. "Just for that half-second, I got a tingling feeling at that line. I said to myself, 'I do, too.' "

The early weeks of the season featured drama high and low. Jack Morris pitched a 4-0 no-hitter against Chicago in the fourth game. The highly anticipated Evans homered on his first swing at Tiger Stadium; after the game, he talked earnestly of having seen a UFO two years before.

Then there was that first inning in Boston in Game 8. The Tigers sent 13 batters to the plate. The teams combined for 13 runs. Lance Parrish, No. 13, made all three outs. The Tigers wound up winning, 13-9, with Parrish scoring the winning run. Yep, it was Friday the 13th.

Everyone appeared to be having a good time except the killjoys in the front office, where the furniture, hairstyles and mind-set suggested 1948, not 1984. President Jim Campbell fought local opinion-makers over the music played on the stadium's scratchy PA system. "I could care less," Campbell said. "I'm a baseball man, not a stage-show manager."

THE AT-BAT

As the fresh northern spring gave way to summer mugginess, the Tigers pressed on. Among many early-season highlights on the field was Dave Bergman's seven-minute at-bat on national TV June 4. It was classic baseball: Tenth inning. Tie score. Two out. Two runners on base. First-place Tigers confronting second-place Blue Jays. Right-handed pitcher battling left-handed hitter.

Digging in against Roy Lee Jackson, Bergman ratcheted

San Diego's Alan Wiggins was out at the plate, and the Padres were finished in five games. Catcher Lance Parrish, who homered during the Series, also uncorked the bubbly when it was all over.

up the drama with each pitch. After Jackson got two strikes on him, Bergman began fouling off pitches. The crowd buzz escalated following each foul. Bergman spoiled seven pitches. Finally, with the clock near midnight, he smashed Jackson's 13th pitch, a low breaking ball, into the upper deck in rightfield. Tiger Stadium exploded. The Tigers leaped to their feet. They had stretched their lead over the Jays, their toughest rival, to 5½ games by rallying in their biggest game of the young season.

By midsummer, the personalities of several new players were becoming apparent. Hernandez was cocky in the clubhouse; his relief pitching was virtually perfect. Boyish Rusty Kuntz, a player of marginal talent who gave teammates high-tech underwear from a friend's store to wear during cold weather, glowed daily with appreciation for simply being on the team. One night, after his hit beat the Yankees, Kuntz proclaimed: "The fairy tale continues. I'm the happiest person in the world."

The 37-year-old Evans turned out to be everybody's big brother. He offered advice and kept the mood light by mimicking a baby's cry of *"waaaaaa"* when the griping got too loud.

One night, between games of a doubleheader in Cleveland, Doug Baker, who had been called up from the minors to replace injured shortstop Alan Trammell, received word from manager Sparky Anderson that he was to return to the minors. Trammell was being activated. The demotion was a shock; the 23-year-old Baker had just won the first game with a bases-loaded triple. Meanwhile, Evans was accepting condolences from teammates. He had just learned that his father had died after a long battle with cancer. Despite his grief, Evans soon was hovering next to Baker, patting him on the back, quietly telling him what a great job he had done and assuring the kid that he likely would be recalled soon.

Playing under intense scrutiny over a 162-game season takes a ➤

April 3, 1989: Rumeal Robinson hit two free throws with three seconds left in overtime as Michigan beat Seton Hall, 80-79, for the NCAA basketball championship.

MARY SCHROEDER/Detroit Free Press

THE TIGERS WERE BLESSED TO HAVE ALAN TRAMMELL, WHO EARNED MVP HONORS AFTER GOING .450 WITH TWO HOMERS AND SIX RBIS IN FIVE SERIES GAMES.

SPARKY ANDERSON, WHO WON TWO WORLD CHAMPIONSHIPS WITH THE CINCINNATI REDS, BROUGHT THE FIREWORKS TO DETROIT AND WON HIS THIRD WORLD SERIES IN HIS SIXTH SEASON AS TIGERS MANAGER.

MARY SCHROEDER/Detroit Free Press

physical and mental toll, even on winners. Some players, such as Evans, Trammell, Lou Whitaker and Parrish, rarely showed self-doubt. But despite the bravado about the need to be mentally tough, many players' psyches bent under constant pressure, and Anderson and his coaches spent a lot of time massaging the highly paid egos.

Pitchers seemed especially vulnerable to emotional distress. Pitching coach Roger Craig, a soft-spoken, friendly Southerner who preached the power of positive thinking and the split-finger fastball, seemed to spend as much time working on the pitchers' minds as he did on their deliveries.

In the spring, Dave Rozema discussed a drinking problem with Craig and the team doctor, and Anderson took him on a couple of early-morning walks to dispense fatherly advice. In June, an agitated Juan Berenguer summoned Anderson, Craig and his friends Hernandez and Aurelio Lopez to announce that he thought the club was having him followed. Gently, Anderson and Craig assured him they were not interfering in his private life.

The season seemed especially painful for Jack Morris, whose competitive nature, temper and tendency to blame others for his mistakes gave him the emotional stability of nitroglycerin. Morris was smart, funny and gregarious. But

APRIL 23, 1989: THE LIONS TOOK RUNNING BACK BARRY SANDERS, THE HEISMAN TROPHY WINNER FROM OKLAHOMA STATE, WITH THE THIRD OVERALL PICK IN THE DRAFT.

during this summer, he frequently pouted and squabbled with teammates. For several weeks, he refused to talk to reporters. "Jack does have a tendency to lose control," Parrish said one day in Kansas City in May after Morris had complained in the dugout that his teammates were not backing him up with enough hits.

During one heart-to-heart talk with Craig, Morris wept. Craig, who loved Morris like a son, told reporters he was "digging deep" for the root of Morris' anger, sort of like a psychiatrist would do with a patient. "You're not happy now," Craig told Morris. "We got to find a way to make you happy." By early September, Craig's constant attention had mellowed Morris, who resumed talking to the media at Anderson's request.

Kirk Gibson was another mercurial talent. Later in his career, he was said to be a mature family man and nice guy. But in the early 1980s, he often was rude and profane. He enjoyed picking on female media members in the clubhouse; he assumed they were trying to catch a glimpse of him naked. "I'm not a male whore," he would say.

Intelligent, high-strung and highly competitive, Gibson had worked hard to learn the subtleties of baseball. Gibson, who grew up in Waterford and was an All-America wide receiver at Michigan State, struggled with the constant pestering that accompanied fame. "It's really hard being Kirk Gibson sometimes," he said.

In 1984, Gibson was rebounding from three mediocre seasons that had brought stinging criticism from reporters and fans. In New York in late June, he was brooding in a darkened hotel room 16 floors above 42nd Street because Anderson wasn't letting him bat against left-handed pitchers. Sprawled on a bed, he talked of being "out of my comfort zone" because of the yo-yo-like publicity over the past 12 months.

"You read all this good stuff . . . you begin to wonder, who is the real Kirk Gibson?" he said. "I have to talk to myself, have my own self-talk, to keep myself sane, so I know who I am."

Gibson told a startling story about the downside of being a celebrity. The previous summer in a bar near Tiger Stadium, a fan had started a torrent of criticism and refused to stop. "I said, 'Enough's enough.' I picked him up by the scruff of his shirt. I said, 'Look, you son of a bitch. You can get on me at the ballpark. I get paid to put up with (bleeps) like you at the park. But not here in public. So say another (bleeping) word, and I'll rip your head off your shoulders.' I threw him back down and slapped him across the face. I was totally in the right. I never felt so right about doing something in my life."

THE ULTIMATE PRIZE

The victory machine rolled on as the days grew shorter. For 12 days in August, the Tigers endured one of the toughest grinds in club history — 16 games, including three doubleheaders in a row.

One of the most spectacular games of the season took place on a steamy August night at Boston's Fenway Park. It was the second game of a doubleheader. In the first game, the Red Sox had won, hammering two grand slams off Morris in 1⅓ innings. Between games, players appeared exhausted in the clubhouse as they snacked. Whitaker lay on the floor with his feet elevated on a stool.

In Game 2, the Tigers bounced back. Parrish hit a two-run homer in the 11th. Outfielder Chet Lemon, who used a ratty old glove, chased

MARY SCHROEDER/Detroit Free Press

JACK MORRIS' CHAMPIONSHIP SEASON INCLUDED A NO-HITTER, TWO WORLD SERIES WINS AND A BEAR HUG FROM LANCE PARRISH.

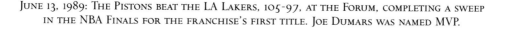

JUNE 13, 1989: THE PISTONS BEAT THE LA LAKERS, 105-97, AT THE FORUM, COMPLETING A SWEEP IN THE NBA FINALS FOR THE FRANCHISE'S FIRST TITLE. JOE DUMARS WAS NAMED MVP.

down a fly ball with his back to home plate, much like the Giants' Willie Mays had done in the 1954 World Series on the famous long fly by Cleveland's Vic Wertz. Lopez won his ninth game in relief, and Hernandez got his 24th save. The Tigers had a come-from-behind victory and a new-found sense of security that they wouldn't lose their lead in the standings — now nine games — for the rest of the year. No one got close during the final six weeks of the season.

In the postseason, the Tigers won the first two games of the best-of-five American League championship series against the Royals in Kansas City. They wrapped up the pennant at Tiger Stadium.

On the Tigers' flight to California for Game 1 of the World Series, "The Natural," naturally, was the in-flight film. The teams split two games in San Diego, which with its canyons, ocean and surfboards, is about as different from Detroit as a city can be. In Game 1, Morris was excellent, pitching an eight-hitter. Back in Detroit, with Tigers fever raging, Marty Castillo's two-run homer helped rubber-armed Milt Wilcox get the victory in Game 3. In Game 4, Morris pitched a five-hit victory, and Trammell, who would be the MVP of the Series, twice hit two-run homers.

That set the scene for Game 5 on a hazy Sunday afternoon before a delirious throng at Tiger Stadium. Gibson scored the go-ahead run in the fifth inning when he tagged up and dashed home on Rusty Kuntz's pop-up to second baseman Alan Wiggins in short rightfield.

In the eighth inning, Gibson batted against Goose Gossage, a grizzly bear of a pitcher whose fastball was once described by author Thomas Boswell as "incomprehensible . . . a quark, something out of a different, smaller dimension." San Diego manager Dick Williams wanted Gossage to walk Gibson, who had homered earlier in the game.

Gossage, however, insisted on pitching to the outfielder. And, while fans screamed "Goosebusters!" to the theme from the movie "Ghostbusters," Gibson drove a Gossage pitch into the rightfield upper deck. Gibson danced around the bases, grinning maniacally, thrusting his fists into the air. The crowd bellowed. The blast increased the Tigers' lead from 5-4 to 8-4, which is how the game ended.

THE EPILOGUE

The Tigers' 104 regular-season victories were their most ever. They had spent each day of the season in first place, making their mark in history alongside the 1913 Philadelphia

Athletics and the 1927 New York Yankees of Babe Ruth and Lou Gehrig. Anderson became the first manager to win World Series in each league.

It was a fantasy world until about 30 minutes after the final pitch. That's when the rioting began.

Reporters from around the nation watched from the stadium roof. It had begun raining by then, and night had fallen. Flames licked wickedly from the smoking police cruiser, which was only one of a number of cars, buses and stores that were damaged. For reporters watching from high above Michigan Avenue, it was difficult to process the harsh image after having absorbed the unabashed joy of such an incredible season.

ROBERT KOZLOFF/Associated Press
THE CITY'S FIRST CHAMPIONSHIP CELEBRATION IN 16 YEARS
WAS MARRED BY HOOLIGANISM FOLLOWING GAME 5.

Detroit's winning image was shattered by the postgame riot. The nationwide picture shifted in a matter of minutes from a leaping Gibson to a pot-bellied Kenneth (Bubba) Helms mugging for the camera.

Helms, 17, was an eighth-grade dropout from Lincoln Park. With friends, he had drunk a fifth of Jim Beam, "smoked a few bad ones" and gone downtown to party. He jumped in front of the burning police car and held high a Tigers pennant and got himself photographed and plastered across front pages around the world.

Typical of the coverage were the words of Palm Beach (Fla.) Post columnist Steve Hummer, who described "explosions and sirens and the baying of a mad mob. They have turned the glory of this city into its shame. The World Series has become one of Detroit's greatest embarrassments."

And, incredibly, things soon got worse. Two weeks after the World Series riot, Detroit erupted in the most incendiary Devil's Night ever, with 808 fires reported over the three-day Halloween period — 600 more than average for a 72-hour period. Firefighters were forced to summon help from suburban departments. The self-immolation of the city made headlines from Paris to Peoria.

In turn, the negative reports touched off a feverish round of finger-pointing as local experts tried to explain why people were saying bad things about Detroit. The Free Press and WDIV-TV commissioned a scientific poll that found Detroit's national image was the worst of 17 major cities.

Not unexpectedly, Mayor Young denounced the poll, the paper and anyone who would criticize his city.

It was the best of seasons and the worst of seasons. If only the real world that year could have been confined to the area between the white lines.   ◆

NOV. 18, 1989: BLAKE EZOR RUSHED FOR A MICHIGAN STATE-RECORD SIX TOUCHDOWNS
IN A 76-14 VICTORY OVER NORTHWESTERN.

DETROITERS PROVED THEY LOVE A PARADE AND TURNED OUT BY THE HUNDREDS OF THOUSANDS AS THE CHAMPIONS PROMENADED THROUGH DOWNTOWN.

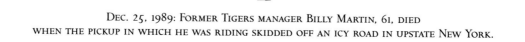

DEC. 25, 1989: FORMER TIGERS MANAGER BILLY MARTIN, 61, DIED
WHEN THE PICKUP IN WHICH HE WAS RIDING SKIDDED OFF AN ICY ROAD IN UPSTATE NEW YORK.

A double-eagle, a double-hit

Double Chen

By Gene Myers

His full name was Chen Tze-chung, but the other golfers called him T.C. for short. When the golf gods chose him to make history, in June 1985, he was an obscure third-year pro from Taiwan, rough with English, slender in build, a smoker to keep himself calm.

Chen would need 280 shots to finish the 85th U.S. Open at Oakland Hills Country Club, one shot too many to tie Andy North and force an 18-hole playoff. Two of Chen's 280 shots, though, would be among the most memorable in golf history.

The first came in the opening round. Chen's drive on the second hole, a 527-yard par five, landed routinely enough in the fairway. He had 256 yards to the pin. He chose a three-wood. The swing was flawless. The ball zoomed right on target. It landed on the green and rolled into the cup. A double-eagle two. The first in U.S. Open history. The few fans around the green started whooping. There weren't more because Chen's threesome didn't tee off until 3:06 p.m. and featured three nobodies. No photograph of the moment exists.

"I thought it would be close," Chen said, "but never thought it would go in."

Everything had changed for Chen. Hundreds of fans rushed to follow his every move. He was challenging for the lead. And Chen did not panic. He smoked, he played smart, he birdied the 17th and 18th holes for a five-under 65, an unimaginable score on a course with the famous nickname of The Monster, one stroke better than Fred Couples.

What a story, right? Yes, and no. Every Open seems to have its T.C. Chen. A Cinderella story. A Roy (Tin Cup) McAvoy who rises from obscurity to lead for a hole or two, sometimes a round or two. Well, Chen followed his 65 with consecutive 69s. After four holes Sunday, a windy and overcast afternoon for the final round, Chen led by four strokes.

Then came his second historic shot, on the 457-yard, par-four fifth hole, as part of a quadruple-bogey eight. A snowman, as golfers call it. An abominable snowman, in Chen's case. His tee shot was perfect — down the middle of the fairway. But he pushed his second shot right of the green,

MARY SCHROEDER/Detroit Free Press

A JOKE STARTED AFTER T.C. CHEN'S TROUBLES AT OAKLAND HILLS: HIS INITIALS STOOD FOR TWO CHIPS.

and his third shot stuck in the tall grass, short of the putting surface. Chen pulled out his pitching wedge. But as he swung to hit the ball, the club hung up in the grass and somehow struck the ball twice. A double-hit. Rarer even than a double-eagle.

Chen was assessed a penalty stroke after the ball came to rest on the collar of the green. From there, he chipped eight feet past the hole and missed the putt, his seventh stroke. "I can't complain," Chen said later. "I just played bad — the double-hit . . . I never play golf like that."

But he did. He lost seven shots in a four-hole stretch. From runaway winner to runaway loser? Not quite. Although Chen shot a six-over 41 on the front nine, he slowly played his way back into contention with a back-nine 36. North helped by bogeying the ninth, 10th and 11th holes. After 13 holes, Chen, North and Dave Barr were tied for the lead at two-under. The drama climaxed on the par-three 17th hole. North and Barr held the lead; Chen was one back. Barr, playing one group ahead, overshot the green, chipped poorly and missed a 35-footer. Bogey. North landed in a deep bunker to the right of the green. Chen still could win the Open, or at least force a playoff. Chen hit the green, but faced a monster putt. North then hit the shot of his life — the ball stopped two inches from the hole. He would get his par. Chen had neither line nor distance on his birdie putt, left it 20 feet short and three-putted for a bogey.

In a few minutes, North would have his second U.S. Open victory, only the 13th player at the time to accomplish the feat. North, in fact, hadn't won a tournament since his first Open, in 1978.

As for Chen, he had had his two shots with golf history. He would win a tournament on the PGA Tour, but within a few years settled into life on the Asian tour, sometimes playing well, sometimes not. One thing he definitely did not do very often was discuss the 1985 U.S. Open. When the Open returned to Oakland Hills in 1996, he refused interview requests and hid from reporters, but finally granted a brief interview to the Free Press:

"So many . . . so many like ESPN, so many . . . I mean, so many reporters want interviews. It doesn't feel good. It doesn't feel good to accept any interviews. I don't know why. I don't think about it anymore. I don't want to think about it anymore. I mean, I play good there except for one hole. I want it to go away. It was 10 years ago. A long time ago."

ARNIE AND JACK

The great golfers believe they have a birthright — to win major tournaments on the historic courses. In the golfing resumes of Jack Nicklaus and Arnold Palmer, under Oakland Hills, there was nothing of significance. "I had a chance in the '61 Open and didn't finish it up," Nicklaus said. "I lost by three and it stuck in my craw. Then I never played that well here since."

Nicklaus and Palmer finally filled in the blanks. They did so by winning the U.S. Senior Open a decade apart. Each won in an 18-hole playoff.

In 1981, fans were just starting to embrace a new concept: senior golf. Two things certainly helped: lowering the age from 55 to 50 and Palmer's winning the Senior Open at Oakland Hills.

Palmer, 51 at the time, could have avoided a playoff but missed a 10-footer for par on the 72nd hole. Tied at nine-over 289 were Palmer, Billy Casper and Bob Stone, a club pro from Independence, Mo. In the Monday playoff, Palmer trailed Stone by six shots after six holes. "My charge, if you wish, was a charge back to par," Palmer said. "This golf course will level you out. I was worried about par — not Bob. There's not a birdie hole on this golf course."

Still, he extracted four. He made 20-footers on the eighth and ninth holes and a 10-footer on the 12th. When he drained a 40-footer on the 15th, he had surged in front by himself for the first time.

On the 16th, a picturesque dog-leg par four with plenty of water, Stone, one back, hit his second shot in the water. Casper, three back, hit his second in the water, too. Palmer watched the events, pulled out a seven-iron and played a safe

shot to the fat side of the green. "You knew I wasn't going to be short," he said. Casper splashed another shot and recorded a quadruple-bogey. Stone bogeyed. Palmer made his par for an insurmountable two-shot lead.

He finished with an even-par 70, to Stone's 74 and Casper's 77. "It's one of the best tournaments I've ever played in," Palmer said. "The field was good and the course is one of the real challenges of golf."

In 1991, Nicklaus, then 51, tamed The Monster like few others. In a playoff with Chi Chi Rodriguez — they finished 72 holes at two-over 282 — Nicklaus shot a 65 that could have been a 60. As it was, he tied the course record set by George Archer in the 1964 Carling World and matched by T.C. Chen in the 1985 U.S. Open. "I was trying to hunt Bear, but I ran out of bullets," said Rodriguez, who shot a 69. "I haven't seen him play that well in maybe 15 years."

Nicklaus birdied three of the first five holes for a three-shot lead before lightning and rain delayed play for nearly two hours. Rodriguez cut the deficit to one by sinking a 35-foot birdie at the sixth green while Nicklaus was three-putting from 40 feet. At the seventh, Nicklaus' seven-iron was short — one of two greens he would miss. But he chipped in from 40 feet for another birdie. Rodriguez had seen this before; he knew there likely would be no stopping the Golden Bear.

Nicklaus made birdies at the 12th (a seven-footer) and the 185-yard 17th (he wired a five-iron within six inches). He had one other birdie putt lip out, almost made two others, and misread another. He shot 31-34—65, with seven birdies, seven 3's and a 2. Only a bogey on the 18th kept him from the course record.

"Course records don't mean anything to me," Nicklaus said. "What matters to me is playing well and winning. I don't think I can play any better than I did."

Nicklaus became the second player to win the U.S. Amateur, the U.S. Open and the U.S. Senior Open. The other? Palmer.

ALAN R. KAMUDA/Detroit Free Press

ARNOLD PALMER ATTRIBUTED HIS HOT PUTTING AT LEAST IN PART TO A HAND-ME-DOWN PUTTER FROM JERRY BARBER.

ALAN R. KAMUDA/Detroit Free Press

IN 1991, JACK NICKLAUS FINALLY HELD A CHAMPIONSHIP TROPHY AT OAKLAND HILLS. HE THOUGHT HE SHOULD HAVE WON THE U.S. OPEN THERE IN 1961.

JAN. 1, 1990: BO SCHEMBECHLER FINISHED HIS MICHIGAN CAREER WITH A BIG TEN TITLE, A 17-10 LOSS TO SOUTHERN CAL IN THE ROSE BOWL AND A 10-2 SEASON.

Winner take all

BY JOHN LOWE

W hat happened at the end of the 1987 season at Tiger Stadium still seems implausible: The teams with the two best records in the major leagues came down to a season-ending, winner-take-all series for their division championship, and then played three games so close, so riveting, that not only were all three decided by one run, but at the end of every inning, the teams were separated by one run or tied.

We have Kirk Gibson and the Milwaukee Brewers to thank for arranging the drama. On the previous Sunday, the Toronto Blue Jays were three outs from sweeping a four-game series from the visiting Tigers and taking a 4½-game lead on Detroit in the American League East with one week left.

Gibson led off the ninth that Sunday with a homer off Toronto relief ace Tom Henke, tying the score. It became the biggest Tigers homer that Gibson ever hit. The Tigers won in extra innings, moving within 2½ of Toronto.

The Tigers came home and split a four-game series with lowly Baltimore. That could have ruined them. But Milwaukee was emphatically sweeping three games in Toronto. So the Tigers gained 1½ games. When the Blue Jays entered Tiger Stadium on Friday, Oct. 2, they led by one game with three to play. To win the division, Toronto would have to beat the Tigers twice — perhaps finally in a playoff game Monday. The Tigers would have to beat the Blue Jays three times — perhaps last in a playoff game Monday.

The Blue Jays arrived displaying cracks of doom. They had lost four straight. Worse, shortstop Tony Fernandez and catcher Ernie Whitt — two of their best hitters — recently had been lost for the season with injuries.

DAYMON J. HARTLEY/Detroit Free Press

LARRY HERNDON SENT A FASTBALL FROM JIMMY KEY OVER THE LEFTFIELD FENCE AND THE TIGERS TO THE PLAYOFFS. LATER, HIS TEAMMATES COULD NOT CONTAIN THEMSELVES.

Manny Lee stepped in for Fernandez and became a central figure in all three games in Detroit. In the second inning Friday night, he hit a three-run homer off new Tigers ace Doyle Alexander. By the third, the Tigers had caught up on homers by Scott Lusader and Alan Trammell off Jim Clancy, then took the lead with an unearned run.

As the chill and tension grew over the final innings, the score did not. The Tigers won, 4-3. The race was tied.

The next afternoon, veteran Toronto left-hander Mike Flanagan pitched 11 heroic innings, allowing one earned run. Yet the longer Flanagan went, the further he seemed from victory. The Blue Jays had been afflicted with the worst possible fate in late-season pressure baseball: a team-wide inability to hit in the clutch.

Jack Morris, the consummate late-season battler, allowed 13 runners in his nine innings, but only two runs. Toronto took a 2-1 lead in the fifth when Lee doubled and scored. In the Tigers' fifth, Lee's throwing error led to the tying run.

There was no more scoring until the 12th, the first inning without Flanagan. Toronto manager Jimy Williams didn't bring in Henke because the Jays weren't ahead. The Tigers jumped on left-hander Jeff Musselman and loaded the bases with one out.

Trammell smashed what could have been an inning-ending double-play ball at Lee. The ball went right between his legs as pinch-runner Jim Walewander — who symbolized the unlikelihood of that Tigers team — scored the winning run. Trammell was credited with a hit, and the Tigers had a one-game lead. Toronto's George Bell, undeservedly voted that

FRANK TANANA, WHO GREW UP IN DETROIT AND PITCHED FOR DETROIT CATHOLIC CENTRAL, WAS ALL SMILES AFTER HE BLANKED THE BLUES JAYS, 1-0.

season's MVP instead of Trammell, sat motionless at his locker for 20 minutes after the game.

On Sunday, Toronto had to win to force Monday's one-game playoff. Larry Herndon hit a second-inning solo homer off ace Jimmy Key. Two innings later, Toronto got a one-out single from a young right-handed hitter who was starting because left-hander Frank Tanana was pitching. His name was Cecil Fielder.

With Lee up, Fielder took off on a hit-and-run. Lee missed the sign and took the pitch. Fielder was thrown out at second. Lee then hit a ball off the fence on which Fielder might have scored.

In 1996, in his seventh Detroit season, Fielder stole his first base in the majors. No big-leaguer then active had gone so many games at the start of his career without a steal. Yet in the biggest game of '87, Fielder had been caught stealing.

Lee was stranded after that fourth-inning triple. The Blue Jays left a runner in scoring position in five innings that day. For the series, they went 3-for-25 with runners in scoring position. Lee, the reserve shortstop, was the only Blue Jay who had an extra-base hit in the three games.

Tanana was the ideal pitcher for this moment. As a product of Detroit Catholic Central High, he was as much a part of Detroit as the packed house that roared for every out he got. As the off-speed master, he threw a variety of speeds and pitches that preyed on the anxiously swinging Blue Jays.

Tanana pitched a six-hitter to magnificently elevate himself into every starting pitcher's dream: a 1-0 complete-game victory that had his teammates embracing him at game's end in title-clinching celebration.

The Tigers had swept the most crucial series ever to end a regular season at Tiger Stadium. They had won their final championship of the 20th Century.

What seemed implausible then soon became impossible. Baseball doubled the size of its playoffs in the mid-'90s. If that format had been in place in '87, the Tigers and Blue Jays would have clinched berths before that season-ending series. One would have been the AL's wild-card team.

By century's end, the season-ending series in '87 was poignant for both teams. The Tigers lost more games than any other team in the '90s, never having a meaningful final few weeks, let alone a meaningful final series. The Blue Jays, despite two subsequent World Series titles, couldn't forget they had lost the last seven games of '87 and let a division title out of their grasp.

In September 1999, on the day of the Blue Jays' final game in Tiger Stadium, veteran Toronto trainer Tommy Craig recalled that final weekend in '87 and said, "Three of the best games I ever saw. . . ."

He spoke more with pain than with enthusiasm, like an art collector discussing a Rembrandt on which he had been outbid.

JUNE 14, 1990: THE PISTONS WON GAME 5 OF THE NBA FINALS AT PORTLAND, 92-90, CLINCHING THEIR SECOND STRAIGHT CHAMPIONSHIP. VINNIE JOHNSON HIT THE WINNING JUMP SHOT WITH 0:00.7 LEFT.

Upper hand in the U.P.

Yooper Dynasty

Lake Superior State University

IN 1992, LAKE SUPERIOR STATE RAISED A FINGER TO SHOW WHO WAS NO. 1. BUT FOR THE LITTLE U.P. SCHOOL, IT WAS TITLE NO. 2.

BY DOUG CHURCH

God must be a Yooper, eh?" Must be. What else could explain the four NCAA hockey championships won over seven years by teams from Michigan's Upper Peninsula?

Divine intervention for the Land Above the Bridge. That's how Joe Shawhan, a radio analyst and former goalie for Lake Superior State, figured it in 1994. The Lakers had just crushed Boston University, 9-1, to add a championship trophy to a case that included ones from '92 and '88.

Throw in Northern Michigan's heart-stopping, three-overtime victory in the 1991 title game and college hockey had itself a true Yooper dynasty.

Before the dynasty, it was a former Yooper — the first Lake Superior State coach, Ron Mason — who ended the state of Michigan's 11-year championship drought.

Mason had built Lake Superior into an NAIA powerhouse and won that title in 1972. He spent six years turning Bowling Green into a national power but never won an NCAA title.

When he arrived at Michigan State in 1979, Mason considered himself a builder, a skill that produced great teams on the ice and speculation off it that he would become a coach or general manager in the NHL. But he preferred to stay in East Lansing.

Entering the 1985-86 season, Mason already had won 443 games in a 19-year career; in the '90s, he set the all-time record for coaching victories. But the ultimate prize — an NCAA championship — had escaped his grasp. His 1983-84 team reached the Final Four but lost to Bowling Green in the semifinals. His 1984-85 team won an NCAA-record 38 games but lost to Providence in the first round when Chris Terreri made 50 saves.

Mason's 1985-86 Spartans were a rebuilding project. Six players had been lost to the NHL; seven freshmen were on the team. But MSU did have one star player, Hobey Baker Award finalist Mike Donnelly; a future star, Joe Murphy, a freshman who would be the first player taken in the '86 NHL draft, by the Red Wings; and a solid goaltending tandem of Bob Essensa and Norm Foster.

The Spartans started slowly but won 23 of 26 games to reach the national championship game against Harvard. They fell behind by two goals three times before taking a 5-4 lead in the third period. Harvard tied the score but Donnelly, fittingly, won it with 2:51 left with his 59th goal.

"It's like heaven," Mason said. "I thought after a while I'd be a Ray Meyer and I wouldn't be able to catch one of those championships."

By 1988, Frank Anzalone was an intense 33-year-old from Brooklyn, N.Y., who in six years had turned Lake Superior State into an NCAA contender. Still, Anzalone couldn't escape the long shadow of Mason's accomplishments in Sault Ste. Marie.

Anzalone's time came at Olympic Arena in Lake Placid, N.Y. Mark Vermette, a Hobey Baker runner-up, scored 4:46 into overtime of the title game against St. Lawrence — an even smaller school than 3,200-student Lake Superior. With their 4-3 victory, the Lakers were on the national hockey map. It wasn't the map used by a CNN sportscaster, who mistakenly offered congratulations to "the folks up there in Marquette, Mich.!"

PAULINE LUBENS/Detroit Free Press

RONALD REAGAN GAVE THE PRESIDENTIAL SEAL OF APPROVAL TO LAKE SUPERIOR STATE AFTER ITS 1988 CHAMPIONSHIP. "HE TOLD US SOME STORIES ABOUT KNUTE ROCKNE," SAID TERRY HOSSACK, A SENIOR DEFENSEMAN FROM WINDSOR, ONTARIO.

Sean Tallaire with 57 seconds left struck the crossbar or the roof of Maine's net before bouncing back into play.

In '94, the Lakers were underdogs again, facing top-ranked Boston U. Goalie Blaine Lacher was back for his third straight final and in the lining of his blocker had a page from a textbook, with a picture of Michelangelo's statue of David. "We keep playing these big, bad schools," Lacher said. "And here we are, this little Lake Superior that always seems to come up big — like David did. It's kind of our little thing. He's the man." The Lakers' 9-1 rout of Boston U. was the most lopsided final in 33 years.

Michigan State University

DESPITE AN 11-7-1 START, THE SPARTANS WERE ABLE TO POSE AS NCAA CHAMPIONS IN 1986 AFTER BEATING HARVARD, 6-5.

With new coach Jeff Jackson, the Lakers reached the finals three straight seasons, 1992-94. Jackson used the biblical story of David and Goliath to motivate his team. In '92, the Lakers were the proud, little underdog school going against the big, bad Wisconsin Badgers. Fab freshman Brian Rolston helped dispatch Wisconsin, 5-3, with the game-winning goal with 4:52 left.

In '93, the Lakers lost, 5-4, to top-ranked Maine, which had Paul Kariya, the first freshman winner of the Hobey Baker. Despite several replay angles, no one knows for certain whether a point-blank shot by Lakers freshman

That was the opposite of the 1991 final between Northern Michigan and Boston U. They were tied at 7 after 60 minutes and a pair of 10-minute overtimes.

The Wildcats overcame a 3-0 first-period deficit and got a hat trick from Scott Beattie and a game-saving stop from Bill Pye on Tony Amonte on a partial breakaway with one second left in regulation. In the first overtime, a shot by BU's Shawn McEachern

caromed off both posts before Pye smothered it on the goal line. Then Northern's Tony Szabo hit the crossbar. Finally, 1:57 into the third overtime, checking-line left wing Darryl Plandowski took a centering pass from Mark Beaufait in the slot and scored the goal that gave his team, his coach and Marquette a measure of respect and accomplishment that only Sault Ste. Marie had in the U.P.

"For me, it's that final step of equality," coach Rick Comley said. "You can work hard and think you're successful. But until you win it, it isn't enough."

An odyssey from Homer

Gold standard

PAULINE LUBENS/Detroit Free Press

GREG BARTON NEVER FOUND HIMSELF UP A RIVER WITHOUT A PADDLE. AFTER ALL, HE BUILT HIS OWN. HE WAS NEVER BETTER THAN IN SEOUL.

BY HELENE ST. JAMES

Greg Barton earned his reputation as the greatest American kayaker with a determination bred on a pig farm in Homer, Mich. There, as a teenager, he would get up before 6 in the morning, load his boat on top of his car, and head to a nearby lake, where he spent an hour powering his kayak with homemade paddles as fast as he could.

"It's hard work," he said at the 1984 Olympics, "but it's also not a bad way to start the day."

Years later, after qualifying for four Olympics and winning four Olympic medals, he credited farm chores with helping to instill the discipline he needed to train early mornings and late evenings, before and after work.

He was inspired to start kayaking by his parents, who enjoyed dabbling in Olympic-style paddling with their friends. They lived in a lovely brick house with 1,000 acres behind it. And maybe 6,000 pigs.

DEC. 14, 1991: MICHIGAN RECEIVER/RETURN SPECIALIST DESMOND HOWARD WON THE HEISMAN TROPHY.

His brother Bruce competed in the 1976 Montreal Olympics, qualified for the boycotted 1980 Moscow Olympics, and later tackled the annual Au Sable Canoe Marathon. Bruce's wife also was on the national team. But Greg's interest was cemented after meeting Marcia Buchanan, a 1964 Olympic bronze medalist.

"It's a sport that sort of grows on you," said Barton, born in 1959 in Jackson, Mich. "At first, you just go out there for fun. Then, when you start improving your speed and stamina, you end up pushing yourself and seeing exactly what you're capable of.

"There's a kind of peacefulness to this sport that appeals to me."

Barton's dedication eventually translated into a 1984 Olympic bronze medal, two golds in 1988, and another bronze in 1992. When he placed third in 1984 in the 1,000 meters, he became the first American to win a kayak sprint medal. His gold medals at the 1988 Games were the first ever for a U.S. kayaker.

In between Olympic Games, Barton became the first American to win gold at the world championships, when he took the 1,000 in 1985 and the 1,000 and 10,000 in 1987.

Not bad for a guy whose clubfeet gave him trouble walking as a child.

"I do the sport because I enjoy it, not because there is a lot of payoff," Barton said before the '88 Olympics in Seoul. "You don't see kayakers get rich or famous. It's a personal goal for myself to see if I can be the best in the world."

His best day came in South Korea. He won the 1,000 meters, and then, 90 minutes later, won the 1,000 doubles with longtime partner Norm Bellingham. Barton's gold medal in singles nearly went to Australian Grant Davies. The kayakers crossed the finish line so close to one another that the electronic scoreboard declared Davies the winner, even though it appeared Barton had won.

"I looked at the scoreboard," Barton said, "and I said, 'Oh, man, I hope someone is up in the photo-finish room.'"

Using freeze-frame film, the judges recanted and switched the names. The final times read: Barton, 3:55.27; Davies, 3:55.28.

In the meantime, Barton already had signed the finish sheet as runner-up. When he found out he had in fact won the gold, he said his emotions "kind of flip-flopped."

PAULINE LUBENS/Detroit Free Press

UNTIL THIS MEDAL WENT AROUND GREG BARTON'S NECK IN 1988, NO AMERICAN HAD WON AN OLYMPIC GOLD MEDAL IN KAYAKING.

Charles Dambach, then the chairman of the U.S. canoe and kayak team, said the finish might have been closer than the .01 difference. "It was 5-1,000th of a second," he said, "but the official results don't go that far. They actually considered awarding two gold medals."

Barton made it two straight golds when he and Bellingham overtook the New Zealand team in the last quarter of the race and spurted across the finish line in 3:32.42.

Ripe with success and the best in the world at age 28, Barton continued to train and earned a spot on his fourth Olympic team by winning the 1992 U.S. trials. (He had qualified for the 1980 team; instead of a trip to Moscow, he received a picture of himself shaking President Jimmy Carter's hand.) At Barcelona, Spain, Barton won a bronze in the 1,000 singles and missed a bronze in the 1,000 doubles by four-tenths of a second.

Although Barton was a versatile and talented athlete — he wrestled and ran cross-country in high school — he was equally dedicated to academics. After graduating as Homer High's salutatorian, Barton went to Michigan, where he graduated summa cum laude with a degree in mechanical engineering.

Barton used the degree to design and build his paddles. He started by ordering supplies of carbon fiber and epoxy and building the paddles at his parents' farm.

"I've been kayaking for 13 years," he said in 1984, "so I'd better know something about it."

Barton retired from Olympic competition after the 1992 Games, at 32. Two summers later, he won the Clean Water Challenge, the world's longest canoe/kayak endurance race, by completing 744 miles in 80 hours, 23 minutes, 13 seconds.

Twenty-four paddlers started in Chicago, spent more than a month covering portions of four Great Lakes, eight rivers and the Erie Canal, and finished with a four-mile trip down the Hudson River to New York City. Barton won almost all of the race's 29 stages.

"It's always fun to be outside," Barton said, "and to pull on the paddle and feel the boat accelerate under your body."

He would know. The fun he had pulling on a paddle won him fame throughout the world, and a reputation for every future American paddler to chase.

JAN. 5, 1992: ERIK KRAMER PASSED FOR 341 YARDS AND THREE TOUCHDOWNS AS THE LIONS BEAT DALLAS, 38-6, IN THEIR FIRST PLAYOFF GAME AT THE SILVERDOME.

One-handed hero

BY MICK MCCABE

In the fall of 1984, Jim Abbott was a rumor. Word spread throughout the state that Flint Central had a quarterback with one hand. The youngster led Central to the state playoffs. And the word was that he was an even better baseball prospect, a left-handed pitcher.

After rejecting an offer from the Toronto Blue Jays, who drafted him in the 36th round in 1985, Abbott entered Michigan and blossomed into a national celebrity.

His first collegiate victory came in his first appearance. He entered an extra-inning game with the score tied, two out and a runner on third. When the catcher threw Abbott's first pitch back to him, the runner broke for home. Abbott caught the ball in his glove on his left hand, tucked the glove under his right armpit, removed the ball and threw to the catcher, who easily tagged out the runner.

Michigan scored a run in the bottom of the inning, and Abbott had the victory without retiring the only batter he faced.

Abbott and his father, Mike, developed the routine of catching the ball and switching the glove at an early age so that they could play catch. By the time Abbott reached college, he had perfected the routine so well that he made the switch with the deftness of a magician. If you didn't know Abbott had only a stump at the end of his right arm, you might not have noticed even after watching him pitch.

During his freshman season, a visitor from another school asked a Wolverine if the one-handed kid was going to pitch. Abbott already had pitched three innings. He liked to play down the notoriety by saying, "I've been blessed with a pretty good left arm and a not-so-good right arm."

Abbott developed into a terrific collegiate pitcher, and in 1987 he became the first American in 25 years to beat Cuba on its home soil. The Cubans cheered wildly for the pitcher they called "El Manco" — the one-hander. A

MARY SCHROEDER/Detroit Free Press

A MAN FOR ALL SEASONS, JIM ABBOTT FIRST DREW THE PUBLIC'S EYE AS A QUARTERBACK FOR FLINT CENTRAL. HE WENT ON TO PITCH FOR THE MICHIGAN WOLVERINES (BELOW), THE U.S. OLYMPIC TEAM, THE ANGELS, YANKEES, WHITE SOX AND BREWERS. HE RETIRED IN 1999.

ALAN R. KAMUDA/Detroit Free Press

month later, in Indianapolis, Abbott carried the U.S. flag in opening ceremonies of the Pan American Games. He then posted a 2-0 record with a 0.00 ERA.

That winter, during his junior year, Abbott received the Sullivan Award as the nation's top amateur athlete, the first Michigander and baseball player so honored. He beat a field that included David Robinson, Janet Evans and Greg Foster. A few minutes after the ceremony, Abbott said: "I was sitting up there with all of these Olympic gold medalists and world-record holders — and all I want to do is make All-Big Ten."

Abbott made All-Big Ten and All-America that spring, and in the fall he pitched the United States to the gold medal in the Seoul Olympics. He pitched a seven-hitter in the finale, a 5-3 victory over Japan.

The California Angels had drafted him in the first round, and in 1989, he went right to the major leagues without a day in the minors. His 10-year pro career, with four teams, included monumental highs and severe lows. In 1991 he finished third in the Cy Young Award voting with an 18-11 record. Two years later, he pitched a no-hitter for the New York Yankees.

He retired in July 1999, at age 31, a couple of years after his fastball disappeared. He had an 87-108 record.

Abbott's career nearly ended in 1996 when he suffered through a demoralizing 2-18, 7.48 ERA season with the Angels. Fans can turn quickly on a millionaire player, but that never happened to Abbott. After one especially rough outing against Baltimore, Abbott received a standing ovation from Angels fans when he was removed. "The fans have treated me well," Abbott said. "I don't know why they gave me that ovation."

Here's why: Abbott was the kind of person who embraced his lot in life as a genuine role model. Abbott became a fan favorite and an

FEB. 9, 1992: MICHIGAN BASKETBALL COACH STEVE FISHER STARTED THE FAB FIVE FOR THE FIRST TIME, AND THE FRESHMEN ACCOUNTED FOR ALL OF THE WOLVERINES' POINTS IN A 74-65 VICTORY AT NOTRE DAME.

PAULINE LUBENS/Detroit Free Press

JIM ABBOTT WAS THE WINNING PITCHER IN THE GOLD-MEDAL GAME IN SEOUL, SOUTH KOREA. THE FINAL SCORE: USA 5, JAPAN 3.

icon for children with disabilities. It wasn't a role he sought, but one he never hid from. He estimated that he averaged at least one scheduled meeting with a child during every road series in his career.

"Most of the kids I met had a limb deficiency — missing hands, a short limb, some sort of birth defect," he said after retiring. "Last year I was meeting kids for the second time, ones who I met years ago in Baltimore. Now they're teenagers and playing sports and accomplishing things. That's tremendously rewarding. It makes me feel pretty good."

Abbott spent years making children with disabilities, as well as baseball fans in general, feel good. He will never be at an induction ceremony in Cooperstown, but that won't change the fact that he was a Hall of Fame person from the time he quarterbacked Flint Central to the time he retired from baseball.

"I feel fulfilled. I feel satisfied," he said. "My career wasn't always great, but it was wonderful. I learned so many lessons and had so many great friends and experiences. My experiences, added up, make me feel like I've had a Hall of Fame career."

A Hall of Fame career? Nope. A Hall of Fame life? Absolutely.

APRIL 6, 1992: DUKE BEAT MICHIGAN, 71-51, FOR THE NCAA CHAMPIONSHIP,
THE FIRST TIME FIVE FRESHMEN STARTED FOR ONE TEAM IN FINAL FOUR HISTORY.

A hoops showplace

Original Palace

Detroit Free Press

THE SPARTANS CLOSED JENISON FIELD HOUSE — THEIR HOME FOR NEARLY 50 YEARS — WITH A 70-61 VICTORY OVER WISCONSIN IN 1989.

BY MICK MCCABE

Decades before the Palace of Auburn Hills was even on the drawing board, Michigan State had a palace of its own, Jenison Field House.

Yes, once upon a time, Jenison was considered a jewel. Later, it proved to be an albatross to the Michigan State coaches who had to recruit to the arena.

"It was the showplace of the state of Michigan," said Dick Kishpaugh, historian for the Michigan High School Athletic Association. "Very, very soon it became known as The Big House. There wasn't anything to

compare it to, so it had that aura in a hurry."

Construction on the Frederick Cowles Jenison Gymnasium and Field House began on Dec. 23, 1938. It was completed March 15, 1940, two months after the inaugural basketball game in which MSU defeated Tennessee, 29-20.

The field house was named after Jenison, a former MSU engineering student who willed his estate to the school, which used the money to construct the state-of-the-art arena.

On Jan. 10, 1948, 15,348 fans jammed into Jenison to

MAY 5, 1992: CHUCK DALY RESIGNED AFTER NINE SEASONS AS PISTONS COACH AND WAS REPLACED BY RON ROTHSTEIN. DALY WOULD GO ON TO COACH THE U.S. OLYMPIC DREAM TEAM, THE NEW JERSEY NETS AND THE ORLANDO MAGIC.

ALAN R. KAMUDA/Detroit Free Press

AN EXTERIOR VIEW OF THE FIELD HOUSE. "JENISON RANKED IN BEAUTY WITH THE BEST OF THE TIME," FORMER BASKETBALL COACH PETE NEWELL SAID.

watch No. 1 Kentucky, led by Alex Groza, Ralph Beard and Wallace (Wah Wah) Jones, defeat MSU, 47-45. It was the largest crowd to attend a game at Jenison. The local fire marshal attended that game, and he ensured that the record never would be broken. He quickly reduced the capacity to 12,500.

In 1972, the fire marshal reduced capacity again to 10,004, but not until after MSU spent $300,000 to install additional exits. The fire marshal said that had the doors not been installed, capacity would have been limited to 7,500.

"I came from the West Coast, and we didn't have big basketball buildings then," said Pete Newell, MSU's coach in 1950-54. "Jenison ranked in beauty with the best of the time. It was a tremendously attractive building — the entranceway with its pictures and trophies."

In the early years, Jenison had a dirt floor and a portable three-foot elevated court for basketball. In the early 1970s a spongy tartan surface was installed, but basketball coach Jud Heathcote eventually had it replaced with a wooden floor.

For many years, Jenison played host to the high school boys basketball state championship games.

"People used to say, 'We're going to Jenison,' " Kishpaugh said. "That meant they were going to the state finals. Jenison was the marvel of the day. It had a charismatic touch to it."

Heathcote, who became MSU's basketball coach in 1976, found nothing charismatic when athletic director Joe Kearney first showed him the place late one night.

"I was interviewed for the job in Chicago and then I went to California to recruit for a week," Heathcote recalled. "When I got to campus, Joe took me in to see Jenison for the first time. It was at night and Joe got a janitor to turn on the lights. When I saw it I said: 'Joe, we had a better place than this at Montana.' Joe said: 'I would hope so.' "

Despite its charm on game nights, Jenison was a hard sell to recruits.

"We brought Granville Waiters in on his visit," Heathcote said. "He looked around and asked: 'Do you play in here?' When we told him yes, he said: 'No, you don't.' He didn't believe us."

Thus disillusioned, Waiters chose Ohio State.

The greatest season in MSU history was the 1978-79 campaign that led to the NCAA championship. Midway through the Big Ten season, MSU was 4-4 heading into a showdown with 8-0 Ohio State.

It was do-or-die for the Spartans that night, but Earvin Johnson sprained an ankle early in the second half and left the court.

"Gregory Kelser was out because he had four fouls," Heathcote said. "He was kneeling at the table to go in, and when he stood up, there was this tremendous ovation. Later, Greg said he knew people would be happy to see him go back, but he didn't expect anything like that. Then he said he turned around and saw Earvin coming back to the bench."

When Johnson left the training room, a few fans noticed and began cheering. The cheering spread throughout the arena like a wave until it was so loud that Jenison literally was shaking. The ovation was deafening. Johnson said he thought the building was going to cave in. MSU won that game in overtime, 84-79, and rolled to the Big Ten title by winning nine of its final 10 conference games.

"That was the loudest of anything I've ever been associated with," Heathcote said. "I still remember when we came in for the opening ceremonies at the Pan American Games in 1975 in Mexico City.

"There were 90,000 people and there was a tremendous cheer for the United States. But that night in Jenison was just unbelievable."

In Jenison's final game, March 11, 1989, the Spartans beat Wisconsin, 70-61.

"It looked like a big jogging barn," Heathcote said, "but it was a great place to play."

◆

OCT. 10, 1992: LITTLE CAESARS PIZZA MAGNATE MIKE ILITCH BOUGHT THE TIGERS FROM DOMINO'S PIZZA MAGNATE TOM MONAGHAN FOR A REPORTED $85 MILLION.

HOOP DREAMS, 1979-1993

And still champion

The Hit Man

ALAN R. KAMUDA/Detroit Free Press

THOMAS HEARNS, FIGHTING OUT OF DETROIT'S KRONK GYM, HAD MORE UPS THAN DOWNS IN A
PROFESSIONAL CAREER THAT BEGAN IN 1977. HE WAS STILL BOXING IN 1999.

BY GEORGE PUSCAS

House lights dimmed at the old Olympia as the pounding beat of a popular boxing movie called "Rocky" filled the arena. A moment later, the lights went off, leaving the arena and 10,000 fans in total darkness.

So the stage was ready. A tall, skinny kid wrapped in a long, red robe covering his head, strode onto the stadium floor, spotlights swallowing his head and creating a dramatic, ominous signal of what was to come.

Hundreds of boxing fans had not yet reached their seats when Thomas Hearns took his first swing at luckless Jim Rothwell. Those who tarried more than a few seconds longer missed one of boxing's great moments.

Hearns slammed his right fist onto Rothwell's head, and Rothwell crumpled onto the canvas. They were just two minutes into the fight, but it was long enough for Hearns to be instantly hailed as boxing's "Hit Man."

Many of Hearns' fights were among the most dramatic of his time. He knocked out Roberto Duran, one of boxing's great champions, with an awesome right-hand punch that frightened all who saw the Panamanian collapse and fall on his face, and then dragged, still unconscious, to his corner.

Hearns the Hit Man was the most appealing, exciting non-heavyweight in boxing during the 1980s. He fought an incredible three-round bout with Marvin Hagler, the first round quickly hailed as one of history's best, and the fight itself as one of the 10 best bouts in a near-century of boxing.

Before Hearns was done, he had won world championships in five weight

NOV. 22, 1992: BARRY SANDERS' 151 RUSHING YARDS IN A 19-13 VICTORY OVER CINCINNATI
GAVE HIM 5,202 FOR HIS CAREER, SURPASSING BILLY SIMS' 5,106 AS THE LIONS' CAREER LEADER.

MARY SCHROEDER/Detroit Free Press

BUT WHEN THOMAS HEARNS FELL, HE FELL HARD. MARVELOUS MARVIN HAGLER KNOCKED OUT THE HIT MAN IN A STORIED BOUT ON APRIL 15, 1985.

divisions, and seven federation titles, at weights from 145 to 190 pounds, unprecedented in boxing.

People say that Joe Louis, the famed Brown Bomber, was Detroit's best boxing product, and maybe the world's, and probably he was. But there are some who would put Hearns no worse than second, ahead of everybody else.

He won 32 bouts in a row opening his career, but then came the first of two defeats that would mar his record and dim his fame. The first was a welterweight showdown with Sugar Ray Leonard in 1981 and the other the loss to Hagler in 1985.

Leonard and Hagler were the accepted kings of the welterweight and middleweight divisions when Hearns fought them, and both narrowly survived.

Hearns, in fact, was ahead on the judges' scoring cards when he suddenly was knocked out by Leonard in the 14th round. Just a few minutes before, Hearns had Leonard in such serious trouble he was being urged in his corner to "finish him off."

KIRTHMON F. DOZIER/Detroit Free Press

HEARNS WON PLENTY OF HARDWARE, PROUDLY DISPLAYED AT HIS HOME IN SOUTHFIELD, MICH.

Instead, Leonard — warned by trainer Angelo Dundee that he might throw in the towel and stop the fight — lashed out with only five minutes left in the bout and caught Hearns with a left-right combination that sent Hearns reeling along the ropes. The bout was stopped.

Unable to obtain a rematch from Leonard, Hearns set sights on Hagler. Hagler wasn't interested, so Hearns turned to Wilfredo Benitez, the super-welterweight champion. He took Benitez's title in a 15-round struggle.

Not until April 15, 1985, could Hearns and manager Emanuel Steward lure Hagler into the ring. Their showdown promised to be a classic.

Hearns' strategy was obvious. Always a fast starter, he would quickly try to stun, then overwhelm and dispose of Hagler.

But Hagler was no fool. He suspected Hearns' plot and prepared for it. He would meet Hearns head-on, challenge and match him blow for blow, may the better man win.

It all began just the way they said it would, Hearns bearing in, forcing the attack, slamming Hagler with a succession of blows to head and body. But before he was done, before Hearns could catch his breath, there was Hagler, suddenly matching him blow for blow.

With only a few seconds left in the first round, Hagler pinned Hearns in a corner and shook him with a series of heavy blows. It was enough to bring an instant change of strategy from Hearns.

Early in the second round, a more cautious Hearns nevertheless opened a long slit on Hagler's forehead, and another along Hagler's nose. The fighting was interrupted to mop blood from Hagler's face, and when they resumed, it was all Hagler, seemingly fighting for his boxing life.

Two minutes into the third round, Hagler caught a retreating, stumbling Hearns and knocked him out, making the Detroiter again only second-best of his weight class.

Hearns lost two more fights, late career upsets to Iran Barkley in 1988 and 1992. But on June 12, 1989, Hearns gained some revenge against Leonard, knocking him down and thoroughly beating him, although the judges gave him only a draw.

Hearns persisted with occasional meaningless fights past his 41st birthday. He already was among sports' richest men, his 60-plus bouts earning purses totaling more than $60 million.

And that might have been the Hit Man's grandest hit of all. ◆

JAN. 1, 1993: A 38-31 VICTORY OVER WASHINGTON IN THE ROSE BOWL CLINCHED AN UNDEFEATED SEASON FOR 9-0-3 MICHIGAN, WHICH EARLIER HAD WON OR SHARED ITS FIFTH STRAIGHT BIG TEN TITLE.

Very good, but not Super

Thumbs up!

BY CURT SYLVESTER

The year was 1991. And for the Lions, what a season it *almost* was.
The year the Lions *almost* made it big. The year they *almost* erased 33 years of frustration. The year they *almost* converted the cynics. The year they *almost* got to the Super Bowl.
Almost.

Barry Sanders, in the third year of his Hall of Fame career, rushed for 1,548 yards and 16 touchdowns. Herman Moore, the rookie wide receiver who would become their all-time receiving leader, caught 10 passes in two playoff games. Offensive tackle Lomas Brown and center Kevin Glover were well on their way to Pro Bowl careers, and legendary linebacker Chris Spielman and hard-hitting safety Bennie Blades were the heart of the defense.

If it hadn't been for the Washington Redskins, the Lions' last NFL championship might well have been Super Bowl XXVI instead of the 1957 NFL championship. The Lions handled everything else the NFL and fate sent their way in that glorious — yet tragic — season.

The Green Bay Packers? No problem, the Lions swept them. They paddled Minnesota twice, Dallas, the Los Angeles Rams and the New York Jets. They eased past Miami and Indianapolis, split with Tampa Bay and Chicago, beat the AFC East champion Buffalo Bills in overtime and, when they clinched the NFC Central Division with a 12-4 record — the best in club history — coach Wayne Fontes lit a victory cigar.

Two weeks later, the Lions hit their post-1957 peak by demolishing the Cowboys, 38-6, for a berth in the NFC championship game.

That's where it all ended, of course. The Redskins, who shocked the Lions to life with a 45-0 blowout in the opener, ended their magical run at their first Super Bowl with an equally convincing, equally devastating, 41-10 whipping.

FANS TOOK UP THE BANNER, AND THE LIONS FINISHED FIRST IN THE NFC CENTRAL THAT YEAR.

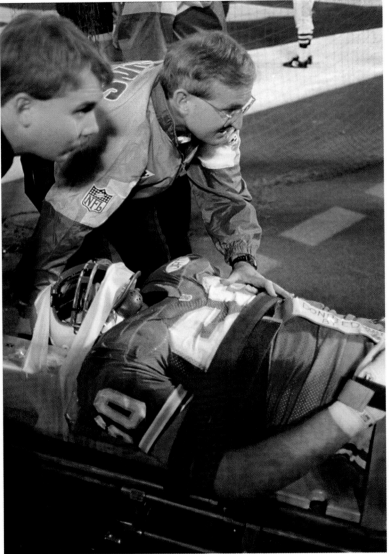

Photos by JULIAN H. GONZALEZ/Detroit Free Press

MIKE UTLEY, WHO SUFFERED A NECK INJURY AT THE SILVERDOME IN 1991, SIGNALED THUMBS UP WHILE BEING TAKEN FROM THE FIELD AND BECAME AN INSPIRATION TO HIS LIONS TEAMMATES.

APRIL 5, 1993: IN A GAME THAT WILL ALWAYS BE REMEMBERED FOR CHRIS WEBBER TRYING TO CALL TIME OUT WHEN MICHIGAN HAD NONE REMAINING, NORTH CAROLINA BEAT THE WOLVERINES, 77-71, IN THE NCAA FINAL.

The Lions, with linebacker Chris Spielman, stopped Emmitt Smith and the Cowboys in the playoffs.

"To put it in a nutshell, we got down early, we gave up some big plays, and they moved the ball on us," Spielman said. "They're a great team. They were the better team. It's hard for me to face that, but they were."

What fans will remember more than the bitter ending, however, was the inspiration the team drew from Mike Utley, a promising but unheralded offensive lineman who suffered a neck injury against the Rams in the 11th game. Blocking against David Rocker, Utley crashed awkwardly to the Silverdome turf, snapping his head in a whiplash effect. A spinal disk had ruptured; his sixth cervical vertebra had been shattered. He was permanently paralyzed from his chest down.

Utley was on the field for several long minutes while doctors and trainers worked frantically. When he was finally carried off on a stretcher, he delivered a thumbs-up signal to his teammates that became the inspiration for the rest of the season.

Quarterback Erik Kramer, originally a replacement player for Atlanta during the 1987 strike, threw three touchdown passes that day. The Lions beat the Rams, 21-10, to improve to 7-4, and then won their five remaining games to finish one game ahead of the Bears.

Although Utley was hospitalized, his teammates never forgot him. They prayed for him, visited him at Henry Ford Hospital in Detroit, and wore Utley thumbs-up T-shirts.

In a special ceremony before the Thanksgiving game 11 days after the injury, Brown addressed Utley with a national television audience looking on. "We want you to know that you are as big a part of this team today as you have ever been, and you will always be a part of this team," Brown said. "Thanks for your courage, your inspiration, and your strength. We're praying for you, we're all pulling for you. So keep the faith — we love you — and thumbs up, Mike."

Nose tackle Jerry Ball suffered a season-ending knee injury in the 14th game against the Jets, but the Lions were on a mission and they were sky-high entering the playoff game against the wildcard Cowboys.

The team that hadn't won a playoff game since the 59-14 NFL championship victory over Cleveland in 1957 took the Cowboys apart, piece by piece. Fontes and offensive coordinator Dave Levy knew Dallas would stack its defense to stop Sanders, so they put the game in the hands of Kramer, who completed 29 of 38 passes for 341 yards and three touchdowns, producing a 38-6 victory.

That was the last of the Lions' magic, however. They couldn't hold up against the Redskins, who beat up on Buffalo, 37-24, two weeks later in Super Bowl XXVI.

During the off-season, Fontes' brother Lenny — the defensive backs coach — died of a heart attack. A month before training camp in 1992, starting offensive guard Eric Andolsek was killed when he was struck by a truck while doing yard work in Louisiana.

The Lions fell to last place at 5-11, and the promise of the stirring 1991 season never was fulfilled.

What a season it was. But what a season it *almost* was. ◆

June 15, 1993: The Red Wings hired six-time Stanley Cup winner Scotty Bowman as coach. Bryan Murray stayed on as general manager.

1979-1993
Our scrapbook

GOING HOLLYWOOD

- Shirley (Cha Cha) Muldowney's tale was told in "Heart Like a Wheel."
- Bubba Smith was a mainstay in the "Police Academy" films.
- Alan Trammell and Lou Whitaker guested on "Magnum PI."
- Roy Scheider played an aging Tiger in "Tigertown" for cable.
- LeVar Burton starred in "One in a Million: The Ron LeFlore Story" (with cameos by Billy Martin, Al Kaline and Norm Cash).

C.D. STOUFFER/United Press International

MAGIC TIME

The signature play of Desmond Howard's 1991 Heisman Trophy season came on a fourth-and-1 play against archrival Notre Dame in Game 2. With Michigan leading, 17-14, and 9:02 left, coach Gary Moeller gave quarterback Elvis Grbac the option of throwing a short pass for a first down or a home run ball from the Irish 25.

Grbac went for it all and appeared to overthrow Howard. But Howard stretched far out, never broke concentration, and caught the ball with safety Greg Davis nipping at his heels in the back of the end zone for a 24-14 victory.

HEY, RALFIE

Two Ralf Mojsiejenko moments, from 1982:
- Sept. 11: Michigan State's Mojsiejenko kicked a 61-yard field goal in his first college attempt, but the Spartans lost to Illinois, 23-16.
- Nov. 20: Iowa safety Ron Hawley crashed into the Spartan Stadium goalpost, knocking it down and breaking the crossbar. Grounds crew had to hold up the post so Mojsiejenko could kick a field goal, but Michigan State still lost the season finale, 24-18.

UPSET CITY

- The University of Detroit's 71-66 basketball victory over No. 4 Memphis State at Calihan Hall in 1985.
- Central Michigan's 20-3 football victory over Michigan State in East Lansing in 1991.
- Central Michigan's 24-20 football victory over Michigan State in East Lansing in 1992.

LOVE COUPLES

- Kirk Gibson and JoAnn Sklarski, above right.
- Dave Rozema and Sandy Sklarski, above left.
- Emily Gail and Pooh.
- Petr Klima and Irena Zelenak.
- Andre Rison and Lisa (Left Eye) Lopes.

PLATONIC COUPLES

- Magic Johnson and Larry Bird.
- Bob Probert and Joey Kocur.
- Ernie Harwell and Paul Carey.
- Desmond Howard and Elvis Grbac.
- Mouse Davis and June Jones.
- Kirk Gibson and Steve Garvey, above.

ANTAGONISTIC COUPLES

BILL FRIEDER AND BOB KNIGHT.
BOB PROBERT AND TIE DOMI.
THOMAS HEARNS AND MARVIN HAGLER.

BEST KISSERS

MORGANNA AND LANCE PARRISH.
MAGIC AND ISIAH.

BROTHERLY LOVE

Ludington's Luke and Murphy Jensen defeated Marc Goellner and David Prinosil, 6-4, 6-7 (4-7), 6-4, for the 1993 French Open title, but ultimately they were known more for dedicating themselves to livin' large and bringing rock 'n' roll sensibilities to tennis.

OVERNIGHT SUCCESS

Eric Hipple made probably the splashiest debut of any Lions starting quarterback, and he did it on the NFL's biggest regular-season stage.

Subbing for injured Gary Danielson, Hipple passed for 336 yards and four touchdowns and ran for two more scores in a 48-17 victory over Chicago on Oct. 19, 1981. That includes a 94-yard TD to Leonard Thompson, at the time the longest completion in "Monday Night Football" history.

"I still think of that Monday night game, too," Hipple said years later. "It still gives me chills. I remember the very first play. It was a 25-yard pass to Freddie Scott. When we completed it, it was like an explosion went off inside of me. I wanted to shout. I felt everything I was going to do was going to work. And it did."

Hipple was cut in '89 after 10 seasons with the Lions, with a broken ankle, dislocated thumb, elbow surgery, cracked ribs, sprained knees, broken nose and other assorted injuries in between.

MARY SCHROEDER/Detroit Free Press

ERIC HIPPLE WAS READY FOR PRIME TIME, EVEN THOUGH HE HAD ONLY HELD FOR KICKS AS A PRO.

WHO'S COUNTING

It was a mad scramble. Seconds were ticking away. Eric Hipple was trying vainly to get the offense set to stop the clock. Special-teams players were running on the field to try a field goal that would break the 24-24 tie with Dallas.

And Eddie Murray did, a 47-yarder that gave the Lions a 27-24 victory on Nov. 15, 1981, at the Silverdome. Nobody noticed till they checked the tapes later that the Lions' peculiar formation had 12 men.

No hard feelings, Cowboys coach Tom Landry said.

"Anybody that could kick a field goal with half of their kicking team and half of their offensive team on the field, deserved it," Landry said. "Any of our cornerbacks could have gone in and blocked it if they knew what was happening, but they couldn't figure out the formation. So they just stood there and watched him kick it.

"I didn't feel bad about the 12 men on the field. They weren't using half of 'em anyway."

NO PLACE LIKE DOME

The NFL had decided it was time a cold-weather city hosted the Super Bowl, so the XVIth game on Jan. 24, 1982, pitted San Francisco against Cincinnati. It also pitted fans against Michigan winter driving conditions, and many of them were still outside when the game started.

On the field, the 49ers won, 26-21.

The Silverdome has certainly seen more than its share of collapses, but none more embarrassing than in March 1985, when wet snow collapsed sections of its inflatable roof.

The Lions' season was long over, but the Pistons were forced to play the final 15 games of the 1984-85 season at Joe Louis Arena (including one at Cobo).

The season before, the Pistons were bumped from the Silverdome by a motocross and had to play the decisive Game 5 of their first-round playoff series with New York at Joe Louis Arena (which they lost, 127-123, in overtime).

No wonder the Pistons announced plans in late '85 to build the Palace of Auburn Hills.

BEAT THE CLOCK

Time was Michigan State's enemy on two straight trips to the NCAA tournament:

■ Midwest Regional semifinals, 1986: Playing on Kansas' near-home-court of Kemper Arena in Kansas City, Mo., the Spartans were leading, 76-72, with 2:21 left when the Jayhawks inbounded the ball, came up the floor and scored a basket. And the clock still read 2:21. MSU coach Jud Heathcote fumed, but officials did nothing about the phantom 15 seconds. Perhaps with the help of the extra time, the Jayhawks tied the game and won in overtime, 96-86.

■ Southeast Regional semifinals, 1990: This time, Georgia Tech's Kenny Anderson tied the game with a three-pointer at the buzzer at the Superdome in New Orleans, and the Yellow Jackets won in overtime, 81-80. Except that TV replays showed the ball still in Anderson's hands when the clock hit 0:00. And Heathcote complained that MSU's previous inbounds play to Steve Smith with six seconds left and subsequent foul by Tech took only one second off the clock when the actual play took about three. "The clock did us in," Heathcote said. "It was a great game, but a tremendous, disappointing loss for us. I'm down, the team is down, but that's basketball."

IT'S A LONG STORY

It was Game 12 of the 1986 season, 2:06 left, and the Lions were two touchdowns ahead at lowly Tampa Bay. What better time to give a rookie quarterback his first NFL playing time.

First-round draft choice Chuck Long came into the game and handed off to fullback Scott Williams for three plays. But on fourth-and-4, Long launched the first pass of his career, and Leonard Thompson gathered it in for a 34-yard TD and a 38-17 victory.

"We decided to let him heave it once," coach Darryl Rogers said, grinning. "He got it over the hog house and everything was fine. . . .

"Hey, he's got a little magic."

Our scrapbook

CAREER MOVES

The early '90s were a time of transition for Michigan legend Bo Schembechler:

■ Dec. 13, 1989: Bo announced his retirement as Michigan football coach after the upcoming Rose Bowl with Southern Cal. "The hardest thing I've ever had to do is give up . . . my football team . . . but I'm doing it. . . . I think I've run my luck about as far as I can take it," he said. Bo's last game would be a 17-10 loss to the Trojans.

■ Jan. 8, 1990: Schembechler resigned as U-M athletic director and went to work for his friend, Domino's pizza magnate Tom Monaghan, as president of the Tigers. He replaced Jim Campbell, who was named chairman of the board, and Jack Weidenbach was named interim AD at Michigan. One of Bo's mandates: Get a new stadium built for the Tigers.

■ Aug. 3, 1992: Monaghan fired Schembechler and Campbell on the eve of selling the Tigers to Little Caesars pizza magnate Mike Ilitch. Bo sued, claiming he had a verbal agreement for a 10-year deal and offered notes on a napkin as proof. The suit was settled.

MUSICAL COACHES

Out	In
Johnny Orr	Bill Frieder
Dick Vitale	Richie Adubato
Les Moss	Sparky Anderson
Darryl Rogers	Muddy Waters
Richie Adubato	Scotty Robertson
Bobby Kromm	Marcel Pronovost
Marcel Pronovost	Ted Lindsay
Ted Lindsay	Wayne Maxner
Wayne Maxner	Nick Polano
Muddy Waters	George Perles
Scotty Robertson	Chuck Daly
Monte Clark	Darryl Rogers
Nick Polano	Harry Neale
Harry Neale	Brad Park
Brad Park	Jacques Demers
Darryl Rogers	Wayne Fontes
Bill Frieder	Steve Fisher
Bo Schembechler	Gary Moeller
Jacques Demers	Bryan Murray
Chuck Daly	Ron Rothstein
Ron Rothstein	Don Chaney
Bryan Murray	Scotty Bowman

TAKE IT TO THE BANK

"I guarantee we will beat Ohio State and go to Pasadena. We might have our backs against the wall where the odds are against us and nobody is giving us a snowball's chance in hell to win, but we'll bounce back and win in Columbus. It's a great feeling to beat Ohio State, and we're going to have that feeling Saturday."

Whoa. Pretty strong words for Michigan quarterback/captain Jim Harbaugh in the week leading up to the 1986 Ohio State game. Did Bo Schembechler approve of Harbaugh serving the Buckeyes such bulletin board fodder?

"I'd worry more," Bo snapped, "if he predicted we'd lose."

Which the Wolverines didn't, of course. No. 6 U-M beat No. 7 OSU, 26-24, for a share of the Big Ten title and that trip to the Rose Bowl. And then a 22-15 loss to Arizona State.

LINGERING DEATH

Like many Lions coaches before and after him, Monte Clark learned to live with rumors that he was about to be fired and even joke about them. After a 21-10 loss to the LA Rams dropped the Lions to 1-4 in Clark's sixth season, he told sportswriters as they left his office: "See you at the cemetery."

But the Lions followed a familiar pattern the rest of that 1983 season: They finished 8-3 and won the NFC Central with a 9-7 record. But then, with a national TV audience watching as Clark prayed on the sideline, they lost in the first round of the playoffs to San Francisco, 24-23, as Eddie Murray missed a 43-yard field goal with 11 seconds left.

"I led it to the right," Murray said. "If I had a hara-kiri knife, I would have committed it right there. Everything we've been working for as a team went down the drain."

Murray actually missed to the left from 43 yards earlier in the fourth quarter. He kicked three field goals in the game, including one from 54 yards, still the Lions' playoff record.

Clark was fired after the Lions went 4-11-1 the next season.

NO BOWL OF CHERRIES

Hey, how about putting on our own bowl game in the Silverdome? It seemed like a good idea when the first Cherry Bowl drew 75,000 fans for Michigan State's 10-6 victory over Army in 1984. But the next year only 23,000 jammed the 80,000-seat stadium to watch Bobby Ross and Maryland beat Syracuse, 35-18.

Cherry Bowl II finished $1.2 million in the red, and the NCAA pulled the plug on the game. But former MSU coach George Perles revived the idea of a Silverdome bowl with the Motor City Bowl more than a decade later, pitting the Mid-American Conference champ against an at-large team.

Ole Miss won the inaugural Motor City Bowl, 34-31, over Randy Moss and Marshall before an announced crowd of 43,340 in 1997. The Thundering Herd came back the next year and beat Louisville, 48-29, before an announced 32,206.

According to eyewitnesses, "announced" apparently meant 10,000-15,000 fewer than actually were in the stands, but the Motor City was one-up on the Cherry — there would be a third game in '99.

ISIAH'S ENEMIES LIST

Sometimes it seemed as if Isiah Thomas had more fights, physical and otherwise, than Thomas Hearns. Some of his sparring partners:

■ BILL CARTWRIGHT: This was a frequent matchup, especially in 1989. On Jan. 31 in Chicago, Thomas took a Cartwright elbow and six stitches above his right eye. The next time the Pistons and Bulls played, April 7 in Chicago, a scuffle broke out when Thomas swatted the ball away from Cartwright and it hit him in the head. As Thomas turned to go upcourt, Cartwright hit him in the neck. Thomas charged Cartwright, they fell to the floor, the benches emptied, and it took about 10 minutes to restore order. Thomas suffered a broken left hand when he punched Cartwright in the head, was fined $5,000 and suspended two games; Cartwright got $2,500 and one game.

■ ADRIAN DANTLEY AND HIS MOTHER: The Pistons traded Dantley in February 1989 — a few months before they won their first title — to Dallas for Isiah's old buddy, Mark Aguirre. Guess who Dantley blamed for masterminding the controversial deal? Dantley seldom blamed Thomas directly, but he told Esquire: "Jack McCloskey didn't make that trade. Isiah runs it in Detroit. It's as simple as that. The bottom line is, it's a business. The Pistons used me up, got their program going, and then, boom, they got rid of me." Or as Dantley's mother, Virginia, put it: "You shouldn't blame Jack McCloskey. He's not the one. It's that little con artist you've got up there. When his royal highness wants something, he gets it." Six weeks after the trade, the Mavs played the Pistons at the Palace. Before the opening tip, Thomas approached Dantley with an open hand. Dantley returned the handshake, put his arm around Thomas and began talking into his ear. Was he making peace, as Thomas' smile indicated? Or dressing down Thomas, as was rumored later? "Ask Isiah," Dantley said. "It's personal," Thomas said.

■ VIRG JACQUES: The Channel 2 reporter claimed Isiah — upset at a story the station ran saying Thomas' name had surfaced in a gambling investigation — choked him in 1990. Thomas eventually was not implicated in the probe.

■ MICHAEL JORDAN: His Airness reportedly was irked ever since an Isiah-led snub to freeze him out of the offense in the 1985 NBA All-Star Game (he scored seven points), not to mention Chicago's decisive victory in the '91 Eastern Conference finals, when Isiah led the dethroned Bad Boys off the court before the game was over. Jordan, some sources say, then kept Thomas off the Dream Team that won the gold medal at the Barcelona Olympics in '92. Both men denied all of this feudin'.

■ BILL LAIMBEER: The two good friends scuffled during a 1993 Pistons practice, and Thomas ended up going on the disabled list. Thomas first threw an air-punch. But later, as Laimbeer turned, Thomas landed one on the back of his head and broke his hand.

■ TOM WILSON: A power struggle? When he retired in '94, Isiah spread word of a $55-million parting package that would make him part owner of the Pistons. Bill Davidson was irked at the leak, and Thomas got little more than a handshake. Wilson is still running the Palace's growing empire; Thomas started up the Toronto Raptors, did TV work and bought the CBA.

BY THE NUMBERS

All taken from the Pistons' 186-184 triple-overtime victory at Denver on Dec. 13, 1983, the highest-scoring game in NBA history:

370
Total points, breaking the NBA record of 337 in San Antonio's 171-166 triple-overtime victory over Milwaukee on March 6, 1982.

145-145
Score at the end of regulation, after Bill Laimbeer intentionally missed a free throw with six seconds left and Isiah Thomas scored on the rebound.

142
Field goals in the game, an NBA record.

74
Pistons field goals in the game, an NBA record.

51
Points by Kiki Vandeweghe, the Nuggets' leading scorer.

47
Points by Thomas, the Pistons' leading scorer.

17
Assists by Thomas.

12
Points by Kelly Tripucka in the second overtime, to account for all of the Pistons' scoring.

2
Number of three-pointers hit in four attempts in that game; one by Thomas and one by Denver's Richard Anderson.

3:11
Time it took to play the game. Summing it up: "Before the game, I told Doug Moe that we should make it the first team to 140 would win the game," Pistons coach Chuck Daly said. "Little did I know how prophetic that would be. They usually say the first team to 100 will win the game, but in this game, that happened in the middle of the third quarter."

Our scrapbook

BEST MARKETING CAMPAIGNS

Bless You Boys

Another One Bites the Dust

Bad Boys

Hammer Time

Restore the Roar

THE OTHER BAD BOYS

While the Pistons were enjoying their glory years, many of the Red Wings were, well, just enjoying themselves. Some of the fuzzy memories include:

■ PETR KLIMA: The Wings spirited the original wild and crazy guy out of then-Czechoslovakia in 1985 and he soon revealed a taste for cars and bars. Police pulled over Klima's GMC Jimmy after a minor accident at about 2 a.m. Oct. 9, 1988, outside a Royal Oak bar. Klima was driving but, already on probation for a 1987 alcohol-related charge, he switched places with a female passenger. Klima spent two days in jail after he pled guilty to DUI and leaving the scene. He was traded to Edmonton in 1989 but returned to Detroit for 13 games in the 1998-99 season.

JOHN COLLIER/Detroit Free Press

PETR KLIMA AND FIANCEE IRINA ZELENAK. THEY WOULD MARRY.

■ BOB PROBERT: One of the most popular Wings, the bruising Probert also led the league in alcohol-related scuffles with the law. After several brushes with the law and attempts at rehab, on March 2, 1989, he was arrested at the Canadian border after U.S. customs agents found 14.3 grams of cocaine hidden in his undershorts. He served three months in a federal facility for that incident, but returned to the Wings in 1990. After another traffic incident in 1994, the Wings released Probert that year. He signed with Chicago but sat out the entire 1994-95 season on league suspension.

■ GOOSE LOONIES: The Red Wings Seven — Steve Chiasson, John Chabot, Darren Eliot, Petr Klima, Joe Kocur, Bob Probert and Darren Veitch — were caught drinking in a well-publicized incident at this Edmonton nightspot on the eve of their Game 5 ouster from the 1988 playoffs. The saddest footnote to this whole era: On May 3, 1999, the popular Chiasson was killed after driving his truck off the road following the Carolina Hurricanes' season-ending party. North Carolina authorities said Chiasson's blood-alcohol level was 3½ times the legal limit. He was 32.

HEROES

KEN MORROW of Flint AND MARK WELLS of St. Clair Shores, who played on the plucky U.S. hockey team that pulled off the Miracle on Ice at the 1980 Winter Olympics, upsetting the mighty Soviet Union and later winning the gold medal.

WILLIE HERNANDEZ, who had 32 saves for the '84 Tigers.

VILLAINS

GUILLERMO HERNANDEZ, for blowing too many save opportunities and dumping a bucket of water on Free Press columnist Mitch Albom, whom he blamed for "turning the fans against me."

DARRYL ROGERS, for messing up two programs, Michigan State and the Lions.

SERVING TIME

More and more athletes were revealing feet of clay, but perhaps none more than Tigers hero Denny McLain in the '80s. McLain was beset by financial problems after his baseball career, and in 1985 he was sentenced to 23 years in federal prison for racketeering, extortion and possession of 6.6 pounds of cocaine.

Released in 1987 after his conviction was overturned, McLain eventually found favor again in Detroit as a broadcaster, especially on the popular "Eli and Denny" show. In the meantime, his retrial ended in a plea bargain, and he was put on probation.

But in 1993, McLain and partner Roger Smigiel bought Peet Packing Co. in Chesaning. The company went bankrupt, and they were convicted of raiding its pension fund. McLain found himself back in prison, serving an eight-year sentence.

Detroit Free Press

DENNY MCLAIN CAME BACK TO DETROIT TO A NICE CAREER IN BROADCASTING. BUT THERE WERE MORE PRISON STRIPES IN HIS FUTURE.

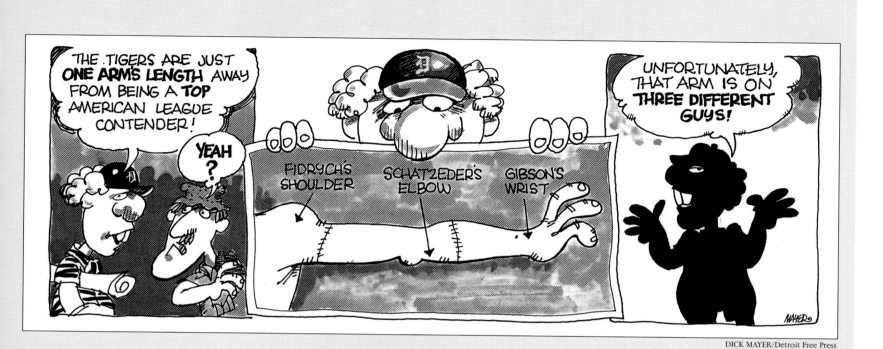

DICK MAYER/Detroit Free Press

SLUGGERS

MARY SCHROEDER/Detroit Free Press

DARRELL EVANS led the major leagues with 40 homers at the age of 38 in 1985.

CECIL FIELDER led the majors with 51 homers in 1990 (second in Tigers history to Hank Greenberg's 58 in '38) and tied Jose Canseco for the lead with 44 in '91.

DUMB IDEA

No argument, the dumbest thing that happened during the Tigers' Monaghan-Schembechler era was the firing of announcer Ernie Harwell. Funny thing, nobody wanted to take credit for it, so Schembechler took the blame from irate legions of Ernie fans.

"I did not recommend the firing of Ernie Harwell," Schembechler said later. "All of you people know that. What I resented was the fact that he called a press conference and said I fired him. That was not true. And when it all came out, you had already bashed me for it, and you weren't going to change that, and you didn't. His contract was with WJR."

After Bo was roasted for about three weeks, the late Jim Long, then WJR's general manager, said he was the one who had fired Harwell.

The Ilitch stewardship brought Ernie back to Tigers broadcasts, first to PASS, then to Channel 50 and finally to WJR, where he finished the century as voice of the Tigers.

WEIRDEST TIGERS LEFT KNEE INJURIES

Pitcher DAVE ROZEMA, who injured himself in 1982 while hurling himself through the air in an attempt to kung-fu kick Minnesota third baseman John Castino during a brawl.

Shortstop ALAN TRAMMELL, who hurt himself when he dressed up as the Frankenstein creature and fell off his monster shoes on Halloween 1983.

TRAFFIC JAM

Formula One racing came roaring to Motown — and through Motown — with the Detroit Grand Prix, won by John Watson in 1982. But the drivers never cared for the course that wound through the streets of downtown Detroit, and after the late Ayrton Senna won his third straight Grand Prix in '88, F1 demanded facility changes.

Negotiations broke off, and the race was switched to CART's Indy-style cars. Emerson Fittipaldi won the inaugural CART race in '89, his first of two Detroit victories. In 1992, the race was moved to Belle Isle.

TONY SPINA/Detroit Free Press

FORMULA ONE CARS ROARED AROUND DOWNTOWN STREETS IN THE FIRST DETROIT GRAND PRIX IN 1982. THE RACE WAS MOVED TO BELLE ISLE AND CHANGED TO CART.

Our scrapbook

1979-1993

OLYMPIC CHAMPIONS

Lake Placid, Winter '80
KEN MORROW, Flint, AND MARK WELLS, St. Clair Shores, hockey: gold.

Los Angeles, Summer '84
GREG BARTON, Homer, kayaking: bronze in 1,000-meter singles.
ALICE BROWN, Jackson, track and field: silver in the 100 hurdles, gold in the 400 relay.
JUDI BROWN, East Lansing, track and field: silver in the 400 hurdles.
BRIAN DIEMER, Grand Rapids, track and field: bronze in the 3,000 steeplechase.
LAURIE FLACHMEIER, Detroit, volleyball: gold.
STEVE FRASER, Ann Arbor, Greco-Roman wrestling: gold in the 198-pound class.
MARK GORSKI, Michigan, cycling: gold in 1,000 sprint.
DOUG HERLAND, Ann Arbor, rowing: bronze in pairs with cox.
EARL JONES, Inkster, track and field: bronze in the 800 meters.
BRUCE KIMBALL, Ann Arbor, diving: silver in platform.
KARCH KIRALY, Ann Arbor, volleyball: gold.
BARRY LARKIN, Michigan, baseball: silver.
STEVE MCCRORY, Detroit, boxing: gold in the flyweight class.
PAM MCGEE, Flint, basketball: gold.
RON MERRIOTT, Ann Arbor, diving: bronze in springboard.
CHRISTINA SEUFERT, Ann Arbor, diving: bronze in springboard.
JON SVENDSEN, Northville, water polo: silver.
FRANK TATE, Detroit, boxing: gold in the light-middleweight class.
KIM TURNER, Detroit, track and field: bronze in the 100 hurdles.
WENDY WYLAND, Jackson, diving: bronze in 10-meter platform.

Calgary, Winter '88
JILL WATSON AND PETER OPPEGARD, Bloomfield Hills, figure skating: bronze in pairs.

Seoul, Summer '88
JIM ABBOTT, Flint, baseball: gold.
GREG BARTON, Homer, kayaking: gold in 1,000 singles and 1,000 pairs.
ALICE BROWN, Jackson, track and field: gold in the 400 relay.
MATT CETLINSKI, grew up in Grosse Pointe and Warren, swimming: gold in 800

JULIAN H. GONZALEZ/Detroit Free Press
DANA CHLADEK, BRONZE IN BARCELONA.

freestyle relay.
JEFF GRAYER, Flint, basketball: bronze.
KARCH KIRALY, Ann Arbor, volleyball: gold.
BRENT LANG, Michigan, swimming: gold in the 400 freestyle relay.
DAN MAJERLE, Traverse City, basketball: bronze.
DEBBIE OCHS, Howell, archery: bronze in women's team event.
CONNIE PARASKEVIN-YOUNG, Detroit, cycling: bronze in the match sprint race.

Albertville, Winter '92
JASON WOOLLEY, Michigan State, hockey: silver (for Canada).
CATHY TURNER, Northern Michigan Olympic Training Center, short-track speedskating: gold in 500.
TURNER, AMY PETERSON, DARCIE DOHNAL AND NICOLE ZIEGELMEYER, Northern Michigan Olympic Training Center, short-track speedskating: silver in 3,000 relay.

Barcelona, Summer '92
MIKE BARROWMAN, Michigan, swimming: gold in the 200 breaststroke.
GREG BARTON, Homer, kayaking: bronze

NEIGH

One Michigan champion left the Barcelona Olympics without a medal: Lectron, a 10-year-old Dutch Warmblood stallion owned by Mary Anne McPhail of Orchard Lake and her daughter Melinda. After helping the U.S. win a bronze medal in team dressage — ending a 16-year American medal drought in the sport — McPhail said Lectron got "lots of sugar, lots of carrots, a great big dinner of hay, lots of hugs and lots of pets. He got lots of everything he loves."

OLYMPIC PIONEER

On Aug. 1, 1984, Ann Arbor's Steve Fraser defeated Ilie Matei of Romania in the 198-pound class at the Los Angeles Games for the first Greco-Roman wrestling gold medal in U.S. history. Fraser, then a Washtenaw County sheriff's deputy, was asked what he would do with the gold medal. "I don't know," he said. "I'll probably keep it for a while. Knowing me, I'll probably bronze it."

in the 1,000 singles.
GUSTAVO BORGES, Michigan, swimming: silver in the 100 freestyle (for Brazil).
CHRIS BYRD, Flint, boxing: silver in the middleweight class.
DAEDRA CHARLES, Detroit, basketball: bronze.
DANA CHLADEK, Bloomfield Hills, kayaking: bronze in whitewater slalom.
DARNELL HALL, Detroit, track and field: gold in the 1,600 relay.
KEVIN JACKSON, Lansing, freestyle wrestling: gold in the 180.5-pound class.
MAGIC JOHNSON, Lansing, basketball: gold.
ZEKE JONES, Ann Arbor, freestyle wrestling: silver in the 114.5-pound class.
MARK LENZI, Ann Arbor, diving: gold in three-meter springboard.
LYNETTE LOVE, Detroit, taekwondo: bronze.
ERIC NAMESNIK, Michigan, swimming: silver in the 400 individual medley.
QUINCY WATTS, Detroit, track and field: gold in the 400 meters and 1,600 relay.

Lillehammer, Winter '94
CATHY TURNER, Northern Michigan Olympic Training Center, short-track speedskating: gold in 500.
TURNER, AMY PETERSON, KAREN CASHMAN AND NICOLE ZIEGELMEYER, Northern Michigan Olympic Training Center, short-track speedskating: bronze in 3,000 relay.
ANDY GABEL, JOHN COYLE, RANDY BARTZ AND ERIC FLAIM, Northern Michigan Olympic Training Center, short-track speedskating: silver in 500 relay.

THE WINNER IS . . .

KENT BENSON: J. Walter Kennedy Citizenship award in 1981-82.

BRAD PARK: NHL's Masterton Trophy in 1984.

SPARKY ANDERSON: American League manager of the year in 1984 and '87.

WILLIE HERNANDEZ: American League MVP and Cy Young awards in 1984.

MITCH ALBOM: APSE columnist of the year in 1986, first of 12 such awards.

ISIAH THOMAS: J. Walter Kennedy Citizenship award in 1986-87.

JACQUES DEMERS: NHL's Jack Adams Award in 1987 and '88.

STEVE YZERMAN: NHL's Lester B. Pearson Award in 1989.

DENNIS RODMAN: NBA defensive player of the year in 1989-90 and '90-91.

DESMOND HOWARD: Heisman Trophy in 1991.

MIKE ILITCH: NHL's Lester Patrick Trophy in 1991.

Michigan State University

MICHIGAN STATE ATHLETES COLLECTED HEAVY METAL IN 1990. FROM LEFT, STEVE SMITH WAS THE BIG TEN MVP, PERCY SNOW WON THE BUTKUS AND LOMBARDI AWARDS, AND KIP MILLER WON THE HOBEY BAKER AWARD.

FASHION STATEMENTS

- Chuck Daly's designer suits.
- Bill Davidson's tieless look.
- Tom Selleck's Hawaiian shirt and Tigers hat, right.
- Lem Barney's British bowler.
- Jack Morris' fur coat.
- Kirk Gibson's whiskers.
- Drago's shaved head.
- Ron Duguay's flowing locks.
- Eddie Murphy's Mumford T-shirt and Lions jacket in "Beverly Hills Cop," right.
- The Fab Five's baggy shorts.
- Mel Farr Superstar's cape.
- Dennis Rodman's tattoos and multicolored hair (first inspired by Wesley Snipes in "Demolition Man"), with messages shaved into it.

OUR STARS

Of his 23 All-Star Games, GORDIE HOWE says he remembers the last one, in 1980, when he received a thundering ovation from Detroit fans at Joe Louis Arena. That was after he had retired from the Red Wings, served an exile in the World Hockey Association, and played in the game as a Hartford Whaler at the age of 51. "I was like a kid again," Howe said. "On my first shift, I had a shot on net, and I missed it by 20 feet. I forgot all the principles of the game. I was nervous as hell. There was no place to hide. Then I went over to talk to (former Wings trainer) Lefty Wilson, and he said, 'Get out of here, you old bastard.' That broke the spell."

Pistons great ISIAH THOMAS was the MVP in two NBA All-Star Games. He gained accolades from his peers after leading the East to a 154-145 overtime victory in 1984 in Denver with 15 assists, four steals, five rebounds and 21 points, but the 1986 trophy was more emotional for him. After scoring 30 points in the East's 139-132 victory in Dallas, Thomas shared a sobbing hug with his

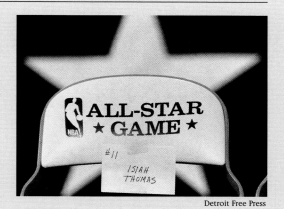

Detroit Free Press

ISIAH THOMAS SAT WITH THE STARS.

mother, Mary, in the middle of the Reunion Arena floor. "I was thinking of the hard times she had and the struggles she had gone through and how great it is for her to be able to come here to Dallas and stay in the Sheraton Hotel and be with the best people and see these things," Thomas said. "And then I think about what a relatively short time she has, I mean, she's not going to live another 60 years. It was very, very emotional."

FANTASTIC FINISH

Freshman Anthony Carter's 45-yard TD reception from John Wangler gave Michigan a 27-21 victory over Indiana in 1979. Carter caught the ball at the 19, darted between two defenders, and raced into the end zone as time expired. Hoosiers coach Lee Corso complained bitterly about the previous play, claiming U-M fullback Lawrence Reid illegally threw the ball out of bounds to stop the clock.

ALPHABET SOUP

For the record, these were the alphabet-soup boxing titles Thomas Hearns won in a career that never seemed to end, courtesy of the Kronk Gym: WBA welterweight, WBC junior middleweight, WBC light-heavyweight, WBC middleweight, WBO super middleweight, WBA light-heavyweight, WBU cruiserweight.

Our scrapbook

DARK VICTORY

The Lions' 1991 season was one of their best in recent memory. It also was one of their darkest.

On Nov. 17, right guard Mike Utley crumpled to the Silverdome floor after a seemingly innocent play in the 21-10 victory over the Los Angeles Rams. He did not get up.

As he was taken off on a gurney, Utley flashed a thumbs-up sign to teammates and fans. The gesture became a rallying point for the rest of the season, after it was discovered Utley was paralyzed.

"We owe it to Mike not to sit around and sulk about him, but to go out and play," offensive tackle Lomas Brown said. "And to show everyone is playing for him, because really the rest of the season is representing Mike. He has been an inspiration to me."

The Lions finished 12-4 in 1991 and advanced to the NFC championship game with a 38-6 victory over Dallas. There, they lost to Washington, 41-10.

Tragedy struck the offensive line again in the off-season, when a truck veered off a rural highway and struck and killed left guard Eric Andolsek while he worked in the yard of his home near Thibodaux, La.

As for Utley, he dedicated himself to staying active in sports such as skiing, scuba diving and skydiving, and to raising funds for the Mike Utley Foundation, which was dedicated to finding a cure for spinal-cord injuries.

And he dedicated himself to walking again. On Feb. 15, 1999, with the help of

MIKE FIALA/Associated Press

FORMER LION MIKE UTLEY FLASHED HIS SIGNATURE THUMBS-UP AFTER TAKING 10 STEPS IN 1999.

friends and with the media watching, he got out of his wheelchair and walked 10 labored feet.

He did it partly to demonstrate the value of continued rehabilitation, partly just to show he could.

"It's a good start," Utley said. "Is it the finish line? Not even close. Will I continue on? Will I walk again? You betcha."

Utley had vowed to one day return to the Silverdome and walk off the field under his own power. "One day I will," he said. "It might not be tomorrow, but someday I will. I guarantee it."

MAGIC'S COURAGE

"It can happen to anybody," Magic Johnson said. "Sometimes you're naive and think it can never happen to you. Here I am saying, 'It can happen to anybody.'"

What happened to Johnson, and caused him to retire from the Los Angeles Lakers at the age of 32, was that he had tested HIV positive. He shocked the world with the announcement Nov. 7, 1991, but left with the assurance that he didn't consider it a death sentence and would work to educate people about AIDS.

"This is not like my life is over,

because it's not," Johnson said. "This is another challenge, another chapter in my life. You have to come out swinging. I'm going to go on, beat it and have fun."

Brave words in the face of tragedy? Johnson went on to play for the NBA Dream Team that won the Olympic gold medal at Barcelona in 1992, coached the Lakers for 16 games in 1994, came out of retirement for 32 regular-season games and four playoff games in 1996, hosted a talk show, and continued playing in exhibitions around the world.

WE SAID IT

The Wings took Steve Yzerman with the fourth pick in the NHL draft on June 8, 1983. The Free Press headline said: "Wings too late for LaFontaine."

HE SAID IT

"I want to be very careful on this assignment," coach Jacques Demers said before naming a new Red Wings captain on Oct. 7, 1986. "I want to be sure whoever it is, is capable of wearing the 'C' for many years to come.

"Steve Yzerman seems to fit the bill. . . . The captain has to be a guy who can play; a guy who on and off the ice shows some class; a guy who wears the Detroit Red Wings sweater with some pride; and a guy who the other players look up to and respect. He doesn't have to necessarily be a rah-rah guy, but someone who will stand up when times get tough and say, 'Let's go, guys, this is it.' And he has to be able to see the coach's side as well as the players' side. There's a lot of pressure."

At 21, Yzerman was the youngest captain in Wings history.

MARY SCHROEDER/Detroit Free Press

STEVE YZERMAN DID THE "C" PROUD.

CHAPTER 8

NEW ICE AGE
1994-1999

By Nicholas J. Cotsonika

Detroit spent its final years of the sports century as a puckhead paradise. The Tigers and Pistons were in decline. The Lions were, well, mostly the same old losing Lions they had been for decades, despite Barry Sanders and a few teasing, fleeting flirtations with success. College sports provided a few thrills. But the Red Wings were religion.

They became the city's identity. Shrewd marketing executives devised a new buzzword, a new theme for Wings games. They plastered it in big, black, arrogant letters across center ice at Joe Louis Arena. They displayed it on bold banners that hung from lampposts along Jefferson Avenue. And it caught on quicker than free beer between periods.

Hockeytown.

In 1955, the Red Wings won their seventh Stanley Cup. They would wait 42 years for No. 8.

Detroit was Hockeytown.

Across the border, Canadians bristled at the thought of an American city usurping their national passion. But what could they do? Hockey was a passion in other places, too. A drive down any Detroit freeway proved that: Thousands of cars and vans and trucks, on their way to work or on their way home or on their way to the game, in winter and summer the same, raised red flags that flapped from their windows.

The flags weren't just a fad. They became a tradition, part of the landscape, like the octopi hurled on the ice at playoff time. They identified the disciples of the new religion. When the Wings eventually won two straight Stanley Cups, more than a million fans flooded the city's streets for the victory parades. For too long, they had suffered the Wings' failures, futility and frustration. They had to be healed by the Cup.

Everyone did. After the New York Rangers won the Cup in '94, the Wings owned the NHL's longest championship drought. They hadn't won since '55. In the '70s and early '80s, they were known as the Dead Wings, the Dead Things. Under coach Jacques Demers in the late '80s, they improved enough to be considered competitive. Under coach Bryan Murray in the early '90s, they inched closer and closer to a championship. But

---

Preceding page: For the first time in 42 years, the Red Wings hoisted the Stanley Cup. Steve Yzerman went first in 1997.

Photograph by MARY SCHROEDER/Detroit Free Press

JULIAN H. GONZALEZ/Detroit Free Press

THE RED WINGS WON THEIR SECOND STRAIGHT CUP IN 1998, AND VLADIMIR KONSTANTINOV JOINED THE CELEBRATION IN HIS WHEELCHAIR.

the playoffs killed them.

Disappointment became an annual ritual. In '91, the Wings lost to St. Louis in seven games. In '92, they were swept by Chicago. In '93, they blew a 2-0 lead to Toronto and lost. Legendary coach Scotty Bowman took over in June 1993, but their fortunes didn't immediately change. In '94, they lost to San Jose in seven games. In '95, they made a ballyhooed return to the finals — but were swept by New Jersey.

Most thought circumstances were as bad as they could get, that things could only get better, meaning a Cup was on the horizon. Then came Colorado. Although the 1995-96 Wings won a record 62 regular-season games, although they expected no less than a summer with Stanley, the Avalanche buried them in the conference finals. Six games. Done. No Cup. Ugh.

"The expectations of our team, and our own expectation, was to get back to the Stanley Cup finals and win, and we didn't do that," captain Steve Yzerman said. "We didn't live

up to expectations. We didn't play as well as the Detroit Red Wings are expected to play, as well as we expected to play.

"Obviously, there's a big difference between playoff hockey and regular-season hockey. We said it, and we meant it when we said it: Winning 62 games in the regular season means nothing. It's not an indicator of what's going to happen in the playoffs. Come playoff time, we didn't respond."

Even worse, the Avs added injury to insult. In the first period of the final game, Colorado's Claude Lemieux hit forward Kris Draper from behind and slammed him into the boards. Draper suffered a broken jaw and nose, a concussion and several displaced teeth. He needed 30 stitches to mend his mouth. His jaw was wired shut for 16 days, forcing him to take his meals through a straw, morning, afternoon and night.

A straw? Well, that was the last straw. Outraged, the Wings vowed revenge, on Lemieux and history itself, knowing the only way to make Draper and their city whole again was by beating Colorado, by reaching the finals once

MARCH 6, 1994: THE RED WINGS
RETIRED GOALIE TERRY SAWCHUK'S NO. 1.

JULIAN H. GONZALEZ/Detroit Free Press

WINNING DIDN'T COME EASY. ROOKIE GOALIE CHRIS OSGOOD COULDN'T HOLD BACK THE TEARS AFTER EIGHTH-SEEDED SAN JOSE ELIMINATED THE TOP-SEEDED RED WINGS IN THE FIRST ROUND OF THE 1994 PLAYOFFS.

more, by winning the Cup this time, so they could harness its healing power.

THE CAPTAIN

Cupless since '55, the city was growing impatient, and the weight of the wait put pressure on Yzerman more than it did on any other player. He *was* the Wings. He was the mayor of Hockeytown. Every boy from Sterling Heights to South Lyon bugged his parents for a No. 19 sweater. Grown men felt comfortable calling him "Stevie" or "Stevie Y" in casual conversation. In more formal situations, people simply — and with affectionate respect — referred to him as "The Captain."

The Wings' first choice (fourth overall) in the 1983 draft, he played his first NHL game Oct. 5, 1983, at Winnipeg. He scored a goal and assisted on another. From that day forward, he never slipped from excellence and never lost his loyalty, joining Gordie Howe and Alex Delvecchio as the

JULIAN H. GONZALEZ/Detroit Free Press

LIKE HIS TEAMMATES, DINO CICCARELLI COULDN'T EXPLAIN LOSING TO THE NEW JERSEY DEVILS IN THE 1995 STANLEY CUP FINALS, FOUR GAMES TO NONE.

only men ever to play 1,000 regular-season games with Detroit.

He had the ability of a deadly scorer. Early in his career, experts considered him the league's third-most-potent player, behind only Wayne Gretzky and Mario Lemieux. Yzerman scored more than 50 goals five times. He racked up more than 100 points six times. But he was unselfish. When Bowman arrived, he asked Yzerman to play a role in a defensive system, although it would cut down on his high production and his high profile. Yzerman did and, although dogged by trade rumors and tough times, never gave up on his first — and only — team.

"Steve Yzerman really wants to win, and he exemplifies that with his heart," owner Mike Ilitch said. "He played with as much heart as you can ask from a player. He played defensive hockey for the good of the team. He sacrificed stats and numbers to help the team win."

APRIL 19, 1994: ISIAH THOMAS PLAYED HIS FINAL GAME WITH THE PISTONS AND SUFFERED A TORN ACHILLES TENDON IN A 132-104 LOSS TO ORLANDO AT THE PALACE.

> "There were summers where I didn't even want to go outside.
> I didn't want to be recognized. I put on my hat, my sunglasses.
> I walked around in a shell."
>
> **STEVE YZERMAN**

JULIAN H. GONZALEZ/Detroit Free Press

THE RED WINGS AND THEIR CAPTAIN WERE BRANDED AFTER ANOTHER PLAYOFF LETDOWN, THIS ONE AGAINST THE AVALANCHE IN 1996.

JUNE 18, 1994: THE SILVERDOME BECAME THE FIRST DOME TO HOST A WORLD CUP SOCCER GAME, A 1-1 TIE BETWEEN THE U.S. AND SWITZERLAND. NATURAL GRASS WAS IMPORTED FOR THE FOUR GAMES PLAYED THERE.

EVEN THE SPIRIT OF DETROIT STATUE CAUGHT RED WINGS FEVER IN JUNE 1997. THE DOWNTOWN LANDMARK TOOK A SIZE 360 JERSEY.

"People are always asking me, 'Who do you think are the great hockey players of all time?' And I say they're the guys who can skate, shoot the puck, play defense, muck it up as rough as anybody, and not hang up at the blue line and cherry-pick. That's Steve Yzerman.

"He probably rivals Gordie Howe more than anybody I've ever seen."

Yzerman was a lot of great things. But he was not yet a winner. The law of sports is simple and unforgiving: no ring, no respect. The most beloved man in the city often didn't feel so high on life.

"There were summers where I didn't even want to go outside," Yzerman said. "I didn't want to be recognized. I put on my hat, my sunglasses. I walked around in a shell."

At times like that, he would try to get away. But it never worked. Once, Yzerman vacationed in Las Vegas, and while he

EVERY DAY WAS FLAG DAY FOR RED WINGS FANS. IN ONE 10-DAY STRETCH, MICHIGANDERS PURCHASED 100,000 FLAGS, AT ROUGHLY $20 A POP.

JUNE 24, 1994: THE PISTONS TOOK DUKE SENIOR GRANT HILL WITH THE THIRD PICK IN THE NBA DRAFT.

sat at a craps table, two guys from Windsor recognized him and made the typical fuss. *Hey, it's Yzerman from the Red Wings!* Then they looked at the gambling action, looked at The Captain, and one of them whispered: "We better get away from here. There's no luck at this table."

Yzerman said he "wanted to slug 'em." But he didn't. Instead, he kept that memory, and hundreds like it, locked away in his mind. It churned around like a sleepless wasp, year after year. Until the magic moment when the Cup set it free.

COMRADES

Having been in Detroit for so long, Yzerman once said that, although he always had worn the same winged-wheel uniform, he felt like he had played for several different teams. Teammates came and went. Coaches, too. In 1996-97, the Wings were still making adjustments — adding forward Brendan Shanahan and defenseman Larry Murphy, subtracting forward Keith Primeau and defenseman Paul Coffey, most notably. But a nifty nucleus had emerged.

There were two sweet Swedes: Tomas Holmstrom, a gutty forward who loved to camp out in the crease, and Nick Lidstrom, who became one of the NHL's top defensemen. There was Martin Lapointe, a forward as capable of mean streaks as scoring streaks. There was Doug Brown, a solid veteran, and Shanahan, quickly embraced by the fans, and goaltenders Chris Osgood and Mike Vernon, subjects of constant controversy. And then there were two groups of guys who caught the city's attention most of all: the Russian Five and the Grind Line.

The Russian Five put the red in the Wings — and made them thankful they were pioneers in the effort to bring Eastern Europe's best players into the world's best league. Since Russian players grew up playing a puck-possession system foreign to most North Americans, Bowman often put his five Russians together on the ice at once.

Defensemen Slava Fetisov and Vladimir Konstantinov anchored the blue line. Once considered the best player in the world, Fetisov was near 40 but still as wily as ever. Konstantinov was among the NHL's nastiest players, a big hitter, a surgeon with a stick as a scalpel, a thorn in the side of every forward who dared come his way.

Forwards Sergei Fedorov, Igor Larionov and Slava Kozlov combined to create a fluid, athletic line. Fedorov's eye-popping talent made him a Hart Trophy winner in '94, but his enigmatic play and personality made him a disappointment at other times. Larionov, the crafty veteran, was responsible for pulling him along — and for developing Kozlov, a young talent with a scoring touch.

In the playoffs, they fought hard against the perception that Russians didn't care about the Cup.

"Look at me," Fetisov said. "I'm 39. It's probably much better

> "We all grew up with our national team, when anything but first place was a tragedy. The NHL is the same situation. Everybody wants to win this Cup and put their names on this trophy also. Russians are no exceptions."
>
> **SLAVA FETISOV,**
> *Red Wings defenseman*

J. KYLE KEENER/Detroit Free Press

AT TIMES, THE WINGS CALLED ON THE NHL'S FIRST ALL-RUSSIAN UNIT. FROM LEFT: SLAVA FETISOV, SERGEI FEDOROV, VLADIMIR KONSTANTINOV, IGOR LARIONOV AND SLAVA KOZLOV.

OCT. 8, 1994: MICHIGAN RETIRED GERALD FORD'S NO. 48.
THE FORMER PRESIDENT WAS A WOLVERINES CENTER IN 1932-34.

MARY SCHROEDER/Detroit Free Press

GABRIEL B. TAIT/Detroit Free Press

KRIS DRAPER CARRIED THE SCARS OF
THE 1996 LOSS TO COLORADO. CLAUDE
LEMIEUX, THE AVALANCHE'S
PROFESSIONAL ANTAGONIST, HAD SENT
HIM FACE-FIRST INTO THE BOARDS IN
GAME 6 OF THE WESTERN FINALS. IN
1997, DRAPER CENTERED THE POPULAR
GRIND LINE, WHICH TRIED TO
ANTAGONIZE OPPONENTS WITH
AGGRESSIVE PLAY AND SPEED. FROM
THE LEFT: DARREN McCARTY, DRAPER,
KIRK MALTBY AND JOE KOCUR.

for me to get season over as soon as possible to get rest. But we're
playing for championship. We're winners.

"We all grew up with our national team, when anything but first
place was a tragedy. The NHL is the same situation. Everybody
wants to win this Cup and put their names on this trophy also.
Russians are no exceptions."

While the Russian Five was the cosmopolitan fan's choice, the
Grind Line seemed designed for the lunch-bucket, blue-collar
crowd. Its mission was simple: crash and bang and frustrate the
bad guys. Draper was the center; Darren McCarty, Kirk Maltby
and Joe Kocur rotated as the wingers. All were scrappy, Kocur
most of all. He was out of hockey, actually playing in beer leagues,
when the Wings signed him in December 1996 to fill an
understood role.

"We're not going to go out there and make the pretty plays the
Larionovs and the Yzermans are going to make," Kocur said. "We
have to go out there and create our own chances, and the best way
to do that is turnovers by their defense, by getting in and being
relentless on them."

By playing Detroit hockey.

JULIAN H. GONZALEZ/Detroit Free Press

HOW SWEDE IT WAS: TOMAS HOLMSTROM AND NICK LIDSTROM, BOTH
FROM SWEDEN, CONTRIBUTED MIGHTILY TO THE TEAM'S SUCCESS.

NOV. 13, 1994: BARRY SANDERS RUSHED 26 TIMES FOR A LIONS-RECORD 237 YARDS
IN A 14-9 VICTORY OVER TAMPA BAY AT THE SILVERDOME.

Photos by TOM PIDGEON/Associated Press

In March 1997, the Red Wings at long last avenged Claude Lemieux's cheap shot on Kris Draper in the '96 playoffs. For several minutes, Darren McCarty pommeled Lemieux, who instead of fighting back assumed the turtle position.

As McCarty fought Lemieux, Avalanche goalie Patrick Roy called out Wings goalie Mike Vernon. Despite a three-inch and 20-pound advantage, Roy left the mid-ice skirmish a bloody mess. Detroit won the game in overtime, 6-5, on a goal by McCarty.

THE CUP

Yzerman and friends had learned the hard way that success in the regular season meant little at playoff time. So nothing made them excited or depressed as the games and months wore on. They were on an incredibly even keel. Fedorov scored five goals in a game against Washington. So what? Their record was 20-13-6 after Game 39, while the season before, they hadn't suffered their 13th loss until Game 76. So what? Down the stretch, they went 2-3-3, blowing third-period leads left and right. So what? Lapointe promised the fans that they would "see a totally different team in the playoffs, for sure," and, for sure, he was correct.

Although the statistics and standings didn't indicate it, the Wings had prepared themselves for war and winning. One night in particular proved that. It was March 26, when Colorado came to town for what became known as Fight Night at the Joe. Still steamed about Lemieux's hit on Draper in the previous season's playoffs, the Wings were ready to fight. And fight they did. McCarty paired off with Lemieux late in the first period, pounding on him as Lemieux retreated into the turtle position, setting off a 3 ½-hour bevy of brawls. Even the goalies fought. Each punch the Wings threw seemed to have the force of the entire, roaring building behind it. Blood speckled the ice.

"I guess it was payback," McCarty said after the Wings' 6-5 victory. "An opportunity presented itself, and something happened. That was a great game. That's one to remember. We stuck together in all aspects of the game. That's old-time hockey. That's the fun stuff."

There would be more fun stuff and more paybacks to come. Afterward, Colorado's Mike Keane said: "I think that team has no heart. Everyone is gutless on that team, and I'd love to see them in the playoffs." He should have been careful what he wished for.

The Wings charged through the playoffs toward a rematch with the Avalanche. After losing the opening game of their first-round series against St. Louis, they got down to business and dispatched the Blues in six. Next, they swept the not-so-Mighty Ducks of Anaheim. After that, they got what they wanted: the Avs in the conference finals. Everyone knew that the team that survived

JULIAN H. GONZALEZ/Detroit Free Press

SERGEI FEDOROV SCORED THE GOAL THAT BURIED THE AVALANCHE ONCE AND FOR ALL IN THE 1997 WESTERN CONFERENCE FINALS.

APRIL 29, 1995: THE RED WINGS
RETIRED FORWARD SID ABEL'S NO. 12.

would not be denied the Cup.

Winning wasn't easy. After splitting the first two games in Denver, the Wings won Game 3, and then the teams squared off for Fight Night at the Joe II. With the Wings ahead, 6-0, in the third period of Game 4, the night descended into savagery. More than 230 penalty minutes were called. Even the coaches got into it, screaming at one another on the benches. But the Wings had the last laugh, 6-0. After losing Game 5, 6-0, they eliminated the Avs in Game 6, 3-1.

Gutless? Had somebody called them gutless? Oh, well. Their pain had been Av-venged. The healing Cup was close enough to touch. As bitter as the past was, the victory, Brown said, was "exactly the opposite of bitter." But no one got carried away. Shanahan proclaimed: "We're not finished yet." And they weren't.

"This team has so much character," said Vernon, who replaced Osgood, the regular-season starter, for the playoffs and performed with aplomb. "Now we're going for the big one."

The Wings had been through too much for their destiny to be anything but victory. The finals? After the Avalanche? No problem. The Wings dominated Philadelphia, winning in a wonderful, resounding sweep on home ice. The Flyers never got off the ground; their coach, Terry Murray, went so far as to suggest they choked. The Wings played Detroit hockey, tough hockey, proud hockey, old-time hockey. Fittingly, a star didn't score the clinching goal; McCarty did, doing his part for the Grind Line.

Hockeytown?

Detroit was Stanleytown.

For the first time in 42 years.

TIME TO CELEBRATE

Suddenly, the agony was over.

"They always say, 'He's a good player, but he didn't win it,' " Yzerman said. "And now they can't say that anymore. No matter what, they can't say it, you know? I don't know how to describe the way I feel.

"I'm glad the game is over, but I wish it never ended. Sometimes, you hold your dream way out there and wonder if you can ever be as good as your dream. It was almost like I wanted to sit back and watch it all and not miss a minute of it."

There was so much to savor. When the final horn of the finals blew, pounds of confetti fell to the ice — startling Bowman, already wearing his Stanley Cup champions hat.

JULIAN H. GONZALEZ/Detroit Free Press

RED WINGS GOALIE MIKE VERNON, CONN SMYTHE TROPHY WINNER AS MOST VALUABLE PLAYER OF THE PLAYOFFS, WAS UNBEATABLE IN THE '97 FINALS. DETROIT SHUT DOWN THE FLYERS, FOUR GAMES TO NONE, AND VERNON ALLOWED ONLY SIX GOALS.

JULIAN H. GONZALEZ/Detroit Free Press

MAY 28, 1995: DETROIT AND CHICAGO COMBINED FOR A RECORD 12 HOMERS AT TIGER STADIUM. THE TIGERS HAD SEVEN — TWO BY CHAD CURTIS, CECIL FIELDER AND KIRK GIBSON, AND ONE BY LOU WHITAKER. THE WHITE SOX WON, 14-12.

"For all the time I spent parading it around and holding it above my head in front of hundreds of people, my favorite memory was of a Saturday afternoon in Toronto, when I took it to my father's grave. The place was totally empty. I just sat there with it."

BRENDAN SHANAHAN

MARY SCHROEDER/Detroit Free Press

SHANNYTOWN: BRENDAN SHANAHAN CRADLED THE CUP IN FRONT OF THE HOCKEYTOWN FAITHFUL AFTER THE SWEEP OF PHILADELPHIA.

AUG. 26, 1995: LLOYD CARR COACHED HIS FIRST GAME FOR MICHIGAN, AN 18-17 VICTORY OVER VIRGINIA. U-M TRAILED, 17-0, IN THE FOURTH. THE GAME'S FINAL PLAY: SCOTT DREISBACH'S 15-YARD TD PASS TO MERCURY HAYES.

Helmets, gloves, sticks and pads flew skyward, then fell scattered. The Wings mobbed Vernon, then slowly lined up to shake hands with the Flyers. "Oh, What a Night!" blared from the loudspeakers. Cheers rained down from the 19,983 standing fans.

A red carpet rolled onto the ice. Yzerman hopped it, skated over to the Wings' bench and embraced Ilitch. Bowman, who had disappeared for a moment, emerged from the tunnel wearing his practice gear and skates. Vernon was presented the Conn Smythe Trophy, and then, at 11 p.m., Yzerman was presented the Cup. He hoisted it high above his head — but wasn't sure what to do next. Celebrating his seventh Cup as a coach, Bowman gave Yzerman some advice, sending him on a counterclockwise trip around the rink, teammates following right behind.

All that was missing was a tooth from Yzerman's smile. After taking a victory lap, Yzerman skated back to the bench and handed the Cup to Ilitch. Then, he took it back and passed it to Fetisov and Larionov, who carried it around the ice together, waving to fans. "I never forget this moment the rest of my life," Fetisov said.

Bowman was next. Most coaches, dignified, dressed in suit and tie, hold the Cup briefly, smile, then pass it on. Not Bowman. Not this time. No one is too old to fulfill the dreams of his youth.

"I always wanted to be a player in the NHL and skate with the Cup," he said. "How many chances do you get to do that? I said, 'If we win, I'll go for it.' I have always dreamt about it."

Vernon was a little worried about the weight of the Cup and Bowman's age, 63. "I just hoped that when they gave it to him, he didn't fall with it and dent the Cup, so I couldn't drink out of it."

Bowman held it just fine, thank you, as did everyone else connected to the Wings: assistant coaches, trainers, even the

JULIAN H. GONZALEZ/Detroit Free Press

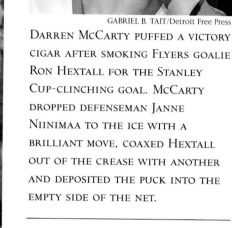

GABRIEL B. TAIT/Detroit Free Press

DARREN MCCARTY PUFFED A VICTORY CIGAR AFTER SMOKING FLYERS GOALIE RON HEXTALL FOR THE STANLEY CUP-CLINCHING GOAL. MCCARTY DROPPED DEFENSEMAN JANNE NIINIMAA TO THE ICE WITH A BRILLIANT MOVE, COAXED HEXTALL OUT OF THE CREASE WITH ANOTHER AND DEPOSITED THE PUCK INTO THE EMPTY SIDE OF THE NET.

Zamboni driver, Al Sobotka. Eventually, the party disappeared into the dressing room, densely packed with reporters and wellwishers. Champagne soaked everything, mixing with tears, turning heads of hair into happy, sticky nests. The pungent aroma of cigar smoke and sweat was so intense, nostrils burned and eyes watered.

"We'll always have tonight," Kocur said. "This is the moment that the city, this team and everyone in this organization has always wanted to be a part of, and no one can ever take it away.

"We're all from different places in the world, and we're all going to different places in the world. But from what we just did here tonight, we're all going to be together in our hearts forever. This is something nobody in this room, as long as they live, will ever forget."

Kocur cracked open a Bud Light that someone had left in his locker before Game 1 in Philadelphia, and he drank it warm with his linemates. Fedorov kept looking for more libations. "I'm telling you, I've been drinking champagne all night long," he said. "It's great. Do we have any more champagne around here? No more champagne?"

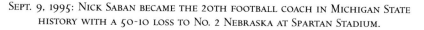

MARY SCHROEDER/Detroit Free Press

WHAT A RIDE: STEVE YZERMAN MADE SURE THE STANLEY CUP WAS SAFELY TUCKED AWAY IN HIS PORSCHE FOLLOWING GAME 4 IN 1997. THEN HE AND STANLEY CAUGHT A WAVE DURING THE OFF-SEASON. EACH PLAYER WAS ALLOWED TO KEEP THE CUP FOR 48 HOURS.

Special to the Detroit Free Press

Oh, yes, there was more champagne. What was gone was the pain. Somewhere in the celebration sat Draper, one year after suffering his horrific injuries. Clenched between his teeth was a fat cigar. His jaw was fine. He smiled and said, "I don't even remember last June anymore."

Numb, everyone let everything soak in. "What a story," Murphy said, nursing a beer while still in full uniform and equipment at 2 a.m. "This team got better as we went along. By the end, no one could touch us. No one. Convincing champions."

At about 3:15 a.m., Yzerman hoisted the Cup again. He walked into the players' parking lot, placed his Holy Grail in the backseat of his Porsche, and drove off as a handful of fans screamed outside.

The city itself seemed to sigh at the sight, satisfied.

TRIUMPH, THEN TRAGEDY

In the days that followed, the Wings basked in glory, unaware of how soon they wouldn't care nearly as much about the Cup. McCarty was at Tiger Stadium, throwing out the first pitch. Vernon was on "Late Night with Conan O'Brien," toting along his Conn Smythe. Shanahan showed off the big prize, the Cup, on

OCT. 1, 1995: SPARKY ANDERSON, THE ONLY MANAGER TO WIN WORLD SERIES IN BOTH LEAGUES, WORKED HIS LAST GAME FOR THE TIGERS, A 4-0 LOSS AT BALTIMORE. IT ALSO WAS LOU WHITAKER'S FAREWELL.

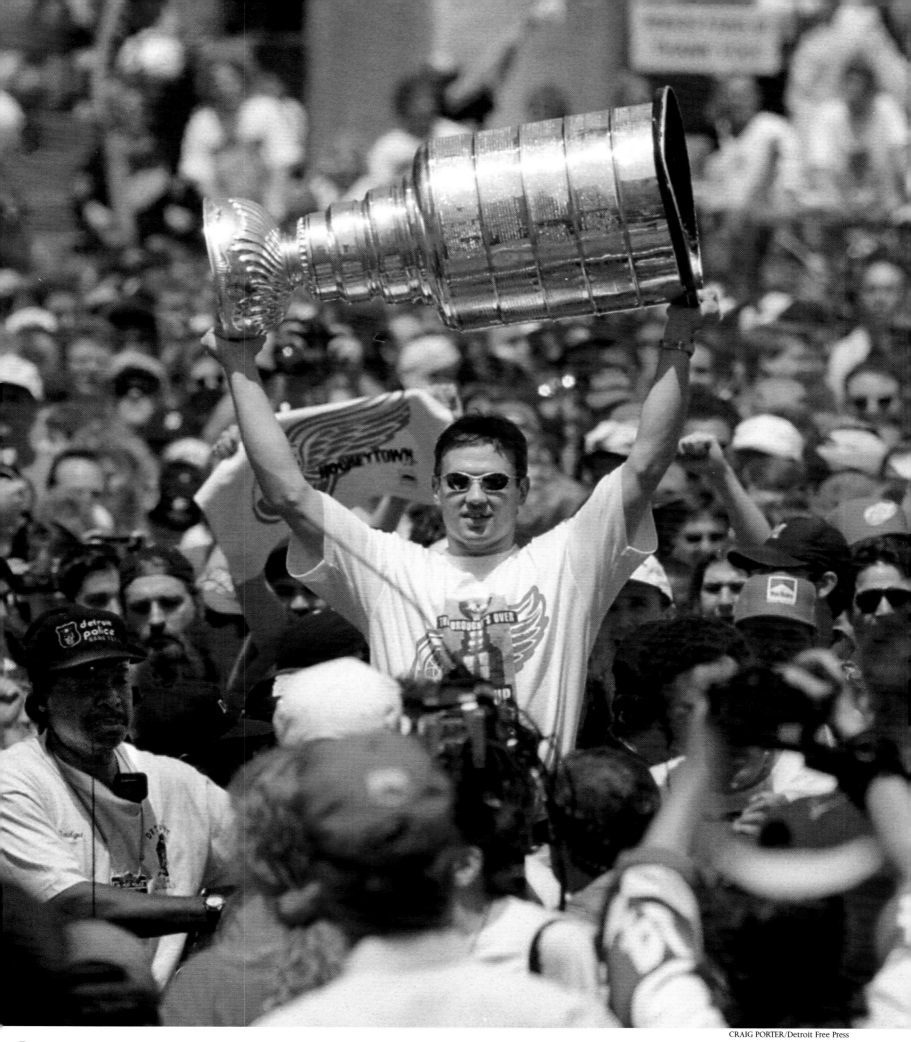

FANS STARTED ARRIVING AT 6 A.M., AND BY THE TIME STEVE YZERMAN PASSED BY, ONE MILLION HAD GATHERED FOR THE DOWNTOWN VICTORY PARADE.

"The Tonight Show with Jay Leno."

Two days after the victory, the team attended a rally for season-ticket holders at Joe Louis Arena. The 2½-hour show was televised to the rest of Detroit, which saw an emotional evening of speeches. Bowman, whose contract was about to expire, said he would be back to do it again. Yzerman, the last to appear on stage, said: "This is the closest group of players, the most unselfish group of players, the hardest-working, most-dedicated team I've ever been a part of."

Three days after the victory, the team's parade drew a million fans to what was normally a near-deserted downtown. They massed into a sea of red and white, holding signs that offered everything from congratulations to marriage proposals. They jammed into every square inch along the mile-long route from the Fox Theatre to Hart Plaza, pushing out along side streets, far from the passage of players. They climbed trees, light poles, ladders, statues — anything to get a better view.

"This is a fabulous day," associate coach Dave Lewis said. "This is a day that grandparents brought their kids who brought their children. That's what this day was all about. I don't think there was another square foot where somebody else could have been. This day was a celebration."

And then, six days after the victory, the celebration ceased.

Konstantinov and team masseur Sergei Mnatsakanov were critically injured when the limousine in which they were riding crashed about 9 p.m. in Birmingham — on Woodward Avenue, the same street on which the Wings had held their parade downtown. Fetisov also was in the vehicle, but he was lucky. He suffered only a chest injury, a bruised lung and a lifetime of haunting memories.

Ilitch heard the news on television and rushed to the hospital, arriving around 10:45, dressed in a team windbreaker. Trainer John Wharton

CRAIG PORTER/Detroit Free Press

AS DOCTORS WORKED TO EVALUATE THE WRECK-INJURED RED WINGS, MANY MEMBERS OF THE TEAM, INCLUDING ASSOCIATE COACH BARRY SMITH AND HEAD COACH SCOTTY BOWMAN, WAITED FOR ANY KIND OF NEWS.

RICHARD LEE/Detroit Free Press

NOT LONG AFTER THE LIMO CRASHED IN THE MEDIAN OF WOODWARD AVENUE IN BIRMINGHAM, FANS TURNED THE SITE INTO A SHRINE. EVENTUALLY, POLICE CLEARED THE AREA OUT OF FEAR IT WOULD DISTRACT MOTORISTS.

GABRIEL B. TAIT/Detroit Free Press

AFTER A FAN GAVE SLAVA KOZLOV THIS ROCK IN THE PLAYOFFS, HE SCORED SIX GOALS IN SEVEN GAMES. HE KEPT IT SAFE AT HIS HOME IN THE SUMMER. "I GIVE IT NOW TO VLADDIE," KOZLOV SAID, "AND HOPEFULLY IT CAN BRING HIM LUCK, TOO."

arrived about 11:30, followed by Yzerman, Shanahan, Fedorov, Brown, Lapointe — about the whole team. Most of the players had been at a golf outing. Konstantinov, Mnatsakanov and Fetisov had left early. But they never made it to Osgood's house. Everyone was supposed to meet there that night for a final victory party. Instead, they met in an intensive care ward. "It was the worst feeling ever," defenseman Mathieu Dandenault said.

Later, news came that the accident could have been avoided. Fetisov said the driver, Richard Gnida, appeared to fall asleep at the wheel and that the players began screaming to wake him. But Gnida never responded. The car crossed two lanes of traffic, jumped the curb and hit a tree. That just made the situation harder to swallow, although Gnida received jail time and community service because of his involvement.

Konstantinov and Mnatsakanov suffered severe brain injuries. At first, they responded to some stimuli — Russian music, kind words from teammates — when they weren't stuck inside their shells. Later, they made some mild improvement. But both remained in wheelchairs and struggled to enunciate every syllable of speech. When Fetisov, Larionov and Kozlov brought the Cup to Russia for the first time in history, Konstantinov and Mnatsakanov weren't able to go with them.

No one could enjoy the Cup now. Not the way they wanted to, anyway. Yzerman took it home to Ottawa. Shanahan took it to his father's grave in Toronto. Kocur allowed his beer-league buddies to take a team picture with it. Others did other things. But all thought of Konstantinov and Mnatsakanov constantly.

"You think you're going to have a good time," defenseman Bob Rouse said. "But then you think that a couple of your brothers aren't doing too well. It's difficult to do anything."

Especially repeat.

OCT. 24, 1995: THE ACQUISITION OF IGOR LARIONOV FROM SAN JOSE GAVE THE WINGS THE RUSSIAN FIVE, WITH SERGEI FEDOROV, SLAVA FETISOV, VLADIMIR KONSTANTINOV AND SLAVA KOZLOV.

BELIEVE

The Wings had won a Cup for their city. Now they went out to win one for their hearts. More healing needed to be done. They dedicated the 1997-98 season to Konstantinov and Mnatsakanov, and to let everyone in the league know it, they sewed special patches on their uniforms that featured the word "BELIEVE" in English and Russian. Before every game, the players looked at Konstantinov's dressing-room stall, still just the way he had left it, and reminded themselves of a few things. There was more to life than hockey. They were blessed men to be healthy, strong, talented, rich, playing a game as their profession. There was only one thing to do: Win for their fallen comrades.

The lineup looked a little different. The Wings, as they had done in the past, traded their Cup-winning goalie; Vernon was now with San Jose. They signed veteran forward Brent Gilchrist from Dallas, which was emerging as a rival equal to that of Colorado. They added defensemen Jamie Macoun and Dmitri Mironov. Fedorov sat out the season's first 59 games because of an ugly contract dispute, which cost him the love of many fans and yet earned him a fortune. But mostly, they were the same Wings, united in their task.

When they raised the Cup banner before the home opener, Irina Konstantinov and Ylena Mnatsakanov represented their husbands, who were still in the hospital, watching the ceremony sadly on television. Tears rolled down Kozlov's cheeks. Fire burned in the bellies of the able-bodied Russians. The Russian Five, reduced to a trio, did what Konstantinov could not do. They led the Wings to a 3-1 victory over Dallas. Fetisov scored a goal on a sweet feed from Larionov. "We say that goal was for Vladdie," Larionov said. "He is very much missed. Tonight was very strange skating without him."

No matter what happened on the ice, the Wings worried more about when

IGOR LARIONOV, SLAVA FETISOV AND SLAVA KOZLOV TOOK THE STANLEY CUP TO RUSSIA FOR ITS FIRST VISIT, WHICH INCLUDED A STOP IN MOSCOW'S RED SQUARE.

they would see Konstantinov and Mnatsakanov next. Twice, they clashed with Colorado in bloody brawls like old times; the fallout from the Draper incident still hung over the Joe. In November, Lemieux went after McCarty right off the opening face-off. In April, the two fought again during another wild night that drew the goalies into the fray. But the Wings cared less and less about the Avalanche, which they didn't even have to face in the playoffs.

What really mattered was the All-Star break, when several team members traveled to Florida, where Konstantinov was convalescing. What really mattered was Jan. 30, when Konstantinov joined them — and the Cup — at the White House, where President Bill Clinton honored them. What really mattered was taking pictures of everything, so Konstantinov, whose short-term memory was shaky at best, could remember the good times somehow, someday. What really mattered was the rousing playoff run that allowed Konstantinov and Mnatsakanov to join them in celebration again.

Bowman reminded his players of their priorities often. "Scotty told us to give our maximum effort for them," Lapointe said. "Scotty said that he would give up all of his Stanley Cup championship rings if the two of them could be standing with us in this locker room today. It was pretty inspiring."

As they had the previous spring, the Wings stumbled down the stretch of the regular season. Once again, it didn't matter much. They beat Phoenix in six. They beat St. Louis in six. They beat Dallas in six, too. All three series were tough tests; all three tough tests were passed. Then, the finals. Once again, the Wings swept right through them. Washington, like Philadelphia, never had a chance. So close to the Cup, the Wings played with relentless passion until, at last, they grabbed it again.

Hockeytown?

Detroit was Stanleytown.

For the second straight season.

Konstantinov was wheeled onto the ice for the celebration in Washington, and the Wings rushed to meet him. He pulled a cigar into his mouth and raised his index finger. He was indeed No. 1 in the hearts of his teammates. Yzerman raised the Cup first, then put it on Konstantinov's lap. Everyone gathered around for a group photo, Vladdie sporting his 1998 Stanley Cup champions hat. "This is Vladdie's Cup," Larionov said.

Back in the dressing room, Draper poured champagne into the Cup and turned to Konstantinov. "You want a sip?" he asked. Konstantinov beamed. Although he didn't speak, he seemed to understand fully what had happened, what was going on. All of his

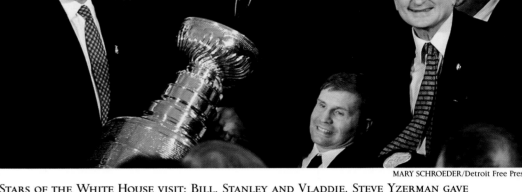

MARY SCHROEDER/Detroit Free Press

STARS OF THE WHITE HOUSE VISIT: BILL, STANLEY AND VLADDIE. STEVE YZERMAN GAVE PRESIDENT CLINTON A RED WINGS JERSEY WITH A "P" INSTEAD OF A "C." "WE'VE EVEN GOT A COUPLE OF AMERICANS ON THE TEAM," THE CAPTAIN SAID.

KIRTHMON F. DOZIER/Detroit Free Press

"WHENEVER WE STRETCH ON THE ICE," FORWARD DOUG BROWN SAID, "I'LL LOOK UP AND SEE OUR BANNER. IT'LL BE SOMETHING SPECIAL."

NOV. 23, 1995: SCOTT MITCHELL COMPLETED 30 OF 45 PASSES FOR A LIONS-RECORD 410 YARDS IN A 44-38 VICTORY OVER MINNESOTA ON THANKSGIVING.

WILLIAM ARCHIE/*Detroit Free Press*

CHRIS OSGOOD ALLOWED SEVERAL GOALS
FROM LONG RANGE IN THE 1998
PLAYOFFS, BUT HE FINISHED WITH A 16-6
RECORD AND A TINY 2.12 GOALS-AGAINST
AVERAGE.

A YEAR AFTER LOSING TO MIKE VERNON,
PATRICK ROY CALLED OUT OSGOOD AND
SUFFERED ANOTHER CENTER-ICE DEFEAT.
OSGOOD'S MOTHER, JOY, HAD FLOWN IN
FROM WESTERN CANADA DREADING A
FIGHT, BUT EVENTUALLY WILDLY YELLED:
"GET HIM, CHRIS! GET HIM! GET HIM!"

JULIAN H. GONZALEZ/*Detroit Free Press*

NOV. 25, 1995: TSHIMANGA BIAKABUTUKA BECAME THE SECOND WOLVERINE TO RUSH FOR MORE THAN 300 YARDS —
WITH 313 IN 37 CARRIES — IN A 31-23 VICTORY OVER NO. 2 OHIO STATE.

NICO TOUTENHOOFD/Detroit Free Press

SCOTTY BOWMAN, UNPREDICTABLE TO THE END, LACED 'EM UP TO SKATE
WITH THE STANLEY CUP IN 1997. WHY? "I ALWAYS WANTED TO BE A
PLAYER IN THE NHL AND SKATE WITH THE CUP." TEAMMATES WERE
WORRIED ABOUT HIS AGE AND THE TROPHY'S WEIGHT. "I JUST HOPED
THAT WHEN THEY GAVE IT TO HIM," MIKE VERNON SAID, "HE DIDN'T
FALL WITH IT AND DENT THE CUP SO I COULDN'T DRINK OUT OF IT."

friends, especially the Russians, stayed by his side all night, sometimes smiling, sometimes seeming as though they were ready to weep. "This is very emotional for us," Larionov said. The summer before, they had six days to celebrate. This they wanted to last a lifetime.

SCOTTY AND TOE

Even in triumph, Bowman wouldn't have been himself unless he were somewhat stoic. The clock wound down and the red gloves went up into the electric air, and Bowman stood behind his bench and watched his Wings rush the ice in front of him. There were hugs for his prized assistants, Dave Lewis and Barry Smith. There was a smile at the sight of Konstantinov. There was even a slight pump of the fist for The Captain, the Conn Smythe winner, who had sacrificed so much at his demand. But Bowman mostly just stood there, seemingly bored with anything but the battle of the game itself.

He handled his eighth Cup as a coach the way his idol and mentor, Toe Blake, probably handled his: with joy for a mission accomplished and sadness for a season ended.

"Going in, I didn't know if we could really win another Cup," Bowman said. "But I knew that the desire and the motivation were there, and fortunately, we did."

The victory made Bowman an equal to Blake in the NHL history books, each coach credited with a record eight Cups. But Bowman had been saying for weeks that the statistic was easily overplayed, and he said the same again after an emotional evening. Blake won his eight Cups in 13 seasons. Bowman took 26 seasons. Yet, in the modern era of free agency and constant expansion, the road to the Cup became ever more treacherous, and in that sense, Bowman often was referred to as the NHL's greatest coach, a worthy successor to Blake.

"He was a real good influence on me, and to be thought of in the same breath is a big honor for me, obviously," said Bowman, who learned from the great Montreal coach while working with the Canadiens' junior team in the late '50s and early-to-middle '60s. "I don't put numbers on Cups, but I just know that he did it with a lot of grace, and I hope I can do the same thing."

If grace is staying true to oneself, no matter the circumstances, then Bowman had plenty of it. Down to the final moments the night of the victory, he stayed in character. At 1:30 a.m., he stood in the hall just outside the Wings' dressing room at the MCI Center, wearing a new, creased championship shirt nearly down to his knees, clutching a videotape in one hand and a cellular phone in the other. He talked to reporters and friends, hugged players' wives — and made sure there was enough pasta on the team bus to the airport.

Finally, at 1:40, Bowman draped his bright blue blazer over his arm and headed down the hall toward the exits. "Well," he said, baggy-eyed, "we're goin' home." Lapointe, sporting sunglasses to shield his bloodshot eyes from the bright glare of camera lights, didn't leave the dressing room with the Cup for 10 more minutes. But Bowman was long gone by then. He had shuffled off ahead without hesitation or thought, feeling no need to wait up for the Cup.

He had seen it before.   ◆

DEC. 4, 1995: HERMAN MOORE CAUGHT A LIONS-RECORD 14 PASSES FOR 183 YARDS
IN A 27-7 VICTORY OVER CHICAGO.

ON A SPRING NIGHT IN WASHINGTON, D.C., VLADIMIR KONSTANTINOV AND THE STANLEY CUP NEVER SEEMED TO BEAM BRIGHTER.

Whack heard 'round the world

Tonya & Nancy

Multnomah County Sheriff

ABC-TV (via Reuters)

NANCY KERRIGAN GRIMACED IN PAIN IN THIS FAMOUS VIDEO FOOTAGE MOMENTS AFTER
HER ATTACK, WHICH A FEW MONTHS LATER EARNED TONYA HARDING A MUG SHOT.

BY MICHELLE KAUFMAN

It would become one of the most stunning, dramatic sports stories of the century, a story that kept America — and much of the world — riveted for weeks. And it all began in a Cobo Arena hallway on a blustery early January afternoon in 1994.

Figure skater Nancy Kerrigan, in a white lace dress and pearl earrings, stepped off the Cobo ice in downtown Detroit after a practice session for the U.S. national championships, and walked through a blue curtain into a hallway that led to the locker room. In less time than it took Kerrigan to do a triple salchow, a large man in a black leather coat and black hat ran toward her from behind and whacked her right knee with a metal baton.

Kerrigan was considered the gold medal favorite for the 1994 Winter Olympics in Lillehammer, Norway, which were a month away. Suddenly, her lifelong dream was in jeopardy.

"Why me? Why now?" she shrieked as she collapsed to the floor.

The assailant bolted down the hall and used his forehead to smash through a Plexiglas door and flee into a snowstorm. An escape car waited for him on Atwater Street, behind Joe Louis Arena.

Figure skating would never be the same.

Less than a week after the attack, an anonymous caller told Detroit police that some Portland, Ore., men connected to Kerrigan's rival, Tonya Harding, had plotted the assault.

DEC. 10, 1995: SCOTT MITCHELL, WITH TWO TOUCHDOWN PASSES IN A 24-17 VICTORY AT HOUSTON,
BROKE BOBBY LAYNE'S 44-YEAR-OLD LIONS RECORD OF 26 IN A SEASON. MITCHELL FINISHED WITH 32.

On Jan. 19, Harding's on-again, off-again husband, Jeff Gillooly, was charged with planning and bankrolling the attack, and three of his friends confessed to being involved. Harding, who won the U.S. title and an Olympic berth in Kerrigan's absence, also was implicated. It was no secret that Harding had been jealous of Kerrigan for years.

An Olympic skating champion stood to make more than $1 million in appearance fees and endorsements, and Gillooly and his buddies were determined to see that money in Harding's hands — and their own — even if it meant injuring Kerrigan. They sat around a living room table in Portland two days after Christmas, and hatched the plan. Gillooly offered $6,500 to each of the three hit men — Derrick Smith, Shane Stant and Harding's bodyguard, Shawn Eckardt. At one point, they discussed staging a car crash to maim Kerrigan, but eventually opted for the knee-whacking.

The U.S. Figure Skating Association, rocked by the news that one of its top skaters might be involved in such a crime, tried to ban Harding from participating in the Olympics, but was unable to do so because she had not been charged with any crimes.

By this point, the story had made front-page headlines across the United States. Television newscasts led with the story. Harding's front lawn in Portland was swarming with reporters, as was the Kerrigan yard in Stoneham, Mass.

More than 35 offers for movie deals poured in.

In England, topless photos of Harding showed up in tabloids.

Harding showed up at the Olympics under a cloud of suspicion and out of shape. Kerrigan, meanwhile, had overcome the injury with a grueling rehabilitation program, received an automatic spot on the Olympic team, and became the undisputed sentimental favorite.

Each skater's every move was chronicled by the world media. Hundreds of reporters showed up at their practice sessions, some as early as four hours in advance to get a good camera spot.

The climax of the saga — the Nancy-and-Tonya Olympic showdown — drew a 48.5 television rating on CBS, the third-highest ever recorded for a sports program of any kind. Viewers got the dramatic show they had hoped for.

Harding finished 10th in the short program,

WILLIAM ARCHIE/Detroit Free Press

NANCY KERRIGAN WAS PICTURE PERFECT AS SHE FINISHED WHAT WOULD BE HER FINAL PRACTICE AT COBO ARENA.

ALAN R. KAMUDA/Detroit Free Press

WITH KERRIGAN OUT OF THE WAY, TONYA HARDING EASILY SKATED TO THE U.S. CHAMPIONSHIP AT JOE LOUIS ARENA.

virtually knocking her out of medal contention. On the evening of the women's final, a hushed crowd was stunned when Harding didn't emerge from the tunnel as her name was called by the arena announcer. The announcer called her name again, and she finally emerged, looking flustered. A skate lace had broken, but she began her program anyway. After missing her first jump, she burst into tears, skated toward the judges' table, and pleaded for time to repair her broken lace. They obliged. Harding went backstage and re-laced her boot. She would fall doing her triple axel and finish in eighth place.

A few minutes later, Kerrigan took the ice in a shimmering gold, $13,000 designer dress and skated the performance of her life.

The crowd went berserk. Hundreds of bouquets of flowers and stuffed animals covered the ice as Kerrigan smiled and waved to the adoring audience. Despite the sore knee and all the distractions, Kerrigan won the silver medal behind Ukrainian teenager Oksana Baiul.

As Kerrigan awaited her marks, carrying all the flowers she could handle, Harding was spotted in a skybox, sobbing into her coach's shoulder.

Shortly after the Olympics, Harding pleaded guilty to hindering the prosecution. She was fined $100,000 and sentenced to 500 hours of community service. She was banned for life by the U.S. Figure Skating Association.

The sport of figure skating benefited greatly from the bizarre tale of Nancy and Tonya. Skating stories moved from the back of newspaper sports sections to the front.

More than 40 skating Web sites sprung up on the Internet. Hoping to cash in on the craze, the entertainment industry produced dozens of made-for-TV skating specials, including a movie chronicling the entire soap opera.

With the increased interest in the sport came big money for every big-name figure skater but Harding. Kerrigan, Katarina Witt, Kristi Yamaguchi and Brian Boitano were able to command as much as $20,000 for a night's work. Teenager Michelle Kwan earned in excess of $750,000 before her 17th birthday.

Harding, meanwhile, dabbled in singing, acting and — perhaps the sport best suited for her considering her episode with Kerrigan — pro wrestling.

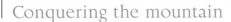

Conquering the mountain

Hail, yes!

By Nicholas J. Cotsonika

Lloyd Carr was not a happy man in the summer of 1997. He flashed his famous Jimmy Stewart scowl too often, because too much was on his mind. His beloved Michigan football program, which had won more games than any other in the history of Division I-A, always had owned a proud place upon the sport's pedestal. But now it appeared to be teetering there, uneasy, poised to fall into the abyss of commonness.

For four straight seasons, the Wolverines had been mired in miserable mediocrity despite their considerable talent, losing four games each year and failing to win even a share of the Big Ten championship. In 1995, their ivory-tower image had been tarnished when Carr's predecessor and best friend, head coach Gary Moeller, was fired because of a very ugly, very public drunken incident at a restaurant.

What had gone wrong? What could Carr do? When he hunkered down, the press called him paranoid. When he lashed out, people called him prickly. He couldn't win, on the field or off. He wasn't Bo Schembechler, no matter how much everyone wanted him to be.

So he retreated to his favorite pastime: reading. He read speeches by battle-hardened generals. He read diatribes by famous philosophers. And then he read "Into Thin Air," a mountain-climbing story by Jon Krakauer, a story that detailed the death and danger that surrounded a group of adventurers who had dared attempt to climb Mt. Everest.

Something hit home. Everest. The tallest mountain in the world. The ultimate challenge. Second only, perhaps, to his

JULIAN H. GONZALEZ/Detroit Free Press

AFTER CONSECUTIVE FOUR-LOSS SEASONS, LLOYD CARR WASN'T EXACTLY SMELLING LIKE A YOU-KNOW-WHAT. THAT ALL CHANGED IN 1997 WITH A NATIONAL CHAMPIONSHIP (AND A VICTORY PARADE).

schedule that season, a brutal slate that most experts considered the nation's strongest. Everest. Carr thought about what he had read, and soon, his countenance brightened. He looked at the schedule and saw a mountain instead, full of cracks and crevices named Colorado and Notre Dame and Penn State and Ohio State.

He smiled. Something told him that his Wolverines, ranked 14th by the Associated Press in its preseason poll, were capable of winning every one of their games. Something told him that with the proper intensity and passion, all the obstacles could be scaled, one at a time, on the path to the summit: the Rose Bowl. "I didn't see any reason why we should lose," he said.

In a few months, he would find out that he was right. Michigan would be back on top of the college football world, national champions for the first time in nearly half a century.

MICHIGAN MEN

Carr loved to speak of his team's character, but when he did so, he really spoke of its characters. The Wolverines were stocked with them.

There was Chris Floyd, the bruising fullback with a face so fierce, he scared students walking to class on campus. There was Jon Jansen, the co-captain who would start 50 straight games at offensive tackle in his career. There was Jerame Tuman, the tight end with pillows for hands. There was Jason Vinson, the punter who didn't start on his high school   ➤

Jan. 17, 1996: Steve Yzerman beat Patrick Roy for his 500th goal, all with the Red Wings, in a 3-2 home victory over Colorado.

TAI STREETS FLOPPED ATOP 1,100 POUNDS OF WOLVERINES, AFTER A JERAME TUMAN TOUCHDOWN PRODUCED A 21-13 LEAD IN THE ROSE BOWL.

SEPT. 29, 1996: ALAN TRAMMELL SINGLED UP THE MIDDLE ON THE FINAL AT-BAT OF HIS CAREER IN A 7-5 LOSS TO MILWAUKEE AT TIGER STADIUM. TRAMMELL, WHO ALSO STARTED HIS CAREER WITH A SINGLE, FINISHED WITH 2,365 HITS.

team, conned his way into a tryout in college, then won a starting job.

There was Marcus Ray, the safety with the motor mouth who served as the emotional leader of a defense that was the nation's best; he had grown up in Columbus, Ohio, in Buckeyes country, and loved to be the nemesis of his hometown. There was Sam

JULIAN H. GONZALEZ/Detroit Free Press

BRIAN GRIESE THREW THREE INTERCEPTIONS IN THE FIRST HALF AGAINST IOWA, BUT RALLIED HIS TROOPS WITH TWO TD PASSES AND A TD RUN IN THE SECOND HALF.

JULIAN H. GONZALEZ/Detroit Free Press

MICHIGAN'S DEFENSE LOVED TO SWARM OVER ITS OPPONENTS, AND MICHIGAN STATE'S SEDRICK IRVIN WAS NO EXCEPTION IN A 23-7 VICTORY IN EAST LANSING.

Sword, the linebacker who thanked his father for forcing him to stick with football after he considered quitting. There was Chris Howard, the tough tailback who ran half the season with broken ribs.

And then there were Brian Griese and Charles Woodson, those most responsible for transforming Michigan from mediocre to magnificent, the team's Sherpas, who would guide the Wolverines up their mountain.

Griese said his career was "like a saga," and he was correct. The son of Pro Football Hall of Fame quarterback Bob Griese, he spurned offers from Georgia Tech and Virginia to walk on at Michigan. In less than a month, he earned a scholarship. By his third year, he was a sophomore starter, heading for a junior season with a promise that matched his father's.

Then, he made a mistake. An incident at a bar. A broken window. "It was an irresponsible thing, and I was responsible," he said. "I was off the team." Carr suspended him from spring drills, forcing him to work out away from his teammates. By fall, he was reinstated. But he had lost his job. Instead of playing quarterback, he pooch-punted.

Until the Ohio State game. In relief of starting quarterback Scott Dreisbach, Griese led the team back from a nine-point deficit to a stunning, 13-9 victory. Life was good again. He started in the Outback Bowl, and although he received his degree, he decided to return for a fifth season rather than attend graduate school.

It turned out to be a wise choice.

Woodson's career was a bit of a saga, too. He grew up in Fremont, Ohio, utterly devoted to his mother, Georgia, who worked 12-hour shifts operating a 3,000-pound clamp truck at American National Can Co. to support the family. Although he had to overcome clubfeet as a child, he gravitated to sports. All sports. Anytime.

Football was his favorite. By the time he got to Michigan, the game had given him so much confidence, he carried himself with a colorful, charismatic bravado that became as much his hallmark as his tremendous talent as a two-way terror. Woodson loved to talk trash. He was frank, honest, brash. Asked early that season whom he thought should win the Heisman Trophy, he

➤

PRECEDING PAGE: FULLBACK CHRIS FLOYD DIDN'T HAVE TIME TO BE BADGERED AS THE WOLVERINES WON THEIR FIRST GAME AS NO. 1.

Photograph by DAVID P. GILKEY/Detroit Free Press

answered, "Me." Everyone laughed at him.

They shouldn't have.

CHAMPIONS OF THE WEST

Everest. As the Wolverines approached the foothills of their mountain, stiff non-conference games against Colorado and Notre Dame sandwiched around a game against Baylor, Carr invited one of the subjects of the book he had read to speak to his team. He also gave each player a climber's ice ax. They were suspended from the ceiling in the team meeting room, to help with the mental climb to come. This would not be easy. No one gave them a chance.

Underdogs against Colorado, making its first appearance at Michigan Stadium since the infamous Hail Mary game of 1994, the Wolverines seemed to need all the karma they could get. But then, karma was what they had most. The Buffaloes fell with a thud in a 27-3 loss at the hands of Michigan's defense, which harassed their quarterbacks rudely. "We just killed their will," Woodson said, "then we kicked them when they were down."

Notre Dame was more difficult. The Wolverines had to withstand a late push by the Fighting Irish before winning, 21-14. But they did it and ascended to the Big Ten schedule with a 3-0 record. They cruised past Indiana (37-0) and Northwestern (23-6), then struggled against Iowa.

Griese threw three interceptions in the first half against the Hawkeyes, and the Wolverines trailed at halftime, 21-7. Carr stood in the locker room and asked his team, "Is there anyone in here who doesn't think we can win?" Silence. "Didn't nobody say a word," Ray said. Win? No problem. They had Griese, who led them back to a 28-24 victory that left them feeling invincible.

The next week, the Wolverines smothered Michigan State with six interceptions. Woodson claimed two of them, one of which was his all-time masterpiece. He leaped and, with one hand, seemed to grab an uncatchable ball straight out of heaven itself. Afterward, he reveled in it, as usual. Asked

ADAM NADEL/Associated Press

CHARLES WOODSON COULDN'T BELIEVE THE FIRST PRIMARILY DEFENSIVE PLAYER HAD WON THE HEISMAN — AND THAT HE WAS THAT PLAYER.

about the Spartans' decision to keep throwing, he said: "I think it was the wrong move."

After beating Minnesota, 24-3, seven days later, Woodson continued to gab. "I want a ring," he said. "I want a big, fat ring with a lot of diamonds." He had three games to go to get it, a murderous stretch of Penn State, Wisconsin, then Ohio State.

Ranked fourth, the Wolverines headed into Happy Valley to face No. 2 Penn State. When the game was over, they were No. 1 for the first time in seven years. They spanked the Nittany Lions in every phase of the game, taking a 24-0 halftime lead and rolling to a 34-8 victory. Rows of red taillights streamed from Beaver Stadium midway through the third quarter, signaling the departure of Penn State from the national title picture and the arrival of Michigan.

"We saw the seats emptying, their fans going home, and we said to ourselves, 'They're leaving! They're leaving!' " linebacker Rob Swett said. "They gave up, and we knew it. We were dominating, and you could feel a wave of fire going down the sideline. There was a feeling like something special was happening."

Something special *was* happening.

In bitter cold the next week, the Wolverines beat the Badgers, 26-16, in Madison, Wis. After that, they dispatched fourth-ranked Ohio State in Ann Arbor, 20-14, to raise their record to 11-0 for the first time since 1971. Woodson capped his standout season with three big plays: a 37-yard reception that set up the game's first touchdown; a 78-yard punt return for a touchdown that put Michigan ahead by 13 points; and an interception in the end zone in the second half.

Clasping a red rose in his right hand, Woodson smiled at the fans who had flooded the field after the game and said, "Can y'all smell that?"

Yes, they could.

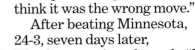

JULIAN H. GONZALEZ/Detroit Free Press

CHARLES WOODSON MADE HIS POINT AFTER HIS SECOND PICK AGAINST MICHIGAN STATE. MARCUS RAY ALSO INTERCEPTED TWO MSU PASSES.

FEB. 8, 1997: THE RED WINGS WON AT PITTSBURGH, 6-5,
MAKING SCOTTY BOWMAN THE FIRST NHL COACH TO REACH 1,000 VICTORIES.

BRIAN GRIESE AND CHARLES WOODSON SHOWED OFF SOME HARDWARE DURING A VICTORY PARADE THAT DREW 100,000 IN 20-DEGREE WEATHER.

ALL ROSES, NO THORNS

The summit was in sight. The Wolverines had won the Big Ten championship that had eluded them for so long, and Woodson had won the Heisman Trophy as he thought he should, giving his school its second of the decade and third of the century. But one goal remained, the goal no Michigan team had dared speak about for years: the national championship, the school's first since 1948.

And so the Wolverines went out and won the Rose Bowl, beating Washington State, 21-16. Ever cool under pressure, Griese threw three touchdown passes, two of them (53, 58) long bombs to wide receiver Tai Streets, who played the second half of the season with dislocated fingers on both hands. Woodson made a crucial interception in the end zone.

All was not perfect. There was a controversial ending, with the Cougars running out of time on their final drive. Nebraska also finished undefeated and claimed a share of the championship. But none of that mattered much. Carr's climb was complete. And after all, Bo never went 12-0.

"I will cherish this game, this university, for the rest of my life," said Griese, voted Rose Bowl most valuable player. "You have opportunities in life, and those who stand out are the ones who take advantage of those opportunities. It's just sweet for us to capitalize on an opportunity to make history."

Hail, yes.

DERBY THE LAB, ALWAYS A FAN OF OTHER ANIMALS, ESPECIALLY WOLVERINES, SAW THE PARADE WITH HIS OWNER.

JUNE 15, 1997: THE VIPERS BEAT LONG BEACH, 2-0, IN GAME 6 OF THE IHL FINALS AT THE PALACE,
MAKING DETROIT THE FIRST CITY TO WIN THE STANLEY AND TURNER CUPS IN THE SAME YEAR.

The Big House

By Nicholas J. Cotsonika

Early in the autumn of 1997, LaVerne (Kip) Taylor returned to Michigan Stadium to remember. Seventy years before, as a nervous 19-year-old making his first start at right end, he had scored the first touchdown in the stadium's first game, a 33-0 Wolverines victory over Ohio Wesleyan.

"Third-down situation, as I recall," he said. "We had the ball on the 28-yard line. Louis Gilbert, our triple-threat man, looked at me and said, 'Listen, sophomore, if I throw it to you, you better catch it.' Well, the ball was so perfect I could have caught it with my teeth. I came across, and there were two players coming at me. I sidestepped one, stiff-armed the other, and ran into the corner."

And Michigan Stadium had its first great moment. Many more would follow in a place that always stayed on the cutting edge of college football.

In the early part of the century, the Wolverines played at Regents Field (1893-1905), then Ferry Field (1906-26). But their popularity grew, and they needed a bigger house. They needed the Big House. So legendary coach and athletic director Fielding H. Yost pushed for a huge new facility fashioned after the Yale Bowl, dug deeply into the earth. Yost received approval for a 72,000-seat stadium, but he boosted its capacity upon completion to 84,401 with temporary stands and influenced plans so it could be expanded to seat more than 100,000.

Bentley Historical Library

MICHIGAN STADIUM DREW AT LEAST 100,000 FANS FOR THE FINAL 154 FOOTBALL GAMES OF THE CENTURY.

Michigan Stadium always was a monument to such vision and ambition. It was the first to use electronic scoreboards, among the first to use artificial turf, and among the first to switch back to grass. It hosted more than 100,000 fans for the final 154 games of the century. Its capacity was increased at least nine times and at the century's end stood at 107,501, the final seat reserved for the ghost of former athletic director Fritz Crisler. It was the largest college-owned stadium in the nation, a humbling hallmark to the game.

"It doesn't matter how old you get," Taylor said, standing in an end zone. "When you get an opportunity to come down here, on the field, you don't feel so big and important." ◆

Oct. 11, 1997: Steve Fisher, his program clouded by an NCAA investigation, was fired as Michigan basketball coach. Brian Ellerbe replaced him.

NEW ICE AGE, 1994-1999

Reign of Tara

Leapin' Lipinski

TARA LIPINISKI LOVED TO COLLECT THINGS — PLUSH FROGS, BEANIE BABIES AND FIGURE SKATING MEDALS. BEANIE COLLECTOR MAGAZINE PUT HER ON ITS COVER AND REPORTED THAT WHEN SHE RETURNED FROM NAGANO, GOLD MEDAL AROUND HER NECK, THE FIRST THING SHE SAID TO A FRIEND WAS, "LOOK WHAT I GOT AT THE OLYMPICS — ERIN THE BEAR!"

BY JO-ANN BARNAS

History won't forget that she was just a kid — 15 years old and 82 pounds, barely taller than the boards at the rink. Too young to stop collecting stuffed toy frogs and Beanie Babies. Too small to shop for clothes in the junior section. Not quite ready for a boyfriend.

But not too young to be Olympic champion.

It happened one glorious night in February 1998 in Nagano, Japan, when Tara Lipinski skated a flawless four-minute long program, smiling through the whole thing, and beat arch-rival Michelle Kwan for the gold medal.

Maybe it was an omen, but Lipinski painted her nails gold that week. She wore six "lucky rings" on her fingers and two favorite pendants, including one that read: "Short but good."

Although her Olympic experience ended in Japan that week, what Lipinski accomplished for the Detroit Skating Club in Bloomfield Hills was for the ages.

The youngest Olympic gold medalist of her sport, Lipinski also had become the club's first Olympic champion — a title

DEC. 13, 1997: CHARLES WOODSON, A CORNERBACK
AND RECEIVER FROM MICHIGAN, WON THE HEISMAN TROPHY.

that might never have come about had her parents not convinced their only child to move to the DSC in December 1995 when Nicole Bobek, then the U.S. women's champion, left coach Richard Callaghan.

It was then that Lipinski and Michigan became indelibly linked.

"I would have never gotten where I am had it not been for the support of the club," Lipinski said. "I'll never forget any of it."

Born in Philadelphia, Lipinski, who grew up near Newark, Del., started skating at age 6 at the University of Delaware Ice Arena. At 9, she moved with her parents, Pat and Jack, to Sugar Land, Texas, near Houston, where she trained for two years before moving back to the Delaware Figure Skating Club while Jack stayed in Houston.

At 12, when Lipinski became the youngest gold medalist at the Olympic Festival, she already was being schooled by private tutors. Soon, an agent and a public-relations firm were hired to help promote her. Bright and perky, Lipinski was sought for endorsement contracts before she competed in her first senior nationals.

JULIAN H. GONZALEZ/Detroit Free Press

IN NAGANO, TARA LIPINSKI CAPTURED HER GOLD MEDAL BY WINNING THE LONG PROGRAM, SCORING 5.9S AND 5.8S.

three finish.

Now 14 — and a week removed from losing her final baby molar — Lipinski became the sweetheart of the skating nationals. She upset the seemingly unshakable and artistically superior Kwan, the reigning world champion, by landing all seven of her triple jumps, including the difficult triple loop/triple loop combination. It marked the first time that combination jump had ever been done in competition, by man or woman.

When the scoreboard flashed her winning marks, Lipinski was christened the youngest U.S. champion in history.

But Lipinski didn't stop there, because when she topped Kwan again a month later in Switzerland for the world title, she became the sport's youngest world champion. (Lipinski was 60 days younger than 15-year-old Sonja Henie, who won her first of 10 world titles in 1927.)

But that world title would be Lipinski's last. Shortly after capturing the Olympic gold medal, Lipinski turned professional two months before her 16th birthday.

Her competitive career over — unless she challenged the International Skating Union to regain her competitive status — Lipinski relocated back to Texas in the summer of 1998. She joined a pro skating tour and began pursuing other ambitions, such as acting.

When she arrived at the Detroit Skating Club, Lipinski — then 13 and 4-feet-8 and 68 pounds — wasted no time putting in champion hours.

Although elfin in stature, Lipinski was determined and tough on the ice. Obsessed with perfection, she often wouldn't leave the rink until she had perfectly executed any problem jump five times in a row.

Training alongside longtime Callaghan student Todd Eldredge, a multiple U.S. men's champion, Lipinski worked on her speed in cat-and-mouse games with Eldredge, chasing him around the rink and collapsing in laughter at the end.

By February 1996, in her first U.S. nationals appearance in the senior division, Lipinski finished third. She followed that with a 15th-place finish at worlds, where she landed seven triple jumps in a dazzling long program that pulled her up from 23rd.

In 1997, Lipinski arrived at the U.S. Figure Skating Championships in Nashville, Tenn., hoping to repeat her top-

Still, Lipinski always will be remembered for the innocence and pure joy she injected into the sport. At the Olympics, millions watched on television when she charged across the ice after her long program. And when she punctuated her happiness in the kiss-and-cry area with a highpitched scream that could be heard throughout White Ring arena, it was hard not to smile with her.

Later, she said she would never forget the words with which Callaghan had sent her onto the ice before her final performance:

"You had a great two weeks here," he said. "You trained hard and had fun. Go out and finish the experience."

Lipinski, the youngest and smallest gold medalist of the Games, did just that.

◆

That old magic

Yabba-dabba-doo!

BY JEMELE HILL

On the surface, the crucial moment of Michigan State's Final Four season in 1998-99 came when Earvin (Magic) Johnson, the biggest hero in East Lansing, gave a pep talk to struggling point guard Mateen Cleaves, the newest hero in East Lansing.

It wasn't.

The crucial moment came in 1995, when Antonio Smith, a center at Flint Northern, decided to come to Michigan State, to take a chance with a young, brash, overworked coach named Tom Izzo.

After Smith came Morris Peterson, a forward from Flint Northwestern. After Peterson came Cleaves, an All-America from Flint Northern. After Cleaves came Charlie Bell, a guard from Flint Southwestern who scored the most points in the history of Flint high school hoops.

The "Flintstones" were born.

In the magical season of 1998-99, when Michigan State made it to the national semifinals after a 20-year absence, the Flintstones proved to be the cornerstone of Spartan success. Cleaves ran the floor show. Smith cleared the boards. Bell guarded the top opponent. Peterson came off the bench first and led all Spartans scorers.

Their mothers even traveled together to home and road games. "They sit behind the bench," Smith said, "and they try to coach us and tell us to keep our head in the game. All of them have a way of getting our attention."

Michigan State, coming off a Big Ten regular-season co-championship, started the season ranked sixth in the country. But the Spartans lost to No. 7 Temple, No. 4 Duke and No. 1 Connecticut and fell to 4-3 in early December. Izzo wondered many times whether he was crazy for creating the

JULIAN H. GONZALEZ/Detroit Free Press

FOR AN ALL-AMERICA, POINT GUARD MATEEN CLEAVES DIDN'T SCORE A LOT — UNLESS THE GAME WAS ON THE LINE IN THE FINAL MOMENTS.

difficult schedule, but he eventually concluded: "It was games like those that got us to where we are."

Early on, Cleaves didn't play like a preseason All-America junior. He shot 3-of-17 against Duke. He was worse against UConn — 2-for-17. In the Big Ten opener, at No. 24 Wisconsin, he was 3-for-11 in a terrible 66-51 loss.

Three days later, everything changed for Cleaves and the Spartans. The Wolverines were in the Breslin Center. And so was MSU's 1979 national championship team. Johnson spoke to the young Spartans and delivered a simple message: "Have fun." During warm-ups, he pulled Cleaves aside and repeated his message, point guard-to-point guard.

"He said when he's not having fun when he's playing, then he's not himself," Cleaves recalled. "That inspired me to go out and have fun. I got caught up in the ratings. I wanted to be too perfect and be too solid."

Cleaves finished with 25 points (on 7-for-10 shooting), eight assists and four steals in an 81-67 victory. "It's great," Izzo declared, "to have our guard back." The Spartans wouldn't lose again until the Final Four.

The Spartans went undefeated at Breslin, where a raucous student section called the "Izzone" took pleasure in frightening opponents. MSU was 15-1 in the Big Ten, then won three times to capture the conference tournament, including a 67-50 wipeout of Illinois in the final.

Cleaves had something special, a desire to win so powerful that it alone powered the Spartans to victory. He nailed an off-balance runner with 0.4 second left to beat Penn State, 70-68. He drove through five Gophers for the game-winning shot with 1.2 seconds left at Minnesota, 84-82. He hit the game-

---

WITH HELP FROM ANTONIO SMITH, HIS FIRST RECRUIT, TOM IZZO MADE THE FINAL CUT AFTER THE SPARTANS WON THE MIDWEST REGIONAL IN ST. LOUIS.

winning floater in the lane with 3.7 seconds left against Northwestern in the first round of the tournament, only his fifth and sixth points of the game. "I swear to God, he waits until the end of the game to do that stuff," Northwestern coach Kevin O'Neill said.

Besides Cleaves, the Spartans won because they were possibly the best rebounding team in the country (only three opponents outboarded them all season), they played ferocious defense, and they were supremely confident they would win any close game. They weren't great shooters (Cleaves, for instance, shot 40.6 percent), so they reveled in winning ugly.

Smith anchored the defense, becoming the third Spartan with 1,000 career boards, and provided fire in the belly. Peterson, who emerged as one of the nation's top sixth men during Cleaves' slump, led a deep bench that included A. J. Granger, a sharpshooter during the NCAA tournament, and Thomas Kelley, a senior guard.

MSU received the No. 1 seed in the Midwest Regional. The Spartans routed Mount St. Mary's, 76-53, and then beat Mississippi, 74-66, with a late 13-0 run. The second-rounder was ugly, but nothing compared to a brutal, 54-46 victory over Oklahoma. Cleaves and Oklahoma's Eduardo Najera collided in the second half, delaying the game 10 minutes and leaving the Sooner bloody and with a concussion and stitches.

In the regional final, defending NCAA champion Kentucky bolted to a 17-6 lead. Smith lit into the Spartans during a time-out. "Antonio is usually the type to be the good cop," Izzo said. "But he was a bad cop, a very bad cop, then. I didn't say anything during that time-out. I just stepped back."

Granger hit a pair of three-pointers and the Spartans were back in the game. They would win, 73-66, because Peterson went 6-for-6 from the free-throw line in the last 29 seconds, MSU shot 52 percent and outrebounded Kentucky, 22-10, in the second half, and MSU held the Wildcats without a basket for three long second-half stretches, from 18:04 to 12:47, from 8:27 to 4:39, and from 3:26 to 0:33.

The Spartans' reward — besides their 33rd victory, the most in Big Ten history — was a semifinal date in St. Petersburg, Fla., with top-ranked Duke. The Spartans couldn't shoot straight (29 percent) and couldn't rebound in the first half (28-14 Duke), which ended 32-20 in Duke's favor. MSU battled in the second half, eventually closing to 51-48, but could draw no nearer. Duke won, 68-62, and the Spartans' dream had been dashed.

Maybe.

Long after the loss, associate coach Tom Crean walked onto the court at Tropicana Field and kissed the Final Four logo. "People doubted us, but we got here, baby," he said. "We'll be back."

MARCH 8, 1998: ROBERT (TRACTOR) TRAYLOR WAS SELECTED MOST OUTSTANDING PLAYER AFTER MICHIGAN WON THE INAUGURAL BIG TEN BASKETBALL TOURNAMENT. U-M BEAT PURDUE, 76-67, IN THE TITLE GAME.

Masters of overtime

Red, maize & blue

By Nicholas J. Cotsonika

TOM UHLMAN/Associated Press

COACH RED BERENSON HUGGED BILL MUCKALT AFTER MICHIGAN ENDED ITS 32-YEAR HOCKEY CHAMPIONSHIP DROUGHT IN 1996. "IT DOESN'T GET ANY BETTER THAN THAT, EH?" BERENSON SAID.

Success didn't rush to Red Berenson. It came slowly, with pain and agony, with so many doubts testing his stern and stoic nature. He said he might not have returned to Michigan, his alma mater, if he had known it would take 12 years to win his first national championship.

When he left the NHL to take control of the Wolverines in 1984-85, they were the laughingstocks of college hockey, a raggedy band of no-talent, no-name players in a once-proud program. They won 11 games and finished ninth in their league. But Berenson remained committed.

The next season, the Wolverines finished in eighth place. After that, they finished seventh, then fifth, then fourth, then fourth again, then second, then finally first in 1991-92. Berenson was pleased with the improvement, but the agony wasn't over.

Although Michigan had returned to prominence, staying there throughout the '90s, one obstacle remained if the school hoped to match the dominance it enjoyed in the '40s and '50s: the NCAA tournament. Particularly, overtime in the NCAA tournament.

In 1993, the Wolverines lost to Maine in the semifinals, 4-3. In overtime. In 1994, they lost to Lake Superior State in the second round, 5-4. In overtime. And in 1995, they lost the longest and perhaps most heartbreaking game in college hockey history, falling to Maine in the semifinals, 4-3. In three overtimes.

Berenson was famous for a rock he

JUNE 13, 1998: THE DETROIT SHOCK, COACHED BY NANCY LIEBERMAN-CLINE, PLAYED ITS FIRST GAME IN THE YEAR-OLD WNBA AND LOST TO THE CHARLOTTE STING, 78-69, BEFORE 15,574 AT THE PALACE.

placed on his desk that bore an inspiring inscription: "OUR DAY WILL COME." But history made it hard to believe. In the triple-overtime thriller against Maine, Michigan's star center, Brendan Morrison, had an opportunity to end the curse with a can't-miss scoring chance. He hit the post.

That seemed to symbolize Berenson's destiny: close, but not quite. And then came 1996. The Wolverines advanced to the NCAA championship game against Colorado College, and when regulation play ended with the score tied at 2, finally, after 12 years of trying, his dream did not die.

The players walked out onto the ice for overtime, passing underneath a sign that read, "SOMETHING TO PROVE." Less than four minutes later, Morrison proved that both he and his school were winners, pouncing on a puck in front of the net and finding net, not iron.

Final score: 3-2, Michigan.

Redemption.

National champions for the first time since 1964, the Wolverines threw their gloves into the air and mobbed Morrison. Overtime? Overjoyed. The black cloud had lifted, allowing goaltender Marty Turco to sum up the situation in four sweet words: "The ghosts are gone."

"When you look back on this, it's incredible," said Morrison, who dedicated the victory to all those Wolverines who rebuilt the program. "It seemed like it took forever to go in the net, but it did. It's incredible."

No one celebrated more than Berenson. He ran around the ice, hugged his teary players, pumped his fists, grinned like a kid. He had been a star at Michigan in the early '60s. He had won a Stanley Cup as a player with the Montreal Canadiens. He had won an NHL coach of the year award with the St. Louis Blues. Still, he considered the title his crowning achievement.

"There's nothing close to this," Berenson said after the game. "We've worked for that day, and we've earned that day, and our day has come."

Their day came again two years later in much the same way.

The '98 Wolverines weren't a powerhouse. They lost seven key players from the '97 team, which won a school-record 35 games and again included Morrison, who won the Hobey Baker Award. They didn't win the Great Lakes Invitational for the first time in a decade. They lost four times to Michigan State. And they didn't win their league.

But perhaps Berenson's previous struggles had earned him a little favor from the hockey gods.

Somehow, some way, the Wolverines squeaked into the NCAA tournament. Somehow, some way, they beat defending national champion North Dakota in a regional final at Yost Ice Arena. Somehow, some way, they sneaked into the NCAA championship game at Boston's FleetCenter, full of

JULIAN H. GONZALEZ/Detroit Free Press

BETWEEN THE PIPES, MARTY TURCO PLAYED LIKE A WALL FOR THE WOLVERINES. HE WON 127 GAMES, MOST IN NCAA HISTORY, AND NINE NCAA TOURNAMENT GAMES, ALSO A RECORD. HE WAS THE MOST OUTSTANDING PLAYER OF THE FINAL FOUR IN 1998.

Bostonians rooting for Boston College, and won, 3-2. In overtime. Of course.

The freshmen, who were supposed to be the reason why the Wolverines wouldn't compete with the nation's elite, provided all the punch. Twice, center Mark Kosick scored to bring them back from one-goal deficits, allowing right wing Josh Langfeld the opportunity to score the winner and give them their unprecedented ninth national title.

"This one is much sweeter," assistant coach Mel Pearson said afterward, as his players sat stunned with euphoria. "We had everything against us, playing in their backyard with their fans and not having the firepower we did last time. But we did it. We did it, in overtime, again, and I just can't believe it."

SEPT. 1, 1998: CITING A CONFLICT WITH GENERAL MANAGER RANDY SMITH, THE TIGERS FIRED MANAGER BUDDY BELL. LARRY PARRISH REPLACED HIM.

There's something about Barry

Always elusive

By Curt Sylvester

An opposing NFL coach once described Barry Sanders as an ice cube. A wet, slippery ice cube. And stopping Sanders, he explained, was just about as difficult as squishing a wet, slippery ice cube with your bare foot. Darned-near impossible.

There would be an occasional meltdown, of course, such as the infamous negative one yard in 13 carries in the playoff loss at Green Bay in 1994.

But for Lions fans of the 1990s, Sanders brought a million magic moments to a team burdened by years and years of frustration.

There was literally nothing Sanders couldn't do when he got a football in his hands. At least that's the way it seemed to the Lions, their fans and their opponents.

He left dozens of defensive players grasping at thin air with a sudden, unexpected change of direction. Others he simply outran to the end zone.

On a cold December day in Buffalo in 1991, he spun like a helicopter blade on top of a pile of would-be tacklers, landed on his feet and continued on his way.

In a game in Tampa Bay in 1997 he had two touchdown runs of 80 yards or more (80/82), something no NFL player had ever done.

In a 1994 game against New England, Sanders turned Patriots safety Harlon Barnett almost inside out with a zig-zag run that was featured on highlight films for years to come.

Sanders was the first NFL player to rush for 1,000 yards in 10 consecutive seasons; the first player to rush for

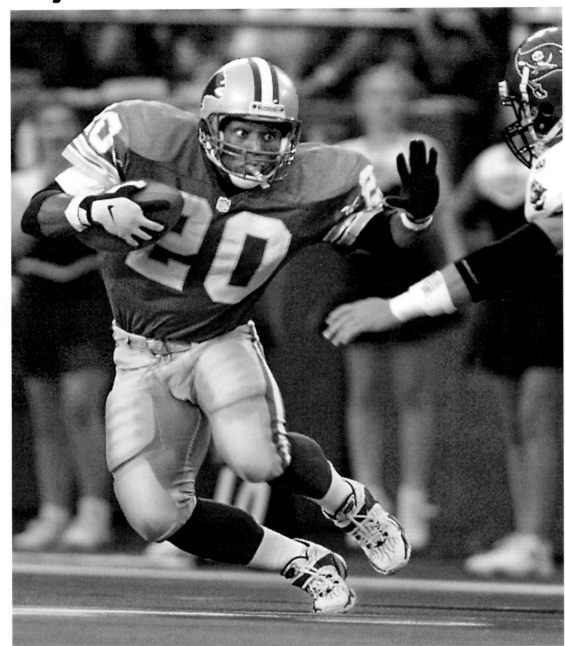

JULIAN H. GONZALEZ/Detroit Free Press

FOR A DECADE, BARRY SANDERS DANCED AND JUKED AND BOBBED AND WEAVED AND SCURRIED AND SCAMPERED HIS WAY INTO THE HEARTS OF LIONS FANS AND THE NFL RECORD BOOK.

SEPT. 20, 1998: CHARLIE BATCH, THE ROOKIE FROM EASTERN MICHIGAN, COMPLETED 20 OF 40 PASSES FOR 160 YARDS IN HIS DEBUT AS LIONS QUARTERBACK, A 29-6 LOSS AT MINNESOTA.

1,500 yards in four consecutive seasons; and the first player to gain 100 yards or more in 14 consecutive games.

Players dreaded playing against the Lions, not only because they feared Sanders but because they feared becoming highlight fodder for Sanders.

"I can see it now," Chicago linebacker Ron Cox once said. "I'll be vacationing on some island someplace, and I'll be watching us in some damn Cadillac commercial — chasing his ass."

It was after the same game — in which Sanders shredded the Chicago Bears for 167 yards in a 55-20 Thanksgiving Day victory in 1997 — that another Bears linebacker, Barry Minter, suggested another comparison. "He was a Lamborghini out there and we were a bunch of Chevy S-10s," Minter said. "I hate to say this, but he showed us why I consider him to be the greatest to put on a uniform and carry the ball."

The Bears weren't the only ones who looked at Sanders that way.

Wayne Fontes, the Lions' coach when Sanders became eligible for the NFL draft in 1989, saw that potential in a workout at Oklahoma State three months after Sanders completed his Heisman Trophy season. Although only 5-feet-8 and barely 200 pounds, Sanders had rushed for 2,628 yards and 37 touchdowns.

Fontes watched Sanders run the 40-yard dash, watched him do the agility drills and the strength tests, saw his vertical leap and his ability to catch the football.

Fontes stuck a thick cigar in his mouth, lit it and smiled. "We're taking him," he announced to the world.

The Lions took Sanders with the third pick in the NFL draft — behind UCLA quarterback

MARY SCHROEDER/Detroit Free Press

IN 1990, THE FREE PRESS GATHERED FOUR OF DETROIT'S MOST PROMINENT STARS AT TIGER STADIUM: BARRY SANDERS, CECIL FIELDER, STEVE YZERMAN AND JOE DUMARS.

Troy Aikman and Michigan State offensive tackle Tony Mandarich, ahead of Alabama linebacker Derrick Thomas and Florida State cornerback Deion Sanders.

And never once did Sanders give the Lions cause to regret Fontes' decision. Although he was not a power back capable of moving the stack or lowering a shoulder and driving through a linebacker, he was widely regarded as one of the best pure runners — if not *the* best — in NFL history.

Wide receiver Brett Perriman was a Sanders teammate for six seasons before playing in 1997 with the Kansas City Chiefs and running back Marcus Allen, another future Hall of Famer.

"They were always saying Marcus Allen's unbelievable, he can cut like crazy," Perriman said. "I said, 'Man, look, that don't impress me. I played with Barry Sanders.' Marcus is no slouch or nothin', but Barry's the greatest back I've ever seen in my life playing football."

Another Sanders admirer was Jimmy Johnson, who won two Super Bowls with Dallas and running back Emmitt Smith before moving on to coach the Miami Dolphins.

"I've been fortunate to be around some good backs over the years," Johnson said, "but Barry is truly special. He is the player who truly keeps you on the edge of your seat; he has a chance to make a big play every time he touches the ball.

"I don't know that there's another player in the entire league that I enjoy watching more than Barry Sanders. The only time I don't like to watch him is when we're playing him."

One of the few who didn't agree was Barry's father — William Sanders, a devoted Cleveland Browns fan. Even as his son was knocking off Lions records and NFL records,

BARRY SANDERS' DECADE WITH THE LIONS:

YEAR	ATT	YDS	AVG	TD
1989	280	1470	5.3	14
1990	255	1304	5.1	13
1991	342	1548	4.5	16
1992	312	1352	4.3	9
1993	243	1115	4.6	3
1994	331	1883	5.7	7
1995	314	1500	4.8	11
1996	307	1553	5.1	11
1997	335	2053	6.1	11
1998	343	1491	4.3	4
Totals	**3062**	**15269**	**5.0**	**99**

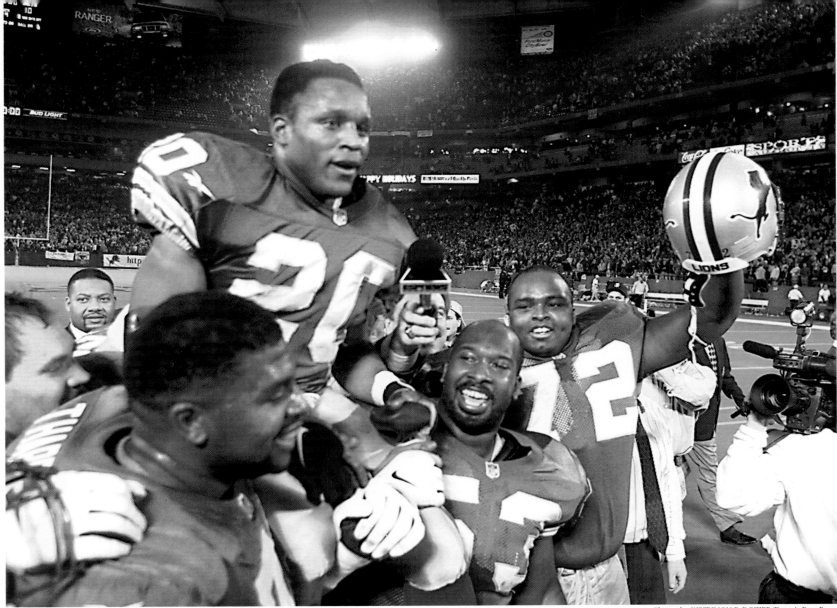

Photos by KIRTHMON F. DOZIER/Detroit Free Press

In the 1997 regular-season finale against the New York Jets, Barry Sanders reached new heights in the Silverdome after this two-yard gain in the fourth quarter. It made him the third player to rush for 2,000 or more yards in a season. He finished the game with 184 yards and the season with 2,053.

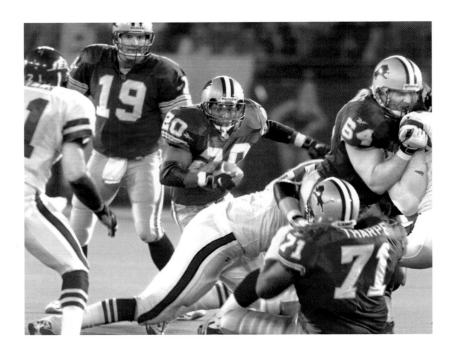

Sept. 27, 1998: Doak Walker, the 1948 Heisman Trophy winner and Lions' All-Pro halfback, died at age 71. He had been paralyzed in January in a skiing accident.

ALASTAIR GRANT/Associated Press

A STRANGER IN A STRANGE LAND, SANDERS ARRIVED AT LONDON'S
GATWICK AIRPORT THE DAY BEFORE TRAINING CAMP OPENED IN 1999.
HE RETIRED FROM FOOTBALL WITHOUT TALKING TO THE LIONS.

A BARRY GOOD SEASON

How Barry Sanders, in 1997, became the third player
to rush for more than 2,000 yards:

OPPONENT	ATT	YDS	AVG	LG	TD
Atlanta	15	33	2.2	12	0
Tampa Bay	10	20	2.0	13	0
at Chicago	19	161	8.5	28	0
at New Orleans	18	113	6.3	19	0
Green Bay	28	139	5.0	46	0
at Buffalo	25	107	4.3	40	0
at Tampa Bay	24	215	9.0	82t	2
NY Giants	24	105	4.4	37	1
at Green Bay	23	105	4.6	18	0
at Washington	15	105	7.0	51t	1
Minnesota	19	108	5.7	21	0
Indianapolis	24	216	9.0	80t	2
Chicago	19	167	8.8	40t	3
at Miami	30	137	4.6	19	1
at Minnesota	19	138	7.3	60	0
NY Jets	23	184	8.0	53	1
Totals	**335**	**2053**	**6.1**	**82t**	**11**

William Sanders maintained that Browns Hall of Fame back Jim Brown was, and always would be, the best running back in NFL history.

"You know what I tell people?" William Sanders said. "Out of all the football players I've ever seen in my life, Barry might be one of the top five great running backs I've ever seen. I'm not going to try to put him No. 1 or No. 2, but I'll put him in the top five and let them argue about who the other four are."

What did Barry say in reply? Not much.

But then, he never said much about anything.

For all of his brilliance carrying the football, however, Sanders was a walking contradiction.

Although he preached and claimed to practice celibacy at one point early in his career, within a couple of years he had a son with a woman he never married.

Although he was considered one of the best backs in NFL history, the Lions were only 78-82 in regular-season games and 1-5 in the playoffs during the 10-year Sanders era.

Although he was one of the most exciting and popular football players of his era, he shunned the spotlight.

Although he broke Lions and NFL records left and right, records and individual honors meant nothing to him.

As a rookie, he left the final game of the season in Atlanta with several minutes to play, rather than go for the 11 yards it would have taken to pass Christian Okoye of Kansas City for the NFL rushing title.

And when he retired suddenly and unexpectedly two days before the Lions were to report for the start of the 1999 training camp, he was within 1,458 yards — one season's work by Sanders' standards — of passing Walter Payton as the NFL's all-time leading rusher.

Oddly enough, he never consulted the Lions before or after making the decision, and all of their efforts to contact him were futile.

As slippery as an ice cube, right to the end.

◆

Chip ahoy!

BY ERIC SHARP

This was how Chip Hanauer liked to leave the Detroit River: carried from his unlimited hydroplane on the shoulders of his pit crew. "It's a lot better than the way I left last time — unconscious in a helicopter," Hanauer said.

It was the summer of '99 and Hanauer, the most important figure on the river since Gar Wood and Bill Muncey, had just captured his 11th Gold Cup, an unprecedented total in boat racing's equivalent of the Indianapolis 500. Hanauer had won Gold Cups with three teams over 17 years (he missed four races because of injuries or brief retirements).

Now 45, he also needed one more victory anywhere to equal the all-time unlimited record of 62 held by Muncey, his late friend and mentor.

Hanauer, a Seattle schoolteacher before a big-time racer, started racing boats at age 9. His first effort in the 200 m.p.h. unlimiteds wasn't auspicious. He got to the Miami course a day ahead of his team and was so broke that he slept under a palm tree on a beach until his teammates arrived the next morning. By the late 1970s he was driving third-rate boats to second- and third-place finishes.

In 1982, Hanauer was hired to drive Atlas Van Lines after Muncey, the Mario Andretti of unlimiteds, was killed in off-season testing. As Muncey's widow, Fran, the boat owner, cheered from a dock on the Detroit River, Hanauer took advantage of a first-rate boat to steal the start from the favorites and win his first Gold Cup.

"I can still remember the emotions of that moment," he said. "I guess it's still the single most rewarding moment of

KEVIN SWANK/Special to the Detroit Free Press

CHIP HANAUER ONCE WROTE IN THE FREE PRESS: "WINNING THE GOLD CUP IS EVERY DRIVER'S DREAM. WINNING THE GOLD CUP IN DETROIT IS THE ULTIMATE."

my racing career."

He also won Gold Cups driving Miller American and Circus Circus and, when that team quit the sport, he spent a year racing cars. He then switched to Miss Budweiser, the fastest and best-financed team that had dominated unlimited racing for two decades.

Hanauer racked up victory after victory in the jet-powered Buds. But while he and the boat were a good match, the same couldn't be said for his relationship with the crew or Bernie Little, the boat's flamboyant and demanding owner.

A self-described "worrywart," Hanauer's intense, reclusive but quietly demanding personality grated on Little and the pit crew. Hanauer believed that mistakes by the technical team were responsible for two serious crashes; in one, four of his vertebrae were broken.

"I never really fit in with the Bud guys," he said. "I was used to a team where we were like a family. We were all friends. At Bud, you got the feeling that you were just the next guy, and if you didn't like it, you could leave because a lot of others were ready to take your place."

The final straw with Budweiser came when he crashed during a Gold Cup heat at Detroit in 1996. Hauled off soaking wet and unconscious by helicopter to a hospital, Hanauer awoke to intensify his criticisms of the boat and crew, and the crew retaliated by questioning his competence as a driver.

Unhappy with his team, feeling uncharacteristic doubts about his own skills, and concerned by a recently diagnosed illness, Hanauer announced in 1996 that he was hanging up

ONLY ONE NAME MATTERED IN HYDROPLANE RACING: CHIP HANAUER'S, NOT THE BOAT'S. IN 1999, HE DROVE MISS PICO TO HIS 11TH GOLD CUP. THE SEATTLE NATIVE ALSO HAD WON THE GOLD CUP DRIVING ATLAS VAN LINES, MILLER AMERICAN, CIRCUS CIRCUS AND MISS BUDWEISER.

his helmet. He spent the next three years putting his priorities in order, getting the disease under control, and learning that there was a lot more to life than boat racing.

He never planned to return to racing. But in 1999, the Miss Pico organization offered him a well-financed team and a boat that would be just slightly slower than Miss Bud. That was too much temptation for a driver who loved the underdog role so much that he often told his pit crew, "You don't have to give me the fastest boat out there. Just get me close, and I'll do the rest."

Hanauer's most frightening challenge came not in a boat but in a hospital, where just before the 1996 season he was diagnosed with spasmodic disphonia. For several years he experienced occasional weakening in his ability to speak and by 1995 had recurrent episodes where his voice disappeared entirely. When doctors couldn't find an organic cause, Hanauer "thought for a while that I was going crazy."

"I became a hermit," he said. "I couldn't answer the phone,

and going out in public was so embarrassing and frustrating I just retreated into myself."

In 1996, a physician who had read a short article on the rare disease referred Hanauer to a New York City specialist. "That's one of the worst things about this disease," Hanauer said. "It's so rare that most people go four or five years before it's diagnosed. You don't know what it feels like to have someone confirm that you aren't going insane."

That didn't mean everything was rosy. Treatment of the disease required regular injections of botulism toxin — the same organism that sometimes causes fatal outbreaks of food poisoning — to paralyze muscles in his throat that go into spasm and paralyze his voice box.

Hanauer knew he could handle it.

After all, he had handled life as an adrenaline junkie, addicted to the incredible rush that comes with running 200 m.p.h. in a jet turbine boat on the razor edge of disaster and hanging your precious butt way over the line time after time. ◆

MARCH 27, 1999: RIOTING IN EAST LANSING FOLLOWED MICHIGAN STATE'S 68-62 LOSS TO DUKE IN THE NCAA TOURNAMENT SEMIFINALS, MSU'S FIRST FINAL FOUR APPEARANCE IN 20 YEARS.

Grand finale at The Corner

Out of the park

BY MITCH ALBOM

Look, there's your father, sitting in the rightfield seats, handing you a hot dog and telling you be careful, don't get mustard all over your shirt. And over there, near the third-base line, that was your grandma, holding her little pencil and writing names delicately in her scorecard, *"Kaline, RF, Horton, LF, Freehan, C . . ."*

And out there, in the bleachers, wasn't that your first girlfriend, looking the way she did back then, her hair in a ponytail, her eyes feigning interest as you pointed out the players and proudly quoted their statistics?

Didn't you see them all there, taking their place with the rest of the remembered, the living and the ghosts, the players and managers, the umpires and owners, all of whom came to wave good-bye to an 88-year-old fading blue palace called Tiger Stadium?

Didn't they gather early, on Sept. 27, 1999, at the corner of Michigan and Trumbull, gazing up fondly at the light towers and the peeling-white walls? Didn't they come through the turnstiles and immediately inhale, sniffing the smells of history mixed with sausage grease?

Didn't they roar for the old players who gathered at home plate before the national anthem? Didn't they laugh and point when Mark (The Bird) Fidrych ran out to the pitcher's mound and scooped up a last bag of dirt? Didn't they get a chill when the great Al Kaline, speaking for everyone who ever wore a Tigers uniform, said, "I again find myself humbled . . . by the events unfolding in front of us."?

Didn't they jump up, the way all baseball fans jump up, when the first pitch was smacked toward centerfield — *Could it be a homer? Will it be a homer?* — and didn't they applaud when it came down in the glove of the Tigers' centerfielder?

On this day, that centerfielder's name was Gabe Kapler, a muscle-bound, 24-year-old stud. But not long ago he was Chet Lemon, and before that Mickey Stanley and before that Johnny

PETE SIMAKAS OF DEARBORN HEIGHTS WAS 43 YEARS OLD WHEN TIGER STADIUM CLOSED — THAT'S 45 YEARS YOUNGER THAN THE OLD BALLPARK.

MAY 18, 1999: AFTER LOSING THE FIRST TWO GAMES, THE COLORADO AVALANCHE WON ITS FOURTH STRAIGHT, 5-2, AND ELIMINATED THE TWO-TIME DEFENDING STANLEY CUP CHAMPION RED WINGS FROM THE SECOND ROUND OF THE PLAYOFFS.

Photos by J. KYLE KEENER/Detroit Free Press

ON SEPT. 27, 1999, THE OLDEST ADDRESS IN PROFESSIONAL SPORTS STAGED ITS FINAL BASEBALL GAME. THE TIGERS BEAT THE KANSAS CITY ROYALS, 8-2. THE PLACE WAS PACKED, AND DOZENS OF FORMER TIGERS ATTENDED THE EVENT. "IT'S ALWAYS BEEN MY FAVORITE BALLPARK, AND I'VE PLAYED IN QUITE A FEW — YANKEE STADIUM, FENWAY, COMISKEY," SAID DICK McAULIFFE, AN INFIELDER FROM THE TIGERS' 1968 CHAMPIONSHIP TEAM.

Groth, Hoot Evers, all the way back to the ornery batting champion, Ty Cobb, who patrolled this same grass in this same building in the 1910s.

Kapler, the kid, seemed to travel through time. He was wearing Cobb's uniform — no number on his back — and for a moment, as the ball dropped out of the sky, it might have been the Georgia Peach himself squeezing it for the out.

History? The place was history.

A LOW CEILING

Look, there's your pal from the old neighborhood, grinning as his hand dove into your popcorn. And over there was your uncle, waiting in his Chevrolet, parked by the church where he said he'd meet you after the game.

There, in the upper deck, weren't those your schoolmates on Safety Patrol Day, having made the long bus trip down from northern Michigan? And down there, along the outfield wall, wasn't that your kid sister, leaning over the rail during batting practice, her big glove dangling from her too-small hand? "Hit one here!" she squealed to the players. "Hit one *here!* . . ."

Weren't they all there for the final game, a day that was, in many ways, perfect for a funeral, so much life-affirming joy to lessen the coming sadness; a sky the color of blueberry ice cream; a breeze that cooled the 84-degree sun; an adoring crowd that included former players Ron LeFlore, Mark Fidrych, Jack Morris, Kirk Gibson, Cecil Fielder, Darrell Evans, even Billy Rogell, the shortstop and former city councilman who played for this team — *in this stadium* — in the 1930s.

The 1930s?

History? The place was history.

"What's funny is how little I thought of this stadium when I first saw it," said Alan Trammell, who played shortstop his entire career in this park. "I came from Southern California, and we were used to big, new stadiums, big parking lots, and I drove by here and the cab driver said, 'That's Tiger Stadium,' and I said, 'Where? That thing? It looks like a fortress!' "

He laughed. "I love it now, but, to be honest, a lot of time I played here, we dreamed of having a new stadium. I mean, for years, we didn't have an indoor batting cage. If it was raining before the game, we didn't get a warm-up. Your first

JULIAN H. GONZALEZ/Detroit Free Press

ROOKIE ROBERT FICK BELTED THE FINAL HOME RUN IN TIGER STADIUM – AN EIGHTH-INNING GRAND SLAM OFF KANSAS CITY'S JEFF MONTGOMERY.

swing of the day was one that counted.

"And then there's that dugout. It's the worst. It's tiny and cramped and the ceiling is so low, you can't see anything but third base."

Trammell got that hazy look.

"I can't tell you how many times guys forgot about how low the ceiling is, and something would happen and they'd pop up to see and — BAM! They'd bang their head on the concrete. Especially big guys like Lance Parrish. Oh, man, that happened all the time!"

Trammell, grinning, was looking off now. Wasn't that his former teammate, rubbing his head, cursing out loud? Out there in the dugout? Did you see him?

A REASON TO CRY

Did you see Joe Louis on the final day? He was there, boxing in a makeshift ring in the outfield, knocking out Bob Pastor, the way he did in 1939. Did you see Jake LaMotta, winning the middleweight crown? Did you hear Billy Graham preaching to the bleachers? Did you see the Lions' Chuck Hughes, lying on the football field, dead of a blood clot he suffered during a 1971 game?

It wasn't just baseball within these walls. It was concerts, football games, prizefights, high school championships, even a summer series called "Opera Under the Stars."

But whatever took place, it was ours. This city. This state. Find another person from Michigan, from a town as far away from yours as you can get. Then find the one place you've both been.

Even money it's Tiger Stadium.

Which is why, at 7:07 p.m. on Monday, Sept. 27, 1999, when the final game ended — a Tigers victory, 8-2 over Kansas City, which included the perfect parting shot, an eighth-inning, monster grand slam off the rightfield roof by a rookie named Robert Fick — when that was over, nobody left. Nobody moved. Cameras flashed. A small cheer went up and then the fans seemed to pause and fall silent, the way you do at an airport gate before letting your loved ones fly away.

Finally, the centerfield gates opened. And one by one, the players who made history at The Corner, where Detroit had played games since 1896, came running out onto the field, squeezed into their old uniforms, Tigers from the '80s, '70s, '60s, '50s, middle-aged men playing boys one more time.

Here came Mickey Lolich, chugging to the mound. Here

MAY 28, 1999: KARIM GARCIA BECAME THE LAST TIGER TO HIT A ROOF SHOT OUT OF TIGER STADIUM, TO RIGHT OFF THE WHITE SOX'S JAIME NAVARRO. ON JULY 9, MILWAUKEE'S JEROMY BURNITZ HIT THE LAST ROOF SHOT, OFF NELSON CRUZ.

came Dan Petry, waving his cap. Here came Tom Brookens, Frank Tanana, Willie Horton, Gates Brown, Eldon Auker, all of them smiling, some of them crying.

It was like watching a rewind reel. And as they ran to their old positions and the sky turned dark and the stirring music sang over the loudspeakers, the crowd fell into a churchlike reverence. It was so quiet, you knew what people were doing.

They were remembering their own lives.

You ask why people cry when baseball stadiums close? This is why. Because some of us found our childhoods inside them.

And some of us left them there.

END OF AN ERA

Look, there were your children, tugging your arm, asking you questions, who is that player, where is the mascot, when can we eat, where is the bathroom? They are the ones you will take to the new place, a new stadium just a mile from this one. There, the walls will not be peeling, the pipes will not be exposed, the sausage fumes will not be melted into the tiling and the dugouts will not cause cranial injuries.

It will not be the same building, but it will be the same idea. You make your memory, and you savor it for years to come. Baseball connects us that way. Just as one day this winter, Sparky Anderson will be sitting on his back porch in Thousand Oaks, Calif., sitting in one of two old wooden seats he owns as souvenirs from Tiger Stadium. He will be thinking of the past. And across town, the rookie, Fick, will be dreaming of the future.

History? The place was history. It was championship celebrations in 1935, 1945, 1968 and 1984. It was Ernie Harwell's voice over a car radio. It was Cobb, Greenberg, Aguirre, Newhouser, Cash, McLain, Lolich, Gibson, Trammell, Whitaker, Morris.

It was the rightfield porch, the flagpole in centerfield, the girders that blocked your view, the home plate that was taken during the final ceremonies and transported to a new park for a new millennium.

It was Opening Days in snowstorms, and a closing day of 84 degrees. It was hot dogs, beer, caramel corn, Cokes, pennants and peanuts, foul balls and souvenirs. It was a house of fun, and a home of memories.

Some you couldn't forget if you tried.

"Hey, Lance," someone said, spotting former catcher Lance Parrish. "Trammell was talking about the dugouts here. He said you have some special bruises."

Parrish grinned. He instinctively grabbed his head. "I banged into that ceiling so many times, I have a permanent lump."

Don't we all?

There was your father, and there was your mother, holding your hand as you walked through the tunnel and saw the dazzling green grass for the very first time. Baseball in Detroit was done for this century. And so was the house in which it was played. We take a new walk now, a mile down the street, and as we glance one more time over our shoulders, at the corner of Michigan and Trumbull, with a lump in our throats — or on our heads — we say good-bye. ◆

J. KYLE KEENER/Detroit Free Press

IN POSTGAME CEREMONIES, LOU WHITAKER AND ALAN TRAMMELL — THE LONGEST-RUNNING DOUBLE-PLAY COMBINATION IN HISTORY — APPEARED TOGETHER AT THE CORNER FOR THE FIRST TIME SINCE 1995.

KIRTHMON F. DOZIER/Detroit Free Press

GROUNDSKEEPER CHARLIE McGEE REMOVED HOME PLATE RIGHT AFTER THE FINAL OUT. IT THEN WENT FOR A SHORT RIDE TO ITS NEW DOWNTOWN HOME — COMERICA PARK.

JULY 28, 1999: BARRY SANDERS ANNOUNCED HIS RETIREMENT. HIS 15,269 YARDS WERE JUST 1,457 SHORT OF WALTER PAYTON'S NFL-RECORD 16,726.

1994-1999
Our scrapbook

BEST MARKETING CAMPAIGN

Red Wings: Hockeytown.

SUGGESTED MARKETING CAMPAIGN

Michigan State: Readin' 'n' riotin' 'n' 'rithmetic.

COMEBACKS

LIONS LINEBACKER Reggie Brown suffered a career-ending spinal injury in the 1997 season finale but regained his ability to walk, an extremely rare occurrence for his condition.

NASCAR DRIVER Ernie Irvan, from near-fatal head and chest injuries suffered in an Aug. 20, 1994, crash during practice at Michigan Speedway. He resumed his career 14 months later and won three more races, the last one at Michigan in 1997. But he decided to retire at age 40 in 1999, after another less-serious crash at Michigan — exactly five years after the first one.

MICHIGAN STATE defensive back Amp Campbell, from a neck injury that was supposed to end his career. A year after he was injured in a 1998 loss to Oregon, Campbell scored on an 85-yard fumble return in the Spartans' season-opening 27-20 victory over the Ducks.

RED WINGS tough guy Joey Kocur, from the beer leagues to play for two Stanley Cup champions.

FIGURE SKATER Nancy Kerrigan returned to Detroit, the site of her 1994 knee-whacking, and performed in "Grease! On Ice."

STILL TRYING
Justin Thompson and Brent Gilchrist.

STILL WAITING
Uwe Krupp and Aaron Gibson.

STEVE SHEVETT/ESPN

A MIRACLE: REGGIE BROWN WALKED AGAIN. NO SURPRISE: HE PICKED UP AN ESPY AWARD FOR BARRY SANDERS, WHO WANTED TO STAY HOME.

NAME CHANGES

Old	New
Brian Williams	Bison Dele
Detroit Neon	Safari
Junior Red Wings	Plymouth Whalers
Detroit Safari	defunct
Oakland University Pioneers	Golden Grizzlies
Wayne State Tartars	Warriors

BY THE NUMBERS

0-11
Michigan State's record in 1994, George Perles' last season as football coach (at least that's what it was after the school, faced with NCAA charges of rules violations, decided in 1996 to forfeit five victories).

2,053
Yards gained by the Lions' Barry Sanders in 1997, second only to Eric Dickerson's NFL-record 2,105 for the LA Rams in 1984.

15,269
Sanders' career yardage when he retired in '99, just 1,457 behind Walter Payton's NFL record.

62
NHL record for regular-season victories set by the 1995-96 Red Wings, before Colorado spoiled it by upsetting them in the Western Conference finals.

0
Number of home runs the Cardinals' Mark McGwire hit against Detroit pitchers en route to his record 70 in 1998 (he had his chance; the Tigers played two games in St. Louis through the magic of interleague play).

$38 MILLION
The Carolina Hurricanes' offer sheet to restricted free agent holdout Sergei Fedorov in 1998. The Red Wings matched, even though the contract would cost them $28 million the first year ($14 million signing bonus, $2 million salary and $12 million for making the conference finals).

111,238
The NCAA-record crowd that watched the Wolverines beat Michigan State, 29-17, in still-growing Michigan Stadium on Sept. 26, 1998. The Big House also set the season standard with 665,787.

PAULINE LUBENS/Detroit Free Press

STARS OF THE SHOCK'S FIRST SEASON: CINDY BROWN, KORIE HLEDE AND SANDY BRONDELLO. THE TEAM CAME WITHIN ONE VICTORY OF THE PLAYOFFS.

WONDER WOMEN

THREE MICHIGAN WOMEN — Lisa Brown-Miller, Shelley Looney and Angela Ruggiero — played on the United States team that won the first gold medal awarded in women's hockey at the 1998 Winter Olympics in Nagano, Japan. Yet even with the pressure to come into Title IX compliance, Wayne State, at the turn of the century, was the only Michigan college to add women's hockey, and in 1999 Ruggiero was told it was against the rules for her to play in a men's pickup game at St. Clair Shores Civic Arena (the rule was soon changed).

THE DETROIT SHOCK made its debut in the summer of '98, the second year of the WNBA. Coached by Nancy Lieberman-Cline, the Shock had a winning record its first year and made the playoffs in its second at the Palace.

KATE SOBRERO of Bloomfield Hills played on the phenomenally popular U.S. soccer team that won the Women's World Cup in 1999.

THE TIGERS hired Heather Nabozny, a Michigan State grad from Milford, as the major leagues' first female head groundskeeper in 1999.

AMERICA'S CUP veteran Dawn Riley of Harrison Township — she was the first female crew member on America³ in 1992 and captain of that boat's mostly female team in '95 — assembled her own San Francisco-based syndicate, America True, for the 2000 regatta in New Zealand.

SCOTT K. BROWN/Associated Press

KATE SOBRERO KEPT A JOURNAL DURING THE WOMEN'S WORLD CUP. "I WANTED TO SOAK IT ALL UP," SHE SAID, "BUT I FOUND THERE'S TOO MUCH TO SOAK UP. NOTHING CAN CAPTURE EVERYTHING THAT HAS HAPPENED."

1994-1999

Our scrapbook

ICONS

Scott Mitchell's clipboard. Tara Lipinski's Beanie Babies. Red Wings car flags. Stanley Cups. Tigers losses.

DAVID STREET/Special to the Free Press; Associated Press (top right); RICK NEASE/Detroit Free Press (bottom right)

TARA LIPINSKI PLAYED 'EM ALL — ON ICE: SPORTY, BABY, POSH, SCARY AND GINGER.

GOING HOLLYWOOD

TARA LIPINSKI as the Spice Girls on her CBS skating special.

KEVIN COSTNER as a Tigers pitcher in "For Love of the Game."

TOMMY LEE JONES as Ty Cobb in "Cobb."

HANK AZARIA as Mitch Albom in "Tuesdays with Morrie."

LOVE COUPLES

■ Pontiac ice dancers Jerod Swallow and Liz Punsalan (married).

■ Piston Grant Hill and singer Tamia, above (newlyweds).

■ Former Piston Dennis Rodman and former "Baywatch" actress Carmen Electra (amicably divorced).

■ Red Wing Sergei Fedorov and tennis star Anna Kournikova (just good friends).

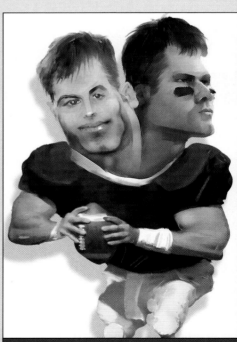

PLATONIC COUPLES

■ Dave Lewis and Barry Smith.

■ Rick Rizzs and Bob Rathbun.

■ Michigan and Nebraska, 1997 football co-champions.

■ Eli and Denny.

■ Denny and his cellmate.

■ Tom Brady and Drew Henson, above.

Special to the Detroit Free Press

THE REAL DEAL OR A FAKE? MITCH ROMPOLA POSED IN THE WOODS WITH HIS MONSTER BUCK.

UNSOLVED MYSTERY

Traverse City bow hunter Mitch Rompola claims he killed a buck Nov. 13, 1998, that measured out at 216 $\frac{5}{8}$ on the Boone & Crockett scale, three inches more than the recognized world-record rack on the buck Saskatchewan hunter Milo Hanson shot in 1993.

But a year later, all Rompola offered for proof was a photograph; he had yet to submit his claim to Boone & Crockett for verification.

EMBARRASSING MOMENTS

Michigan led, 26-21, with six seconds left in a Sept. 24, 1994, game in Ann Arbor when Colorado's Kordell Stewart heaved a Hail Mary more than 70 yards down-field toward a crowd of receivers and defenders. Michael Westbrook (Detroit Chadsey) caught it with 0:00 showing on the clock for a 27-26 Buffaloes victory, silencing most of the 106,427 in the stands.

Lucy (Xena) Lawless, right, popped out of her top while singing the national anthem before a 1997 Red Wings-Mighty Ducks playoff game in Anaheim.

Associated Press

FASHION STATEMENTS

■ The Pistons' new teal uniforms and horsehead logo.

■ Doug Collins' collarless shirts.

■ Ernie Harwell's beret.

■ Michigan Stadium's halo.

■ Spirit of Detroit's Wings jersey.

■ Sergei Fedorov's white skates.

■ Wayne Fontes' Mickey Mouse cap.

■ Scott Mitchell's Wayne Fontes Halloween costume.

SUPER FANS

Courtesy Joe Crachiola

JOE (THE BROW) DIROFF, above, who died in 1997. He showed up at games to cheer and airports to greet returning players for all the home teams, complete with signs and props.

JOHN SPIRIT, aka John Frederic Sheldon II. He paints his 6-foot-6, 230-pound body green with a big white "S" on his chest for his beloved Spartans, though he's been known to change color schemes for teams like the Red Wings. In '96, his red, white and blue body was kicked out of the Atlanta Olympics swimming venue for creating a disturbance.

MO CHEESE, aka Scott Stebbins, or Lard of the Dance. Wearing a Red Wings jersey, he dances up and down the steps at Joe Louis Arena to Three Stooges music, sort of like a chubby Roberto Benigni.

Our scrapbook
1994-1999

GIMMICKS

KIRTHMON F. DOZIER/Detroit Free Press

Anthem singer Karen Newman bungee-jumped from the Joe Louis Arena ceiling before Red Wings playoff games in '98.

MARY SCHROEDER/Detroit Free Press

Gordie Howe, then 69, played the opening shift with the IHL's Detroit Vipers in the 1997-98 season, making him the first to play pro hockey in six decades.

YOU MAKE THE CALL

Heads we win, tails you lose. That's pretty much how the Pittsburgh Steelers felt they were scammed in a Thanksgiving '98 loss at the Silverdome. Here's what happened:

Referee Phil Luckett and players from both teams congregated on the field for the coin toss to start overtime, with Jerome Bettis (Detroit Mackenzie) out to call the toss for the Steelers.

The coin landed on tails, and Luckett awarded the toss to the Lions.

With Luckett's field microphone still on, Bettis was heard protesting immediately, claiming he had called "tails." And the audio on TV replays seemed to back him up.

No matter. The Lions got the ball and won on Jason Hanson's 42-yard field goal just 2:52 into overtime, 19-16.

"I'm in shock right now," Bettis said

afterward. "I can't actually believe the referee thought I said heads. When he went to flip the coin it almost hit him, so he jumped away from it. And I have to believe that caused him to forget what I said, but I said tails as clear as day.

"It was the most bizarre situation that I've ever been associated with. I'll take this to my grave as the craziest call a referee has ever made."

Luckett told reporters after the game that Bettis said "heads-tails" as the ref tossed the coin. Luckett said he went with the first thing he heard.

Lions earwitnesses on the field shed little light on the incident. "All I can say is happy Thanksgiving," Robert Porcher said. "We had a lot of bad calls in the first half, and when we really needed it, they came through."

MUSICAL COACHES

Out	In
Gary Moeller	Lloyd Carr
George Perles	Nick Saban
Don Chaney	Doug Collins
Sparky Anderson	Buddy Bell
Jud Heathcote	Tom Izzo
Wayne Fontes	Bobby Ross
Steve Fisher	Brian Ellerbe
Doug Collins	Alvin Gentry
Buddy Bell	Larry Parrish

BY ANY OTHER NAME

How well have you been paying attention this century? What are the given names of the following sports types? (Answers below.)

A: Sparky Anderson

B: Bubba Baker

C: Red Berenson

D: Scotty Bowman

E: Mud Bruneteau

F: Potsy Clark

G: Mickey Cochrane

H: Rocky Colavito

I: Duffy Daugherty

J: Gus Dorais

K: Sonny Grandelius

L: Chick Harbert

M: Magic Johnson

N: Red Kelly

O: Night Train Lane

P: Heinie Manush

Q: Biggie Munn

R: Buddy Parker

S: Bo Schembechler

T: Bubba Smith

U: Turkey Stearns

V: Bubba Trammell

W: Muddy Waters

ANSWERS — A: George. B: Al. C: Gordon. D: William. E: Modere. F: George. G: Gordon. H: Rocco. I: Hugh. J: Earl. K: Everett. L: Melvin. M: Earvin. N: Leonard. O: Dick. P: Henry. Q: Clarence. R: Raymond. S: Glenn. T: Charles. U: Norman. V: Thomas. W: Frank.

JULIAN H. GONZALEZ/Detroit Free Press

THE RISE AND FALL OF SCOTT MITCHELL

■ March 6, 1994: The Lions signed Miami Dolphins quarterback Scott Mitchell, an unrestricted free agent, to a three-year, $11.1-million deal. "This," said coach Wayne Fontes, "is the future of the Detroit Lions."

■ Feb. 5, 1997: The Lions re-signed Mitchell to a four-year, $21-million deal.

■ Sept. 16, 1998: Two games into his second season as coach, Bobby Ross demoted Mitchell to third string and named rookie Charlie Batch the starter. Mitchell never played another down for the Lions.

■ March 16, 1999: The Lions traded Mitchell to Baltimore for two draft picks. The legacy: Mitchell's 12,647 passing yards were second only to Bobby Layne's 15,710 on the Lions' career list, and he still owned team season records for yards (4,338) and TD passes (32), both set in 1995.

PITCHMEN

SERGEI FEDOROV for Nike (until the contract was terminated in '99).

GRANT HILL for Sprite.

BARRY SANDERS for Cadillac and McDonald's.

CHRIS SPIELMAN for Cintas, the uniform people.

ERNIE HARWELL AND MICKEY REDMOND for Tuffy Muffler.

MIKE THOMPSON/Detroit Free Press

BEST QUOTES BY A LIONS COACH

WAYNE FONTES, Sept. 18, 1995, after a 20-17 loss to Arizona dropped the Lions to 0-3:

"I'm like that big buck that's in the field. They're trying to hunt him down, trying to shoot him. I just keep dodging those bullets. Everybody wants my rack on the wall. Sure, I feel the heat from the fans and the media. Am I under close scrutiny by my owners? No. I have a job to do and if I don't do it, then when the season's over we'll see."

"I'm not low, I'm ticked off! I take the blame, I get all the damn criticism, people hammerin' at me. I'm a good coach. I know what the heck's supposed to be done. I'm not going to second-guess myself one time. That was terrible what we did out there today. We shot ourselves in that last drive! We get two holding penalties, a motion penalty — you think I coach that stuff? I don't coach that stuff. I work on that stuff. I spend time on that stuff. And I'm gettin' all the damn heat, each and every one of y'all hammerin' my tail."

BOBBY ROSS, Nov. 8, 1998, after a 10-9 loss at Philadelphia dropped the Lions to 2-7:

Our scrapbook

BELIEVE IT OR NOT, PART I: NO ONE WAS SERIOUSLY HURT. BELIEVE IT OR NOT, PART II: A CAR WRECK WOULD COST STEVE FISHER HIS JOB.

TOM PIDGEON/Associated Press

THE M FILES

Michigan's program is still proud, but it ran afoul of the law on more than a few occasions in the late '90s. A few lowlights:

■ Football coach Gary Moeller, right, resigned and pleaded no contest to charges of disorderly conduct and assault and battery in connection with an April 28, 1995, drunken incident at a Southfield restaurant. Moeller paid a $409 fine and reportedly collected some $325,000 in parting gifts from the university.

■ Maurice Taylor rolled his grandmother's Ford Explorer — the basketball team's SUV of choice — on M-14 returning to Ann Arbor from a Feb. 17, 1996, field trip to Detroit. Taylor and teammates had been showing Flint Northern recruit Mateen Cleaves a good time, including a visit to booster Ed Martin's house. Not only did Cleaves end up signing with Michigan State and suing Taylor, the incident helped spawn an NCAA investigation.

■ In December 1998, cornerback William Peterson was charged with stealing $46 from a stripper's purse after she showed up to perform at a dormitory birthday party. The woman told police: "The guys . . . were expecting someone else, a stripper they knew." Peterson, who said he was not involved in hiring the stripper, said they "did not think she was attractive and decided they did not want her to perform." The woman left but forgot her purse, and Peterson lifted the money. Peterson was kicked off the football team, but charges were dropped in a plea bargain on another charge.

■ In 1999, offensive linemen Maurice Williams and Jonathan Goodwin were sentenced to one-year probation after pleading guilty to felony embezzlement in connection with a shoplifting scheme at an Ypsilanti Township Kmart. Linebacker Anthony Jordan faced a misdemeanor charge. Authorities said the players were part of a six-person ring that stole, with inside help, thousands of dollars of merchandise through a checkout lane.

NEXT GENERATION

Good-bye	Hello
Isiah Thomas	Grant Hill
PASS	Fox Sports Detroit
Mike Vernon	Chris Osgood
Korie Hlede	Jennifer Azzi
Ladbroke DRC	Millennium Park, a shopping complex anchored by Meijer Thrifty Acres
Barry Sanders	Ron Rivers

VILLAINS

ED MARTIN, whose cakes and other favors brought down the Michigan basketball program.

STEVE FISHER, who brought us the Fab Five but lost his job in the U-M hoops scandals.

JEFF GILLOOLY, Tonya Harding's ex-husband and mastermind? of the attack on Nancy Kerrigan.

CLAUDE LEMIEUX, for the cheap shot on Kris Draper.

RICHARD GNIDA, the limo driver in the accident that injured Vladimir Konstantinov, Sergei Mnatsakanov and Slava Fetisov.

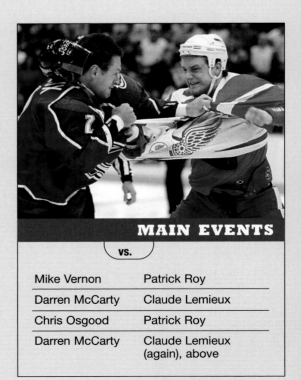

MAIN EVENTS

	vs.	
Mike Vernon		Patrick Roy
Darren McCarty		Claude Lemieux
Chris Osgood		Patrick Roy
Darren McCarty		Claude Lemieux (again), above

OLYMPIC CHAMPIONS

AT 27, SHEILA TAORMINA OF LIVONIA BECAME THE FIRST AMERICAN MASTERS SWIMMER TO WIN OLYMPIC GOLD. IT CAME IN THE 800-METER RELAY AT THE ATLANTA OLYMPICS.

Atlanta, Summer '96

GUSTAVO BORGES, Michigan, swimming: silver in 200-meter freestyle, bronze in 100 free (for Brazil).

DANA CHLADEK, Bloomfield Hills, kayak: silver in singles slalom.

TOM DOLAN, Michigan, swimming: gold in 400-meter individual medley.

SETH GREISINGER, Tigers pitcher, baseball: bronze.

GRANT HILL, Pistons, basketball: gold.

KARCH KIRALY, Ann Arbor, beach volleyball: gold with Kent Steffes.

MARK LENZI, Ann Arbor, diving: bronze in three-meter springboard.

TOM MALCHOW, Michigan, swimming: silver in 200-meter butterfly.

FLOYD MAYWEATHER, Grand Rapids, boxing: bronze in featherweight division.

ERIC NAMESNIK, Michigan, swimming: silver in 400 individual medley.

JEFF PFAENDTNER, Detroit, rowing: bronze as part of lightweight four without coxswain.

ANNETTE SALMEEN, Detroit, swimming: gold in 800 freestyle relay.

KENT STEFFES, Ann Arbor, volleyball: gold.

SHEILA TAORMINA, Livonia, swimming: gold in 800 freestyle relay.

SHELLEY LOONEY OF TRENTON, RIGHT, SCORED THE GOAL THAT BEAT CANADA FOR THE GOLD MEDAL.

Nagano, Winter '98

LISA BROWN-MILLER of Union Lake, SHELLEY LOONEY of Trenton and ANGELA RUGGIERO of Grosse Pointe Woods, hockey: gold.

SERGEI FEDOROV, Red Wings, hockey: silver (for Russia).

MARK GRIMMETTE, Marquette, luge: bronze in doubles with Brian Martin.

TARA LIPINSKI, Detroit Skating Club, figure skating: gold.

CHRIS THORPE, Marquette, luge: silver in doubles with Gordy Sheer.

Our scrapbook

1994-1999

QUESTIONS FOR THE NEXT CENTURY

So, when are they going to hold Barry Sanders Day at the Silverdome?

Do Red Wings fans have to wait until 2040 for another Stanley Cup?

Are they going to call our new favorite AHL team the Toledo Mud Wings?

How long before they try to tear down Tiger Stadium?

How long before they try to get us to build a replacement for Comerica Park?

And will Comerica Park have a cellar, so the Tigers will feel at home?

Is the Discovery Channel ever going to have "Carp Week"?

BUFF

HANS DERYK/Associated Press

ANNA KOURNIKOVA: LOVE MATCH.

BUFFER

Special to the Detroit Free Press

GABE KAPLER: BIG MUSCLES, BIG BAT.

BUFFEST

KIRTHMON F. DOZIER/Detroit Free Press

SPARTY: THE PRIDE OF MSU.

THE WINNER IS . . .

SPARTY: Named nation's buffest mascot by Muscle and Fitness Magazine in '98.

KEVIN VANDAM: Bass Anglers Sportsman Society Angler of the Year in 1992, 1996 and 1999.

SERGEI FEDOROV: Hart Trophy as NHL most valuable player in 1993-94, Selke Trophy as top defensive forward in 1993-94 and 1995-96, Lester Pearson Award as outstanding player in 1993-94.

JOE DUMARS: NBA's J. Walter Kennedy Citizenship Award in 1993-94, inaugural Sportsmanship Award in 1996-97.

PAUL COFFEY: Norris Trophy as NHL's top defenseman in 1994-95.

GRANT HILL: NBA co-rookie of the year in 1994-95 with Dallas' Jason Kidd.

CHRIS OSGOOD AND MIKE VERNON: Jennings Trophy for lowest goals-against average in 1995-95.

SCOTTY BOWMAN: Jack Adams Award as NHL's top coach in 1995-96.

BRENDAN MORRISON: Hobey Baker Award winner for Michigan in '97.

MIKE VERNON: Conn Smythe Trophy as Stanley Cup playoffs MVP in '97.

CHARLES WOODSON: Heisman Trophy winner for Michigan in '97.

BARRY SANDERS: Associated Press NFL co-most valuable player in '97, with Green Bay's Brett Favre.

STEVE YZERMAN: Conn Smythe Trophy as Stanley Cup playoffs MVP in '98.

INDEX

Compiled by George Sipple

INDEX

INDEX

INDEX

INDEX

NEXT PAGE: CHARLES WOODSON LET THE 1998 ROSE BOWL CROWD KNOW THAT MICHIGAN HAD FINISHED NO. 1 FOR THE FIRST TIME IN 49 YEARS.

Photograph by JULIAN H. GONZALEZ/Detroit Free Press